Through the Roof

Housing is a defining issue of our time, driving a persistent affordability crisis, financial instability, and economic inequality. *Through the Roof* examines the crucial role of the state in shaping the housing markets of two economic powerhouses – the United States and Germany. The book starts with a puzzle: Free-market America has vigorously supported homeownership markets with generous government programs, while social-market Germany has slashed policy support for both homeownership and rental markets throughout the past century. The book explains why the two nations have adopted such radically different and unexpected housing policy approaches. Drawing on extensive archival material and interviews with policymakers, it argues that contrasting forms of capitalism – demand-led in the United States and export-oriented in Germany – resulted in divergent housing policies. In both countries, these policies have subsequently transformed capitalism itself.

Alexander Reisenbichler is Assistant Professor of Political Science at the University of Toronto. His work explores the political economies of Western Europe and the United States, with a focus on housing, credit, and social policy.

Cambridge Studies in Comparative Politics

Other Books in the Series

Luis Schiumerini, *Incumbency Bias: Why Political Office is a Blessing and a Curse in Latin America*
Alexander Reisenbichler, *Through the Roof: Housing, Capitalism, and the State in America and Germany*
Raúl L. Madrid, *The Birth of Democracy in South America*
Nicholas Kuipers, *States against Nations: Meritocracy, Patronage, and the Challenges of Bureaucratic Selection*
Nicholas Barnes, *Inside Criminalized Governance: How and Why Gangs Rule the Streets of Rio de Janeiro*
Isabel M. Perera, *The Welfare Workforce: Why Mental Health Care Varies Across Affluent Democracies*
Graeme Blair, Fotini Christia, and Jeremy M. Weinstein, *Crime, Insecurity, and Community Policing: Experiments on Building Trust*
Georgia Kernell, *Inside Parties: How Party Rules Shape Membership and Responsiveness*
Volha Charnysh, *Uprooted: How post-WWII Population Transfers Remade Europe*

Continued after the index

Through the Roof

Housing, Capitalism, and the State in America and Germany

ALEXANDER REISENBICHLER
University of Toronto

CAMBRIDGE
UNIVERSITY PRESS

CAMBRIDGE
UNIVERSITY PRESS

Shaftesbury Road, Cambridge CB2 8EA, United Kingdom

One Liberty Plaza, 20th Floor, New York, NY 10006, USA

477 Williamstown Road, Port Melbourne, VIC 3207, Australia

314–321, 3rd Floor, Plot 3, Splendor Forum, Jasola District Centre, New Delhi – 110025, India

103 Penang Road, #05–06/07, Visioncrest Commercial, Singapore 238467

Cambridge University Press is part of Cambridge University Press & Assessment, a department of the University of Cambridge.

We share the University's mission to contribute to society through the pursuit of education, learning and research at the highest international levels of excellence.

www.cambridge.org
Information on this title: www.cambridge.org/9781009596602

DOI: 10.1017/9781009596619

When citing this work, please include a reference to the DOI 10.1017/9781009596619

First published 2025

A catalogue record for this publication is available from the British Library

Library of Congress Cataloging-in-Publication Data
NAMES: Reisenbichler, Alexander author
TITLE: Through the roof : housing, capitalism, and the state in America and Germany / Alexander Reisenbichler.
DESCRIPTION: Cambridge ; New York, NY : Cambridge University Press, 2025. | SERIES: Cambridge studies in comparative politics | Includes bibliographical references and index.
IDENTIFIERS: LCCN 2024051230 (print) | LCCN 2024051231 (ebook) | ISBN 9781009596602 hardback | ISBN 9781009596657 paperback | ISBN 9781009596619 ebook
SUBJECTS: LCSH: Housing policy – United States | Housing policy – Germany | Housing – United States – Finance | Housing – Germany – Finance | Housing development – United States – History | Housing development – Germany – History
CLASSIFICATION: LCC HD7293 .R365 2025 (print) | LCC HD7293 (ebook) | DDC 363.50973–dc23/eng/20250320
LC record available at https://lccn.loc.gov/2024051230
LC ebook record available at https://lccn.loc.gov/2024051231

ISBN 978-1-009-59660-2 Hardback
ISBN 978-1-009-59665-7 Paperback

To my mother

Contents

Figures

Tables

Acknowledgments

Affordable housing was the fortunate norm when I grew up in the eastern German city of Leipzig in the post-unification years. For my family, cheap rent was a ticket for entering the middle class, as it allowed us to save money for occasional vacations, restaurant meals, and sport and cultural activities. Despite rising housing costs in recent years, long-term apartment rentals remain an attractive option for middle-class households in Germany. In the United States, by contrast, entry to the middle class – and fulfilling the American Dream – is inextricably tied to homeownership. Most American families aspire to own their home as a means to building wealth and financial security in old age. What fascinates me about these different American and German housing experiences is the distinct role of the state in each country's housing market. As the following pages will show, American and German governments struck very different balances between supporting homeownership and rental housing, between facilitating or restricting access to housing credit, and between steering public and private capital into housing or other sectors of the economy. The aim of this book is to explain the two countries' divergent housing policy trajectories and choices over the past century.

I have incurred many debts writing this book. I would like to first express my appreciation to my interviewees on both sides of the Atlantic. I am grateful that they took the time out of their schedules to provide me with a deeper look behind the scenes of the complex processes of housing policymaking in both countries.

This book started as my dissertation at the George Washington University's political science department. It was a privilege to work with an incredibly supportive committee that profoundly shaped how I think about political economy and long-term political processes. From the early dissertation stage to this day, Kimberly Morgan has been a mentor and inspiration. She encouraged me to pursue this research project – at a time when housing was rarely a topic of political science dissertations – and I benefited immensely from her guidance and thorough feedback. Both were crucial for the development of the book's main ideas. I am grateful for her continued support, mentorship, and collaboration. Henry Farrell and Abe Newman pushed me to sharpen the argument and think bigger about its implications. I thank them for their guidance, advice, and the many exchanges over the years. My committee's scholarly dedication set an example I strive to emulate. For financial support, I would like to extend thanks to the Horowitz Foundation for Social Policy, the Berlin Program for Advanced German and European Studies at the Free University Berlin, and the American-German Institute at Johns Hopkins University at the dissertation stage.

The University of Toronto provided an exceptionally supportive environment. I am grateful to the political science departments – at both the Mississauga and St. George campuses – for offering financial support for my research and cultivating a scholarly community in which comparative-historical scholarship is valued. I am privileged to have benefited from my departmental colleagues' generous advice, feedback, and guidance on this project and beyond.

I am also immensely thankful to the University of Toronto's Center for European and Eurasian Studies and its wonderful community. The center provided substantial financial and intellectual support that helped me finish the book. I am especially grateful to former director Randall Hansen for offering extensive feedback on this book and many other projects. His mentorship has been invaluable in helping me navigate the world of book publishing and academic life as a new faculty member. I also thank current director Ed Schatz and the center's staff, as well as Rob Austin and Mark Manger for their support, advice, and good humor.

I completed a draft of this book as John F. Kennedy Memorial Fellow at the Minda de Gunzburg Center for European Studies at Harvard University during the 2021–2022 academic year. It is difficult to imagine a more intellectually stimulating environment for working on the political economies of Germany and the United States. I am grateful to the center for the financial support it provided. I am also thankful for the conversations I had there about my work with Peter Hall and Kathleen Thelen, as well as Jeffry Frieden, Edward Glaeser, Hanno Hilbig, Torben Iversen, Hans-Helmut Kotz, Arie Krampf, Charles Maier, Florian Meinel, Gunnar Trumbull, and Daniel Ziblatt. I am indebted to Winnie van Dijk and the participants in the center's New Research in Europe seminar for their valuable comments on a draft book chapter. For excellent research assistance, I am grateful to Aden Barton. Finally, I was fortunate to be part of a wonderful cohort of Kennedy Fellows – together with Charlotte Bartels, Moritz von Brescius, Pascal König, and Christoph Nitschke – with whom I enjoyed numerous conversations about each other's work. I am especially grateful to Pascal König for his permission to present some of our joint survey findings in the last chapter of this book.

Back at the University of Toronto, I benefited tremendously from a book workshop held in the fall of 2022. The workshop received generous funding from the Center for European and Eurasian Studies, the political science department, and the German Academic Exchange Service (Deutscher Akademischer Austauschdienst) with funds from the German Federal Foreign Office. I am grateful to Randall Hansen, Stephan Heblich, Martin Höpner, Sebastian Kohl, Daniel Mertens, Darius Ornston, Sarah Quinn, and Chloe Thurston for carefully reading the manuscript and offering valuable comments on it. Their excellent and thorough feedback undoubtedly improved the book.

It has been truly rewarding to be part of a vibrant community of scholars working on the political economies of housing, credit, and economic growth, and I appreciate the ongoing exchanges with them. I thank Karen Anderson, Ben Ansell, Lucio Baccaro, Mark Blyth, Dorothee Bohle, Asli Cansunar, Greg Fuller, Lindsay Flynn, Anke Hassel, Alison Johnston, Desmond King, Sebastian Kohl, Paulette Kurzer, Ronen Mandelkern, Matthias Matthijs, Daniel Mertens, Jonas Nahm, Bruno Palier, Jonas Pontusson, Philip Rathgeb, Aidan Regan, Sidney Rothstein, Waltraud Schelkle, Herman Mark Schwartz, Mallory SoRelle, Chloe Thurston, Andreas Wiedemann, and James Wood for their insights, advice, and collaboration. Special thanks go to Sebastian Kohl, who has hosted me at the Free University Berlin's John F. Kennedy Institute for North American Studies over several summers, as well as to Ingrid Hobbis and Hanno Balz at Cambridge University, who welcomed me as Munk-Cambridge Fellow in summer 2023.

I thank my editor Rachel Blaifeder at Cambridge University Press for her guidance and for shepherding this book through publication with unparalleled professionalism. Additional thanks go to the anonymous reviewers for their excellent feedback on an earlier version of the manuscript.

My family and friends offered immeasurable support during the long and rewarding journey of completing this book. Above all, Jona listened to and commented on every breakthrough and setback with patience and empathy. I am grateful for her encouragement, perspective, and contagious kindness. Family and friends helped put things into perspective, and they always offered a welcome and comforting distraction from the book and academic life. I am immensely fortunate to have them in my life. Finally, this book would have been impossible to write without the unconditional support and love of my mother. I am forever grateful for all her sacrifices, support, and encouragement that made my academic journey possible, even though the journey took me a great distance from home. I dedicate this book to her.

Abbreviations

BdL	Bank deutscher Länder (Bank of German States)
CDU	Christlich Demokratische Union (Christian Democratic Union)
CEA	Council of Economic Advisers
CRA	Community Reinvestment Act
CSU	Christlich Soziale Union (Christian Social Union)
DGB	Deutscher Gewerkschaftsbund (German Trade Union Confederation)
DM	Deutsche Mark
ECB	European Central Bank
Fannie Mae	Federal National Mortgage Association
FDP	Freie Demokratische Partei (Free Democratic Party)
Fed	Federal Reserve System
FHA	Federal Housing Administration
FHLB	Federal Home Loan Bank
FNMA	Federal National Mortgage Association = Fannie Mae
FOMC	Federal Open Market Committee
Freddie Mac	Federal Home Loan Mortgage Corporation
FSLIC	Federal Savings and Loan Insurance Corporation
Ginnie Mae	Government National Mortgage Association
GSE	government-sponsored enterprise
HOLC	Home Owners' Loan Corporation
HUD	Department of Housing and Urban Development
ICT	information and communication technology
KfW	Kreditanstalt für Wiederaufbau
MBA	Mortgage Bankers Association
MBS	mortgage-backed securities
MID	mortgage interest deduction
NAHB	National Association of Home Builders

NAR	National Association of Realtors
NAREB	National Association of Real Estate Boards
OFHEO	Office of Federal Housing Enterprise Oversight
OPA	Office of Price Administration
RFC	Reconstruction Finance Corporation
S&L	savings and loan association
SALT	state and local taxes
SPD	Sozialdemokratische Partei Deutschlands (Social Democratic Party of Germany)
VA	Department of Veterans Affairs, previously Veterans Administration

1

Introduction

Home ownership is the West's biggest economic-policy mistake.

—*The Economist* (January 16, 2020)

In January 2006, two months after taking office, German Chancellor Angela Merkel eliminated the country's largest government program for subsidizing homeownership. It was one of her first major policy initiatives as chancellor and marked a significant shift from a key conservative policy she had passionately defended just a few years earlier. In a 2002 parliamentary debate, Merkel had rebuked her leftwing opponents for proposing just such a reform, saying: "You do not at all comprehend what you are doing to the people! Do you know what this means for a family who wants to build a house?"[1]

Merkel's center-right party, the Christian Democratic Union (Christlich Demokratische Union, CDU), had been the country's strongest advocate of the homeownership program (the *Eigenheimzulage* or homeownership allowance) since the founding of the Federal Republic of Germany in 1949. It was a stunning U-turn, made in the context of a reeling German economy. A decade after reunification, Germany faced skyrocketing unemployment, exploding fiscal deficits, a collapsing housing market, and back-to-back recessions. These economic problems led to a deep crisis of confidence in the German model of capitalism, which had previously been envied by its European neighbors. As part of larger efforts to save that model, the Merkel government sacrificed the homeownership subsidy, the country's largest tax subsidy, which was costing taxpayers EUR 11.5 billion annually.[2] The policy shift was permanent:

[1] Merkel, A. (October 29, 2002), *Remarks in the 15th Bundestag, 4th session (Plenarprotokoll 15/4)*, 63. Unless otherwise stated, all translations from German into English are my own.

[2] Bundesregierung (March 22, 2003), *Bericht der Bundesregierung über die Entwicklung der Finanzhilfen des Bundes und der Steuervergünstigungen für die Jahre 2003 bis 2006 (20. Subventionsbericht, BT-Drs. 16/1020)*, 103–104.

German homeownership programs have never returned to their previous levels despite the country's return to prosperity during the 2010s.

Meanwhile, a house-price bubble of epic proportions was about to burst on the other side of the Atlantic. When it did, the American economy collapsed. The 2008–2009 housing crash was America's own systems-threatening crisis, as economic growth plummeted, unemployment doubled, and house prices were in freefall.

But the American response could not have been more different. A housing bust of this magnitude could – and arguably should – have led policymakers to question the generous homeownership programs that had helped to inflate the bubble. Instead, American politicians did the opposite: They expanded government support for housing. In response to the crash, Republican President George W. Bush effectively nationalized the country's mortgage lending system. In September 2008, President Bush placed the battered Wall Street mortgage giants Fannie Mae and Freddie Mac under direct government control, assuming all their commitments and obligations – a staggering USD 5.2 *trillion* in mortgage debt at the time.[3] The president felt deeply uneasy about his course of action, as he confessed in a speech: "I'm a strong believer in free enterprise. So my natural instinct is to oppose government intervention. I believe companies that make bad decisions should be allowed to go out of business."[4] More than fifteen years after the crash, and several American presidents later, the country's mortgage market remains de facto nationalized even though the US housing market has long returned to growth. In 2024, the American state directly backed USD 9 trillion or 70 percent of all homeowner debt through public agencies, meaning that millions of indebted American homeowners receive a massive subsidy via lower mortgage rates.[5]

These contrasting German and American policy responses violate widely held assumptions about these two global economic powerhouses. The United States is the world's quintessential liberal market economy and rhetorical champion of free markets, emphasizing minimal government interference in capitalist activity. In contrast, Germany is the archetypal social market economy with a stronger tradition of government involvement in market affairs. An entire research agenda in political economy, the influential "varieties of capitalism" framework (Hall and Soskice 2001), is based on the two countries' differing economic models. In the case of housing, however, both German and American responses deviated from these well-established academic

[3] Before 2008, Fannie Mae and Freddie Mac were privately operated yet government-sponsored enterprises that enjoyed the *implicit* backing of the US federal government. Their 2008 nationalization made the backing of the federal government *explicit*. See Figure 4.3 for their mortgage commitments and obligations.

[4] Bush, G. W. (September 24, 2008), *President's Address to the Nation*, The White House, Office of the Press Secretary.

[5] Federal Reserve Board (2024), *Financial Accounts of the United States Z.1*, www.federalreserve.gov/releases/z1/.

expectations. Germany eliminated what economists consider market-distorting subsidies, while the United States entrenched major subsidies for American homeowners by effectively nationalizing one of the world's largest debt markets in response to the 2008 crash.

These divergent policy decisions exemplify a much broader historical pattern of government support for housing markets in the United States and Germany. In good economic times and bad from the Great Depression onward, American policymakers have added layer upon layer of support for mortgages through generous tax subsidies and the government's backing of private mortgage debt. The culmination of this decades-long process of policy expansion was the nationalization of America's mortgage market. When it comes to subsidizing mortgage debt, the United States occupies one end of the spectrum. Germany occupies the other, as the country's policymakers have outright retrenched tax subsidies and credit programs for homeownership over time. It was America, not Germany, that socialized housing finance. This book asks why.

The book's argument, in brief, is that the different natures of American and German capitalism – demand-led in the United States and export-oriented in Germany – created different housing policymaking trajectories over the past century. The American political economy is demand-led and relies heavily on institutions and government programs that promote consumption and credit, and housing is a key sector through which American policymakers can generate such consumption and credit. From the Great Depression onward, successive US governments have concluded that housing programs fuel the overall level of demand in the economy through a virtuous cycle: Subsidizing households' mortgage debt boosts mortgage lending, housing activity, house prices, and household wealth, which in turn stimulates more consumer lending and spending. Central to this cycle are rising house prices that allow American homeowners to use their homes as credit cards, borrowing money against the value of their homes for consumer spending. Over time, American housing programs have become interwoven with the very functioning of the US economy; withdrawing housing support would be an assault on the economy itself. Housing finance, in short, is America's unnamed national champion, able to deliver demand-led growth via credit and consumption.

By contrast, the German political economy is export-oriented, relying on institutions and government programs that restrain inflation and wages, which in turn keeps German exports competitive compared to those of nations with higher inflation and wage growth. For German policymakers, housing programs were thus not American-style engines of domestic growth but served the opposite purpose: To *restrain* growth in house prices and housing costs, consumer credit, and personal consumption, often with the implicit or explicit goal of keeping inflation and wages in check. In the decades after World War II (WWII), which were characterized by massive housing shortages, German housing programs for both rental and owner-occupied housing reinforced the export-oriented economy by producing more affordable housing supply that also prevented wage-cost spirals detrimental to export-led growth.[6] Once housing shortages were overcome in the 1970s, however, policymakers soon attacked many of these programs for contradicting the priorities of the export-oriented economy by channeling capital away from the country's avowed national champion: Manufacturing. Over time, politicians duly retrenched homeownership programs in the name of strengthening Germany's export-oriented economy.

In explaining the radically contrasting approaches to housing in the United States and Germany, this book also relates to some of the defining challenges of our day: Financial instability, racialized wealth inequality, and a chronic shortage of affordable accommodation in cities across Europe and North America. Housing finance programs directly shape the world's largest asset class – residential housing with an estimated value of USD 288 trillion in 2022[7] – by encouraging or deterring housing investments. In good times, such programs can help create massive private wealth, as housing is the most important asset that most households will ever own. However, such programs can also fuel overinvestment, resulting in speculative bubbles, financial turmoil, and sudden losses in household wealth, as evidenced by the well-known American housing crash of 2008 and the lesser-known German housing slump of the late 1990s.

Housing is also a significant driver of wealth inequality. In recent decades, the return on capital has risen faster than wages, particularly from housing assets (Piketty 2014; Rognlie 2015; Fuller et al. 2020). As a result, inequality between the haves and the have-nots is on the rise. In the United States, housing also contributes to racial wealth disparities. In 2024, 74% of white households owned their homes, compared to only 46% of Black, 50% of Latino, and 62% of Asian households.[8] In the case of Black Americans, this is largely a consequence of policy choice. For decades, the federal government deliberately excluded them from homeownership programs (Thurston 2018). When federal policy finally included racialized minorities from the late 1960s, it often drove them into the hands of predatory lenders (Taylor 2019).

German and American policy approaches to housing have been highly divergent, but they recently converged on one outcome: A lack of affordable

[6] Throughout this book, I use "Germany" to refer to the Bundesrepublik Deutschland (BRD, the Federal Republic of Germany), including during the period 1949–1990 before it was joined by what had been the Deutsche Demokratische Republik (DDR, German Democratic Republic). Statistics and policy descriptions from 1945 to 1990 refer to the BRD.

[7] Tostevin, P. and Rushton, C. (September 2023), *The total value of global real estate: Property remains the world's biggest store of wealth*, Savills, www.savills.com/impacts/market-trends/the-total-value-of-global-real-estate-property-remains-the-worlds-biggest-store-of-wealth.html.

[8] US Census Bureau (April 30, 2024), *Quarterly Residential Vacancies and Homeownership, First Quarter 2024* (Release No. CB24-62), www.census.gov/housing/hvs/files/currenthvspress.pdf.

accommodation. Between 2012 and 2022, real house prices increased by a staggering 60% in Germany and 70% in the United States.[9] American real house prices have since continued to climb, standing 80% above their 2012 levels at the time of writing, while German house prices have declined from their 2021 peak (although German prices remained 25% above their 2012 levels in mid-2024). Both the German withdrawal of housing support and the American expansion of that support exacerbated the crisis of affordable housing supply in such cities as Berlin, Munich, New York, and San Francisco, where both buyers and renters are being pushed out of the market. The American failure was one of omission: Housing policy favored single-family homes in suburbs to the detriment of affordable multifamily rental housing in cities. The German failure was one of commission: In its zeal to remove distorting subsidies, the country withdrew them from both homeowners *and* rental landlords. Paradoxically, these policy actions ultimately harmed the growth regimes that they were meant to serve in their respective countries, as they inflated property prices into bubble territory in the United States and crippled affordable housing programs that could have helped to deflate housing costs in Germany.

DIVERGING HOUSING FINANCE POLICIES IN AMERICA AND GERMANY

Despite housing's role in the economy, personal wealth, and inequality, scholars have long treated housing as a technical and apolitical arena. It is, however, a deeply political one. All governments intervene in their housing sectors to varying degrees, making political choices about whether to subsidize the cost of homeownership or rental housing, control or liberalize rents, expand or restrict access to credit, raise or lower taxes on property, and tighten or loosen land-use regulations (cp. Vogel 2018; Quinn 2019; Fligstein and Goldstein 2012; Schwartz 2020; Fligstein 2021). To provide a focused comparison, this book's emphasis is on housing finance programs – those that subsidize the cost of financing owner-occupied housing and, to a lesser degree, rental housing. As the preceding discussion shows, the United States and Germany have adopted radically different housing policy approaches, and it is the goal of this book to make sense of these differences.

Housing finance programs are complicated webs of fiscal policies and credit programs. Both types of policy reduce the cost of financing homes, which in turn stimulates housing investment relative to other investments (Schelkle 2012). In other words, policymakers can deploy the infrastructural power of the state – using state capacity to achieve desired private-market outcomes – to steer private capital into or away from housing (cp. Mann 1984;

9 Own calculations, based on Organisation for Economic Co-operation and Development (OECD) (2024), *Housing Prices*, www.oecd.org/en/data/indicators/housing-prices.html.

Krippner 2011; Hyman 2011; Braun 2020; Wansleben 2022; Schwartz 2020). Fiscal policies are tax subsidies or direct spending programs for households, builders, or financial institutions that subsidize the costs associated with building or acquiring homes. Credit programs can take the form of cheap government loans to households or government guarantees on homeowners' mortgages that protect banks against mortgage defaults, which in turn allows banks to offer mortgages at lower rates.

Cross-National Variation

Comparing housing finance programs in the United States and Germany reveals two puzzling dimensions of variation: One cross-national and the other historical. The United States has developed a *government-sponsored* housing finance model, generously subsidizing the cost of financing homeownership through a plethora of fiscal and credit programs. In contrast, Germany offers few fiscal and credit subsidies for financing homeownership. This characterization is consistent with recent studies that compare housing finance programs in advanced economies, concurring that the United States stands out in its generosity and Germany in its restrictiveness (International Monetary Fund 2011; Fuller 2015; Wiedemann 2021; Johnston et al. 2021).

The degree of American government support for housing finance is remarkable. In 2022 alone, the American government provided USD 72 billion in tax subsidies for homeowners through mortgage interest deduction and capital gains exclusion.[10] In the primary mortgage market, where banks loan mortgages to consumers, the Federal Housing Administration (FHA) and the Department of Veterans Affairs (VA) together insured 1.6 million new mortgages worth USD 483 billion in 2022, guaranteeing 22 percent of all new mortgage debt that year.[11] In the secondary market, where mortgages are pooled together and traded as bonds in financial markets, the American state has an even larger presence. In fact, the American government dominates one of the largest bond markets in the world: US mortgage-backed securities. In 2024, the US government directly backed USD 9 trillion in mortgage-backed securities, or 70 percent of the entire US mortgage market, through quasi-public agencies such as Fannie Mae and Freddie Mac.[12] Even the country's independent central bank, the US Federal Reserve (the Fed), which usually does not attempt to pick winners in the economy, has joined the federal government in providing direct housing support. By the end of 2024, the Fed held USD 2.2 trillion in

[10] US Joint Committee on Taxation, *Estimates of Federal Tax Expenditures for Fiscal Years 2022–2026* (December 22, 2022), www.jct.gov/publications/2022/jcx-22-22/.

[11] FHA (2023), *Single Family Market Share*, www.hud.gov/sites/dfiles/Housing/images/FHASFMarketShare2023Q1.pdf; US Department of Veterans Affairs (2024), *VA home loans*, www.benefits.va.gov/HOMELOANS/Lender_State_Volume.asp.

[12] Federal Reserve Board, *Financial Accounts of the United States Z.1*.

mortgage-backed securities issued by Fannie and Freddie, artificially lowering the cost of mortgages for homeowners.

The German state provides marginal government support for financing homeownership. In fact, there are currently only two permanent programs that do so, and both are limited. The first is the exclusion of capital gains tax on the sale of homes, but only after ten years of ownership (as opposed to just two years in the United States).[13] The second is a set of small-scale, subsidized homeownership loans, offered by the country's development bank, Kreditanstalt für Wiederaufbau (KfW), amounting to merely EUR 4.5 billion in credit volume in 2023 – just 2 percent of all new mortgage debt in Germany that year.[14] These programs pale in comparison to American ones. In Germany, one is hard-pressed to find something akin to the American mortgage interest deduction, although the country briefly experimented with it on two separate occasions in the 1980s and 1990s, as Chapters 5 and 7 detail. The German government similarly does not offer large-scale government guarantees to protect financial markets against losses in the case of mortgage defaults. In Germany, housing finance receives few privileges relative to other sectors.

These different housing finance models have profoundly shaped the two countries' political economies. As the American state absorbs a great deal of risk in financial markets, US banks can offer the country's beloved thirty-year, fixed-rate mortgage as a standard option – making the US an outlier among wealthy democracies. With fewer government protections, German banks tend to offer shorter mortgage durations (twenty-five years) with a fixed interest rate for only ten to fifteen years. As Table 1.1 shows, the abundance of American mortgage subsidies has contributed to generally higher mortgage indebtedness among American households compared to German ones.

Relatedly, Germany's restrictive mortgage system, which requires relatively high down payments for home purchases, partly explains the lower number of German housing transactions per capita compared to those in the United States. In addition, low government support for homeownership is an important factor in why Germany's homeownership rate is lower than that of the United States.

Historical Variation

The historical dimension of variation is no less intriguing. In the early and mid-twentieth century, both the United States and Germany started in a similar

[13] The German finance ministry does not publish estimates of this tax exemption.

[14] European Mortgage Federation (EMF) (September 2024), *Hypostat 2024*; Kreditanstalt für Wiederaufbau (December 31, 2024), *Förderreport KfW Bankengruppe*. In 2024, the KfW's homeownership programs included (1) a subsidized loan for homebuyers (EUR 5.3 billion in total credit volume) and (2) a subsidized loan specifically for low- and middle-income families to buy or build energy-efficient homes (EUR 920 million in total credit volume).

TABLE 1.1 *Key housing indicators in the United States and Germany in 2020 (or latest year available)*

	Outright homeowners as a share of households	Mortgaged homeowners as a share of households	Housing transactions per 1,000 residents	Typical down payment on house purchase	Typical mortgage term	Average mortgage debt per capita (total population)
USA	25.3%	40.1%	14.2	9% for first-time buyers; 23% for repeat buyers	30 years (fixed interest rate for 30 years)	USD 40,000
Germany	25.3%	15.5%	4.7	20–30%	25 years (fixed interest rate for 10–15 years)	USD 23,000

Data sources: EMF Hypostat; OECD Affordable Housing Database, Housing Tenures; National Association of Realtors Profile of Home Buyers and Sellers.

place of offering a high degree of government support for housing finance. However, their policy trajectories diverged over time. While the United States incrementally *expanded* housing finance programs, German policymakers had *retrenched* theirs to a minimum by the early twenty-first century.

The American government-sponsored housing finance model originated in response to the Great Depression. While the country went into the depression with virtually no national housing finance programs, it emerged with an expansive toolkit of programs that would forever change the American housing market. At the height of the depression between 1929 and 1933, millions of households lost their homes, housing prices and construction plummeted, and mortgage lending came to a halt. In response, American policymakers adopted federal homeownership programs – such as FHA mortgage insurance – to resuscitate the housing market. After the depression, however, policymakers did not withdraw the government from housing finance as originally planned. On the contrary, they kept *expanding* the state's role. As the country emerged from the depression during the WWII years – a period marked by significant housing shortages of 3.7 million homes as civilian housing production stalled to secure resources for military production – policymakers broadened homeownership support to returning veterans. By the early 1950s, the US government was directly subsidizing half of all new residential construction and directly backing 44 percent of all mortgage debt through federal credit programs (Grebler et al. 1956, 146; see Figure 2.1).

Importantly, as Figure 1.1 shows, America's generous housing finance programs originated in the depression era when the country was still a nation of renters. Even with a majority-renter population at that time, though, the US government prioritized support for homeowners over renters; it has continued to do so to this day. The reason, as this book will go on to argue in more detail, lies in the macroeconomic heft of homeownership finance programs vis-à-vis rental housing programs, the latter of which have remained a footnote in the American political economy.

US policymakers' relentless expansion of the state in housing finance has continued well into the twenty-first century. First, from the late 1960s to the 1990s, American policymakers developed a new *government-backed* housing bond market, one in which domestic and global investors started trading mortgage-backed securities equipped with a government guarantee. This market, centered around the quasi-public agencies Fannie Mae and Freddie Mac, grew to over USD 2 trillion and was providing close to 50 percent of all mortgage funding in the country by the late 1990s.[15] Second, American politicians

[15] A government-sponsored enterprise (GSE) is a for-profit agency that enjoys the implicit backing of the federal government as well as many other privileges that private competitors do not (Koppell 2003). As Chapter 2 of this book shows, although Fannie Mae was established during the Great Depression, it was not until much later that it became a dominant market player. See Figure 4.3.

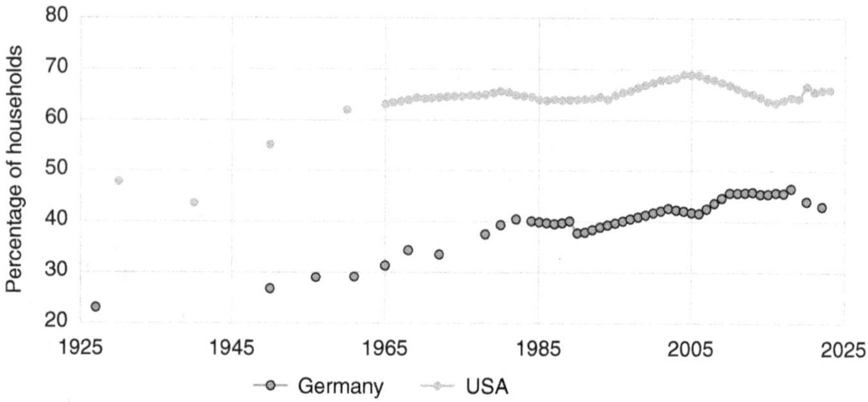

FIGURE 1.1 Homeownership rates in the United States and Germany, 1925–2023: Percentage of households living in owner-occupied housing
Data sources: Kohl (2017) for data until 2017; US Census Bureau, German Federal Statistics Office, and OECD Wealth Distribution Database for data from 2017 onward.

repeatedly strengthened tax breaks for homeowners, such as the mortgage interest deduction. During rare moments of comprehensive tax reform, such as President Ronald Reagan's 1986 Tax Reform Act, they retained housing tax breaks while eliminating those for other consumer loans. Third, the housing crash of 2008–2009 led policymakers to expand housing programs yet again: They bailed out Fannie Mae and Freddie Mac, effectively nationalizing America's housing finance system. For its part, the Fed started to directly support American mortgages through large-scale housing-bond-buying programs as a crisis measure in 2008 and has sustained that support ever since. Supporting US mortgages with ever more government programs is a constant in the history of the American political economy.

Germany's policy path similarly started with generous housing finance programs, but it diverged over time. Like their American counterparts, in the early to mid-twentieth century German policymakers adopted large-scale housing programs to stimulate homebuilding. After WWII, their priority was to overcome the severe shortage of 4.6 million homes. Unlike their American counterparts – who, as noted, also faced considerable post-WWII housing shortages – German policymakers chose to strongly support the construction of *both* rental *and* owner-occupied housing. Landmark social housing programs, for example, offered cheap loans to homeowners and rental investors alike. With private capital scarce, the German government directly provided close to 50 percent of all mortgage funding in the early 1950s. Until the late 1960s, the federal government subsidized more than 5.6 million homes (51 percent of the 10.9 million total new homes) through social housing programs alone, including 1.4 million homes for homeowners and 4.2 million rental units.[16] The German government also offered tax subsidies for both owner-occupied and rental markets to encourage housing investments. In short, the German state dominated the country's postwar housing finance market – arguably even more so than the American state in this period – offering generous housing finance programs for homeowners and rental investors as part of the country's broader effort to build more houses after the war.

During the mid-1970s, however, German housing programs reached a turning point. As the housing market recovered from postwar shortages, German policymakers wound down rental housing programs to a minimum by the late 1980s. At the same time, they initially protected homeownership programs, including tax breaks and social housing loans for homeowners. Like President Reagan's 1986 tax reform, Chancellor Helmut Kohl's tax reform in the same year strengthened the homeownership allowance, making it a "sacred cow" in the German tax code (Stimpel 1990, 62). Germany's reunification led to a temporary revival of housing programs in the early 1990s, aimed at modernizing the housing stock in eastern Germany and remedying shortages in the west. To that end, German policymakers even briefly experimented with a mortgage interest deduction. However, these programs contributed to a crisis, now often forgotten, of housing overproduction in the late 1990s. Instead of responding with ever more subsidies, as the Americans did in response to their own 2008 housing crisis that included large-scale vacancies, German policymakers *retrenched* homeownership programs. Despite the popularity of the homeownership allowance among voters and the housing lobby, the Merkel government eliminated it. Since then, housing finance programs have remained marginal in Germany.

What explains these contrasting housing policy trajectories in the United States and Germany? Why has the United States continuously expanded housing programs, while Germany has ceased offering such generous programs?

ARGUMENT

This book's argument is that the differing natures of American and German capitalism – demand-led in the United States and export-oriented in Germany – produced contrasting political dynamics that have resulted in diverging housing policy trajectories over the past century. Policymakers and governments are the primary drivers of policy action in this book's historical account. They have repeatedly wielded state power to pursue different housing market objectives in the name of strengthening their respective political economies. Before delving further into the historical argument, it is important to establish how

[16] Own calculations, based on annual social housing reports (1951–1970) presented in *Bundesbaublatt*, a monthly housing trade journal published by the German federal housing ministry.

the American and German political economies differ, and how their housing markets exhibit different macroeconomic complementarities.

Macroeconomic Complementarities: Growth Regimes and Housing

The two countries' economic models rely on distinct sources of economic growth – demand-led in the United States and export-oriented in Germany – and different economic institutions and macroeconomic policies that support these different patterns of growth. To capture these differences, I use the term "growth regimes" (Hall 2020, 2021, 2024; Hassel and Palier 2021; Thelen 2019). A growth regime can be defined as the components of an economy that are key for producing growth and prosperity – chiefly exports or domestic demand (Baccaro and Pontusson 2016; Baccaro et al. 2022; Stockhammer 2015) – and the economic institutions and government actions that support these components (Amable 2003; Iversen and Soskice 2012; Prasad 2012).[17] While some advanced economies such as Germany are organized in ways that promote exports, others including the United States have developed an institutional shape that promotes domestic demand as a source of economic growth. Importantly, as Peter Hall (2024, 262) notes, "[w]hat renders a growth regime more than a disparate collection of practices, however, is how the practices of firms and governments interlock to reinforce each other and yield distinctive patterns of growth" (also cp. Iversen and Soskice 2012). In other words, economic activity is structured by economic institutions and government programs that are often – but not always – mutually reinforcing parts of a coherent growth regime. Setting aside, for now, the question of whether governments intentionally design such complementarities, I will detail here the macroeconomic complementarities between the American and German growth regimes and their respective housing sectors.

The American economy is a quintessential demand-led growth regime, whereas Germany's is an archetypal export-led growth regime. Germany's institutional economic foundations first arose in the late nineteenth century (Abelshauser 2005; Manow 2020; Herrigel 1996) and the United States' in the early twentieth century (Prasad 2012; see Chapters 2 and 3 of this book).

[17] Using the concept of "growth regimes" reconciles the insights of two paradigmatic bodies of comparative political economy scholarship on the US and Germany. On one side of the debate, the "varieties of capitalism" perspective (a supply-side approach) emphasizes the differences in both countries' economic institutions, such as in business–labor relations, vocational training systems, intercompany relations, and corporate governance structures (Hall and Soskice 2001). On the other side, the more recent "growth model" perspective (a demand-side approach) privileges the drivers of economic growth, such as exports and domestic demand (Baccaro and Pontusson 2016). My approach considers the demand and supply sides of both countries' political economies together. As the historical argument and analysis show, governments – the main actors of this book – often adopt or reform public programs or institutions with a desire for macroeconomic effects on the demand side, such as boosting exports or domestic consumption.

From the post-WWII years, as Figures 1.2 and 1.3 show, private consumption as a share of the economy tended to be much higher in the United States than in Germany, while exports as a share of the economy have been significantly larger in Germany than in the United States, and the contrast has become starker over time. By 2022, private consumption was 68% of gross domestic product (GDP) in the United States and 51% in Germany, whereas exports were only 12% of GDP in the US and 51% in Germany.

The American demand-led economy relies, above all, on household consumption for economic growth. From the depression era to today, consumption of goods and services in the large domestic market – such as healthcare, education, consumer goods, entertainment, real estate, and financial services – has been the strongest driver of US economic growth. Underlying the American growth regime are institutional features that promote domestic demand. Importantly, the country has developed a large and liquid credit system in which households have relatively easy access to credit for purchasing homes, financing consumer spending, smoothing income losses, or "keeping up with the Joneses" (Wiedemann 2021; SoRelle 2020; Iversen and Soskice 2012). Debt-financed household spending became particularly important from the mid-1970s, when the postdepression period of wage and

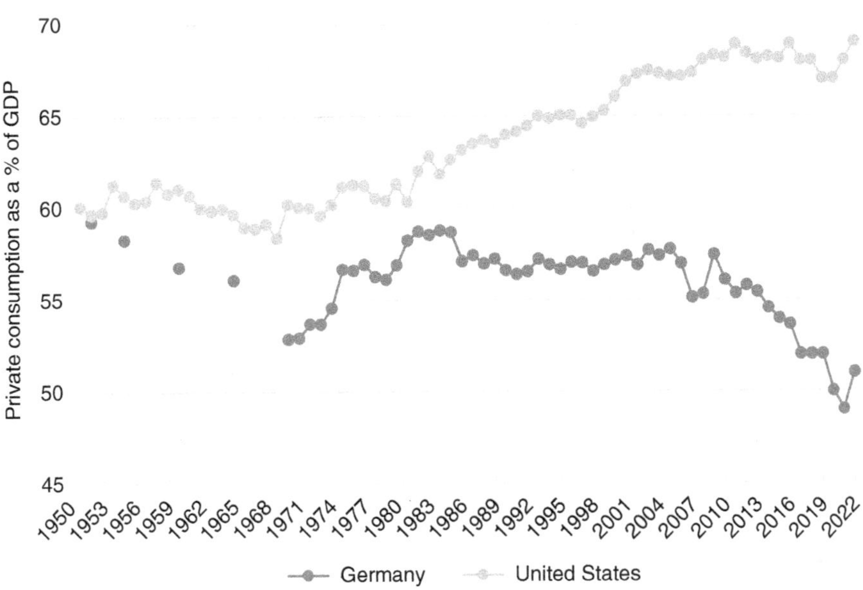

FIGURE 1.2 Private consumption as a percentage of GDP, United States and Germany, 1950–2022
Sources: US data from Federal Reserve Economic Data (FRED, series: DPCERE1Q156NBEA); Germany data prior to 1970 from Logemann (2012, 23) and since 1970 from World Bank Open Data (series: NE.CON.PETC.ZS).

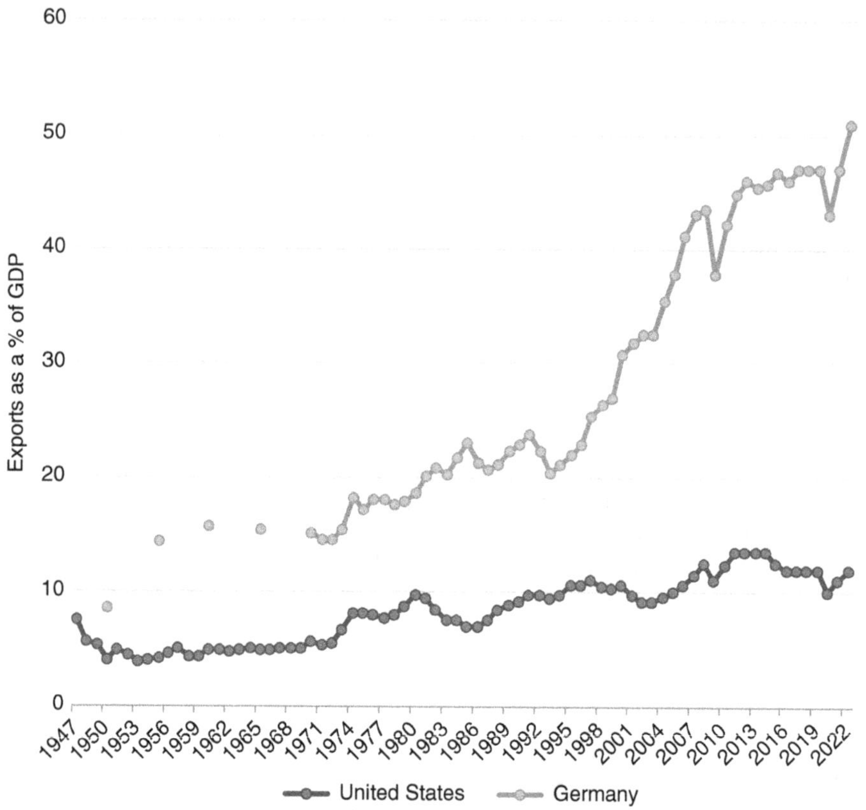

FIGURE 1.3 Exports as a percentage of GDP, United States and Germany, 1947–2022
Sources: US data from FRED (series: B020RE1Q156NBEA); Germany data prior to 1970 from Abelshauser (2011, 217) and since 1970 from World Bank Open Data (series: NE.EXP.GNFS.ZS, v. 03/28/2024).

welfare growth gave way to a post-Keynesian period of stagnating wages and declining welfare (Baccaro et al. 2022; Stockhammer 2015). In 2021, the finance, insurance, and real estate sectors made up a much larger share of the American economy (21% of GDP) than manufacturing (11% of GDP).[18]

This is not to reduce the complex US economy to just household consumption and credit. Knowledge-intensive sectors – such as information and communication technology (ICT), education, computing, and software – have driven employment, innovation, cutting-edge technology, investment, and economic growth both domestically and globally (Iversen and Soskice 2019; Soskice 2022; Hacker et al. 2021; Mazzucato 2015). The United States is also the world's largest funder of research and development, having spent USD 658 billion in 2019, while Germany spent USD 147.5 billion (both representing approximately 3%

[18] OECD (2024), *Value Added by Activity*, https://data-explorer.oecd.org/?lc=en.

of GDP).[19] While manufacturing has declined as a share of the US economy in recent decades, the country remains a major producer and exporter of cars, airplanes, energy, and pharmaceuticals, making it the world's second-largest exporter overall.[20] However, within the massive US economy, it is private consumption, not exports, that remains the most important driver of growth.

Housing is a key sector reinforcing the American growth regime. The housing sector itself is a large component of the US economy, with housing construction, home improvements, and rental payments making up a share of 16% of GDP in 2022.[21] Moreover, housing is also central to the country's business cycle. Edward Leamer (2015) famously noted that "housing really is the business cycle," indicating that housing downturns often preceded economic recessions in the postwar US economy and thus served as reliable warnings signs (cp. Jordà et al. 2016b).

Moreover, housing also indirectly stimulates the key elements of the American growth regime: Credit and consumption. The first mechanism is the *wealth effect*, where growing house and asset prices boost homeowners' sense of their own wealth, increasing their propensity to consume and discouraging them from saving (Case et al. 2013; Calomiris et al. 2013).[22] The second mechanism is the *credit effect*, suggesting that growing house prices – and the associated growth in homeowners' equity – allow homeowners to borrow money against their homes. American homeowners can leverage growing home equity by taking out home equity loans or refinancing their existing mortgages with larger ones, using these funds for consumer spending, home improvements, financial emergencies, health care, education, or travel (Aron et al. 2012; Greenspan and Kennedy 2008; Mian and Sufi 2011).[23] The third mechanism is the *global capital flow effect*. As the world's financial hegemon, the United States finances its large current account deficits via foreign

[19] US National Science Foundation (2022), *The State of U.S. Science and Engineering 2022*, https://ncses.nsf.gov/pubs/nsb20221/u-s-and-global-research-and-development.

[20] In 2022, in aggregate terms, the volume of American exports of goods and services was USD 3 trillion, while that of Germany was USD 2 trillion (current USD). See World Bank (2024), *Exports of Goods and Services*, https://data.worldbank.org/indicator/NE.EXP.GNFS.CD.

[21] National Association of Home Builders (NAHB), *Housing's Contribution to GDP*, www.nahb.org/news-and-economics/housing-economics/housings-economic-impact/housings-contribution-to-gross-domestic-product#.

[22] Case et al. (2013) estimate that a house-price boom, such as the one from 2001 to 2005 that increased housing wealth by USD 10 trillion, would increase consumer spending by 4.3 percent. Similarly, Calomiris et al. (2013) found that a one-dollar increase in housing wealth stimulates household spending by an average of eight cents.

[23] According to Greenspan and Kennedy (2008), US consumers extracted an average of USD 590 billion *annually* in home equity (i.e., through home equity loans, refinancing, and proceeds from the sale of homes) between 1991 and 2006 to finance personal expenses. In another study, Mian and Sufi (2011) show that US homeowners extracted 25 cents for every dollar in house-price gain from 2002 to 2006, resulting in USD 1.25 trillion in additional household borrowing during that time.

savings, such as through mortgage-backed securities or Treasury bonds. In 2022, foreign countries – above all, China, Taiwan, and Japan – owned USD 1.2 trillion in US mortgage-backed securities, a share of 13 percent of the entire mortgage-backed securities market.[24] When foreign capital flows into US bonds, long-term interest and mortgage rates fall, stimulating house prices, credit, and consumption (Ansell et al. 2018; Schwartz 2009; Schwartz and Blyth 2022). However, as seen during the 2008–2009 crash, declining house prices can also produce a vicious cycle of falling consumer spending (Mian et al. 2013).[25] Housing is thus deeply interlinked with America's large and globally competitive financial sector (Iversen and Soskice 2012).

By contrast, the German growth regime is export-oriented, with a strong focus on manufactured goods. From the postwar period to today, Germany has been far more reliant on exports for growth and prosperity than the United States (Wallich 1955; Kreile 1977; Eichengreen 1994; Lindlar and Holtfrerich 1997; Giersch et al. 1992). As Lucio Baccaro and Martin Höpner (2022, 240–241) show, export-led growth has been especially strong in the post-unification period from the 1990s, when exports became by far the most important contributor to growth (cp. Stockhammer 2015; Baccaro and Pontusson 2016).[26] Germany is a major exporter of high-value-added manufacturing goods such as cars, machine tools, chemicals, pharmaceuticals, and, increasingly, renewable energy components such as wind turbines (Nahm 2021). The manufacturing sector constituted 20% of the economy in 2022, while the finance, insurance, and real estate sector's share was considerably smaller at 14%.[27] Germany's information and communication sector (5% of GDP in 2022) is also smaller than its American counterpart (7.5% of GDP). In short, Germany's export-oriented manufacturing sector is the backbone of the economy, whereas the service sector remains underdeveloped and less productive compared to that of the United States (Falck and Wölfl 2018).

The foundation of the German growth regime lies in a set of economic institutions that have enhanced the nation's export competitiveness by *restraining* wages, private consumption, and household credit. From the post-WWII years, this moderation of domestic demand has maintained low inflation, resulting in competitive prices for German exports due to lower production and labor costs. Three institutional features stand out in restraining domestic demand and inflation. First, the country's coordinated wage bargaining

[24] Ginnie Mae (2022, September), *Foreign Ownership of Agency MBS*, www.ginniemae.gov/newsroom/publications/Documents/foreign_ownership_of_agency_mbs_september2022.pdf.

[25] Mian et al. (2013) find that for every dollar lost in housing wealth, consumers reduce spending by 5–7 cents. Similarly, Case et al. (2013) estimate that a 35% decrease in housing wealth, such as the one from 2005 to 2009, would produce a 3.5% decrease in consumer spending.

[26] In the postwar decades, German exports were an important driver of economic growth, but not always *the* most important driver compared to domestic demand. Even so, the postwar German economy was export-oriented, meaning that macroeconomic policies and institutions privileged export growth over domestic demand (cp. Eichengreen 2008; Iversen and Soskice 2012).

[27] OECD, *Value Added by Activity*.

system has successfully limited real wage growth and kept labor costs low relative to its European competitors (Iversen and Soskice 2012). The collective bargaining system gives Germany a competitive edge in the eurozone, as many of its southern neighbors lack similar structures to limit wage growth (see, e.g., Höpner 2019; Matthijs and Blyth 2015). Second, strict fiscal and monetary policies have reinforced Germany's low inflation regime, a regime in which the country's conservative central bank, the Bundesbank, historically threatened monetary tightening should unions demand higher wages or governments engage in inflationary fiscal spending (Hall and Franzese 1998; Manow 2020). Even within the eurozone, the Bundesbank continued to promote hawkish monetary policy (Reisenbichler 2020b). Third, the country has developed a restrictive credit and mortgage lending system that *limits* credit expansion and debt-financed consumption (Mertens 2015; Wiedemann 2021). Instead of going into debt, German households have high levels of savings. In 2023, German households saved 10.4% of disposable income, while American households saved just 4.7%.[28] In short, since the post-WWII years, these institutions have protected export-oriented industries by systematically lowering domestic costs and boosting export competitiveness (Baccaro and Höpner 2022; Höpner 2019).

In Germany, the housing system serves the opposite economic purpose to that of the United States: It *restrains* housing demand and prices, household credit, and consumption. As in the United States, housing is an important component of the German economy. In 2023, it comprised a share of 19 percent of the country's economy, including housing construction, housing services, the real estate industry, and mortgage lending sectors.[29] However, the key difference between the two countries is that German property is *not* a transmission belt to stimulate household spending or borrowing in the wider economy. Unlike the American case, there is no evidence for *wealth* or *credit effects* in Germany, meaning that rising house prices do not produce higher consumer spending or lending (Voigtländer 2014; Kofner 2014; Geiger et al. 2016; Stockhammer et al. 2021). If anything, high down payments and rising property prices incentivize aspiring German homeowners to save more (Geiger et al. 2016). The absence of wealth and credit effects is the result of the country's conservative mortgage system, which does not routinely offer home equity loans to fund personal spending. In contrast to American homeowners, Germans do not use their homes as credit cards.

[28] Federal Reserve Economic Data (2024), *Personal Savings Rate*, https://fred.stlouisfed.org/series/PSAVERT#0; German Federal Statistics Office, *National Accounts*, www.destatis.de/EN/Themes/Economy/National-Accounts-Domestic-Product/Tables/domestic-product-important-economic-indicators.html?nn=22776.

[29] This definition is broader than the common measure of housing as a share of the economy in the US, which does not include the mortgage lending sector, for example. Hellwig, M. (2024), *Die Bedeutung der Immobilienwirtschaft in Zahlen*, Zentraler Immobilien Ausschuss, https://zia-deutschland.de/wp-content/uploads/2021/05/Bedeutung-der-Immobilienwirtschaft-in-Zahlen.pdf.

Germany's conservative mortgage market complements the macroeconomic priorities of the export-oriented growth regime. First, stable house prices and housing costs – achieved through restricted access to credit and rent controls – help keep down wage demands and inflation, which are conducive to export competitiveness (cp. Muellbauer 2018; Führer 1995; 2015). The country's wage bargaining institutions not only restrain wages but also depresses demand for mortgage-financed homeownership (Johnston and Regan 2017). Second, rising house prices and the associated profit-making opportunities in real estate can shift labor and capital into housing and away from Germany's key manufacturing sector, thereby hurting the sector's export competitiveness (Égert and Kierzenkowski 2014). Sebastian Kohl and Alexander Spielau (2022) identify a trade-off between the strengths of a country's housing sector vis-à-vis its export sector. The two sectors tend to have contradictory macroeconomic needs: The housing sector might favor stronger mortgage lending or higher wages to stimulate housing, while the export sector benefits from low wages and low domestic demand. For these and other reasons, export-oriented Germany has had a "repressed" housing market, especially in recent decades (Kohl and Spielau 2022).

A Historical Institutionalist Explanation: Growth Regimes and Policy Feedback

These macroeconomic complementarities between the two countries' growth regimes and housing markets were the cumulative result of political actions and policy feedback that unfolded over long periods of time. The historical account in this book suggests that each country's growth regime initiated distinct policy actions and feedback effects, which *expanded* American housing programs while *undermining* German ones over time. In the American case, early housing programs reshaped the demand-led growth regime by making it more dependent on housing-based growth. As housing became ever more central to American capitalism over time, political leaders retained or expanded housing programs in subsequent policymaking rounds. In Germany, early housing programs initially reinforced the country's export-oriented growth regime by addressing post-WWII housing shortages, reducing housing costs, and keeping wages low. However, rather than increasing the German economy's reliance on housing-based growth, policymakers started viewing housing programs as creating frictions with the export-oriented growth regime once housing shortages were resolved. The increasingly peripheral role of housing to the German export-oriented economy ultimately enabled policymakers to retrench housing programs.

Governments drove this long-term policy divergence, using state power to shift public and private resources either into housing or away from it. As Torben Iversen and David Soskice (2012, 37) note, "governments … are deeply concerned with promoting the high value-added sectors of their economies, in which they enjoy comparative institutional advantage." In other words, governments tend to create policy landscapes that they believe benefit the key sectors of their economies (Hall 2024). While housing finance is a core sector in the American demand-led economy, it is more peripheral in Germany's export-oriented economy in which manufacturing industries are the national champions. The different positioning of housing within each country's growth regime has created distinct housing policy dynamics in the two countries, including a century-long American bipartisan consensus supporting housing programs and a German cross-party consensus favoring the eventual retrenchment of these programs.

The American demand-led growth regime fostered political dynamics that led to a century-long expansion of housing programs. During the Great Depression, US politicians across the spectrum viewed the struggling housing market as holding back domestic demand. In response, they adopted policies to steer capital into housing and boost domestic demand by stimulating housing construction, employment, and wages. Importantly, depression-era housing programs fundamentally transformed American capitalism. First, the new housing-based growth machine relied on government support for its functioning and survival. Indeed, these programs created a new market for consumer-friendly and cheap mortgages that private actors were unable to provide on their own. Second, they made housing finance a national champion deeply intertwined with the emerging American demand-led growth regime to the point where their economic priorities became indistinguishable. Following the depression, successive governments expanded these housing programs as a routine measure to stimulate the economy well into the postwar period, including providing support for veterans.

From the 1960s to the 1990s, US politicians across the spectrum continued expanding housing programs, which made them ever more integral to the financializing American growth regime in this period. When inflation and rising interest rates threatened housing-based growth, policymakers sprang into action to rescue the housing finance architecture they had helped build in earlier decades. Their actions once again transformed the American growth regime by further deepening its dependence on housing-based growth. First, policymakers utilized the power of the state to create what would become a multi-trillion-dollar market for mortgage-backed securities, which relied on government support for its survival. This move also elevated the quasi-public agencies Fannie Mae and Freddie Mac to become America's most important mortgage players and pro-housing-policy lobbyists. Second, policymakers expanded housing programs to stimulate economic activity in marginalized communities. However, this growth strategy was fraught with challenges, as racialized minorities remained disproportionately targeted for predatory lending. Third, these housing programs turned American homes into credit cards. As homeowners experienced massive gains in home values, they began borrowing against their homes for consumer spending, all while policymakers subsidized this practice through the mortgage interest deduction. The growing role of housing in America's financializing economy thus gave policymakers additional reasons to expand housing programs.

By the time of the 2008–2009 housing crash, American housing programs were already deeply embedded in the demand-led growth regime. Even though housing programs had contributed to the housing bubble, policymakers felt compelled to double down on these programs. Politicians expanded the programs with bipartisan support, as they saw housing as both the root of economic disaster and the key to recovery. They bailed out Fannie Mae and Freddie Mac – institutions created and championed by earlier generations of policymakers and housing programs – which effectively quasi-nationalized America's multi-trillion-dollar mortgage market. Additionally, the Fed offered unusual support for housing. Remarkably, these housing policy expansions, intended as temporary measures, became entrenched. The "new normal" of a quasi-nationalized mortgage market and direct central bank support is the culmination of a century-long process of housing policy expansion to promote housing-based growth. Despite growing discomfort among policymakers about the American state's excessive role in the housing sector, its importance to the demand-led growth regime led policymakers to retain expanded housing programs. Even long after the country's economic recovery, policymakers feared that reducing the state's role could disrupt the housing sector and the American growth regime; such fears trapped them in the expanded housing policy landscape.

This is not to discount other factors reinforcing America's spectacular housing policy expansion. As these programs helped increase the number of homeowners over time, policymakers had strong incentives to protect the interests of a growing homeowning voting constituency. In addition, well-organized housing groups lobbied aggressively for retaining or expanding housing programs. Crucially, the central positioning of homeowners and these interest groups within the American demand-led growth regime made politicians responsive to their demands. In other words, these groups' material interests were perfectly congruent with the larger macroeconomic objectives of the American demand-led economy. In short, these political factors reinforced macroeconomic ones, creating a multiplicity of forces that drove policymakers to expand housing programs over time.

In contrast, the German export-oriented growth regime fostered political dynamics that *undermined* housing programs over time (cp. Jacobs and Weaver 2015). Early post-WWII housing programs were initially highly complementary to the export-oriented economy. With broad support from across the political spectrum, German policymakers established generous housing programs for both owner-occupied (favored by right-leaning parties) and rental housing (favored by the left) to address postwar housing shortages. Importantly, these policies simultaneously strengthened the fundamentals of the country's export-oriented economy. First, early housing programs alleviated labor shortages in industrial areas and improved labor mobility. Second, they were anti-inflationary policies that limited housing costs and thus curbed inflationary wage demands that would have been detrimental to export-driven growth. Third, policymakers retained a restrictive housing finance system that encouraged household savings over easy access to credit. In essence, early German housing programs were more than just housing initiatives – they functioned as a form of wage and industrial policy, supporting the needs of the export-oriented economy.

From the mid-1970s, however, policymakers' perception of postwar-era housing programs changed: They came to view them as *contradicting* the German export-oriented growth regime. When housing shortages abated and the country experienced rising unemployment, public debt, and inflation, policymakers increasingly viewed these programs as structural economic problems rather than solutions. They started criticizing them for creating fiscal deficits, steering capital away from manufacturing, and creating excess demand and house-price inflation in times of sufficient housing supply. The influential Bundesbank and Council of Economic Experts (Sachverständigenrat für Wirtschaft) provided the economic rationale for these criticisms. As a result, German politicians on the left and right started scaling down housing programs, especially those for rental housing. For the time being, however, they retained homeownership support to promote conservative family life, create household wealth, and privatize old-age provision, yet decidedly not as a long-term economic growth strategy.

In the 2000s, German policymakers developed a broad-based consensus in favor of retrenching the remaining large-scale homeownership and rental housing programs, perceiving them as clashing with the export-oriented growth regime. Unlike in the United States, early German housing programs had not transformed the country's model of capitalism into one reliant on housing-based growth. Quite the opposite. When German policymakers experimented with American-style housing policies, such as a mortgage interest deduction, to stimulate the eastern economy in the post-unification years, it resulted in a prolonged housing slump that exacerbated the country's economic problems of the late 1990s and early 2000s. To strengthen the core of the German economy – export-oriented manufacturing – Christian Democrats and Social Democrats decided to retrench these programs and utilized the power of the state to redirect capital from housing to the industrial sector. The peripheral, and to some extent even contradictory, role of housing programs within the export-oriented economy facilitated their retrenchment.

The existing literature on policy feedback provides several reasons for why German policy retrenchment should *not* have occurred. German homeownership programs, for example, enjoyed support from a powerful housing lobby, (aspiring) homeowners, and the mass public, as well as ideological backing from the Christian Democrats (Pierson 1993; van Kersbergen 1995; Campbell 2012; Mettler and SoRelle 2018; Béland et al. 2022). However, the *macroeconomic* imperatives of the country's export-oriented growth regime ultimately prevailed over these factors.

CONTRIBUTIONS AND IMPLICATIONS

This book adds to an established literature that places housing squarely in the center of the comparative and American political economy scholarship on capitalism, welfare states, and financial markets (Aalbers 2016; Ansell 2019; Einstein et al. 2020; Fligstein 2021; Fuller 2019; Hankinson 2018; Hyman 2011; Immergluck 2009; Johnston and Kurzer 2021; Kohl 2017; Krippner 2011; Logemann 2012; Marble and Nall 2021; McCabe 2016; Mertens 2015; Prasad 2012; Quinn 2019; Schwartz and Seabrooke 2009; Schwartz 2009; Taylor 2019; Thompson 2010; Thurston 2018; Wiedemann 2021). This is a curiously recent development. While news outlets have repeatedly emphasized the importance of housing, social scientists have paid much less attention to it. This book highlights the massive macroeconomic and distributive consequences of housing programs: They shape the world's largest asset and financial markets, influence the distribution of wealth in society, and spur economic activity well beyond the housing sector itself.

This book first advances upon an important literature on diverse capitalist models by investigating the *politics of economic policy* behind these models with rich historical detail. The paradigmatic "varieties of capitalism" (Hall and Soskice 2001; Amable 2003) and "growth model" literatures (Baccaro et al. 2022; Hassel and Palier 2021) offer systematic understandings of how the German "coordinated" or "export-led" and the American "liberal" or "demand-led" economies operate and differ. While numerous studies have investigated the ever-changing institutional arrangements of these models (e.g., Thelen 2014; Streeck 2009), fewer have focused on the role of the state – that is, the politics and history of economic policy behind these models (exceptions are Manow 2020 and Prasad 2012).[30] This book delves into the co-evolution of the two countries' growth regimes and key economic policies over the past century through the lens of housing. It shows that American and German policymakers embarked on different housing policy paths, because they viewed stimulative housing programs respectively as constitutive to American demand-generated prosperity and, by contrast, as inimical to German export-generated prosperity. These divergent state actions have subsequently transformed the very natures of American and German capitalism.

Relatedly, the literature on capitalist diversity has rarely investigated in-depth *sectoral government policy* within and across countries over long periods of time. While existing studies have privileged the role of sectoral producer groups – and coalitions between them – in bringing about institutional changes in collective bargaining, vocational training, and the labor market

[30] An older comparative political economy literature was centered more strongly on the active role of the state in the economy and economic policymaking (cp. Hall 1986; Martin 1991).

(e.g., Thelen 2014), this book emphasizes the role of the state through *sectoral* government policy (Ornston and Vail 2016; Nahm 2021). The book demonstrates that different economic models rely on different sectors for producing prosperity and that policymakers tend to privilege core sectors over peripheral ones in aiming to generate prosperity (cp. Bohle and Regan 2021; Iversen and Soskice 2012; Haffert and Mertens 2021; Hall 2024; Hassel and Palier 2021; Prasad 2012; Thelen 2019). This book's sectoral logic is as follows: The contrasting American and German growth regimes, in which housing plays different macroeconomic roles, led to contrasting political dynamics and sharply divergent policy trajectories in the two countries. In the United States, housing is a key sector for producing growth, prosperity, and employment, whereas it is much less significant in Germany. Consequently, housing finance became a policy-privileged national champion in America, but not in Germany, where export industries remain the national champions.

Second, the book contributes to scholarship on *policy feedback* in historical institutionalism by treating growth regimes as a novel source of policy feedback. Existing studies have fruitfully examined how new policies create constituencies, mass publics, interest groups, and state capacities that in turn strengthen or undermine these same policies over time (Béland et al. 2022; Pierson 1993; Campbell 2012; Thurston 2015; Busemeyer et al. 2021; Mettler and SoRelle 2018; SoRelle 2020). Yet such studies rarely directly compare the feedback effects of similar policies across countries. This book shows that American and German homeownership programs exhibited contrasting feedback effects, attributable to policymakers' different macroeconomic priorities, leading to the expansion of American programs and the retrenchment of German ones over time. Without discounting the influence of interest groups or homeowning constituencies, this book argues that American policymakers expanded homeownership programs mainly because they viewed such support as congruent with, if not constitutive of, the demand-led growth regime. In contrast, against the opposition of lobby groups and homeowning constituencies, German policymakers eliminated homeowner programs, as they ultimately viewed such subsidies as contradicting the export-oriented economy.

Relatedly, the book shows the importance of considering the positioning of interest groups within a growth regime. My findings suggest that similar kinds of interest groups can have varying degrees of political influence across countries, based on their positioning at the core or periphery of a growth regime. Both the United States and Germany are home to powerful housing lobbies, such as realtors, homebuilders, and mortgage bankers in the United States (e.g., Howard 1997) and Germany's building societies and construction firms and unions (e.g., Egner et al. 2004). The centrality of the housing sector within the American growth regime places the housing lobby in a comparatively powerful position, enabling it to advocate demands that are congruent with the objectives of the growth regime. Nonetheless, as the empirical discussion in this book demonstrates, the American housing lobby did not dictate housing policy; policymakers often pursued their own strategies of supporting the country's housing market autonomously. While American policymakers and the housing lobby generally pursued the same goal of supporting the country's housing market, they often differed on how to achieve it. In Germany, where housing plays a less central role to the growth regime, the housing lobby held a comparatively weaker structural position from which to defend housing programs over time, as their demands and interests were less congruent with the objectives of the export-oriented economy (cp. Kohl and Spielau 2022).

Third, the book demonstrates important yet previously neglected differences in how policymakers deploy the infrastructural power of the state for economic objectives (cp. Mann 1984; King and Lieberman 2009; Krippner 2011; Morgan and Orloff 2017; Vogel 2018; Quinn 2019; Schwartz 2020; Braun 2020; Wansleben 2022). American policymakers have repeatedly used state power to absorb risk in financial markets to channel private capital, which otherwise might have gone elsewhere, into housing. In doing so, the American state crafted a financialized home lending system that became addicted to government support. In Germany, policymakers ultimately used state power to steer capital *away* from housing – preventing a financialization of the sector – and into manufacturing. As this book suggests, the difference can be explained by policymakers' different macroeconomic priorities: Boosting domestic demand in the United States versus export-oriented manufacturing in Germany.

Fourth, my findings challenge political economy scholarship on party politics by showing that party positions regarding housing are not fixed and are more nuanced than merely reflecting the material interests of a party's core constituencies (Beramendi et al. 2015; Ansell 2014). The common wisdom is that center-right parties favor homeownership programs, as they represent affluent asset owners, while left-of-center parties support rental housing programs, given their propertyless constituencies. Scholarship has also described homeownership as an ideological mainstay of center-right Christian Democratic parties in Europe, as homeownership is seen as promoting conservative values such as traditional family life in single-family homes and private ownership over public welfare (Esping-Andersen 1990; van Kersbergen 1995). Yet macroeconomic imperatives can override constituency concerns and party ideology, resulting in high levels of bipartisanship. In Germany, the center-right Christian Democrats *and* the center-left Social Democrats agreed to eliminate homeownership programs. In the United States, Democrats *and* Republicans share a consensus in favor of supporting homeownership despite intense polarization in many other policy areas (Schelkle 2012; McCarty et al. 2013). Contrasting macroeconomic imperatives explain both the degree of bipartisan consensus and the divergent policy outcomes in both countries.

Fifth, the book contends that housing is an important yet overlooked element of Germany's capitalist model (Logemann 2012; Mertens 2015; Kohl 2017). Recent scholarship on the United States has successfully integrated housing as an area of investigation in the American political economy (Prasad 2012; Thurston 2018; Quinn 2019). In contrast, influential scholarship on the German political economy has rarely investigated housing, focusing instead on other areas of the economy: Collective bargaining, welfare and labor programs, vocational training, corporate governance, and monetary and fiscal policy (Manow 2020; Hall and Franzese 1998; Streeck 2009; Thelen 2014). Yet housing is an important part of the German model, as government actions have helped to establish low-cost housing that contributed to wage compression, low inflation, productivity, and restrained credit and consumption. It is partly for this reason that Germany remains, to the mystification of Anglo-American observers, a nation of renters.

ORGANIZATION OF THIS BOOK

The book traces the co-evolution of each country's housing programs and growth regime across three distinct historical periods (cp. Hall 2020, 2021, 2022). It begins with the Great Depression in the United States and WWII in Germany, extending into the postwar "Golden Age" of capitalism through the late 1960s. It then examines the turbulent post-Keynesian period from the early 1970s to the 1990s. The book concludes with the Great Recession of 2008–2009 and its aftermath up to today. Each historical era, along with its developments in the international political economy, produced distinct economic challenges for the American and German growth regimes that profoundly influenced the housing policymaking context (Blyth and Matthijs 2017).

The first part of the book compares the origins and early evolutions of the two countries' growth regimes and housing programs. Chapter 2 tells the story of how American policymakers established housing programs as an engine of economic growth during the Great Depression. They discovered that subsidizing mortgage debt via government guarantees was an effective countercyclical tool to help overcome the depression and even permanently stimulate the economy. While the country went into the depression with virtually no national housing programs, it emerged from it with an expansive toolkit of demand-side housing programs deeply interlinked with the American demand-led growth regime.

Chapter 3 discusses the origins of housing programs in post-WWII Germany and how these programs reinforced the country's postwar export-oriented economy. To overcome severe housing shortages after the war, the German government implemented a range of generous housing programs for rental housing and homeownership. Critically, these programs strengthened the export-oriented growth regime and contributed to the country's postwar economic miracle. They established low-cost housing for workers and the middle class, which helped improve both competitiveness by limiting wage inflation and productivity by improving labor mobility.

The second part of the book analyzes the diverging housing policy trajectories in the United States and Germany during the post-Keynesian period. Chapter 4 details how American policymakers expanded housing programs into new areas of the home lending market between the late 1960s and the early 1990s. Amid rising inflation and interest rates, they feared that impaired mortgage lending could threaten housing-based growth. In response, they established a new market for housing bonds underwritten by the American state to ensure the availability of cheap mortgages. As mortgage credit became ever more plentiful, policymakers discovered the growth potential of leveraging homes for consumer spending in times of stagnating wages.

Chapter 5 shows that German housing programs reached a turning point in the mid-1970s. While these programs had reinforced the country's postwar export-oriented growth regime during severe housing shortages, policymakers later came to view them as increasingly conflicting with the economy's needs once shortages abated. German economic elites and policymakers criticized these programs for increasing public debt, diverting capital from export-oriented manufacturing, and creating inflation. Consequently, policymakers started withdrawing rental programs. However, they retained homeownership programs, prioritizing ideological factors – such as creating household wealth or old-age security through homeownership – over the potentially damaging effects of these programs on the German growth regime.

The final part of the book contrasts the retrenchment of German housing programs with the striking expansion of American housing programs during and after the Great Recession of 2008–2009. Chapter 6 demonstrates that American policymakers doubled down on housing programs in response to the housing crash. By bailing out Fannie Mae and Freddie Mac, they nationalized the country's housing finance market. Their goal was to rescue and revive the country's reeling economy. Even the Fed established a new layer of government support for housing in the postcrisis period. Remarkably, these crisis measures, initially designed to be temporary, became entrenched features of the American demand-led growth regime.

Chapter 7 explains the retrenchment of German housing programs in the mid-2000s. After reunification, the country experienced a housing boom and bust that left it with one million vacant homes. In response, German policymakers eliminated the remaining large-scale housing programs for homeownership and rental housing. At a time when Germany was considered the sick man of Europe, they viewed these programs as structural economic problems that contradicted the macroeconomic needs of the reeling German export-oriented economy.

The book's conclusion, Chapter 8, highlights paradoxes of American and German housing policymaking amid surging house prices during the 2010s and early 2020s. While the US housing market is one of the country's greatest economic strengths, it could also be the source of its undoing, as housing programs can fuel financial bubbles and create turmoil. In contrast, German policymakers retrenched the housing programs that once supported the country's growth regime by deflating housing costs. This retrenchment left them grappling with mounting housing affordability problems that threatened inflation and wage demands detrimental to export competitiveness. The conclusion also extends this book's lessons to other advanced economies such as Austria, Canada, the Netherlands, Sweden, and the United Kingdom.

2

Discovering Housing-Based Growth in America

America's housing finance market did not become a national champion overnight. The roots of the country's government-supported housing model lie in the Great Depression. As the country experienced skyrocketing unemployment, millions of households faced the prospect of defaulting on their mortgages and losing their homes, with little government support in place to cushion the blow for either households or banks. Faced with foreclosure in 1931, a married couple in Illinois took drastic measures. Just days before the new owner was to take over their foreclosed home, they left a note: "We will be gone by Saturday." That Saturday, on March 14, 1931, they were found dead in their home, having ended their lives over the loss of their home.[1] Their tragic case is emblematic of the desperation many households experienced during the depression. As President Franklin D. Roosevelt (FDR) expressed in a radio broadcast in May 1933: "The country was dying by inches ... there was actually in process of destruction the property of millions of people."[2] For FDR, reviving the economy and solving the problem of housing were intertwined priorities that required radical measures.

It was in this context that American policymakers *discovered* the economic growth potential of housing programs. They realized that these programs could be not only effective countercyclical tools to mitigate the worst effects of the Great Depression but also permanent tools to stimulate the economy beyond the depression. Housing became America's government-sponsored engine of growth. The logic was straightforward: Subsidized mortgages would produce cascade effects throughout the economy, stimulating bank lending, construction, employment and wages, and consumer spending.

[1] "Couple end lives over loss of home" (March 15, 1931), *New York Times*.

[2] Roosevelt, F. D. (May 7, 1933), *Second fireside chat*, The American Presidency Project, www.presidency.ucsb.edu/documents/second-fireside-chat.

Producing an "ever-growing output of new homes," as Leo Grebler (1960, 109) described it, became a "national objective."

The Great Depression was the key moment in establishing America's government-supported housing model. As Price Fishback and colleagues (2020, 857) note, "the federal government entered the Depression with essentially no role in the nation's housing market." However, it emerged from the depression with an expansive toolkit of *demand-side* housing programs that would forever change the American political economy.[3] The presidential administrations of Herbert Hoover (1929–1933) and FDR (1933–1945) both took action to stop the foreclosure crisis and stabilize the mortgage market, but FDR took things much further. For his administration, the homeownership market – not public housing – was the key lever to turn the economy around. The core idea behind New Deal housing programs was not direct government spending; rather, it was the transformation of mortgage markets to lower costs for borrowers and minimize risk for creditors. To get banks back to lending and consumers back to spending, the FDR administration created the Federal Housing Administration (FHA) in 1934 to provide banks with insurance against mortgage defaults. In turn, the FHA required banks to offer cheap and consumer-friendly mortgages to households. In 1938, the FDR administration created the public mortgage association Fannie Mae to buy FHA-insured mortgages from banks, enabling banks to issue even more mortgages. The strategy worked, as the housing sector and the economy began to recover by the late 1930s. By then, policymakers had made a valuable discovery: The seemingly endless economic potential of housing-based growth.

Depression-era housing programs profoundly reshaped the American political economy and its politics of housing policy well into the future. First, these housing programs created a housing-based growth machine at the center of the American demand-led economy – although one that excluded racialized minorities from its prosperity-creating potential. For policymakers, housing became a strategic sector crucial for generating domestic demand through a virtuous cycle of mortgage lending, housing construction, employment and wage growth, and private consumption. As Charles Abrams (1946, 55) noted, the "dominating motive" behind these housing programs was "the vitalizing effect of building operations on economic activity." Second, the emerging housing-based growth machine depended on these programs for its functioning and survival. These programs formed the foundation of a highly liquid, stable, and affordable mortgage market – including the beloved 30-year fixed-rate mortgage – that private market actors would have been unable to provide without government support (Hyman 2011, 46). As housing held a "special position" (Grebler 1960, 15)

[3] I define demand-side programs as "per-unit subsidies to demanders" irrespective of whether demanders build new homes or buy existing homes, while supply-side programs are subsidies to builders of *new* homes (Glaeser and Gyourko 2008, 137–141).

in the American political economy, policymakers had strong incentives to expand – or at least retain – housing programs in subsequent policymaking.

This is precisely what happened in the post-WWII period. Although wartime economic activity had revived the American economy, it also led to massive housing supply shortages and fears of an economic slowdown once the war ended. The political response was to expand housing programs, drawing inspiration from New-Deal-era initiatives. Policymakers extended homeownership programs to millions of (predominantly white) veterans returning from WWII and the Korean War (Katznelson 2005), hoping that veterans would fuel the housing-based growth machine by stimulating construction, employment, and mass consumption of consumer goods to fill new suburban homes. The strategy worked again, leading to a booming postwar economy with housing as a major driving force.

SETTING THE STAGE: THE AGRICULTURAL ORIGINS OF HOUSING POLICY

The origins of America's consumption- and credit-based growth regime lie in the early twentieth century (Prasad 2012). At that time, the American economy experienced rapid urbanization and industrialization alongside a strong but gradually diminishing agricultural sector (Levy 2020, 236; Quinn 2019, ch. 5). Although there were virtually no permanent national housing programs prior to the Great Depression, policymakers had already experimented with credit and tax programs in the area of agriculture during the late nineteenth and the early twentieth centuries. These programs subsequently served as templates and inspirations for national housing programs during the Great Depression. Just prior to the depression, in the 1920s, residential housing had gained importance in an economy increasingly based on mass production, consumption, and consumer credit (Levy 2020, ch. 12; Prasad 2012; Quinn 2019; Cohen 2003). As nonfarm jobs grew in industrial areas, urban housing and mortgage markets boomed, with households benefiting from better-paid commercial and industrial jobs in urban areas. Their increased purchasing power not only raised housing expectations, such as the aspiration to own a home, but also fueled middle-class aspirations of acquiring consumer goods such as radio sets, refrigerators, vacuum cleaners, electric irons, and cars – goods that were increasingly financed with personal loans (Quinn 2019, ch. 5; Jacobs 2007, ch. 2). In other words, residential housing became an important part of an emerging yet fragile consumption- and credit-based growth regime (Prasad 2012, 81).

The preludes of modern housing finance programs lie in the field of agriculture. The fundamental problem in nineteenth-century agricultural financing was that capital was abundant in the country's northeast, while the peripheral south and west faced a scarcity of capital (Quinn 2019). Without a national capital market to efficiently allocate capital flows among regions, the peripheral credit system experienced severe fluctuations in credit availability and high credit costs (Prasad 2012, 73). The response to this problem was a government-sponsored system of farm credit that became a precursor to the depression-era housing finance programs. The Federal Farm Loan Act of 1916 established the Federal Farm Loan System, which channeled private capital into agriculture and supplied farmers with long-term loans, stable credit, and below-market interest rates compared to private banks (Shaw 2019, 514; Radford 2013, 42). Notably, this system did not offer direct government loans to farmers but created quasi-public Federal Land Banks that raised *private* funds by issuing tax-privileged bonds (Quinn 2019, 80).[4] In short, US policy-makers used the power of the state to steer capital into areas that the private market did not serve, a precedent for depression-era housing interventions (Quinn 2019, ch. 4; Radford 2013, 11; Shaw 2019).

Intriguingly, the American farm credit system was partly inspired by Germany's system of agricultural credit based on *Landschaften* (mortgage cooperatives) and the "covered bonds" (*Pfandbriefe*) that they issued.[5] American policymakers held the German system in high regard, as it had provided stable credit to nobles, landholders, and farmers from the eighteenth century onward. It did so by drawing capital from urban merchants into more rural agricultural areas through merchants' investments in covered bonds issued by the *Landschaften* (Quinn 2019, ch. 4; Wandschneider 2015). In the early twentieth century, several US government reports, commissions, and delegations endorsed the adoption of aspects of the German model (Quinn 2019, ch. 4). While the eventual American farm credit system was not a simple emulation of the German model, it was an "Americanized version" of it (Quinn 2019, 81) that similarly distributed credit across the entire country, offering stable, long-term credit to farmers. Both systems attracted private capital into credit cooperatives by issuing bonds against the collateral of mortgages. However, they

[4] The act established the Federal Farm Loan Board, which was in charge of creating a system of twelve regional quasi-public Federal Land Banks that would lend money to newly created regional farmers' cooperatives and, through those cooperatives, to individual farmers. Most importantly, the federal government's *implicit* backing of the Federal Land Banks and their tax-privileged bonds (issued against the security of cooperatives' farm loans) attracted private capital into the system. By the late 1920s, the land banks were financing 20 percent of all farm debt in the country (Quinn 2019, 83).

[5] *Landschaften* were German credit cooperatives that originated in Prussia in the late eighteenth century and provided farm mortgages to their members. They financed their activities by issuing "covered bonds," which were secured either individually by the borrower's estate or jointly by all members' estates. Covered bonds were relatively conservative financial instruments (i.e., estate values were estimated conservatively, and lending was restricted to 50–60 percent of the value), making them historically low-risk investments. While the German state legally treated these covered bonds preferentially as "senior" debt in the case of default, it did not directly back these institutions or bonds in the case of defaults; rather, the *Landschaften* themselves – through members' pools of assets – were responsible for backing covered bonds (Wandschneider 2014, 2015; Quinn 2019, ch. 4).

differed in how each system managed the risk of credit defaults. The German system managed risk *privately*. The state did not back the *Landschaften* nor their bonds; rather the *Landschaften* and their members *jointly* backed the system, and conservative lending regulations ensured that there was little speculative activity. The American system relied more heavily on the state to manage risk, with the state *implicitly* backing the farm lending system and providing tax privileges on the bonds of land banks. Indeed, the US federal government repeatedly delivered financial assistance to the system during the 1920s and 1930s (and even the 1980s) (Glock 2021). The American and German mortgage stories are thus connected at the root. As the remainder of this book shows, however, they diverged profoundly over time.

In the area of taxation, the American mortgage interest deduction (discussed in detail later in this chapter) has subsidized mortgage credit since well before the Great Depression, again with some important agricultural roots. In fact, its origins had little to do with stimulating residential housing or homeownership. Rather, it allowed taxpayers to deduct the interest on all kinds of personal and business loans from their declared income, not just mortgage interest. The Revenue Act of 1913, which established the federal income tax code, specified that taxpayers could deduct "all interest paid within the year by a taxable person on indebtedness."[6] Notably, the Congressional Record does not indicate that the deduction's creation was related to boosting homeownership or housing. Congressional hearings do not reveal interest group pressure, probably because only the richest two percent of US households were subject to America's progressive income taxation system at the time (Morgan and Prasad 2009). As Dennis Ventry (2010, 241) argues, "the better interpretation for why legislators included the deduction in the original Revenue Act is that it was extraordinarily difficult, both practically and administratively, to differentiate between the personal and profit-seeking expenses of family-run farms, small businesses, and individual proprietors." Christopher Howard (1997, 54) similarly suggests that agricultural politics probably played a role in establishing the deduction, as "[a]gricultural workers comprised nearly one-third of the labor force and frequently incurred heavy debts." However, since most people in the US did not pay income tax until WWII, the deduction remained dormant until policymakers transformed it into a narrower, housing-specific tax program in the post-WWII period.

In urban America, despite growing housing shortages and rising housing costs in the early twentieth century – driven by immigration, urbanization, and industrialization – policymakers ignored the housing problem until WWI. At that time, the United States was still a nation of renters, with a homeownership rate of only 45 percent (Kohl 2017). Much like in Europe, WWI exacerbated urban housing shortages due to a slump in civilian housing production and an

[6] Revenue Act of 1913, ch. 16, 38 Stat. 114 (1913).

influx of workers into war production areas. Like their European counterparts, American policymakers responded with emergency housing programs and adopted rent controls in several states to limit housing costs. First, in 1917, the federal government created new housing for workers in war production areas, built and owned by temporary US government agencies.[7] However, these programs expired with the war's end in 1918, having produced only 15,000 single-family homes and another 15,000 temporary housing units such as dormitories for workers. As policymakers believed in the superiority of private housing solutions over public ones, they privatized most of these units immediately after the war (Harloe 1995, 85; Quinn 2019; Snowden 2013). Second, they adopted rent controls, supported by labor unions, to cope with rising urban housing costs (Harloe 1995, 135). However, rent controls were implemented only at the state and local levels, such as in New York and Washington, DC, and most such provisions had expired by the time of the 1920s housing boom that alleviated housing shortages (Fogelson 2013; Radford 1996, 46). In contrast to Germany (as Chapter 3 shows), where public housing programs and rent controls were well established by the 1920s, US policymakers eliminated similar measures. As Michael Harloe (1995, 133) puts it, "the dynamism of the American economy, with a housing-led boom, meant that even most lower-middle-class and skilled, better-paid working-class households could look to the private market for accommodation."

By the 1920s, the American economy had transitioned further away from agriculture and toward the mass production of industrial and consumer goods. Residential housing became a crucial element of the emerging, yet fragile, growth regime based on private demand, credit, and consumption. Demand for urban and suburban housing surged in the 1920s, owing to pent-up demand after WWI, the rise of the automobile, and demographic factors such as the continued influx of workers into metropolitan areas and general population growth. America's urban population increased from less than 30 percent in the 1880s to more than 50 percent in the 1920s in pursuit of job opportunities in commercial and industrial centers (Quinn 2019, 89). Such jobs paid higher wages, which, in turn, increased households' aspirations of living in single-family homes. At the same time, credit was abundant and investor confidence high, partly due to the establishment of the Federal Reserve (Fed) in 1913, which bolstered financial market confidence and stabilized mortgage rates (White 2014). In addition, private market innovations in the housing bond market spurred increased bank lending.[8] The result was that the housing

[7] Among these were the US Housing Corporation and the Emergency Fleet Corporation.

[8] During the 1920s, financial institutions – real estate bond houses and mortgage guarantee companies – developed urban mortgage bonds based on commercial and residential mortgages and sold them to investors and to millions of households. These companies also offered *private* insurance on the payments of these bonds to investors, yet without a government guarantee (Quinn 2019, 109; Snowden 2013). By 1930 this was a sizable USD 6 billion market, representing 14

market experienced an unprecedented boom from the early to mid-1920s: Residential mortgage debt tripled, far exceeding outstanding farm debt, real house prices of newly constructed homes rose by 43 percent (White 2014, 122), and a housing construction boom produced almost one million homes during the peak in 1925, up from roughly 250,000 produced in 1920 (Wickens 1941, 296). The booming housing market was a wealth-generating machine that also stimulated the wider economy by increasing the demand for other consumer and capital goods. The growing use of retail credit and early versions of credit cards supported this trend, allowing consumers to borrow and spend money on good such as refrigerators, with 75 percent of all such sales on credit (Persons 1930, 112; Trumbull 2014, 13).

There are two takeaways from this brief historical discussion. First, industrialization and urbanization transformed residential housing into a vital sector of the emerging yet fragile American demand-led growth regime of the 1920s, which increasingly relied on private demand, credit, and consumption. Housing stimulated domestic demand directly through credit-financed construction and indirectly through associated consumer spending. As Sarah Quinn (2019, 104) notes, "residential housing was taking its place as part of the American economic growth machine." Second, since the late nineteenth century policymakers had already been experimenting with agricultural credit and tax programs in support of credit and consumption in the American economy (Prasad 2012). These programs served as templates for later growth-generating housing programs central to America's demand-led growth regime. However, it took the Great Depression for policymakers to create a government-supported housing model.

HOUSING AND THE GREAT DEPRESSION

The Great Depression was one of the longest and most severe economic crises in US history, featuring a housing crash that resulted in mass foreclosures and a mortgage credit crisis. In the early 1920s, housing market activity had surged, driven by extensive investment and construction amid strong economic growth, low unemployment, low interest rates, and WWI-related housing shortages. Property values increased by roughly 40 percent in real terms between 1921 and 1926 (White 2014, 122), and the country's mortgage credit volume more than tripled from USD 9 billion to USD 30 billion between 1921 and 1929 (Fishback et al. 2013, 148). The boom reached its peak in 1925, with almost one million new housing units produced that year (White 2014, 119). In the second half of the 1920s the housing market began its downturn, with sales, prices, and construction trending downwards, although the worst was yet to come with

percent of outstanding commercial and residential mortgage debt. However, the real estate bond market all but disappeared when the country experienced large-scale mortgage defaults during the Great Depression. It took decades for a new housing bond market to emerge, and it took the federal government to create it, as Chapter 4 shows.

the onset of the Great Depression (Gjerstad and Smith 2014, 90). At the time, mortgage lending was characterized by short-term mortgages of three to five years with high down payments, variable interest rates, and large "balloon" or "bullet" payments at the end of the mortgage period (Green and Wachter 2005).[9] These mortgage terms were supposed to protect banks from the risk of credit default or interest-rate fluctuations. But they did not protect banks from the risk of mass unemployment resulting in large-scale mortgage defaults.

The economic shock of 1929 produced just that result. Between 1929 and 1933, the economy shrank by 30 percent (Fishback et al. 2020, 856), and the number of unemployed workers surged from 1.5 million in 1929 to 12 million in 1932.[10] As homeowners became unable to pay their mortgages, the housing market collapsed. Property values declined by a median of 31 percent from their 1925 peak to the 1933–1934 trough (Gjerstad and Smith 2014, 95; Brocker and Hanes 2014). At the depth of the collapse in 1933, banks foreclosed on a quarter of a million homes, up from 68,000 in 1926, and construction activity plummeted by 89 percent (Field 2014, 65–70). Relatedly, residential investment, which was around 6 percent of GDP in 1925, dropped to just one percent in 1933 (Field 2014, 64–65). This drastic decline meant that only 90,000 housing units were produced in the entire country in 1933, down from almost one million in 1925. The mortgage market also ground to a halt as banks, overwhelmed by large-scale mortgage defaults and foreclosed properties, were unable to lend.

Economic historians have found that the housing crisis deepened the severe fall in aggregate demand during the depression. Jonathan Levy (2020, 367) writes that declining wealth and dried-up credit "inevitably depressed all kinds of spending, both investment and consumption." More specifically, Steven Gjerstad and Vernon Smith (2014, 88) estimate that durable goods expenditure declined by 49 percent between 1929 and 1933. They argue that the housing crisis was directly related to declining consumer spending, as problems in housing affected aggregate demand:

> The first and most direct [channel] is reduced residential construction. The second channel was the damage to household balance sheets from the fall in home prices, and the negative impact from damage to household balance sheets on household demand for consumer durables and nondurables. The third channel was the reduction in firms' inventories, production, and fixed investment that resulted from the household consumption decline. The fourth channel was the feedback effect from declining production and investment to declining household income, which then circled back to affect each of the first three factors. The fifth factor was the damage to banks' balance sheets, which accentuated the troubles of both firms and households when loans could not be extended or rolled over due to the need for banks to deleverage.

9 The savings and loan associations (S&Ls) had already been offering medium-term (8–12 years) amortizing mortgages, whereas commercial banks often offered bullet or balloon mortgages.

10 Lebergott, S. (July 1948), *Labor Force, Employment, and Unemployment, 1929–39: Estimating Methods*, US Bureau of Labor Statistics.

Similarly, Michael Brocker and Christopher Hanes (2014) found that cities experiencing extensive construction and house-price booms in the mid-1920s, which were not sustained by an associated increase in the number of households, also faced the steepest declines in home values and the highest rates of foreclosure during the depression. For example, Birmingham (Alabama) and San Diego (California) each suffered a house-price decline of almost 50 percent between 1930 and 1934 (Brocker and Hanes 2014, 171; Galbraith 1979). As Brocker and Hanes (2014, 198) note, "the 1920s real estate boom contributed to the Great Depression through wealth and financial channels."

Not entirely unlike the Great Recession of 2008–2009, a significant housing downturn and falling real estate values preceded the Great Depression, creating a vicious economic circle (Gjerstad and Smith 2014, 112). Indeed, contemporary observers acknowledged the central role of housing in the economy and financial markets (Wickens 1941, 1–2):

> The important role real estate values play in the economy is most clearly evident at such times [the Great Depression]. Not only the owners of real estate and the holders of real estate mortgages but also bank depositors and other persons whose savings are committed to financial institutions having substantial real estate investments may feel directly or indirectly the effects of radical fluctuations in real property prices. The disturbing effect of interrupted financing, of fluctuations in income from real property and hence in its value and salability, inevitably makes less secure the status of financial institutions and of their owners and depositors.

Another sobering account highlighted the limits of credit-led growth and the role of excessive (mortgage) credit expansion in contributing to the Great Depression (Persons 1930, 129–130):

> Nor can over expansion of credit be practiced without dire penalties being visited on the family guilty of such excesses, and in case the mistake is widely indulged, on the industries generally and the nation at large … The depression into which the nation fell in the latter year [1929] was undoubtedly due in part at least to these developments in our complicated economic structure.

But what did policymakers think about the role of housing in the economy when deliberating solutions to overcome the Great Depression? What were their primary motivations when designing housing programs at that time?

HOOVER'S HOUSING RESPONSE: TOO LITTLE, TOO LATE

President Herbert Hoover (1929–1933), a longstanding proponent of private homeownership, made addressing the housing crisis an economic priority.[11] His political actions aimed to stabilize mortgage lending and stop the growing

[11] As secretary of commerce, in 1922, Hoover helped launch a grassroots campaign called "Better Homes in America" to promote homeownership and modernize homes (McCabe 2016, ch. 2; Hornstein 2005, ch. 5).

foreclosure crisis. But his ambitions ended there. Compared to the later New Deal programs, Hoover's housing policy agenda was relatively modest and did not envision using housing markets as a vehicle for economic growth. Nonetheless, Hoover's initiatives provided a crucial first step in tackling the housing crisis and laying the foundation for America's government-sponsored housing model.

The Hoover administration planned to provide government support for owner-occupied housing, albeit within limits (Weiss 1987). During the depression in 1931, he convened a housing conference where policymakers, interest groups, and experts worked to devise solutions for the crisis. The conference, attended by 3,000 participants, developed a set of recommendations for future housing policy. Hoover emphasized that the goal was "not to set up government in the building of homes but to stimulate individual endeavor and make community conditions propitious."[12]

Hoover's plan aimed to restore mortgage liquidity and provide low-cost mortgages to households. To achieve this, he advocated for creating a "system of home loan discount banks," akin to a federal reserve system for housing. Under this system, any mortgage lending institution – such as life insurance companies, commercial banks, and savings and loan associations (S&Ls) – would gain access to cheap long-term funding for mortgage lending. In turn, this would encourage banks to resume lending at better mortgage rates and with safer mortgage terms compared to the pre-crisis period. As a representative of the National Association of Real Estate Boards (NAREB) lamented in Congress, "mortgage money has practically disappeared."[13] Hoover's plan, in short, sought to repair and restore mortgage lending.

However, the administration adopted only limited support for a specific segment of the housing finance market – the S&Ls – excluding other major mortgage lenders affected by the housing crash. In 1932, it created the Federal Home Loan Banks (FHLB), a system of twelve quasi-public regional banks.[14] Inspired by the Federal Land Banks, the FHLBs provided cheap short-term and long-term funding exclusively to S&Ls, but not to other crisis-affected financial institutions such as life insurance companies or commercial banks.[15] At that time, S&Ls were

[12] Hoover, H. (December 2, 1931). *Address to the White House Conference on Home Building and Home Ownership*, The American Presidency Project, www.presidency.ucsb.edu/node/206990.

[13] US Senate (January–February 1932), *Creation of a System of Home Loan Banks: Hearings before the US Senate Committee on Banking and Currency on S. 2959* (testimony of W. Schmidt), 323.

[14] Another federally sponsored credit institution (funded by the US Treasury and by issuing bonds) that originated during the Hoover presidency was the Reconstruction Finance Corporation (RFC), which initially provided funding for distressed banks and later helped fund public works and other New Deal initiatives (Quinn 2019, 132–133). It was in place from 1932 until 1957.

[15] Given their government-sponsored status, the FHLBs could borrow funds at attractive rates in financial markets by issuing agency bonds.

important lending institutions, as prominently featured in the 1946 movie *It's a Wonderful Life*, and accounted for almost 25 percent of mortgage lending in the 1920s (White 2014, 135; Weiss 1987, 33). At the signing ceremony, Hoover said:

> The purpose of the system is both to meet the present emergency and to build up home-ownership on more favorable terms than exist today. The immediate credit situation has for the time being in many parts of the country restricted the activities of building and loan associations, savings banks, and other institutions making loans for home purposes, in such fashion that they are not only unable to extend credit for the acquirement of new homes, but in thousands of instances they have been unable to renew existing mortgages with resultant foreclosures and great hardships.[16]

The immediate goals were to repair the dysfunctional mortgage market and to stop foreclosures. The long-term objective was to stimulate home lending, increase liquidity, and reduce the cost of home mortgages. However, these were overly ambitious aims given the limited nature of the FHLB system.

Why did Hoover adopt a limited response focused solely on supporting the S&Ls? His original, broader proposal faced opposition from the banking and insurance industries and thus found only lukewarm support in Congress (Hoffmann and Cassell 2010, 33; Mason 2004, ch. 3). The Mortgage Bankers Association (MBA) and the American Bankers Association (ABA) opposed a government support system for mortgage lenders, fearing it could lead to an overheated housing market. They also questioned the need for a permanent institution with strong government presence, arguing that it would be unnecessary once the depression was over (Mason 2004, ch. 3). Given this resistance, Morton Bodfish, chief S&L lobbyist, successfully made the case for a government support system centered around the S&Ls only. The S&L lobbyists argued that such a system would "place resources at the command of the home-financing institutions, which will lead, first, to lower costs of mortgage credits, and, second, to higher percentage loans to the sturdy, honest, home purchaser."[17] NAREB initially supported Hoover's original, broader proposal (Davies 1958; Jones and Grebler 1961, 113), but they ultimately backed the narrower S&L-focused proposal, viewing it as better than no proposal at all.

Hoover's actions were insufficient to turn the housing market and the economy around. The FHLB system somewhat improved the financial situation of the S&Ls, but its scale was too limited to improve overall mortgage lending (Fishback, Rose, and Snowden 2013, 48).[18] Above all, the system was unable

[16] Hoover, H. (July 22, 1932), *Statement about Signing the Federal Home Loan Bank Act*, The American Presidency Project, www.presidency.ucsb.edu/node/207247.

[17] US House of Representatives (March 1932), *Creation of a System of Home Loan Banks: Hearing before the US House Committee on Banking and Currency on HR. 7620* (testimony of W. Best), 29.

[18] By 1935, the FHLBs had only USD 100 million in loans to S&Ls outstanding, while the New Deal's HOLC had more than USD 3 billion in loans outstanding. See US Department of Commerce (1936), *Statistical Abstract of the United States: Money and Banking*, 258–259.

to stop mortgage defaults and foreclosures on existing homeowners (Snowden 2013). Rescuing the housing market, and the American economy, would require more ambitious and radical housing programs.

HOW HOUSING BECAME THE US ECONOMY'S "WHEEL WITHIN THE WHEEL"

For the incoming President FDR, the housing market was not just an economic problem that needed fixing. It was also the key to revitalizing the economy. He believed that housing-based growth could address the nation's economic woes, such as low consumer demand, deflated prices, and stifled investment.

Housing held a special place in FDR's New Deal agenda, as the administration considered it the key to overcoming fear and spurring growth. One of FDR's main housing policy architects was Marriner Eccles, a respected banker and economist from Utah. In February 1934, Eccles became FDR's assistant secretary of the Treasury; a few months later he became the chair of the Fed, a role he held until 1948. As assistant secretary, Eccles saw housing as the pivotal lever to stimulate growth, as he recalled (1951, 144–145):

> The significance of a new housing program that could revive the economy was not lost on President Roosevelt. He knew that almost a third of the unemployed were to be found in the building trades, and housing was by far the most important part of that trade. A program of new home construction, launched on an adequate scale, not only would gradually help put those men back to work but would act as the wheel within the wheel to move the whole economic engine. It would affect everyone, from the manufacturer of lace curtains to the manufacturer of lumber, bricks, furniture, cement, and electrical appliances. The mere shipment of these supplies would affect the railroads, which in turn would need the produce of steel mills for rails, freight cars, and so on.

President Roosevelt put it this way:

> The long-continued lag in building is a drag on all industry and trade. This presents an urgent problem which is the common concern of industry, labor, and government. All business needs the infusion of orders and the diffusion of purchasing power that come when building is thriving. Great numbers of people look directly or indirectly to the construction industry for employment. *This industry, to a greater extent than any other, can put idle funds to work and thus speed up the circulation of the nation's money supply. This, in turn, would increase national income, reduce unemployment ...* The government, however, can take the initiative by bringing about a reduction of financing costs, by making it easier for families of moderate means to buy or rent new houses, and by providing mechanisms to make it practicable for private enterprise to engage in large-scale housing operations for the mass market.[19]

[19] Roosevelt, F. D. (November 27, 1937), *Message to Congress on Legislation for Private Construction of Housing*, The American Presidency Project, www.presidency.ucsb.edu/node/209024. My emphasis.

In other words, if households started purchasing homes again, it would stimulate housing activity and create employment, which in turn would boost private spending power and consumer activity (Jacobs 2007, 150).

After Hoover's failures, the question was how to kick-start housing-based growth. The FDR administration, particularly Eccles (1951, 151–152), favored generating economic activity by stimulating *private* housing without using even "one penny of government money." Achieving housing-based growth without increasing direct public spending was a tall order. Following the trauma of millions of mortgage defaults and home foreclosures, banks needed reassurance to lend to consumers again. Eccles and others envisioned what Michael Mann (1984) referred to as the "infrastructural power" of the state. The strategy involved the state absorbing *risk* to restore confidence in the mortgage industry, with the larger goal of generating economic growth. Instead of lending directly to consumers or building housing directly, the government would *guarantee* private mortgages, encouraging banks to offer consumer-friendly loans. The hoped-for result was to increase mortgage lending, construction, and associated consumer spending while limiting budget deficits (Koppell 2003; McCabe 2016; Green and Wachter 2005; Freund 2007). This approach appealed to both the left, with its preference for state-led economic planning, and the right, with its emphasis on fiscal conservatism.

Winfield Riefler, a Federal Reserve economist and part of FDR's economic team, was the key policy entrepreneur credited with designing what became the core New Deal housing programs: Government guarantees on home mortgages (Hyman 2011, 53). Much like Eccles, Riefler viewed credit-financed housing construction as an effective way to overcome high unemployment and stimulate the economy. As a memorandum that crossed his desk – and may even have been authored by him – noted:

> the housing problem is the key log in the economic jam ... a sort of vicious circle: unemployment is maintained at a high figure because of the absence of facilities for financing new construction, while at the same time the financial burden of the existing mortgage debt is becoming increasingly difficult to carry because of the continuing large volume of unemployment.[20]

Government guarantees, in Riefler's view, could stimulate the financing of new housing construction and break the logjam in the economy caused by the housing crisis.[21]

[20] *The Housing Problem* [memorandum] (ca. May 1934), Winfield W. Riefler Papers, US National Archives and Records Administration, Box 1, Folder 6, https://fraser.stlouisfed.org/archival-collection/winfield-w-riefler-papers-rflr-1929-71-1345/box-1-folder-6-469393.

[21] Riefler, W. (1934, December 31). *The Housing Problem* [paper presentation]. American Association for the Advancement of Science, Riefler Papers, Box 1, Folder 6.

Government guarantees on home mortgages became quintessential New Deal programs. Much like other New Deal initiatives, they were not Keynesian spending policies (Levy 2020, ch. 13). Instead, they stimulated private market activity – mortgage lending and construction – by leveraging the infrastructural power of the state to reduce the cost of home financing for borrowers and mitigate the risk for creditors. Although fiscal deficits were inevitable given the severity of the depression, FDR prioritized balancing budgets (Katznelson 2013, 230). His administration only undertook outright countercyclical fiscal policy to address the recession of 1937–1938.

Implementing these economic principles and plans was no easy feat, as it required fundamental restructuring of complex mortgage markets and, indeed, of the role of the state within them. There was also the question of the duration of government support – whether the American state should subsidize housing beyond the depression. If Hoover's programs had failed, how would the New Deal housing experiment ultimately help turn the economy around?

THE NEW DEAL HOUSING REVOLUTION

FDR's policies, supported by strong Democratic majorities in Congress, were more aggressive and far-reaching than Hoover's. Their key innovation – one that would forever change the American mortgage market – was to have the American state absorb risk in housing, thereby unleashing housing-based growth in the entire economy. By the end of the depression, policymakers had not only created a government-sponsored housing model that fundamentally transformed the mortgage market but also recognized the permanent demand-led growth potential of housing programs.

The New Deal housing revolution started with the establishment of the Home Owners' Loan Corporation (HOLC) in 1933, marking the first step in fundamentally re-organizing America's mortgage market. The goal of the HOLC was not to directly boost economic growth but instead to stabilize mortgage lending by stopping mortgage defaults, curbing the foreclosure crisis, and halting the freefall of property values – key issues holding back the American economy. As FDR stated, the priority was to end the "deflation which was rapidly depriving many millions of farm and home owners from the title and equity to their property."[22] This quasi-governmental agency acted as a "bad bank," purchasing mortgages at risk of default and refinancing them into longer-term, amortizing mortgages with below-market, fixed interest rates.[23] It was a win-win: Homeowners benefited from better mortgage terms at lower cost, while private banks offloaded toxic assets

[22] Roosevelt, F. D. (June 13, 1933), *Statement on Signing the Home Owners Loan Act*, The American Presidency Project, www.presidency.ucsb.edu/node/208223.

[23] The HOLC financed its activities by issuing bonds and receiving financial support from the US Treasury in the amount of USD 200 million.

(Fishback et al. 2013, 79).[24] The HOLC's efforts were massive. Between 1933 and 1936, it restructured over one million mortgages valued at USD 3 billion – approximately 20 percent of total mortgage debt at the time – into the types of mortgages we know today: Longer-term (initially 15 years), amortizing mortgages with fixed interest rates (Grebler et al. 1956, 444). The HOLC was dissolved in 1951 after these loans were paid off. An equivalently scaled program today would amount to USD 2 trillion and eight million refinanced mortgages (Fishback et al. 2013, 54).

While housing-related lobby groups generally welcomed government help for private housing, not all of them supported the HOLC. Parts of the S&L industry outright opposed the legislation, citing concerns about the federal government taking on "dubious liabilities" and fearing that no one would invest in HOLC bonds.[25] Realtors were more supportive and had "no criticism to offer on the [HOLC] bill," but they also noted that the bill would not meet "the exigencies of the situation." Instead, they supported their long-standing Hoover-era proposal of "a permanent discount system for long-term financing, comparable to the Federal Reserve System for short-term financing."[26] The divided housing lobby gave FDR significant legislative leeway in establishing the HOLC.

The HOLC even found an unlikely supporter in the Fed. Typically, the Fed has refrained from directly financing housing activities. However, during the depression, it provided direct but modest support for the HOLC by channeling funding into the agency. To enable the Fed to do so, President Roosevelt changed the Federal Reserve Act in 1934, authorizing the Fed to purchase HOLC bonds. The administration also elevated the status of HOLC bonds to being fully backed by the US government, whereas HOLC bonds previously "had not been clearly guaranteed as to principal by the United States" (Hackley 1973, 95). FDR's goal in proposing the amendment was to "assure the continued progress on a self-sustaining basis of the making of loans for the purpose of refinancing home mortgages without interruption."[27] The Fed used its new authority under none other than chairman Eccles. By 1939, the Fed had purchased roughly USD 6 million in HOLC bonds, a number that increased to USD 36 million in 1943.[28] The Fed's depression-era monetary interventions were mostly symbolic, as the HOLC was authorized to issue up

[24] Banks received HOLC bonds as a form of payment in exchange for their distressed mortgages.

[25] US Senate (April 20 and 22, 1933), *Home Owners' Loan Act: Hearing before the US Senate Committee on Banking and Currency on S. 1317* (testimony of C. Hennesy), 72.

[26] US Senate (April 20 and 22, 1933), *Home Owners' Loan Act: Hearing before the US Senate Committee on Banking and Currency on S. 1317* (testimony of W. Schmidt), 44.

[27] Roosevelt, F. D. (March 1, 1934), *Message to Congress Recommending Legislation to Guarantee the Principal on Home Owners Loan Bonds*, The American Presidency Project, www.presidency.ucsb.edu/node/208421.

[28] Federal Reserve Board (1939), *Annual Report*, 38; Federal Reserve Board (1943), *Annual Report*, 66.

to USD 4.75 billion in bonds to finance its activities, with the Fed owning only a small fraction of that total.

Despite its successes in restructuring *existing* mortgages, the HOLC did little to stimulate *new* mortgage lending and housing activity. Banks remained hesitant, viewing new mortgage lending as too risky during the depression. An internal 1934 memorandum from the FDR administration captured this sentiment:

> new lending on real estate by private agencies ... remains at an abnormally low and wholly inadequate figure. This great deficiency and lag in mortgage lending and home-improvement financing *constitutes the most serious problem that the American industrial system has to grapple with. At the same time, however, it points the way to our greatest industrial opportunity – namely, the field of modern housing.*[29]

As a result, the FDR administration began devising new housing programs, viewing them as an industrial opportunity to revive the economy.

The key institution aimed at stimulating new mortgage lending – and the hoped-for economic ripple effects – was the Federal Housing Administration (FHA), established as part of the National Housing Act of 1934. The FHA's main innovation was to offer government insurance on mortgages, guaranteeing the principal and interest payments to banks. Through the FHA, the American state began absorbing *risk* in private mortgage lending, soon exercising "an extraordinary degree of control over real estate development patterns" (Weiss 1987, 145). As risk was absorbed through FHA guarantees, the program encouraged banks to resume lending and "lower the cost of mortgage money to the borrower"[30] without an increase in direct public spending. The resulting credit expansion was expected to boost housing activity, "provide employment, and stimulate industry."[31] In short, the FDR administration believed that stimulating mortgage lending was essential to generate construction activity and employment, increase household spending power, and "stimulate the so-called service industries."[32]

The FHA developed two mortgage insurance programs to kick-start economic activity. The first program ("Title I") offered FHA insurance on consumer loans for home improvement and repairs (Trumbull 2014, ch. 2). According to an internal memorandum, these subsidized home improvement loans would result in the "re-employment of large numbers of skilled workers."[33] The second, and more significant, program ("Title II") provided FHA

29 *Memorandum on National Housing Program* (May 9, 1934), Riefler Papers, Box 1, Folder 6. My emphasis.

30 *Memorandum on Mutual Mortgage Insurance* (May 9, 1934), Riefler Papers, Box 1, Folder 6.

31 US House Committee on Banking and Currency (June 4, 1934), *National Housing Act: Report to Accompany H.R. 9620 (No. 1922)*, 1.

32 *The Housing Problem* [memorandum] (ca. May 1934), Riefler Papers, Box 1, Folder 6.

33 *Memorandum on Home Improvement Credit* (May 9, 1934), Riefler Papers, Box 1, Folder 6.

insurance on mortgages for the purchase of homes. In return for guaranteeing mortgage debt, the FHA specified the terms of the loans that could be insured: Long-term, fixed-rate, amortizing mortgages (e.g., 20 years) with lower down payments (i.e., loans up to 80 percent of house value). By 1939, the FHA had insured 2.3 million home improvement loans and 500,000 mortgages, with a total insurance volume of USD 3 billion.[34]

A further major innovation resulting from New Deal housing legislation was the creation of a national secondary mortgage market to further stimulate FHA-insured mortgage lending – although this had mixed initial results. The idea was to create a secondary market in which mortgages could be traded nationally. Policymakers hoped that such a market would not only improve financial flows into capital-poor housing finance markets in the south and west (Hyman 2011, 54) but also make "lower cost money available for home financing."[35] To achieve this, the 1934 National Housing Act ("Title III") allowed for the creation of National Mortgage Associations. The act authorized the FHA to approve public or private associations that would buy and sell FHA-insured mortgages in the secondary market by financing their activities through issuing bonds. Policymakers envisioned that these mortgage associations would emerge organically from the private market. But they did not. By 1937, the FHA had not approved a single association (Jones and Grebler 1961, 116). Private investors were hesitant to establish such associations partly because the FHA-related mortgage market was simply not yet large enough. In addition, there was uncertainty about how much longer the US Treasury would explicitly back the FHA insurance fund – primarily financed through the collection of borrower fees – as the Treasury's guarantee on the fund was set to expire initially in 1937 or, after an extension, in 1939.[36]

The FDR administration did not give up on their idea of supporting FHA-insured mortgage lending through a secondary mortgage market, which led to the creation of a new government agency to achieve that goal.[37] As a recession loomed in 1937, FDR was dissatisfied with the slow pace of improvement in the housing market, but he maintained his belief that "housing constitutes the largest and most promising single field for private enterprise" capable

[34] FHA (1940), *6th Annual Report*, 2–3.

[35] *Memorandum on National Mortgage Associations* (May 9, 1934), Riefler Papers, Box 1, Folder 6.

[36] As an internal memorandum described it, the "limitation of governmental guaranty to FHA debentures issued prior to July 1, 1937" created uncertainty in the FHA market. See *Reasons Why Current Operation of Title III Is Impracticable* [memorandum] (ca. January 1935), Marriner S. Eccles Papers, University of Utah, Box 27, Folder 2, https://fraser.stlouisfed.org/archival-collection/marriner-s-eccles-papers-1343/reasons-present-operation-title-iii-impracticable-460619.

[37] FDR had initially formed the public–private RFC Mortgage Company in 1935 (dissolved in 1947) to demonstrate the feasibility of a secondary market for commercial mortgages (Hyman 2011, 68; Quinn 2019, 143). Later on, this company also covered residential buildings (particularly old ones) while Fannie Mae covered new FHA-financed homes (Jones and Grebler 1961, 118).

of driving economic recovery. As a result, the administration amended and expanded many provisions of the 1934 National Housing Act in early 1938, including measures to ensure that "one or more such [national mortgage] associations may be promptly organized."[38] The amendments improved the conditions for operating such an association, most notably by reassuring investors that the US Treasury would *permanently* back the outstanding volume of FHA-insured mortgages, even if the FHA fund were depleted due to catastrophic losses. As the amendment stated, "[i]n the event that the [FHA] Fund … fails to pay upon demand, when due, the principal or interest on any debentures issued … the Secretary of the Treasury shall pay to the holders the amount thereof."[39] This permanent government backing made it easier to attract investments in any new mortgage association dealing with FHA-insured mortgages. By permanently absorbing the risk of FHA-insured mortgage debt, the American state laid the foundation for a robust secondary mortgage market.

Just one day after the amendments came into effect, the administration incorporated the National Mortgage Association of Washington and quickly changed its name to Federal National Mortgage Association (FNMA or Fannie Mae). This new public agency was established to purchase and sell FHA-insured mortgages in the secondary market.[40] It financed these activities by borrowing from the US government and issuing obligations. When Fannie issued its first USD 25 million in obligations in 1938, they were oversubscribed, partly because their obligations were tax-exempt (Snowden 2013, 82). In the same year, Fannie began trading its first FHA-insured mortgages with major financial institutions, including banks, mortgage lenders, and insurance companies.[41] By 1940, the mortgage portfolio of Fannie Mae (and the RFC Mortgage Company) had grown to roughly USD 200 million, which represented about 8 percent of total outstanding FHA-insured mortgage debt.[42] Although modest in scale, Fannie offered yet another layer of government support in the mortgage market. Fannie's creation bolstered confidence in FHA-insured mortgages, generated profits for the US government,

38 Roosevelt, F. D. (November 27, 1937), *Message to Congress on Legislation for Private Construction of Housing*, The American Presidency Project, www.presidency.ucsb.edu/node/209024.

39 "Text of amendments to National Housing Act as made law by president" (February 5, 1938), *New York Times*.

40 The amendments also included a reduction of down payments, lower interest rates, and longer mortgage terms (raised from 20 to 25 years) on FHA-insured mortgages, and an extension of the FHA's "title I" guarantees on home repair loans. It also made available better mortgage insurance for rental properties. See *Immediate Measures to Stimulate Housing Construction* [White House memorandum] (November 10, 1937), Eccles Papers, Box 5, Folder 7, https://fraser.stlouisfed.org/files/docs/historical/eccles/005_07_0012.pdf.

41 In 1948, Congress revoked the charter for setting up private national mortgage associations (Quinn 2019, 144).

42 FHA (1941), *7th Annual Report*, 53.

contributed to standardizing the mortgage market, and attracted private funds into housing (Hyman 2011, 67; Quinn 2019, 144; Jones and Grebler 1961, 122).

The housing lobby was divided over FHA guarantees and the creation of Fannie Mae,[43] providing the FDR administration considerable room for maneuver. The S&Ls were the main opponents of these measures, as they were concerned about the potential competition from commercial banks in mortgage lending.[44] To appease the S&Ls, FDR created the Federal Savings and Loan Insurance Corporation (FSLIC) under "Title IV" of the National Housing Act of 1934. Modeled after the Federal Deposit Insurance Corporation (FDIC) for commercial banks, the FSLIC insured household deposits held in S&Ls (Eccles 1951, 153–155). Despite the FDR administration's concessions, the S&Ls continued their opposition to the FHA. In contrast, realtors and community builders supported the FHA and Fannie Mae as solutions to the "nonliquidity" problem in the mortgage market (Weiss 1987, 145; Slater 2021, 104).[45] However, their preference remained the creation of a mortgage reserve system, a proposal that they had been advocating for years but that the FDR administration ignored.[46]

Some of FDR's housing programs were initially designed as *temporary* measures but were made *permanent* to secure demand-led growth beyond the depression. Policymakers wanted to maintain the economic cascade effects generated by a vibrant housing market. For example, Title I loans on repairs and maintenance were originally set to expire after 1936 but were extended with amendments in 1937 and 1938 – and have remained in place today (Snowden 2013, 80). Similarly, government guarantees behind the FHA's mortgage insurance fund (Title II) were initially intended to be temporary. However, the 1938 amendments made the US Treasury's guarantee on FHA debentures – debt instruments with which the FHA paid banks when FHA-insured mortgages defaulted – permanent. Even though the FHA mortgage insurance fund was self-supporting through the collection of borrower fees and was in good financial shape with negligible losses, policymakers chose to maintain the Treasury's guarantee to ensure that the

[43] Two parallel government-sponsored housing finance subsystems with different political interests generated friction with one another, which is reflected in these legislative conflicts. On the one hand, the S&L industry enjoyed access to cheap funding through the quasi-public FHLB system. On the other hand, the FHA's guarantees (and Fannie Mae) supported mortgage lending by insurance companies and commercial banks (Jones and Grebler 1961, 119).

[44] US House of Representatives (May/June 1934), *National Housing Act: Hearings before the US House Committee on Banking and Currency on H.R. 9620* (testimony of M. Bodfish), 249.

[45] US Senate (May 16–24, 1934), *National Housing Act: Hearings before the US Senate Committee on Banking and Currency on S. 3603* (testimony of W. Schmidt), 280.

[46] US House of Representatives (May/June 1934), *National Housing Act: Hearings before the US House Committee on Banking and Currency on H.R. 9620* (testimony of H. Potter), 226.

FHA's operations "should not be hampered by the loss of this guarantee."[47] As Kenneth Snowden (2013, 80) notes, "federally guaranteed home mortgage insurance had become a permanent and broad feature of residential mortgage finance, even though it was designed ... to be a stand-alone insurance fund that was supported by guarantees only temporarily in order to stimulate home construction." As these programs delivered housing-based growth, policymakers no longer considered withdrawing government support as an option.

Together, the New Deal measures helped revive the housing market and the economy. They contributed to a significant increase in housing construction, from a trough of 93,000 new homes in 1933 to half a million in 1939 (Grebler et al. 1956, 332). As the FHA wrote in 1939: "The sharp rise in these credit-insurance activities was largely instrumental in the vigorous revival in the residential construction industry which was one of the earliest and strongest forces acting for recovery in business and employment from the recession in late 1937 and early 1938."[48]

In sum, New Deal housing programs had not only transformed the country's housing market but also set housing policy on a path of government-sponsored, housing-based growth. As Monica Prasad (2012, 93) describes it, these programs represented a form of "'mortgage Keynesianism' in which mortgage finance was a primary mechanism for sustaining economic growth."

THE PATH NOT TAKEN

There was also a brief push for the establishment of European-style affordable rental housing projects (Radford 1996, 195). However, this effort was unsuccessful as policymakers viewed rental housing as a less effective economic stimulus than homeownership programs. A group of labor unionists, New Dealers such as Harold Ickes (FDR's secretary of the interior, responsible for the Public Works programs), and public housing activists advocated for innovative, high-density urban rental housing projects to address the nation's housing crisis (Hyman 2011, 50–53; Thurston 2018, 64).[49] Indeed, FDR's New Deal policies also included public rental housing programs. Initially part of the 1933 Public Works Administration, these programs became federal initiatives under the Wagner-Steagall Act in 1937 (McDonnell 1957). Like other New Deal programs, FDR intended these to generate employment and economic activity through increased housing construction and to

47 "To extend FHA guarantee" (January 28, 1937), *New York Times*.

48 FHA (1939), *5th Annual Report*, vii.

49 The Labor Housing Conference was one such group in the mid-1930s – led by Catherine Bauer, a housing activist – pushing for noncommercial housing solutions, including cooperatives, to improve the nation's housing situation (Radford 1996).

improve urban living conditions of the poor during the recession of 1937–1938. While public housing programs helped create 400,000 housing units between 1934 and 1958 (Goetz 2013), that number is marginal considering the size of the entire housing market. Despite activists' attempts to broaden these programs to include the middle class, they remained focused on the poor and were notoriously underfunded.

The brief opportunity for establishing large-scale public housing quickly faded, if it ever truly existed. The main reason was that direct spending programs were expensive and did not stimulate construction, employment, and private consumption as effectively as off-budget FHA homeownership programs (Harloe 1995, 196). The beneficiaries of public housing programs were primarily urban and low-income working-class households and, increasingly, racialized minorities.[50] These groups did not have as powerful a lobby as the housing industry, which criticized public housing programs for interfering with private market activities (Goetz 2013; Weir 2005; Pierson 1994, ch. 4; Radford 1996). Public housing programs never enjoyed the bipartisan support that homeownership policies did. Republicans viewed direct spending on public housing programs as too costly and socialist. Even members of labor unions and New Dealers such as Eccles questioned these programs – particularly their effectiveness in expanding economic growth compared to other programs (Goetz 2013; Radford 1996, 207). As Eccles (1951, 148) recalled: "in a depression the proper role of government should be that of generating a maximum degree of *private* spending through a minimum amount of public spending … A large-scale *public* housing program would not meet the foregoing specification. It would call for public ownership and government financing. This would increase the public debt." Instead of public housing programs, American policymakers privileged homeownership programs, believing they could turn the economy around (Shonfield 1965, 308).

The "public" that ultimately benefited from the government-supported housing model was a limited one, as these housing programs privileged white households and discriminated against women and racialized minorities (Thurston 2018; Freund 2007; Slater 2021). The FHA's *Underwriting Manual*, which set out explicit criteria for evaluating financial risk in terms of location, property, and the borrower, included the racial and ethnic composition of a neighborhood. The 1938 manual, for example, warned appraisers that a "change in social or racial occupancy generally leads to instability and a reduction in [property] values" and advised that "possible infiltration of

50 Initially, both white and Black families lived in segregated public housing projects. After the depression, many white households moved out of poverty and into the suburbs, partly owing to prosperity-generating housing programs from which Black households were excluded (Goetz 2013, 36). The proportion of Black households living in public housing correspondingly increased.

inharmonious racial groups" should warrant lower property appraisal ratings. Ethnically diverse urban neighborhoods were considered a higher risk to future house prices, while white homogeneous neighborhoods, often in suburban areas, were seen as financially more desirable.[51] As a result, borrowers in diverse neighborhoods were denied access to credit owing to "redlining" practices (Rothstein 2017, 65).[52] These FHA practices reinforced a government-sponsored system of housing segregation, preventing different racial groups from living in the same communities (Rothstein 2017; King and Smith 2011, ch. 5). In addition, women were held to a higher credit standard than men, as their income was often considered to be temporary or supplemental. Lenders were concerned about pregnancies and often requested "baby letters" from women's doctors confirming the patient's use of birth control (Thurston 2018, 144; Ryan et al. 2011, 484).

In short, America's government-supported housing model was deeply exclusionary and discriminating. It privileged white homeowners, who were positioned centrally in the American demand-led growth regime, as the health of their properties was seen as being linked to the health of the economy. Meanwhile, it excluded racialized minorities, renters, and women.

Finally, while German policymakers were institutionalizing strong rent controls to secure affordable housing as early as the beginning of the twentieth century (see Chapter 3), American politicians did not implement such measures on a permanent basis. As noted earlier, state and local politicians had experimented with rent controls around the time of WWI but allowed these provisions to expire when the 1920s housing boom alleviated housing shortages (Fogelson 2013; Radford 1996, 46). During the Great Depression, the FDR administration focused on the construction of new single-family homes and, to a lesser extent, public housing, yet it did not adopt rent controls as part of its housing policy mix. While the depression-era housing slump also meant falling rents, which declined by 19 percent in real terms from 1924 to 1933 (Gjerstad and Smith 2014, 97), widespread unemployment during that period still made it difficult for many tenants to pay rent (Harris 2024). In contrast, German policymakers were requiring nationwide rent reductions from landlords in the deflationary early 1930s (Führer 1995, 194). Meanwhile, the only US federal policy effort in that direction – a bill to protect renters in the District of Columbia – failed at that time (Willis 1950).

51 FHA (1938), *Underwriting Manual: Underwriting and Valuation Procedure Under Title II of the National Housing Act*, 936–939 & 1358–1360, www.huduser.gov/portal/sites/default/files/pdf/Federal-Housing-Administration-Underwriting-Manual.pdf

52 These redlined districts were based on maps evaluating mortgage risk in American cities that the HOLC had originally designed.

This reluctance to adopt rent controls, however, does not imply that the FDR administration generally opposed price interventions. In fact, the National Industrial Recovery Act of 1933 included provisions that encouraged industry-wide price, wage, and production controls and stabilizations. The act was an attempt to remake America's industrial organization through state-led economic steering, collective bargaining between business and labor, and sectoral self-regulation, with the goal of preventing prices and wages from further spiraling downward (Hawley 1995; Katznelson 2013, ch. 7). As part of the act, the FDR administration briefly implemented price interventions in such industries as manufacturing and textiles. However, these price and production controls expired just two years later, when the Supreme Court declared the National Industrial Recovery Act unconstitutional. Facing growing business complaints about government interference, the FDR administration let the matter rest (Hawley 1995, 130).

More broadly, the FDR administration came to view price interventions and rent controls as obstacles to a key driver of the economy: Private demand. However, this stance shifted as the economic changed dramatically during WWII, prompting a reconsideration of rent controls.

REPRESSING HOUSING-BASED GROWTH DURING WWII

Before housing programs expanded further in the postwar period, there was another potential opening for the establishment of European-style low-cost rental housing in wartime America. But the exigencies of the demand-led economy again defeated these attempts. As the wartime economy risked overheating owing to massive defense spending – more than 40 percent of GDP in 1943–1944[53] – FDR established the Office of Price Administration (OPA) in 1941 and expanded its interventionist powers in 1942. Working alongside agencies such as the War Production Board, the OPA regulated prices and rents, while other agencies managed wages, profits, and production to tame inflation and redirect resources from civilian to military needs. As a result, households not only faced shortages of consumer goods, from automobiles to refrigerators, but were also discouraged from making such purchases because credit for these items was restricted. Housing was no exception to deep wartime interventions. The FDR administration imposed relatively strict rent controls and a housing construction moratorium. Instead of promoting housing-based growth and associated consumer spending, the US government encouraged households to increase savings – the personal savings rate (relative to disposable income) reached an all-time high of well over 20 percent between 1942 and 1945 (Higgs 1999, 609) – and invest in

[53] Vandenbroucke, G. (February 4, 2020), *Which war saw the highest defense spending? Depends how it's measured*, Federal Reserve Bank of St. Louis, www.stlouisfed.org/on-the-economy/2020/february/war-highest-defense-spending-measured.

war bonds to finance the war. The strategy proved successful, as inflation was held in check, averaging 5.7% between 1941 and 1946.[54] During this period, the United States briefly resembled a statist economy. But not for long. American policymakers quickly lifted wartime price controls after the war to return to credit-financed housing growth and consumer spending. In contrast, German politicians retained strict price controls in the housing sector well into the 1960s, even after overcoming wartime shortages, as part of their export-oriented growth regime that thrived on low inflation and housing costs.

The US war economy opened a small but temporary window of opportunity for establishing low-cost rental housing. During WWII, housing production came to a halt, owing to a moratorium on nondefense residential construction. As a result, the growing number of workers in war production centers had to find shelter in subpar housing, including converted chicken coops, garages, and trailers. More than one million households were forced to double-up in shared living arrangements.[55] To counter rising rental prices caused by housing shortages in war production centers, the OPA adopted strict rent controls, covering around 80 percent of the rental housing stock (Fetter 2016, 1002). However, key actors within the country's demand-led growth regime, such as lobby groups representing property owners, worked diligently to limit the scope of broad-based rental programs. Southern Democrats also aimed to maintain racial hierarchies by limiting the centralized power of the OPA (also cp. Quinn 2019, 128–129; Rothstein 2017, 31).

While *building* new owner-occupied housing was severely restricted in the US wartime economy, the *purchase* of homes remained relatively unrestricted. Indeed, although the Fed curtailed instalment and retail credit to suppress credit-driven inflation and channel savings into the wartime economy, it exempted housing loans, underlining the special status of mortgage lending in the country.[56] The combination of limited housing construction and available mortgage credit resulted in house prices increasing by 56 percent between 1940 and 1945. Simultaneously, homeownership climbed from 43 percent in 1940 to 55 percent in 1947 (Fetter 2016). Such dramatic

54 Federal Reserve Bank of Minneapolis (2024), *Consumer price index, 1913-: Historical data from the era of the modern U.S. consumer price index (CPI)*, www.minneapolisfed.org/about-us/monetary-policy/inflation-calculator/consumer-price-index-1913-.

55 National Housing Agency (April 1944), *Housing for War and the Job Ahead*, 15, www.huduser.gov/portal//portal/sites/default/files/pdf/US-National-Housing-Agency-Housing.pdf.

56 The Fed unsuccessfully demanded authority for curtailing housing loans. See Federal Reserve Board (July 29, 1941), *Changes to Include All Housing in Consumer Credit Order* [memorandum], Eccles Papers, Box 41, Folder 3, https://fraser.stlouisfed.org/files/docs/historical/eccles/041_03_0009.pdf; also see Vest, G.B. (May 12, 1945), *Summary of Proposed Executive Order Regulating Real Estate Credit* [memorandum], Eccles Papers, Box 32, Folder 2, https://fraser.stlouisfed.org/archival-collection/marriner-s-eccles-papers-1343/summary-proposed-executive-order-regulating-real-estate-credit-462558?page=2.

jumps are highly unusual within a few years, as homeownership rates tend to be rather "sticky." As Daniel Fetter (2016) shows, rent controls led landlords to disinvest in rental properties and sell them as owner-occupied ones. Many tenants purchased the apartments they lived in, investing their increased savings accumulated during the war. Yet this transition was not always voluntary. In 1942 the *New York Times* cited OPA investigations that found that many landlords gave tenants the "choice" of buying their occupied unit at an inflated price or facing eviction so that the landlord could sell to another buyer.[57]

Interest groups lobbied fiercely to remove OPA restrictions from housing, arguing that they would impede housing activity. Realtors, in particular, issued a range of formal complaints about the agency's alleged overreach in housing markets and property rights (Lebowitz 1981). While NAREB begrudgingly accepted some forms of rent control in the fight against inflation, they criticized the OPA's rental price baseline as too low, inflexible, and punitive for landlords.[58] In addition, NAREB argued that the OPA's policies were overly restrictive in the homeownership market by requiring a 33 percent down payment (later reduced to 20 percent) for the sale of rented apartments and a three- to six-month eviction moratorium.[59] The OPA had implemented these measures to prevent predatory real estate deals and give tenants enough time to find another home in the case of a sale. NAREB also proposed that the OPA consider a homebuying program to channel excess savings into homeownership in addition to war bonds, but the OPA dismissed the proposal. In a letter to the realtors cited in Congress, the head of the agency's rent department, Paul Porter, wrote that the OPA was "not in favor of stimulating a program promoting home buying and home ownership as an anti-inflation measure ... [because] it would seem preferable for the worker to purchase War bonds directly rather than to depend on noninflationary use of these funds by the home seller."[60]

While Germany's strict rent controls remained in place until long after WWII to support a low-inflation export-oriented growth strategy, American price controls were comparatively short-lived and succumbed to the demands of a mass consumption economy by 1947. Toward the end of the war,

[57] "OPA plans limits on sale of houses" (August 20, 1942), *New York Times*.

[58] US House of Representatives (April–June 1943), *To Investigate Executive Agencies: Hearings before the Special Committee to Investigate Executive Agencies pursuant to H. Res. 102* (testimony of H. Nelson), 211.

[59] OPA (1946), *Some Answers to Landlords' Questions about OPA Rent Control*, www.govinfo.gov/content/pkg/GOVPUB-PR32_4200-fa30a7def978540376a7bf813fa9b6e9/pdf/GOVPUB-PR32_4200-fa30a7def978540376a7bf813fa9b6e9.pdf.

[60] Porter, P. (August 4, 1942), *Memorandum: Proposed Program to Encourage Home Buying*, cited in US House of Representatives (April–June 1943), *To Investigate Executive Agencies: Hearings before the Special Committee to Investigate Executive Agencies pursuant to H. Res. 102* (testimony of H. Nelson), 215–217.

the OPA lost political support amid growing pressure from Republicans and conservative Democrats to lift controls (Lebowitz 1981). The powerful pro-business lobby – including mass manufacturers, realtors, builders, and agricultural companies – advocated for the removal of price controls to restore private enterprise. On the other side of the political debate were labor unions, which saw a "corporatist moment" of cooperation between business and labor during the war. Unionization rates rose to an all-time high of 35 percent of nonfarm workers in 1945 (Levy 2020, 459). Moreover, many African Americans benefited from lower rents due to price controls and increased wartime labor market participation. However, they remained excluded from the administrative structure of the OPA and suffered from weaker enforcement of price controls in their neighborhoods, alongside ongoing segregation and discrimination (Cohen 2003, 86). White women also benefited from the wartime economy as their labor market participation rate increased by 10 percent, and they attained key positions in the OPA. The wartime economy advanced women's roles outside the home and challenged the traditional male-breadwinner model, as women were seen as steering and representing "good citizenship and good consumership" (Cohen 2003, 83). Women, labor unions, and Black Americans were thus vocal activists in the fight against inflation and demanded that some price controls stay in place even after the war.

President Harry S. Truman, who assumed the office after FDR's death in April 1945, favored a gradual approach to the phasing out of wartime price controls to manage the risk of postwar inflation (Geselbracht 2019). But the imperatives of the American demand-led economy made his gradual plan unfeasible. Although Truman managed to extend price controls into 1947, the pro-business lobby pressured the Democratic Congress to force him into signing a diluted price-control bill in 1946 already. The meat industry led the charge, withholding meat in protest and triggering public outcry, which led Truman to lift price controls for meatpacking and other sectors (Lebowitz 1981). A few months later, the Republican-controlled Congress dissolved the OPA, leaving Truman with little choice but to begrudgingly oversee the elimination of price controls, including a gradual winding down of rent controls by 1949. As Lizabeth Cohen (2003, 101) notes, the business lobby believed that "a flourishing mass consumption economy with competitive, unregulated pricing of new cars, new suburban homes, and new products to fill them would better protect the general good," and policymakers across the political spectrum ultimately agreed.

ADDING ANOTHER LAYER: HOUSING SUPPORT FOR VETERANS

The war had brought the US economy back to life, but new economic problems were on the horizon. The US government's role was crucial in this resurgence, stimulating unprecedented industrial production during the war. By 1945, unemployment had fallen to 2 percent and real incomes were rising, and the economy had expanded by more than two-thirds during the war.[61] A key postwar question became how to transition the wartime economy to a peacetime economy without slipping into a recession, as military spending dramatically decreased from 38 percent of GDP (90 percent of federal spending) in 1945 to just 4 percent of GDP (31 percent of federal spending) in 1948.[62]

Stimulating housing-based growth was a key part of the answer. Before the war's end, the FDR administration had planned to sustain the economic momentum into peacetime. With home repairs and construction on hold during the war, the result was massive housing supply shortages of around 3.7 million homes nationwide, especially concentrated in manufacturing hubs such as San Diego and Los Angeles.[63] To stimulate economic growth and address housing shortages, FDR expanded demand-side homeownership programs.

Foreseeing macroeconomic benefits, the FDR administration adopted mortgage guarantee programs for veterans as part of the Servicemen's Readjustment Act of 1944, commonly known as the G.I. Bill. The bill also included higher-education tuition benefits and job-training programs to reintegrate veterans into civilian life (Mettler 2005). But FDR was particularly attuned to the bill's potential to stimulate the economy, noting that a major goal was to address "the serious problem of economic reconversion and readjustment after the war, so that private industry will be able to provide jobs for the largest possible number ... A sound postwar economy is a major present responsibility."[64] Then-Representative Albert Gore, Sr. (Democrat, Tennessee) emphasized the dual purpose of the bill: "We should pass it not only to do justice to the returning veterans ... but to safeguard our national economy."[65] Housing industries, particularly realtors, were enthusiastic about the bill, estimating that an active housing sector could provide jobs for about 5 million returning veterans.[66]

61 Fishback, P. (November 12, 2019), *World War II: America's spending, deficits, multipliers, and sacrifice,* Centre for Economic Policy Research, https://voxeu.org/article/world-war-ii-america-spending-deficits-multipliers-and-sacrifice.

62 Tassava, C. (February 10, 2008), *The American economy during World War II,* in Whaples, R. (ed.), *EH.Net Encyclopedia*, https://eh.net/encyclopedia/the-american-economy-during-world-war-ii/.

63 Wheildon, L. (1946). "National housing emergency, 1946–1947." *CQ Researcher*, https://doi.org/10.4135/cqresrre1946121700.

64 Roosevelt, F. D. (June 22, 1944), *Statement on Signing the G.I. Bill*, The American Presidency Project, www.presidency.ucsb.edu/node/210867.

65 Gore, A. (May 17, 1944), *Remarks in the US House of Representatives, Congressional Record* 90(04), 4623.

66 US House of Representatives (November 1943 – March 1944), *Post-War Planning: Hearings before the Committee on Public Buildings and Grounds* (testimony of H. Nelson), 50.

Much like the New Deal housing programs, housing programs for veterans were designed to stimulate the economy without direct government spending.[67] Policymakers across the spectrum agreed that the federal government should support private homebuilding via subsidized mortgages. Using the model of depression-era FHA guarantees, the Veterans Administration (which became the Department of Veterans Affairs, VA, in 1989) offered returning veterans mortgages guaranteed by the US government with very low down payments and interest rates. The G.I. Bill's home loan provisions were specifically designed to support veterans who had been unable to accumulate savings or build credit history during the war (Thurston 2015, 262). These provisions would make veterans "a good banking risk," as US Representative Paul Cunningham (Republican, Iowa) remarked after the bill's passage.[68] The American Legion, with 3 million members at the time, was the main sponsor of the bill (Frydl 2009; Mettler 2005). Realtors even called the G.I. Bill's housing provision the "greatest single stimulant" for the housing sector.[69] To further support the VA-insured mortgage market, in 1948 policymakers authorized Fannie to buy and sell VA mortgages in the secondary market (Jones and Grebler 1961, 123).[70]

While housing programs for veterans expanded America's housing policy toolkit for stimulating demand-led growth, their exclusionary nature did not change. As Ira Katznelson (2005, ch. 5) notes, the G.I. Bill was effectively for "white veterans only." Much like FHA programs, VA housing programs excluded roughly one million Black veterans, as private banks continued to follow redlining guidelines, realtors refused to show them homes, and bankers denied them loans (Thurston 2018; Freund 2007). Consequently, Black households were still denied middle-class entry via property ownership and remained excluded from America's most important driver of wealth, prosperity, and growth.

POSTWAR HOUSING SUPPLY SHORTAGE, DEMAND-SIDE RESPONSE

In light of persisting housing shortages in the immediate postwar years, it would not have been unreasonable to pursue a German-style supply-side

[67] The Council of Economic Advisers underlined that these programs "do not add much if anything to Government expenditures ... credit guarantees of various sorts on the part of the Government, such as in housing, provide a stimulus to private investment." See Council of Economic Advisers (1953), *Annual Economic Review*, 117.

[68] US House of Representatives (June–July 1945), *World War Veterans' Legislation: Hearings before the House Committee on World War Veterans' Legislation on H.R. 3749* (testimony of P. Cunningham), 52.

[69] Cooper, L. (July 1, 1944), "Realty men adopt post-war report," *New York Times*.

[70] Fannie's portfolio grew steadily to USD 2.5 billion until 1954, particularly driven by an expansion of VA mortgages.

housing response by building affordable rental housing for the masses. Indeed, there were some political efforts to boost rental housing in postwar America. However, the American growth strategy of stimulating private mortgage lending and homeownership remained dominant, largely due to the perceived successes of earlier demand-side housing programs in addressing the depression. Consequently, public and rental housing remained marginalized elements of the American political economy.

Between 1945 and 1949, President Truman and some congressional Democrats pushed for strengthening public housing programs, albeit with limited success (Thurston 2018, 67; Jacobs 2007, 242). Public housing programs faced familiar challenges: They were seen as budgetary burdens rather than growth-generating measures. With the adoption of the Housing Act of 1949, the Truman administration – supported by labor unions and housing activists but opposed by the real estate lobby and southern Democrats – initially strengthened public housing efforts (Dreier 2000). The act included funds and provisions for urban clearance and renewal as well as ambitious public housing goals (McCabe 2016, ch. 3; Thurston 2018, 67). The real estate lobby could not prevent the bill's passage, but they successfully pushed for liberalizing the terms of FHA mortgages for homeowners – such as requiring lower down payments and allowing higher loan limits – as part of the bill. The act's public housing goals were ambitious on paper but modest in reality. It envisioned the construction of 800,000 public housing units over six years, but only 240,000 new units had been built or were being built by 1955.[71] One reason for this shortfall was that Truman cut public housing construction as early as 1950, fearing inflationary pressures and shortages of labor and material resulting from the Korean War. As often happened, public housing programs succumbed to other macroeconomic priorities, while homeownership programs remained intact.

Soon after, it was business as usual when Truman extended homeownership benefits to Korean War veterans in 1952. The construction of public housing units was no longer a priority. The administration of President Dwight D. Eisenhower (1953–1961) followed suit, further liberalizing the lending terms of VA and FHA mortgages in 1954. According to the Fed, these housing measures provided "additional stimulus to housing markets."[72] A few years earlier, the Fed had similarly concluded that government programs contributed to a residential building boom in 1949, as "[a]n important factor in the demand for both new and old residential properties was the large volume of Government guaranteed mortgage funds available from banks and other lenders on very

[71] Shaffer, H. (April 20, 1955), "Public housing, 1955," *CQ Researcher*, https://doi.org/10.4135/cqresrre1955042000.

[72] Federal Reserve Board (1954), *Annual Report*, 10.

favorable terms."[73] Finally, in 1954, the administration partially privatized Fannie's operations, raising private funds to expand the agency's activities in the secondary market while reducing its reliance on the US Treasury for funding (Jones and Grebler 1961, 36).[74] This move was a prelude to the 1968 "privatization" of Fannie Mae (discussed in Chapter 4).[75]

The demand-side, housing-based growth strategy worked. After wartime controls were lifted, residential investment reached a peak of 7.3 percent of GDP in 1950 and remained relatively high until the mid-1960s.[76] In 1950, almost two million units were built nationwide, up from just 326,000 in 1945. Construction of new housing units remained between 1 and 2 million per year until the 1960s. The outstanding mortgage volume for the owner-occupied market increased from USD 15 billion in 1934 to USD 131 billion in 1959, with 41 percent backed by the federal government in the latter year (see Figure 2.1; Grebler et al. 1956, 286). By 1957, veterans had taken out 5 million VA mortgages, and by 1970 an additional 2.3 million. The FHA numbers were even more impressive, with 4.6 million mortgages insured from 1934 to 1957 and another 5.8 million between 1958 and 1970.[77] Over time, the terms of FHA and VA mortgages have become longer and required lower down payments.[78] Although the FHA was authorized to insure mortgage loans for

[73] Federal Reserve Board (1950), *Annual Report*, 16. In 1950, the Fed was temporarily granted the authority to curtail real estate lending through Regulation X as part of broader efforts to control inflation during the Korean War.

[74] Despite the partial privatization, the American state continued to back Fannie Mae debt, as a press report confirms: "While the [Fannie] notes will not be guaranteed by the US government ... the Treasury would lend FNMA any amount that might be needed to pay interest and principal on time"; see "FNMA to market $500,000,000 notes" (December 30, 1954), *New York Times*.

[75] A presidential advisory committee on housing, consisting of representatives from the home-building, realty, and mortgage banking industries, hoped to eventually close Fannie Mae and replace it with an agency that was federally chartered but privately financed and without the explicit endorsement of the federal government. However, as a dissenting participant notes, a new and more privatized agency detached from the Treasury would "reduce the volume of mortgage lending; to tend towards increase of down payments on mortgage loans; shorten mortgage maturities; and have a tendency to increase interest rates." The participant cautioned that the creation of a new and "untried" facility would take time, require efforts to gain the trust of investors, possibly "shock" the mortgage system, and require handling Fannie's massive portfolio. Policymakers heeded these concerns by reforming and partially privatizing Fannie rather than replacing it. See Cole, A. (December 1953), *A Report by the Advisory Committee on Government Housing Policies and Programs*, www.huduser.gov/portal/sites/default/files/pdf/President-Advisory-Committee-Dec14.pdf.

[76] Federal Reserve Economic Data (FRED) (2024), *Private Residential Fixed Investment*, https://fred.stlouisfed.org/series/A011RE1Q156NBEA.

[77] US Census Bureau, *Historical Statistics of the United States: Colonial Times to 1970*, Series N 180–185.

[78] The median loan-to-value ratio for VA loans was 91 percent in 1950 and increased to 95 percent in 1970. The median loan-to-value ratio for FHA loans increased from 79 to 93 percent

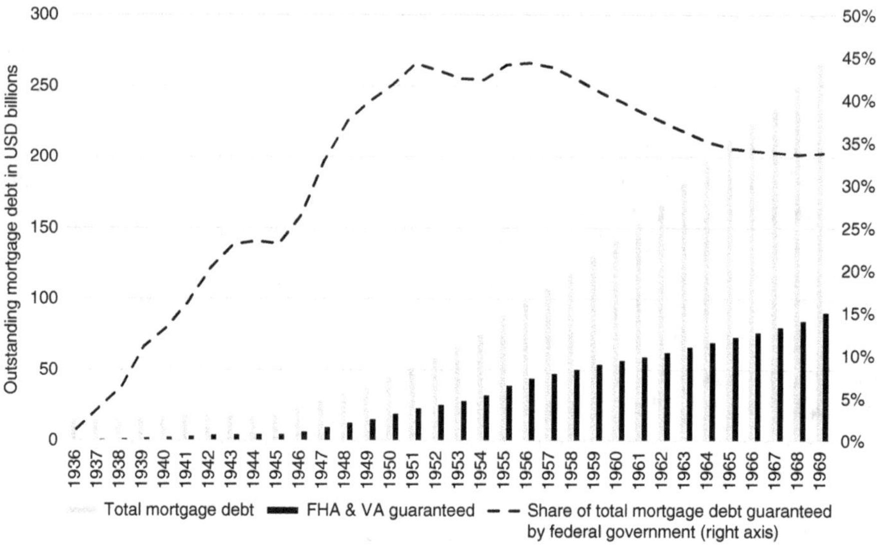

FIGURE 2.1 Homeowner mortgages guaranteed by the US federal government, 1936–1969
Note: Data covers mortgage debt for one- to four-family homes. *Data source:* Historical Statistics of the United States (1975), Series N 273–277.

rental properties, it did not do so on a large scale (Weiss 1987, 155). Between 1934 and 1962, the FHA had funded only one million rental units (with a mortgage insurance volume of USD 10 billion) compared to 6.4 million owner-occupied units (USD 56 billion).[79] By the early 1960s, the political economy was thus squarely centered around owner-occupied housing-based growth.

It was not only government programs that fueled the housing boom. Population growth and real wage increases also contributed to growing housing demand. Between 1940 and 1960 the US population grew by over 50 million, while the average annual real wage increased by around 2 percent, in line with high rates of productivity growth. The strong housing demand was met with an increasing supply: During the 1950s, housing starts totaled 15 million, many of these in suburban areas and the Sunbelt, compared to 7.4 million total new homes in the 1940s and only 2.7 million in the 1930s (see Figure 2.2). Despite the postwar housing boom, from 1950 to 1970, real house prices remained relatively stable. Nominal house prices had increased mostly in line with construction costs, a

between 1950 and 1970 (Fetter 2013). In addition, the median loan term of FHA and VA mortgages increased from 20 years in 1950 to 29 years in 1970, while that of conventional mortgages increased from 11 to 21 years during the same time period.

[79] FHA (1962), *29th Annual Report*, 18.

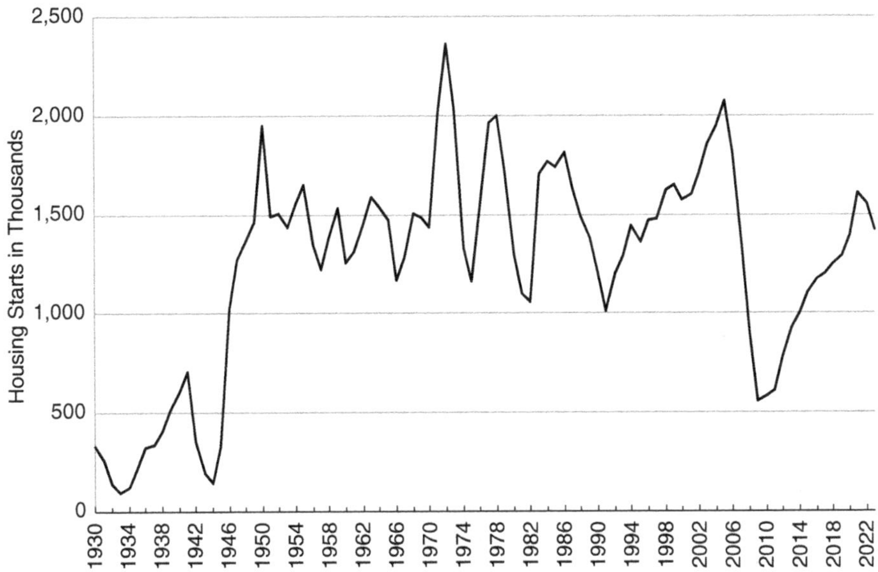

FIGURE 2.2 Housing starts in the United States, 1930–2023
Notes: The historical average between 1960 and 2000 is 1.5 million homes per year.
Data sources: US Census Bureau (1975), Historical Statistics of the United States (Series N 156–169) for data until 1959; FRED (series: HOUST) for data after 1959.

development that can be attributed to relatively few building restrictions, which helped expand the country's housing supply (Glaeser 2013, 30; Glaeser and Gyourko 2018). In short, America's demand-led growth regime was in full swing, fueled by subsidized housing credit that supported new housing construction, employment, and private spending on consumer goods.

Economic experts not only confirmed but also endorsed the stimulating effects of housing programs, underscoring the broad-based consensus among American political and economic elites. The Council of Economic Advisers (CEA), established as an advisory body to the president in 1946, repeatedly recommended expanding the FHA and VA programs. These programs, they argued, would help create "mortgage availability [that] will influence housing demand considerably. If funds remain readily available, gains in household incomes are likely to strengthen the demand for new homes."[80] At the same time, the CEA correctly pointed out that the American state had become deeply intertwined with the mortgage market:

> Housing loans insured or guaranteed by the Federal Government now represent over two fifths of the entire home mortgage debt. For this reason, if for no other, the Government has a direct responsibility in helping to maintain a sound housing and

[80] Council of Economic Advisers (1962), *Annual Economic Review*, 65.

> mortgage market. It has a corresponding duty to use its own programs wisely, so as to promote stable economic growth … The objective of stable growth is clearly in the national interest. It is also in the long-term interest of those who have so greatly benefited from the Federal housing programs – the millions of consumers with a stake in their homes, jobs, and debt obligations, the hundreds of thousands of workmen in the construction industry, and the thousands of enterprises engaged in home building and mortgage lending.[81]

In short, generating demand-led growth via housing became a national objective shared across the political spectrum and among influential interest groups and economic elites. As a result, presidential administrations kept injecting government support into housing to keep the housing-based growth machine running, with few counterbalancing forces standing in their way.

HOUSING FORDISM AND SUBURBAN MASS CONSUMPTION

The United States emerged as the world's postwar superpower, achieving prosperity through vast Fordist industrial production capacities that supported both a domestic mass consumer market and the export of goods abroad (Link 2020; Maier 1977). Housing programs further reinforced postwar mass production and consumption.

Few developments better embody such production and consumption than the emerging and rapidly expanding Levittowns, named after the homebuilders Levitt & Sons from Long Island, New York (Jackson 1985). Both FHA and VA programs enabled white households to buy single-family homes in the postwar years, contributing significantly to America's postwar suburbanization (Weiss 1987, 156). Levitt & Sons transformed their small-scale industry into a mass-producing enterprise, streamlining every aspect of the housing production process from purchasing land to construction and sale. The result was entire neighborhoods of low-cost, mass-produced cookie-cutter homes in suburban areas of the northeast, helping to alleviate housing shortages in former war production areas. Kenneth Jackson (1985, 234) details the hyperefficient, standardized Fordist mass production process:

> After bulldozing the land and removing the trees, trucks carefully dropped off building materials at precise 60-foot intervals. Each house was built on a concrete slab (no cellar); the floors were of asphalt and the walls of composition rock-board … New power hand tools like saws, routers, and nailers helped increase worker productivity. Freight cars loaded with lumber went directly into a cutting yard where one man cut parts for ten houses in one day.

The family-owned business would soon build over 140,000 homes, sometimes up to thirty houses per day. Other homebuilders and developers in Texas and

[81] The White House (1956), *Economic Report of the President*, Washington, DC, 40.

California followed suit. Between 1948 and 1958, 11 million homes (out of 13 million total new homes) were built in suburbs where land was cheap and housing production simple (Levy 2020, 492). Subsidized credit by the FHA and the VA were "among the main forces behind the growth of the suburbs."[82] Physical infrastructure followed, including highways, schools, and shopping malls, which generated economic activity and a "material landscape of consumerism" (Levy 2020, 502; Ryan et al. 2011, 468).

Although housing programs were not explicitly designed to stimulate private mass consumption, they did so implicitly as part of cascade effects emanating from housing activity. Jonathan Levy (2020, 485) notes that "new home construction meant fresh demand for consumer durables to fill garages, living rooms, and kitchens." As Nick Bunker (2014) finds, "the largest driver of growth during this period was personal consumption expenditures," followed by government expenditure and private investment, while "net exports were a very small part of growth" (Bunker 2014). Unlike German housing programs, American ones were not scaled down when US housing shortages were declared to be over in 1960.[83] Instead, they continued to stimulate domestic demand and, indirectly, consumption in the economy. The CEA repeatedly emphasized housing as a key sector – if not *the* key sector – of the postwar growth regime: "The higher standard of living made possible by economic growth results from increased output of a wide variety of goods and services. Among these is one item which, by virtue of its economic importance … deserves special attention in a discussion of economic growth. *This item is housing*."[84]

In short, as Lizabeth Cohen (2004, 237) writes, housing became "the bedrock of the postwar mass consumption economy."

FROM RACIAL EXCLUSION TO PREDATORY INCLUSION

For white households, buying a house was as easy as buying a mass-manufactured car, while Black households were largely excluded from property markets and tended to remain in cities. This exclusion meant that Black households were sidelined from the core of America's demand-led growth regime: Credit-financed homeownership. As a result, in 1960, Black households had a homeownership rate of only 38 percent compared to 64 percent for white households.[85] By 1960, only 5 percent (or 2.5 million people) of the suburban, mostly property-owning, population was Black (Nicolaides and Wiese 2017). As suburban areas boomed due to new investments and population growth, urban areas experienced the flip side of the coin: Population flight, underinvestment, and poverty.

[82] Council of Economic Advisers (1965), *Annual Economic Review*, 155.

[83] The White House (1960), *Economic Report*, 1960, 2.

[84] Council of Economic Advisers (1962), *Annual Economic Review*, 139. My emphasis.

[85] Devaney, F. J. (1994), *Tracking the American Dream – 50 Years of Housing History from the Census Bureau: 1940–1990*, 29, www.huduser.gov/portal/Publications/pdf/HUD-7775.pdf.

Black Americans faced discrimination not only in homeownership but also in urban rental markets; this exacerbated housing shortages in cities, forcing many Black households into dilapidated neighborhoods and buildings owned by white property owners who saw little incentive to invest in these rental properties. Meanwhile, rich white households continued to populate luxury apartments in affluent neighborhoods (Taylor 2019, 30). As the share of the American population living in suburbs increased from 13 percent in 1940 to 37 percent in 1970 (Nicolaides and Wiese 2017), American cities were in crisis. Thomas Sugrue (1996, 23) highlights Detroit as an example of these developments, with the city experiencing a population decline of 340,000 people (mostly white households leaving for the suburbs) from 1950 until 1970. Services declined, capital fled, crime increased, and neighborhoods deteriorated (McCabe 2016, 57), all of which "added further legitimacy to the stereotype that poor and working-class Black people posed a threat to the property values of white property owners" (Taylor 2019, 22). One result of such poor living conditions was urban riots in as many as 150 cities starting in 1964 (Thurston 2018, 193).

In response to urban housing problems, the presidential administration of Lyndon B. Johnson (1963–1969) began to open America's government-sponsored housing model to racialized minorities. It adopted two key pieces of legislation to help end discrimination in real estate, stimulate homeownership in minority markets, and promote urban development.[86] The first was the Fair Housing Act of 1968, which aimed to end racial discrimination in real estate sales and was later amended to end sex discrimination as well (Thurston 2018, 27).[87] The second was the bipartisan Housing and Urban Development Act of 1968, which we will revisit in Chapter 4 for a discussion on how it revolutionized America's housing finance market. This act included measures to stimulate homeownership among minority and low-income households[88] as well as rental housing initiatives that expanded rent supplements, increased public housing funding, and made building rental housing more attractive to private developers.

These measures stimulated housing and growth in Black communities but did not eliminate prevailing practices of racial discrimination and exploitation (McCabe 2016). Homeownership programs for low-income people and African Americans often resulted in "predatory" lending – unequal, more

86 Prior to these reforms in 1968, the Johnson administration had adopted the Housing and Urban Development Act of 1965, which included new rental subsidies and funds for urban renewal and rehabilitation, and it also liberalized FHA and VA mortgage terms. Shortly thereafter, President Johnson established the US Department of Housing and Urban Development (HUD).

87 President Kennedy's 1962 "stroke of the pen" executive order (11063) had preceded the 1968 act and was intended to limit discrimination in real estate and federal housing programs.

88 The act's Section 235 was the homeownership program for poor and minority households. The 1954 Housing Act had already included a small-scale provision to support minority households displaced by urban renewal in obtaining financing for homeownership (Section 221).

expensive, and exploitative lending to Black borrowers (Taylor 2019, 7; Krippner 2017). As Keeanga-Yamahtta Taylor (2019, 3) powerfully describes, for many Black households homeownership "was not the fulfillment of the American Dream; it was the beginning of an American nightmare."

THE FINAL LAYER: MORTGAGE INTEREST DEDUCTION

The final expansion of America's postwar government-sponsored housing model occurred with the growing impact of the mortgage interest deduction (MID). Unlike other housing programs, the MID was not specifically designed to support housing or economic growth. As noted earlier, its origins trace back to 1913, when policymakers introduced an interest deduction that applied to all kinds of consumer interest, not just mortgage interest. However, as mortgage debt and homeownership rose in the postwar years, policymakers *discovered* the MID as a major tool to support housing-based growth and allowed for its expansion. The rise of the MID as a third rail in American politics is a story of deliberate political inaction (see Chapter 4).

In the initial post-WWII years, the MID garnered little attention. Politicians and interest groups were more focused on the taxation of capital gains on the sale of homes. Lobby groups, particularly NAREB, viewed the capital gains tax as an unfair burden on homeowners, arguing that it would limit labor mobility.[89] For these and other reasons, the *Washington Post* endorsed the tax exemption of capital gains, stating that it "would be in the public interest."[90] After decades of advocacy led by NAREB, these efforts bore fruit. The Revenue Act of 1951 excluded these capital gains from taxation if they were reinvested in a new home, a provision that still exists in modified form today.[91]

It was not until much later in the postwar period that the MID gained significant political attention, driven by the growth in the number of households claiming the deduction. Two key developments favored this expansion. The first was President Roosevelt's actions to increase tax rates and broaden the tax base to finance the country's WWII activity, transforming the "class" tax system into a "mass" tax system.[92] As more households began paying

[89] US House of Representatives (July 1947), *Revenue Revisions, 1947–48: Hearings before the House Ways and Means Committee on Proposed Revisions of the Internal Revenue Code* (testimony of H. Nelson), 1382.

[90] "Relief for home buyers" (June 25, 1951), *Washington Post.*

[91] In 1954, policymakers adopted a tax provision for the accelerated depreciation of buildings, a subsidy that benefited rental and commercial real estate investors (Hanchett 1996). The subsidy for accelerated depreciation for residential buildings was subsequently reduced in 1969 and ultimately eliminated in 1986.

[92] At the same time, the Roosevelt administration introduced the standard deduction to reduce the administrative burden of processing income tax returns and alleviate the tax burden of households. Yet the standard deduction was fixed and not inflation-adjusted, while itemized

income tax, the number of households claiming deductions also increased. The second development was the booming US economy, which included rising homeownership and mortgage debt in the 1940s and 1950s – partly the result of generous FHA and VA programs. Homeownership rates rose from 44 percent in 1940 to 62 percent in 1960 (Kohl 2017), while the volume of mortgage debt grew almost tenfold from USD 17 billion to USD 141 billion during that period. These developments led to an increase in the number of mortgaged households from 4.8 million in 1940 to 15.8 million in 1960, many of which claimed the deduction.[93] Importantly, policymakers did not actively boost the MID; it grew automatically due to rising mortgage debt and homeownership.

Tax economists and officials at the US Treasury noticed the MID's growth and sounded the alarm during the 1960s (Kahn 1960; Surrey 1973). They expressed concern about the increasing number of households claiming itemized deductions – not just in housing but also other areas of the economy – that escaped taxation. Indeed, the number of taxpayers claiming itemized deductions doubled from 12 million taxpayers in 1951 to 24 million in 1960. Concomitantly, the total dollar amount of itemized deductions claimed by taxpayers increased from USD 12 billion in 1951 to USD 35.3 billion in 1960.[94] Deductions on credit interest, including on mortgages, were among the largest categories, rising from USD 2.2 billion in 1952 (16 percent of total claimed deductions) to USD 8 billion in 1960 (25 percent of total deductions).[95]

Stanley Surrey, assistant secretary for tax policy at the US Treasury from 1961 until 1969, was one of the most vocal critics of these tax breaks. He argued that they violated the principle of tax neutrality, strained the country's budget, and often privileged high-income households. Surrey not only started publicizing the precise cost of these deductions – later included in the US Treasury's annual tax expenditure reports – but also played a key role in developing reform plans to limit their growth. From the 1960s onward, the MID was no longer "hidden" in the tax code, as some scholars have claimed (e.g., Howard 1997). On the contrary, its growing visibility made the MID subject to political debate.

Surrey and the Treasury faced significant opposition in their efforts to curb the MID. Policymakers discovered that, like other housing programs, the MID supported housing-based growth. In 1963, under President John F. Kennedy, the Treasury – with Surrey as a key tax official – developed a

deductions, such as the mortgage interest deduction, kept growing along with mortgage debt and house prices.

[93] US Department of Commerce (1970), *Statistical Abstract of the United States, Construction and Housing*, 687.

[94] US Treasury Department (1962), *Statistics of Income: Individual Income Tax Returns for 1960*, 98–102, www.irs.gov/pub/irs-soi/60inar.pdf.

[95] Other notable tax deductions were those on real estate (USD 4.1 billion in claimed deductions in 1960) and charitable contributions (USD 6.8 billion).

tax reform plan to limit itemized deductions, including the MID.[96] The plan was met with resistance from policymakers in Congress and interest groups. Policymakers in Congress immediately discussed the Treasury proposal's potential "injurious effect on the building of homes and financing of homes," as stated by Representative Howard Baker Sr. (Republican, Tennessee).[97] NAREB preferred maintaining the status quo, arguing that curbing the deduction would "affect our economy not only within our business, but in many other businesses, including the construction business and all of the allied businesses that fit into construction."[98] Congress correspondingly left the MID intact. Similarly, the Tax Reform Act of 1969, signed by President Richard M. Nixon, did not touch the deduction. As a result, Surrey (1973, 235) lamented the massive growth in the value of homeownership tax breaks that were in place by 1970: "The tax expenditure items for housing – deductions for mortgage interest and property taxes – constitute the largest items in the Government program to assist private housing, far in excess of direct expenditure programs in the housing area. Thus, for 1970, these tax expenditures came to $5.4 billion, and the direct expenditures came to $2.7 billion." Homeownership tax breaks had become much larger than direct government spending on housing.

In sum, policymakers discovered the MID as another housing program to stimulate housing-based, demand-led growth in the postwar period. Policymakers believed that curbing the deduction would harm the housing market and the economy and thus tolerated its expansion. The MID became the latest addition to America's government-sponsored housing model.

CONCLUSION

Depression-era housing programs made housing finance a national champion, capable of serving as a vehicle for creating prosperity at the heart of America's demand-led economy. First, policymakers realized that depression-era housing programs could be not only countercyclical but also *permanent* tools to stimulate the economy though housing-based growth, acting as "levers and pulleys" to manage the economy (Krippner 2011, 61). For policymakers, stimulating housing became synonymous with stimulating economic growth. Second, depression-era housing programs created a consumer-friendly and affordable

96 Tax Foundation (February 11, 1963), *Tax Reduction and Reform: A Summary of the President's Tax Proposals.* The proposal envisioned broadening the tax base by incentivizing households to claim the standard deduction and bringing down wartime tax rates.

97 US House of Representatives (January–February 1963), *President's 1963 Tax Message: Hearings before the House Ways and Means Committee on the Tax Recommendations of the President* (remarks by H. H. Baker), 607.

98 US House of Representatives (January–February 1963), *President's 1963 Tax Message: Hearings before the House Ways and Means Committee on the Tax Recommendations of the President* (testimony of D. Sheehan), 890.

mortgage market highly dependent on state support for its functioning – a market that private actors would have been unable to provide on their own. As a result, American policymakers assumed responsibility for this newly created market over which they had imperfect control. These and other factors made supporting housing-based growth a default economic response well into the subsequent decades, as outlined in Table 2.1.

TABLE 2.1 *American housing finance programs adopted or reformed between 1913 and 1968*

Type of program	Program/agency	Years active	Description
Tax	Revenue Act of 1913: mortgage interest deduction	1913–	Allowed taxpayers to deduct interest on personal loans
Tax	Revenue Act of 1951: capital gains exclusion	1951–	Allowed homebuyers to exclude capital gains from taxation
Tax	Revenue Act of 1913: property tax deduction	1913–	Allowed homeowners to deduct state and local property tax from federal tax
Credit	Federal Home Loan Banks (FHLB)	1932–	Created government-supported credit system for S&Ls
Credit	Home Owners' Loan Corporation (HOLC)	1933–1951	Refinanced underwater mortgages – those worth more than the homes – at better terms
Credit	Federal Housing Administration (FHA)	1934–	Mortgage insurance program for homebuyers
Credit	Federal Savings and Loan Insurance Corporation (FSLIC)	1934–1989	Deposit insurance scheme for S&Ls
Credit	Federal National Mortgage Association (Fannie Mae)	1938–	Initially bought FHA mortgages, then also VA mortgages; supports secondary mortgage market
Credit	Veterans Administration (VA)	1944–	Mortgage insurance program for veterans (part of the G.I. Bill)
Credit	Housing and Urban Development Act of 1968: Section 235	1968–1987	Homeownership program for low-income and minority households
Central bank	HOLC bond buying program: 1934 change in Federal Reserve Act	1934–1951	Granted Fed authority to buy HOLC bonds

In the United States, demand-side housing programs for owner-occupied markets – but notably not for rental and public housing – became a cornerstone of the postwar demand-led economy. In contrast, as Chapter 3 will detail, Germany's post-WWII housing approach was markedly different and emphasized supply-side housing programs for both owner-occupied and rental homes to boost the country's housing supply and support German manufacturing industries.

3

Germany's Postwar Housing and Export Miracles

By the end of World War II, the German housing market was devastated: 2.5 million homes had been destroyed and another 1.6 million severely damaged (Diefendorf 1993, 125). This devastation, together with prewar housing shortages and war-related migration flows, left the first postwar West German government with a housing shortage of 4.6 million homes in 1949.[1] Around one-quarter of households – especially the millions of refugees from former eastern territories – was living in barracks, bunkers, cellars, camps, or overcrowded housing arrangements. These housing shortages also held back the economy, as workers needed adequate and affordable housing in order to fill industrial jobs in metropolitan areas. Unsurprisingly, Chancellor Konrad Adenauer made rebuilding the housing stock a priority to "lead the German people to a political, economic, ethical and cultural recovery."[2] For decades to come, postwar housing programs – above all, tax subsidies and credit programs for residential housing construction – shaped the country's housing market and helped produce an affordable rental market and a slowly increasing homeownership rate.

As seen in Chapter 2, in postdepression and postwar America, housing finance programs became a vehicle to stimulate domestic demand. Similarly, German housing programs were integral to the country's postwar economic success story, albeit in a different way. Postwar German housing programs, as this chapter demonstrates, directly supported the country's reemerging export-oriented growth regime. To overcome the severe housing shortages, the Adenauer government adopted *supply-side* housing programs that

[1] The post-WWII coverage in this chapter discusses developments in West Germany. For a historical overview of housing developments in East Germany, see Michelsen and Weiß (2010).

[2] Adenauer, K. (February 24, 1950), *Remarks in the 1st Bundestag, 41st and 42nd session*, 1388.

supported builders of new residential homes while also strengthening the manufacturing-based, export-oriented economy.[3]

German policymakers designed postwar housing programs with at least three macroeconomic goals in mind. First, increasing the housing supply would not only address housing shortages but also boost industrial productivity in manufacturing by alleviating labor shortages and promoting labor mobility to industrial areas, where housing and labor shortages were most acute. As Henry Wallich stated (1955, 174), "at that time to aid housing was to aid productivity." For these reasons, manufacturing industries and labor unions alike supported large-scale housing programs. The second goal was to build *low-cost* housing for most households, especially for workers in industrial areas, to keep the cost of living and wages down. Given wartime destruction, demand for housing vastly exceeded supply. Without government intervention, housing costs would have risen, fueling wage-cost spirals detrimental to export-oriented growth. Finally, policymakers created strong incentives for households to save – such as through homeownership savings programs (*Bausparen*) – while discouraging private consumption and easy access to credit. These measures helped limit inflationary tendencies that would have been detrimental to exports.

In the postwar period, housing programs were thus more than just housing or social policies; they also functioned as industrial and wage policies. Most importantly, the Adenauer government implemented social housing programs (*sozialer Wohnungsbau*) to construct new rental *and* owner-occupied homes, with a particular focus on the housing needs of industrial regions. By 1970, these programs had supported an astonishing 5.8 million new homes (out of 11.4 million total new homes), including 1.5 million owner-occupied units and 4.3 million rental units (see Figures 3.1 and 5.1). Relatedly, the Adenauer government adopted tax subsidies for constructing new rental and owner-occupied homes to further mobilize private investment and direct it into housing. These programs not only helped improve the much-needed supply of homes but also alleviated labor shortages in industrial regions that had held back production.

Moreover, postwar housing programs also had a *price-deflating* effect – keeping the cost of living and wages down – that was essential for export-oriented success. The German government built millions of low-cost social housing units, which significantly stabilized the cost of living and wage growth in the postwar decades, aligning with the country's "deliberate policy of deflation" (Kreile 1977, 777). In addition to supporting *new* low-cost social housing, the Adenauer government also extended nationwide rent freezes for *older*, prewar housing until the early 1960s. Germany's influential unions were the most vocal proponents of measures securing low-cost housing, threatening wage

[3] I define supply-side programs as subsidies to builders of *new* homes (Glaeser and Gyourko 2008, 137–141).

demands if housing costs increased. For Adenauer, lowering housing costs was a means to limit wage growth and inflation, thereby boosting the competitiveness of German firms.

By the early 1960s, Germany was experiencing not only an economic miracle – with fast-growing exports at its center – but also a housing miracle, building more new homes per capita than any other advanced economy at the time. Despite these successes, the center-right Adenauer government was unnerved by the relatively low number of owner-occupied homes built as part of social housing programs. Yet the federal states (*Länder*), responsible for allocating social housing funds, often viewed low-cost rental housing as better suited to their regional economic and industrial needs. It is partly for this economic reason that Germany remained a "nation of renters."

In contrast to American housing programs designed to stimulate housing as a vehicle for demand-led economic growth, German housing programs supported the country's own national champions found in the export-oriented manufacturing industries. In short, Germany's housing and export miracles are inextricably linked in previously underappreciated ways.

SETTING THE STAGE: THE ORIGINS OF EXPORT-ORIENTED GROWTH AND HOUSING PROGRAMS

Many features of Germany's current export-oriented growth regime and housing market originated well before WWII, dating back to the late nineteenth century (Abelshauser 2005; Manow 2020; Streeck and Yamamura 2001; Herrigel 1996). After the country's unification in 1871, Germany rapidly industrialized and developed the core features of its emerging manufacturing-based and export-oriented growth regime: Cooperative business–labor relations, vocational training systems, and long-term finance relations between banks and industrial firms. These pillars later became the foundation of Germany's "diversified quality production" of goods in the chemical, electrical engineering, and manufacturing sectors (cp. Streeck 2009), making Germany the second-largest exporter in the world after the United Kingdom by 1914. Importantly, from the late nineteenth century onward, policymakers and social partners also experimented with solutions to housing problems for workers in industrial areas. The reasons were both social and economic: Low-cost housing allowed industries to attract skilled workers and suppress wages, reinforcing the country's nascent industrial and export-oriented economy. While German elites did not simply recreate these old institutional features after WWII, they became the foundation from which to launch Germany's consolidated postwar export-oriented growth regime.

During the late-nineteenth-century industrialization of the German Empire (1871–1918), the country experienced a housing crisis and experimented with solutions developed by business and labor that aligned with the needs of the industry-based economy. While the imperial state avoided the problem (Wollmann 1985; Von Beyme 1987), business and labor developed housing solutions that would later shape Germany's post-WWII housing response. The crisis at that time was less about the quantity and more about the quality of housing. Cramped and unhygienic living arrangements for workers made the so-called housing question a pressing social issue. The country's population grew by around 25 million from 1870 to 1914, while workers flocked to industrial regions and overcrowded cities. At the time, there were no national housing programs in place, and "[b]ecause the construction and management of low-cost housing is not particularly profitable, municipal governments of the Imperial era took only limited measures to deal with the housing problem" (Silverman 1970, 116).

With the imperial state avoiding the problem, labor developed one solution: They helped finance affordable rental housing with capital from the country's pension and accident insurance fund that they were co-administering (Manow 2020, 20; Kohl 2017, 102; Kohl and Sørvoll 2021, 571–572). The unions' chosen partners were the limited-profit housing associations and member-based cooperatives (*gemeinnützige Baugesellschaften* and *Baugenossenschaften*), which emerged from the housing reform movement and specialized in building affordable multifamily homes (Jaedicke and Wollmann 1990, 205–206).[4] By 1914, these associations and cooperatives had grown their housing stock to a modest 1.3 percent of all housing units (Zimmermann 1991, 161).

Industrial firms, such as Krupp, developed their own solutions. In the late nineteenth century they started employer-based housing projects for workers (*Werkswohnungsbau*), which amounted to another 1.2 percent of all housing units by 1914 (Zimmermann 1991, 156). The reason was not charity but profitability, meaning that then already, "in Germany, the direct links between industrial needs and housing policy were especially strong" (Harloe 1995, 48). Or as historian Michael Honhart (1990, 9) observed, "[e]mployers found that shortages of affordable housing hindered them in efforts to recruit employees from other areas and to keep current employees from leaving or demanding higher wages." Without much state support, however, these corporatist solutions remained marginal components of Germany's political economy.

From WWI onward, the German state became more interventionist in addressing growing housing shortages and costs, with policymakers experimenting with housing programs as anti-inflationary tools to suppress wages. During the war, the imperial government implemented rent controls and

[4] Some housing cooperatives and associations also built affordable single-family homes, but they were less prominent than their rental housing projects. Moreover, homeownership savings banks – *Bausparkassen* – gained momentum only in the 1920s, at which point the rental-based limited-profit housing associations had developed a key role in the country's housing economy.

tenant protections to prevent evictions and exploitations amid rising housing costs in war production areas. After WWI and throughout the Weimar Republic (1918–1933), policymakers continued renewing rent controls and tenant protections, albeit for a different reason: To limit wage increases and inflation (Führer 1995). During the 1920s, Germany experienced significant housing shortages, ranging between 600,000 and 1.4 million, which threatened to drive up housing costs (Silverman 1970, 119). This shortage resulted from halting housing production during the war, capital shortages, and skyrocketing inflation and interest rates after the war. To prevent rising housing costs from leading to higher wage demands during the inflationary and economically turbulent 1920s, Weimar-era policymakers extended rent controls.[5] The outcome was affordable housing for renters, largely at the expense of property owners (Führer 1995, 129). Historian Dan Silverman (1970, 138) provides one rationale: "As one popular phrase stated it, the *Wohnfrage* [housing question] was really a *Lohnfrage* [wage question]. Rent increases did heat up the demand for wage increases ... Higher wages might have reduced Germany's international trade advantage, throwing her economy into a downturn." During the Weimar period, policymakers thus linked housing to broader economic issues of wage suppression and trade.

The flip side of rent controls was that they stifled *new* housing construction, leading Weimar governments to adopt large-scale affordable rental housing programs, albeit with mixed success. After the hyperinflation of the early 1920s that had halted housing construction, policymakers – especially the Social Democrats – adopted housing programs to subsidize the construction of low-cost rental housing (Jaedicke and Wollmann 1990, 204). These programs were partly funded by a tax on property owners and landlords (*Hauszinssteuer*), which directed funds to *Länder* governments for building affordable housing. The strategy worked to a degree, and housing construction picked up from 1924 until the end of the decade. On average, about 50 percent of new housing construction between 1924 and 1931 received public support in the form of cheap loans or subsidies (Silverman 1970, 123). Limited-profit housing associations were the greatest beneficiaries of these programs, as private housing companies were still deterred by strict rent controls and high financing costs. Despite these successes, housing shortages persisted, and the 1929 economic crisis crippled both the housing sector and the public finances that supported housing programs. Another issue was that the national government had little formal authority over how the *Länder* implemented housing programs, and the *Länder* often decided to consolidate their budgets instead of financing new housing with the tax revenue they collected.

[5] While rent controls persisted throughout the Weimar period, policymakers tightened and loosened controls in response to changing economic conditions such as hyperinflation in the early 1920s, an improving housing supply in the late 1920s, and mass unemployment in the early 1930s (for more details, see Führer 1995).

Once the Nazis had seized power in 1933, they promised to solve the country's housing shortages with their much-publicized antiurban ideal of building millions of single-family homes in settlements. But they utterly failed in both respects (Harloe 1995, 174). By 1936, a housing shortage of 1.5 to 1.8 million remained. By 1939, the regime had created a total of only about 150,000 settlement homes through its housing programs, while overall housing construction numbers largely mirrored those of the final years of the Weimar period, averaging 250,000 units per year (Harlander 1995, 180; Silverman 1970, 120). Despite the propaganda, the Nazi regime mobilized too little capital for housing construction; indeed, subsidies for new housing construction were higher during the Weimar years, as the Nazi regime's priority was military, not civilian, production. Unable to address the housing problem, the Nazis *froze* rents of *all* apartments in 1936. The reasoning was, again, to limit rent increases that could produce wage demands and inflation (Führer 1995, 210).

In sum, German post-WWII housing programs did not come out of the blue. Since the late nineteenth century, the country had experimented with rent controls, employer-based housing, and labor-supported limited-profit rental housing to address housing shortages. These early programs already exhibited some complementarities with the emerging German manufacturing-based, export-oriented economy. German industries found much macroeconomic merit in affordable housing policies, which helped them attract skilled workers, increase productivity through better housing conditions, and pay lower wages. However, it was only in the post-WWII period that policymakers adopted massive national housing programs that would become essential pillars of Germany's consolidated postwar export-oriented growth regime.

POSTWAR HOUSING SHORTAGES: HOLDING BACK INDUSTRIAL PRODUCTION

As WWII left the housing stock in German cities and industrial centers severely damaged or destroyed, industries faced massive labor shortages that held back the core engine of the economy: Industrial manufacturing. At the same time, housing shortages also meant that, without government intervention, living costs and wages would have exploded, which would have hurt export competitiveness. Solving the housing problem was thus much larger than just social policy of providing adequate living for the population. It was also industrial policy to revive the full capacity of the German export machine.

By 1950, the German government estimated the housing shortage to be 4.6 million units.[6] In other words, there were only 9.4 million units for 14 million households in the country. Most of these shortages were in large cities – Hamburg, Berlin, Munich, Frankfurt, Stuttgart, Düsseldorf, Bremen,

[6] Fey, W. (1953), "Das Wohnungsdefizit," *Bundesbaublatt* 1(1), 3.

and Hannover – and in the highly industrialized Ruhr area where aerial bombings had been most pronounced (Hansen 2009). Experts calculated that restoring sufficient supply would take until the 1980s (Schulz 1994, 44). The precarious housing situation was exacerbated by the influx of 12 million displaced individuals from eastern territories and the return of millions of prisoners of war, including mass returns from the Soviet Union in 1955, particularly affecting Schleswig-Holstein and Lower Saxony. Many families were forced to share apartments, while others lived in barracks, bunkers, cellars, and even holes in the ground.

For German industries, housing shortages in industrial areas led to labor shortages, as workers could not easily move to these areas to fill industrial or construction jobs, nor did they have adequate places to rest after demanding physical jobs. Due to housing-related labor shortages, manufacturing industries were underutilizing their production capacities, which held back production at the core of Germany's postwar export-oriented growth regime (Wallich 1955, 86–87; Häußermann and Siebel 1996, 147). In a joint letter of 1949, manufacturing industries urged the government to build new housing in industrial areas: "[E]mployees must travel long distances to work, which not only means higher costs but also lost time for them. It is very much justified for *macroeconomic reasons* to especially support building new housing for employees."[7]

Given the lack of housing in industrial centers, Germany's rural population increased by 6.7 million people due to the influx of refugees and expellees, while cities lost around 2.4 million people from 1939 to 1946 (Vonyo 2018, 69). The national unemployment rate of 14 percent also masks important regional differences: Unemployment in industrial centers such as North Rhine-Westphalia and Baden-Württemberg was below 5 percent, while unemployment in rural areas such as Schleswig-Holstein reached over 20 percent in 1950 (Vonyo 2018, 54). Housing shortages meant that many workers were trapped in rural unemployment or faced overly long commutes, even while industrial areas faced labor shortages.

The limited housing stock also meant that demand for housing grossly exceeded the available supply, posing a threat to German industries and exports. Rising housing costs would have increased the cost of living, resulting in a wage-cost spiral detrimental to the competitiveness of industries. Without state intervention, housing costs would have skyrocketed, since "[t]o the small extent that houses could be built without government aid, rentals greatly exceeded the paying-power of the average wage earner" (Wertheimer 1958, 344). Such a scenario was unacceptable for Germany's

[7] Deutscher Industrie- und Handelstag, Ausschuß für Wirtschaftsfragen der industriellen Verbände, Gesamtverband des Groß- und Außenhandels & Hauptgemeinschaft des Deutschen Einzelhandels (November 24, 1949), *Stellungnahme zu dem Entwurf des Gesetzes zur Änderung des Einkommensteuergesetzes* [statement], Frankfurt, BArch K B126/11676. My emphasis.

influential labor unions. Time and again, they demanded low rents in the context of relatively low postwar household income, threatening higher wage demands should rents increase (Führer 1995; Zündorf 2006). Providing low-cost shelter was thus crucial not only for reintegrating uprooted families but also for reviving the manufacturing-based economy.

Before the creation of the Federal Republic of Germany in 1949, the Allied powers did not prioritize new housing construction. Rather, they mostly adopted laws to coordinate who could live in available housing units (*Wohnraumbewirtschaftung*) – giving priority to victims or opponents of the Nazi regime, families with children, and disabled persons – and extended rental freezes that had been in place since 1936. Housing repairs and new housing construction were primarily managed by local authorities, housing associations, and residents (Diefendorf 1993, 130–131; Von Beyme 1999).

In 1949, political parties of the newly established Federal Republic prioritized adopting *supply-side* housing programs to address the housing crisis, and they did so with the industrial economy in mind. The Social Democratic Party (Sozialdemokratische Partei Deutschlands, SPD) promoted housing construction not only as social policy but also as a macroeconomic tool to support the manufacturing-based and export-oriented growth regime. Their 1949 housing proposal stated that "[t]he recovery of our macroeconomy [*Volkswirtschaft*], particularly the strength of our *exports* ... depends on an intensive focus on housing construction."[8] The proposal further states that housing was inextricably linked with industrial success, as "full industrial capacity can only be reached if workers live in proximity to the workplace." The party emphasized that new affordable housing "will create the necessary conditions for labor mobility,"[9] and made it a major task to tackle the "housing shortages in the hotspots of labor need."[10] To achieve this, the SPD privileged low-cost rental housing for the masses, especially the working class. Their focus on low rents was closely connected to concerns about wages: Low rents could protect household wages and purchasing power while ensuring wage restraint and price stability (Schulz 1994, 97). As Erich Klabunde, the SPD's housing spokesperson, noted: "[W]e do not want [rental price] increases above current levels, because there would be consequences in terms of wage policy."[11] Indeed, the

[8] SPD (May/June 1949), *Wohnungsbauprogramm der SPD für die Trizone* [housing program proposal], Parlamentsarchiv des Deutschen Bundestags PA-DBT 4000 I/26. My emphasis.

[9] SPD (1949), *Für ein freies Deutschland in einem neuen Europa* [party manifesto], 5, https://library.fes.de/spdpd/1949/490801-sondervers.pdf.

[10] SPD (1953), *Wahlprogramm* [party manifesto], 9, https://library.fes.de/pdf-files/bibliothek/retro-scans/fa86-01385.pdf.

[11] SPD (1948), *Protokoll der Verhandlungen des Parteitages der Sozialdemokratischen Partei Deutschlands* [transcript of party convention], Düsseldorf, 165, https://library.fes.de/parteitage/pdf/pt-jahr/pt-1948.pdf.

German Trade Union Confederation (Deutscher Gewerkschaftsbund, DGB) persistently threatened higher wage demands should housing costs increase (Schulz 1994, 173).[12] While the SPD prioritized affordable rental housing, it did not oppose subsidizing homeownership (Kohl 2020; Kohl and Sørvoll 2021). On the contrary, the SPD viewed homeownership as a way to both free up rental units for low-income families and make capital available for rental markets, as homeowners would use much of their own capital for financing their home.

Solving the housing problem was equally important for the Christian Democrats (Christlich Demokratische Union Deutschlands, CDU), but they emphasized homeownership over rental housing as the solution (Kohl 2020). For ideological reasons, the CDU argued that modest single-family houses would be the ideal home for male-breadwinner families, helping them attain freedom and self-determination through property. As Josef Brönner, the CDU's housing spokesperson, put it: "We would like to see an emphasis on homeownership in residential construction. The man who owns his home is a frugal, satisfied, and happy man; whose family lives a completely different life from those who are crammed into apartments in multifamily buildings ... The more homeownership, the more satisfied the population."[13] While the CDU's long-term goal was to create a nation of homeowners, they also supported low-cost social rental housing to tackle the immediate housing crisis, including "apartments with socially bearable rents for broad segments of the population."[14] Pragmatic CDU Bundestag members acknowledged that building single-family homes to tackle housing shortages would be unrealistic, particularly in densely populated cities, which required multifamily housing construction that offered more efficient and cost-effective use of construction material and land.[15] More generally, as the following sections will show, the CDU's ideological efforts to boost homeownership repeatedly ran up against the macroeconomic needs of the German export-oriented and industrial-based growth regime.

RENT CONTROL AS WAGE POLICY

The center-right Adenauer government – a coalition of the CDU with the Free Democratic Party (Freie Demokratische Partei, FDP) – took several steps to solve the housing crisis. One major action was to retain strict rent controls

[12] Stenzel, A. (1950), "Die Lohn-Preis-Schere," *Gewerkschaftliche Monatshefte*, 1(7), 316.

[13] Brönner, J. (February 24, 1950), *Remarks in the 1st Bundestag, 41st and 42nd session*, 1395.

[14] CDU (July 15, 1949), *Düsseldorfer Leitsätze über Wirtschaftspolitik, Landwirtschaftspolitik, Sozialpolitik, Wohnungsbau* [party program], 29, www.kas.de/de/web/geschichte-der-cdu/dokumente-zur-geschichte-der-cdu/-/content/1949-duesseldorfer-leitsaetze-cdu; CDU (November 10, 1949), *Leitsätze für ein Bundesgesetz über den Wohnungsbau* [housing program proposal], PA-DBT 4000 I/26.

[15] Neuburger, A. (1949), *Gedanken zum Wohnungsbau und seiner Finanzierung* [memorandum], PA-DBT 4000 I/26.

for the existing housing stock that had survived the war. While the United States' short-lived rent controls, designed to support its wartime economy during WWII, quickly gave way to the demands of a consumption-oriented economy, Germany's strict rent controls remained in place for much longer. It is intriguing that the German center-right government, guided by market-liberal principles and representing a core constituency of property owners, retained strict rent controls while lifting other price controls in the economy. The reason was macroeconomic. Through rent controls, the Adenauer government could keep unions' wage demands in check, thereby securing wage and price stability, which were central to the macroeconomic objective of boosting exports.

When the Adenauer government took office, it extended rental price freezes for the entire housing stock. Rents had been frozen since 1936, a measure that the Allied powers extended after the war as part of broader price controls across many areas of the economy – food, consumer goods, housing, transportation, and raw materials. The goal of these price controls was to prevent price increases for households during times of postwar shortages, thereby stabilizing the cost of living and ensuring that households could purchase basic needs. While prices for consumer goods had been liberalized by the late 1940s, strict rent controls remained in place until the 1960s (Zündorf 2006).

The reason for retaining strict price controls in housing was to secure price stability, a key principle on which the export-oriented economy rested. Economics minister Ludwig Erhard, a committed market liberal and architect of the German postwar economic miracle, believed that stabilizing the cost of living, of which housing is a major component, would contribute to export competitiveness. Erhard wrote the following with respect to evaluating Germany's export strength:

> These surpluses are certainly the result of the strength of the German economy. But it would be misleading to attribute this development to strength alone. To a considerable degree, the surplus is also due to the fact that West Germany resisted the temptations of an inflationary path compared to other economies, in other words, that we did not sin as much as our trading partners. Our price trend is relatively low by international standards. In 1962 (basis 1950 = 100) the cost of living index was 128, while important European trading partners experienced price increases of up to 144 (Netherlands), even 160 (Great Britain), and even beyond that (France 186). These circumstances naturally entail great export chances.[16]

Erhard believed that sacrifices were necessary to achieve price stability and export competitiveness. These sacrifices included a strictly regulated housing market even if it contradicted his market-liberal principles.

[16] Erhard, L. (1997), *Wohlstand für alle*, ECON Verlag, 321–322. He also stated that he took action "against any avoidable price increases" and "against any wage increase that was not justified by productivity progress" (p. 92).

Erhard made exactly this point in a 1951 speech in front of the Zentralverband der Haus- und Grundbesitzer, an organization representing property owners. The organization had long criticized the rent freezes that had hurt owners of prewar buildings. Erhard wholeheartedly agreed and began his speech by lamenting that there was "no relationship whatsoever" between the principles of a market economy and the housing sector, calling it "a form of capitalism that does not deserve the name."[17] He showed much compassion for property owners who had not been able to increase rents since the 1930s and tried to appease them by promising "to create order" and "establish market principles" following the example of consumer goods that had already been liberalized. However, Erhard then seamlessly transitioned to lecturing property owners at length about the importance of price and wage stability to boost export competitiveness. As he noted, "the competitiveness of our German economy can only be guaranteed if we are able to ... keep our German price level somewhat stable," while "[b]oosting exports is the fateful task of our people." For all his support for liberal market principles (Mierzejewski 2004), Erhard's speech provided the macroeconomic reasons, rooted in Germany's export-oriented growth regime, for why massive housing interventions were justified and why property owners needed to make sacrifices: Price stability and export competitiveness.

The Adenauer government retained strict rent controls throughout the 1950s, fearing increases in the cost of living and higher wages. Initially, the Korea crisis of 1950/51 – triggering global demand for German products (Abelshauser 2011) but also inflationary fears due to skyrocketing commodity prices (Temin 1995) – prevented the government from increasing rents (Zündorf 2006, 137–138; Führer 1995, 268).[18] The concern was that higher rents could result in demands for higher pensions and wages (cp. Wallich 1955, 174). Erhard's ministry was aware of the unions' resistance to rent increases but authorized two moderate increases for prewar buildings in the 1950s to allow property owners to fund repairs and maintenance: One by 10 percent in 1952 (which Erhard estimated would increase the cost of living by a tolerable 1 percent) and another by 10 percent in 1955. In the 1952 case, housing minister Eberhard Wildermuth (FDP) wanted to increase rents by 20 percent, but Adenauer's cabinet decided on 10 percent not least due to the influence of the unions.[19] As Wildermuth acknowledged, low rents were "the

[17] Erhard, L. (September 13–17, 1951), "Wohnungswirtschaft und soziale Marktwirtschaft" [speech]. In *Aktuelle Fragen der Wohnungswirtschaft: Vorträge auf dem Verbandstag des Zentralverbandes*, Wiesbaden/Mainz, 95–100.

[18] The German economy experienced a short-lived balance-of-payment crisis due to rising prices and wages, all while consumers and producers spent cash instead of depositing money (Wallich 1955, 88–89). However, the balance of payment quickly improved again in mid-1951 and inflation was brought under control.

[19] Bundesregierung (October 23, 1951), *181. Kabinettssitzung* [cabinet protocol], https://kabinettsprotokolle.bundesarchiv.de/protokoll/b2cdfd23-97d9-4f45-b345-9f2d5beaef70.

political price to pay for keeping wages low."[20] Indeed, the news magazine *Der Spiegel* wrote in 1955 that "nobody in the country fought rent increases like the national union federation" and quoted a DGB official who stated, after the passing of the second rent increase, that the union had "made these rent increases the subject of new wage demands."[21] Even after these moderate increases, rents constituted only about 8–9 percent of a typical household's budget in 1958 (Zündorf 2006, 243).[22]

In short, the Adenauer government struggled to strike a balance between the interests of property owners, who required income for maintaining older homes, and the imperatives of Germany's export-oriented growth regime, which required low inflation and wages. For macroeconomic reasons, it prioritized the latter. As Hellmut Wollmann (1985, 138) accurately noted, property owners had to make sacrifices to "contribute, through low real estate prices and low rents, to maintaining wage levels. In this way, the industrial production cost level would also be kept down which, in turn, was regarded as an indispensable precondition for the economic recovery of postwar Germany." Or, as a housing official wrote, the German political economy followed "a decades-long approach that tied wage levels to frozen and subsidized rents."[23]

SOCIAL HOUSING AS INDUSTRIAL AND WAGE POLICY

In addition to rent controls, new housing construction was a top priority for the Adenauer government. It could kill two birds with one stone: Increasing the much-needed housing supply and reviving the industrial economy. To increase the housing supply, German policymakers stimulated both rental and owner-occupied housing via *supply-side* social housing programs.

These landmark social housing programs became an essential pillar of the country's export-oriented growth regime and welfare state. First, they alleviated housing and associated labor shortages in industrial areas. Second, they enhanced workers' productivity by improving their living conditions. Third, they produced low-cost housing for workers, which helped suppress

20 Wildermuth, E. (January 30, 1952), *Industrie und Wohnungsbau* [speech], Ausschuss für Wohnungs- und Siedlungswesen der Spitzenverbände der Wirtschaft, Rheinisch-Westfälisches Wirtschaftsarchiv, RWWA-1-773-3.

21 "Gewerkschaften – Miet-Erhöhung: Der unrentable Hausbesitz" (September 28, 1955), *Der Spiegel*. Note that the measure was part of a larger bill (*Bundesmietengesetz*) that also liberalized prices for *newly concluded* rental contracts in prewar buildings (Führer 1995, 275).

22 Although housing costs were relatively low at the time, many households struggled to afford other basic goods due to generally low wages and often paid high prices in black markets in the early postwar years (Führer 1995, 252).

23 Klein, A. (1964), "Die amerikanische Wohnungsbaufinanzierung: Eine Zauberformel für die Eigenheimfinanzierung?" *Bundesbaublatt*, 13(4), 198.

the cost of living and unions' wage demands. Even though social housing programs funded both new rental *and* owner-occupied housing units, establishing low-cost rental housing better suited the macroeconomic objective of reviving industrial export-oriented manufacturing. The German approach thus stands in stark contrast with the American one, which stimulated owner-occupied housing with *demand-side* programs to fuel economic growth as an end in itself.

The Adenauer government's First Housing Law of 1950 was not only a housing program but also an industrial one. Although there were precedents during the Weimar Republic, it was the country's first *national* housing program to provide cheap or subsidized housing loans to builders of homes.[24] It aimed to expand the housing supply by 1.8 million affordable rental and owner-occupied homes by 1956. As the law's official announcement states, the program would help increase labor productivity and alleviate labor shortages: "Tackling the [housing] problem can simultaneously solve a series of urgent economic problems: a) crowded living conditions inhibit, physically and psychologically, workers' output. Increasing that output is prerequisite for the recovery of the German economy. b) As a result of housing shortages, and despite job vacancies in industrial and manufacturing professions, 11.5 million workers remain unemployed."[25] A related priority was the establishment of low-cost rental housing. The Ministry of Economics spelled out the relationship between low rents and wages in a 1950 report, stressing that low rents "have the effect of manipulating the real wage by artificially keeping down nominal wages."[26] In turn, wage moderation was crucial to the export competitiveness of German industries.

The 1950 law represented a broad consensus and was adopted unanimously in the Bundestag. All parties agreed on its two core propositions: To boost housing supply and create low-cost housing for the working and middle classes. Indeed, 70 percent of the population was eligible to live in social housing units at the time (Kramper 2008, 48). Both the CDU and SPD considered the passage of the law a triumph.[27] Paul Lücke (CDU), the future housing minister, stated that the law would initiate a "century of social housing," while Erich Klabunde (SPD) called the law the country's "constitution [*Grundgesetz*]

[24] In addition, property tax reductions (*Grundsteuervergünstigung*) for ten years could be claimed by rental landlords and homeowners if new property was built with social housing funds. The *Länder* also granted property tax transfer exemptions (*Grunderwerbsteuerbefreiung*) for new properties financed with social housing funds.

[25] Der Bundesminister für Wohnungsbau (May 20, 1950), "Amtliche Bekanntmachungen: Begründung zum Ersten Wohnungsbaugesetz," *Gemeinsames Ministerialblatt* 1(4), 49–56.

[26] Wissenschaftlicher Beirat des Bundeswirtschaftsministeriums (May 6–7, 1950), *Stellung des Wohnungswesens in der sozialen Marktwirtschaft* [report], Bonn, RWWA-1-237-7.

[27] The law bears the SPD's signature, as many aspects of the legislation were adopted from the SPD's 1949 housing proposal.

in the housing area."[28] Economics minister Erhard had mixed feelings about social housing programs. On the one hand, he viewed them as necessary tools to rebuild housing and restraining wages; on the other, he had concerns that these and other programs would have market-distorting effects in the property sector.[29] In his ranking of priorities, however, price stability was more important than a liberal housing market.

American Marshall Plan funds supported German housing programs, with the goal of improving productive capacities in the German industry (cp. Maier 1977). As the American High Commission emphasized with regard to Marshall Plan funding in 1950: "[H]ousing is allocated with the view to increasing the general productivity of the German economy by bringing workers closer to their work, and by relieving labor shortages and inefficiencies" (quoted in Diefendorf 1993, 141). Housing funds were thus not distributed for political or ideological reasons. Instead, as Jeffry Diefendorf (1993, 141) notes, "economic growth rather than rewarding political loyalty guided American policy." Marshall Plan funds for housing amounted to only roughly DM 500 million between 1950 and 1954, a share of only 2 percent of total housing funding for those years.[30] The vast majority of housing funds that rebuilt the German housing market came from domestic sources: Public funds constituted roughly 40% of total housing funding between 1950 and 1954.

Unlike American public rental housing programs, most German social housing rental units were *not* government- but privately operated. German social housing programs were public–private market arrangements, mobilizing both public *and* private capital for the construction of rental homes. Specifically, they offered cheap or subsidized credit to virtually *anyone* willing and able to build new and affordable rental housing: Private companies, limited-profit housing associations (e.g., church-based, union-based, and municipal associations, as well as cooperatives), and even private households. In return for subsidized housing loans (typically up to 50 percent of the total financing costs for a rental home), builders had to comply with certain housing standards and offer below-market rent to tenants for as long as builders received program benefits, often for more than 30 years (Häußermann and Siebel 1996, 152). While landlords had to offer below-market rents, they were allowed to turn a small profit to encourage investment in the first place.

Even though unions wanted to see even lower rents, they supported the 1950 housing law as these programs kept rents just low enough. The unions

[28] 1st Bundestag (March 28, 1950), *53rd session* [remarks by P. Lücke & E. Klabunde], 1936 & 1942.

[29] Erhard, "Wohnungswirtschaft und soziale Marktwirtschaft," 98.

[30] Fey, W. (1955), "Der Wohnungsbau in der Bundesrepublik 1954 und seine Finanzierung," *Bundesbaublatt*, 4(4), 169.

considered social housing programs to have a "special macroeconomic role" in keeping rents low and preventing increases in the cost of living associated with higher wage demands.[31] As ever, their support was conditional: "An expansion of rent as a share of the cost of living would be a legitimate reason for wage increases."[32]

Few commentators have appreciated the fact that German social housing programs also subsidized building new owner-occupied homes (see Figure 3.1). However, homeowners were subsidized to a much lower degree than builders of new rental housing, which better served the economic needs of German industrial regions. Policymakers viewed subsidizing homeownership and rental housing as complementary, contributing to increasing the housing supply for different income groups. The CDU's Josef Brönner emphasized that the creation of owner-occupied homes would free up rental apartments for lower-income families,[33] while the SPD's Erich Klabunde noted that homeownership subsidies would encourage middle-income households to finance their own homes, which in turn would free up capital for financing affordable rental housing.[34] Prospective homeowners, excluding high-income earners,[35] could apply for cheap or interest-free loans to finance the construction of new owner-occupied homes (typically up to around 40 percent of the total cost of an owner-occupied home).[36] In principle, funding applications for owner-occupied and multifamily homes received equal treatment. In practice, the *Länder* – responsible for administering, cofinancing, and implementing social housing programs (Scharpf et al. 1976) – distributed most funds toward the rental sector, which better served their regional economic needs.[37]

While social housing programs were a resounding success, the Adenauer government was unnerved by the low share of owner-occupied units within these programs. From 1950 to 1953, the country built 1.8 million new homes,

[31] DGB (January 25, 1950), *Stellungnahme zum Wohnungsbaugesetzentwurf* [statement], PA-DBT 4000 I/26.

[32] Stenzel, A. (1950), "Ein Wohnungsbauprogramm für den sozialen Wohnungsbau," *Gewerkschaftliche Monatshefte*, 1(1), 21–25; also see Zündorf (2006, 134 and 191).

[33] Brönner, J. (February 24, 1950), *Remarks in the 1st Bundestag, 41st and 42nd sessions*, 1395.

[34] Martens, H. (2011), "Erich Klabunde und das Erste Wohnungsbaugesetz von 1950," in Heinrich-Kaufmann-Stiftung, *Miteinander geht es besser* (November 3–4, 2006), 73–79, Hamburg.

[35] In 1957, homeowners' income limits for this benefit were identical to those that qualified a renter to move into a social housing rental home.

[36] The funding plans for financing owner-occupied homes were rather complex and often involved multiple government programs in addition to homeowner equity, a private-sector mortgage, and the social housing loan. They were also dependent on rules in different states and on family income.

[37] In 1956, for example, the federal government spent roughly DM 700 million on social housing, while the federal states contributed DM 900 million in the same year. See Fey, W. (1959), "Die Quellen der Wohnungsbaufinanzierung in der Bundesrepublik im Jahre 1958," *Bundesbaublatt*, 8(4), 174.

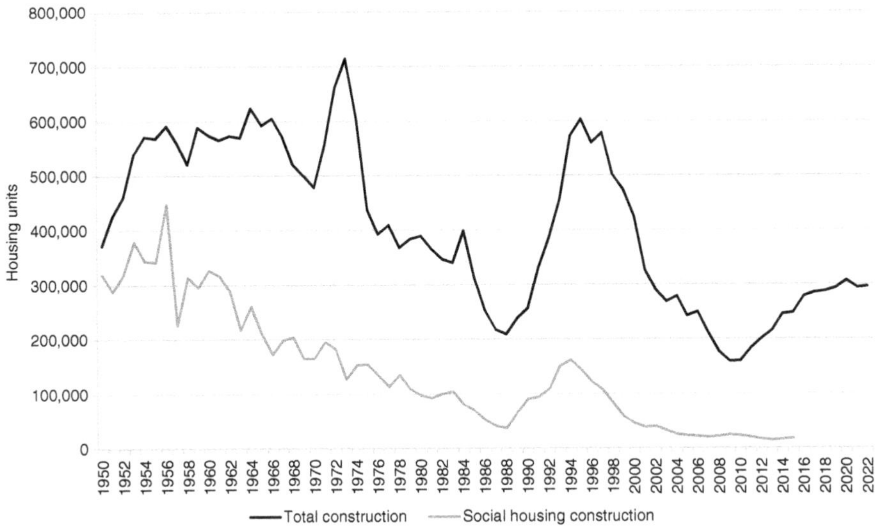

FIGURE 3.1 Total housing construction and social housing approvals in Germany, 1950–2022

Note: Social housing construction includes newly supported social rental and owner-occupied units per year. *Data sources:* Total construction data from German Federal Statistics Office (Destatis); social housing data based on annual social housing reports in *Bundesbaublatt* until 2003, German Federal Statistics Office between 2004 and 2006, and Bundesregierung, *Sozialer Wohnungsbau in Deutschland – Entwicklung, Bestand, Perspektive* (BT-18/8855), between 2007 and 2015.

of which 1.3 million were social housing units, a share of over 70 percent (see Figure 3.1). Most social housing units were low-cost rental units, with far fewer owner-occupied homes. In 1952, for example, only around one-quarter of all social housing units approved for construction were owner-occupied – that is, 90,000 owner-occupied units out of 320,000 total social housing units that year. In an internal report, Brönner (CDU) complained that "[t]he CDU's core demand of creating property for the population through residential construction, with the goal of allowing uprooted people to become settled again and providing them with the opportunity to own their home, could not be realized in ways we desired."[38] From this point on, the Adenauer government tried – but struggled – to "make the [single] family home the norm of social housing."[39]

The CDU's attempts to make owner-occupied housing the standard of social housing failed, as they ran up against the regional industrial needs of

[38] Brönner, J. (n.d.), *Überblick über das Erste Wohnungsbaugesetz* [memorandum], PA-DBT 4000 I/26.

[39] Lücke, P. (January 21, 1953), *Remarks in the 1st Bundestag, 245th session*, 11685.

Germany's growth regime. As a result, such attempts were either watered down in the legislative process or outright ignored by the *Länder*. In 1953, the Adenauer government updated its social housing goals from building 1.8 million social housing units to 2 million by 1956, while simultaneously shifting funding priorities toward owner-occupied housing. To achieve this, the Adenauer government planned to adopt strict quotas mandating that most social housing funding would go to homeowners.[40] Yet the measure was watered down in the legislative process. The *Länder* and the SPD wanted to preserve the autonomy of the federal states in implementing housing programs with respect to their regional and economic needs. Some FDP members considered the CDU's exclusive focus on homeownership "removed from reality" (Schulz 1994, 256). German industries, similarly, criticized the intended prioritization of homeownership over rental housing.[41] While the CDU managed to establish some funding priorities for homeowners, meaning that "[a]n appropriate amount of social housing funds should be used to subsidize single-family homes," it was still up to the federal states to decide what exactly "an appropriate amount" was.[42]

In 1956, the Adenauer government launched another attempt to strengthen homeownership vis-à-vis rental housing. It adopted the Second Housing Law of 1956, which became the "Magna Carta" of social housing for the next 50 years, with the goal of building another 1.8 million social housing units by 1962.[43] The legislation continued to provide strong subsidies for both rental housing and homeownership, also partly to "increase productivity," as noted by the departing housing minister Victor-Emanuel Preusker (FDP).[44] The law also expanded the social housing finance toolkit by offering a wider array of interest-rate and annuity subsidies and government guarantees (Krummacher 1981).[45] This time, the Adenauer government managed to establish funding priorities for homeownership over rental housing – at least on paper. The new

40 CDU (1953), *Entwurf eines Gesetzes zur Schaffung von Familienheimen* (Drs. 5) [draft law].

41 Vereinigung der Industrie- und Handelskammern des Landes Nordrhein-Westfalen (January 14, 1955), *Bau- und wohnungswirtschaftlicher Ausschuss* [report], Düsseldorf, RWWA-1-773-3.

42 "Gesetz zur Änderung und Ergänzung des Ersten Wohnungsbaugesetzes" (1953), *Bundesgesetzblatt* 5(54).

43 Fischer-Dieskau, J. (1956), "Das zweites Wohnungsbaugesetz (Wohnungsbau- und Familienheimgesetz)," *Bundesbaublatt* 5(7), 320.

44 Preusker, V.-E. (February 16, 1957), *Wirtschaftspolitik und Wohnungsbau* [speech], Ausschuss für Wohnungs- und Siedlungswesen (Gemeinsamer Ausschuss des Deutschen Industrie- und Handelstages, des Bundesverbandes der deutschen Industrie und der Bundesvereinigung der Deutschen Arbeitgeberverbände), RWWA-1-773-4.

45 The German state guaranteed a much lower volume of mortgage debt than the United States, an average annual insurance volume of DM 700 million during the 1960s. In the same period, the American government's FHA and VA mortgage insurance volume was around USD 10 billion per year; see Eckart, W., and Klein, A. (1988), "Wohneigentumsförderung in der Bundesrepublik Deutschland," *Der Langfristige Kredit* 39(70), 70. Also see Bundesrat (July 22, 1997), *Bericht der Bundesregierung über das Program zur Bürgschaftsübernahme* s. 550/97) [report].

law states: "[B]uilding single-family homes has priority over other forms of housing."[46] Wherever possible, social housing funding was supposed to be given to homeowners. Where single-family homes were unfeasible, funding should be allocated to create affordable multifamily rental homes, especially for low-income groups.

Yet again, Adenauer's homeownership push faced opposition from important actors in the German growth regime who believed building rental housing better served their economic interests. Labor unions, limited-profit housing associations, the *Sparkassen* (local deposit-based savings banks), and associations representing cities had opposed prioritizing homeownership over rental housing, partly because such a measure would not meet the economic needs of many regions.[47] Manufacturing industries, as they had before, continued to support subsidizing both homeownership and rental housing so long as these measures served to tackle housing shortages in cities.[48] Interest groups representing property owners and conservative family values supported Adenauer's homeownership push, but they had few arguments to convince the federal states to distribute the lion's share of funding to homeowners.[49] In fact, the federal states continued to channel the vast majority of social housing funding into the rental sector. From 1956 to 1962, the country started building another 2.2 social housing units, including 1.6 million rental units and only 600,000 owner-occupied units.[50]

Finally, the Adenauer government faced significant pressures from unions to prevent rental price increases in social housing units. While the center-right

[46] "Zweites Wohnungsbaugesetz" (June 28, 1956), *Bundesgesetzblatt* 8(30).

[47] E.g., Gesamtverband Gemeinnütziger Wohnungsunternehmen (September 1, 1954), *Entwurf zu einem Zweiten Gesetz zur Änderung des Ersten Wohnungsbaugesetzes* [statement], PA-DBT 4000 II/272; Deutscher Sparkassen und Giroverband (January 5, 1954), *Entwurf eines Gesetzes zur Schaffung von Familienheimen* [statement], PA-DBT 4000 II/272; Deutscher Städtebund (April 27, 1956), *Entwurf eines Zweiten Wohnungsbaugesetzes* [statement], PA-DBT 4000 II/272; DGB (March 15, 1956), *Wohnungsbau- und Familienheimgesetz, Das Thema des Monats*, Düsseldorf, PA-DBT 4000 II/272.

[48] Gemeinsamer Ausschuß des Deutschen Industrie- und Handelstages, des Bundesverbandes der deutschen Industrie und der Bundesvereinigung der Deutschen Arbeitgeberverbände (February 16, 1953), *Stellungnahme zum Entwurf eines Gesetzes zur Schaffung von Familienheimen* [statement], PA-DBT 4000 II/272; Wendt (February 1, 1957), *Die betriebliche Wohnungsfürsorge unter dem Zweiten Wohnungsbaugesetz* [speech], Ausschuss des Deutschen Industrie- und Handelstages, des Bundesverbandes der deutschen Industrie und der Bundesvereinigung der Deutschen Arbeitgeberverbände, Bonn, RWWA-3-146-8.

[49] Bundesvereinigung Deutscher Heimstätten (October 30, 1954), *Verstärkte Förderung des Baues von Eigenheimen und Kleinsiedlungen* [statement], PA-DBT 4000 II/272; Familienbund der deutschen Katholiken (April 24, 1955), *Den Kindern ein Vaterhaus* [statement], PA-DBT 4000 II/272; Deutscher Siedlerbund (September 14, 1955), *Novelle zum Bundeswohnungsbaugesetz* [statement], PA-DBT 4000 II/272.

[50] The total housing funding made available through social housing programs was around DM 2.3 billion in 1953, DM 3 billion in 1961, and DM 3.7 billion in 1965. See *Bundesbaublatt*, annual housing finance reports, 1952–1970.

coalition generally accepted the macroeconomic benefits of low-cost social rental housing, it tried to increase the rental income and profits of owners of social housing units. The 1953 reform allowed social housing landlords to charge somewhat higher rents – although still well below market prices – because construction costs had increased from 1950 to 1952, partly due to the Korea boom. Predictably, the unions opposed the measure. In 1953, they argued that "today's wage levels do not provide any room for rent increases. The implementation of those planned measures must thus lead to consequences in terms of wage demands."[51]

Modest increases in social housing rents were, in essence, a compromise between the interests of property owners and the unions (Schulz 1994, 305). The 1956 Second Housing Law increased social housing rents further by allowing social housing landlords to calculate rents more flexibly based on their costs (*Kostenmiete*) – as opposed to setting a fixed amount of rent – and to increase rent moderately along with rising costs in the construction sector (Zündorf 2006, 243).[52] The DGB opposed the measure, arguing that it would "increase the cost of living which would force trade unions to adjust their wage policy."[53] This stance reflected a broader logic: Germany's influential labor unions had linked their wage demands to rent levels and housing programs.

REGIONAL GROWTH REGIMES AND SOCIAL HOUSING

Despite the CDU's ideological preferences in favor of homeownership, the *Länder* used their considerable autonomy to distribute most social housing funds to the rental sector, because low-cost rental housing served the regional growth regimes that were often based on manufacturing. The Association of German Cities (Deutscher Städtetag) captured the regional growth-regime logic well in their 1949 housing policy demands:

> Building new homes should concentrate on damaged cities and regions. Here are the most urgent housing needs with regard to industrial production, as *industrial production and exports* will be of increasing importance in the coming years ... Supporting new housing construction in cities and regions is in the interest of our entire economy [*Gesamtwirtschaft*], as it provides housing for people working in productive sectors.[54]

[51] "Wohnungsmieten – Wie unter Kaiser Wilhelm" (December 22, 1953), *Der Spiegel*.

[52] Construction prices rose by 32 percent from 1954 to 1960. See "Grunddaten zur Wohnungs- und Bauwirtschaft" (1960), *Bundesbaublatt*, 9(12).

[53] DGB (April 17, 1956), *Erklärung des DGB Bundesvorstandes zum Wohnungsbau- und Familienheimgesetz* [statement], PA-DBT 4000 II/272.

[54] Deutscher Städtetag (September 3, 1949), *Begründung und Erläuterung der 12 Forderungen des Deutschen Städtetags zum Wohnungsbau* [statement], PA-DBT 4000 I/26. My emphasis.

In industrial regions, multifamily housing was not only more cost-effective than owner-occupied single-family homes but also provided a larger number of housing units on available land, thus concentrating large numbers of workers near plants.[55]

Is it possible that there were not enough aspiring homeowners applying for social housing funding? A closer look reveals that more than 100,000 homeownership applications per year remained unprocessed in the late 1950s and 1960s.[56] The *Länder could* have done more to boost homeownership if they had prioritized these applications. A 1955 survey also shows that voters would have liked such actions, as more than half of respondents preferred to own their own home, a number much higher than the homeownership rate of less than 30 percent at the time.[57] Housing minister Paul Lücke (CDU) urged the housing sector to build more owner-occupied housing and federal states to process homeowner applications with priority, as specified in the Second Housing Law.[58] But to no avail.

The federal states privileged their regional industrial growth regimes over creating homeownership, emphasizing housing for as many workers as possible to boost production and economic growth. As a housing ministry official noted in 1958: "Housing shortages ... are increasingly found in big cities and industrial, metropolitan areas. However, building single-family homes cannot meet the housing needs there because of a lack of land ... Better conditions for that are usually found in rural areas and in small towns."[59] These policies also saved costs: Subsidizing dense rental housing allowed these regions to contain urban sprawl and suburbanization, including the infrastructural costs associated with it, for which they would have been on the hook. The mayor of Stuttgart, Arnulf Klett, called the Christian Democrats' efforts to boost homeownership "artificially bloated."[60]

Actors that were linked in dense economic networks in industrial regions – including manufacturing industries, housing associations, the banking sector, and social partners – mostly preferred the construction of affordable multifamily housing. Limited-profit associations (*gemeinnützige Wohnungsunternehmen*) and housing cooperatives (*Baugenossenschaften*) had specialized in building

[55] Housing minister Wildermuth (FDP) told Adenauer precisely this in a written statement (Schulz 1994, 256).

[56] Own calculations based on *Bundesbaublatt* annual reports of unprocessed social housing homeownership applications ("Die unerledigten Anträge von Familienheimen und Eigentumswohnungen").

[57] Hoff, H. (November 3, 1955), "Neue Umfrage: Wie möchten Sie wohnen?" *Die Zeit*.

[58] Lücke, P. (1958), "Die Aufgaben der nächsten Jahre," *Bundesbaublatt*, 7(2), 49–55; Lücke, P. (1958), "Familienheimgesetz und Wohnungsbaugenossenschaften," *Bundesbaublatt*, 7(9), 469–472.

[59] Fischer-Dieskau, J. (1958), "Der Wohnungsbau an der Jahreswende 1957/58," *Der Langfristige Kredit*, 9(1).

[60] Quoted in Preusker, V.-E. (1955), "Gemeinden und sozialer Wohnungsbau," *Bundesbaublatt*, 4(9), 410.

multifamily homes since the late nineteenth century (Kohl 2017). These housing associations were owned by unions, employers, churches, and municipalities. The union-owned corporation Neue Heimat quickly became West Germany's – and later even Europe's – largest housing company, building 240,000 housing units by 1970, most with the help of social housing programs (Kramper 2008, 620–621). Industrial employers also criticized the federal government's intended prioritization of homeownership over rental housing as too "dirigiste."[61] Instead, they revived their nineteenth-century efforts of supplying employer-based housing, building around 450,000 social housing units for their workers after WWII (Krummacher 1988, 442).[62] Volkswagen, for instance, started building 1,400 rental housing units in 1953, as half of its workforce had to commute up to 80 kilometers every day in the early 1950s.[63] Meanwhile, mortgage banks (*Hypothekenbanken*) had historically extended credit not mainly to homeowners, but rather to housing associations for the creation of multifamily housing in urban areas (Kohl 2017). Heinz Simon (1964, 47), representing the German Association for People's Settlement Homes (Deutsches Volksheimstättenwerk), thus argued:

> None of the parties involved in the production of housing are actually interested in building owner-occupied homes, except homeowners themselves. Urban planners fear ... sprawl. To underline their concern, they refer to the negative examples of large American cities. Local communities shy away from what they believe is an inevitably higher usage of land and higher cost of land development. For architects, the planning and designing of multifamily homes are less time-consuming and much more lucrative than dealing with individual homeowners and their extra wishes, whose properties are often scattered... For banks, processing a mortgage of DM 500,000 for a multifamily home is hardly more work than the DM 10,000 to DM 15,000 mortgages of single-family homes... It makes the local government employee's hair stand on end when he processes incomplete and flawed applications of homeowners ... Who can blame him for preferring the application of a housing association, which is all too well known for providing complete and flawless applications? The fact that the municipality might have a stake in this very housing association does not make his decision any harder.

Boosting affordable multifamily rental housing was thus in the interest of key actors in dense regional and industrial networks. Until the early 1960s, limited-profit housing associations – receiving their funding mainly from

[61] Vorwerk, W. (February 16, 1957), *Ausschuss für Wohnungs- und Siedlungswesen: Gemeinsamer Ausschuss des Deutschen Industrie- und Handelstages, des Bundesverbandes der Deutschen Industrie und der Bundesvereinigung der Deutschen Arbeitgeberverbände* [minutes of meeting], Bonn, RWWA-3-146-8.

[62] Uhlmann, S. (June 26, 2020), "Werkswohnungsbau: Wohnen beim Chef," *Süddeutsche Zeitung*.

[63] Volkswagen Group (2024), *1950 bis 1960 – Internationalisierung und Massenproduktion im Wirtschaftswunder*, www.volkswagen-group.com/de/volkswagen-chronik-17351/1950-bis-1960-internationalisierung-und-massenproduktion-im-wirtschaftswunder-17356#1953.

social housing programs and mortgage banks[64] – helped build between 40–50 percent of all social housing units and roughly 25–30 percent of all new housing units in the country.[65] The vast majority of those units were rental housing units, as rental units were at least 30 percent cheaper to build than owner-occupied units due to more efficient land and material use (Kramper 2008, 200).

At the regional level, partisanship was not the driving force when it came to distributing social housing funding for homeownership or rental markets. Rather, it was the degree of housing shortages in industrial and urban areas (Wollmann 1985; Von Beyme 1987; Jaedicke and Wollmann 1990). For example, the three city-states – West Berlin, Hamburg, and Bremen – followed by the highly industrialized North Rhine-Westphalia subsidized homeownership the least, with a share of around 25 percent of all social housing units from 1957 to 1967. Notably, North Rhine-Westphalia was led by the Christian Democrats (1947–1956 and 1958–1966) and still subsidized much more rental housing, owing to its populous industrial areas that required dense and affordable housing for workers. Moreover, labor unions were strong in industrial areas and demanded housing programs that secured low rents (Schulz 1994, 321). Even the CDU-led Baden-Württemberg, known as the land of homebuilders, subsidized homeowners with a share of only 35 percent of all social housing units between 1957 and 1967, as the state suffered from severe housing and labor shortages in industrial regions.[66] The state's policymakers knew that industrial productivity depended on affordable rental housing, acknowledging that rents could not exceed the purchasing power of households.[67] For these reasons, most but not all *Länder* continued to primarily fund social housing rental units over owner-occupied social housing units well into the 1980s, as Figure 3.2 shows.

In sum, the *Länder* subsidized both rental housing and homeownership as part of social housing programs to increase the much-needed housing supply. However, they tended to privilege rental housing over homeownership, which better aligned with their regional growth regimes.

[64] In 1959, the limited-profit housing associations received 36 percent of their housing finance funds through government programs and 20 percent from the *Hypothekenbanken*. The rest was financed through their own capital, *Sparkassen*, and other sources. See Fey, W. (1962), "Die Quellen der Wohnungsbaufinanzierung in der Bundesrepublik 1961," *Bundesbaublatt*, 11(4), 177.

[65] Fey, W. (1966), "Tendenzen und Merkmale des Wohnungsbaus 1965," *Bundesbaublatt*, 15(5), 195–196.

[66] All other states subsidized owner-occupied units less than rental units as a share of total social housing units between 1957 and 1967: Hesse (28% owner-occupied units); Bavaria (31%); Schleswig-Holstein (36%); Lower Saxony (39%); Rhineland-Palatinate (42%). For an excellent study on social housing programs in Lower Saxony in the 1950s, see Lüning (2005).

[67] Land Württemberg-Hohenzollern, Wirtschaftsministerium (May 3, 1949), *Zum Problem des Wohnungsbaus* [statement], PA-DBT 4000 I/26.

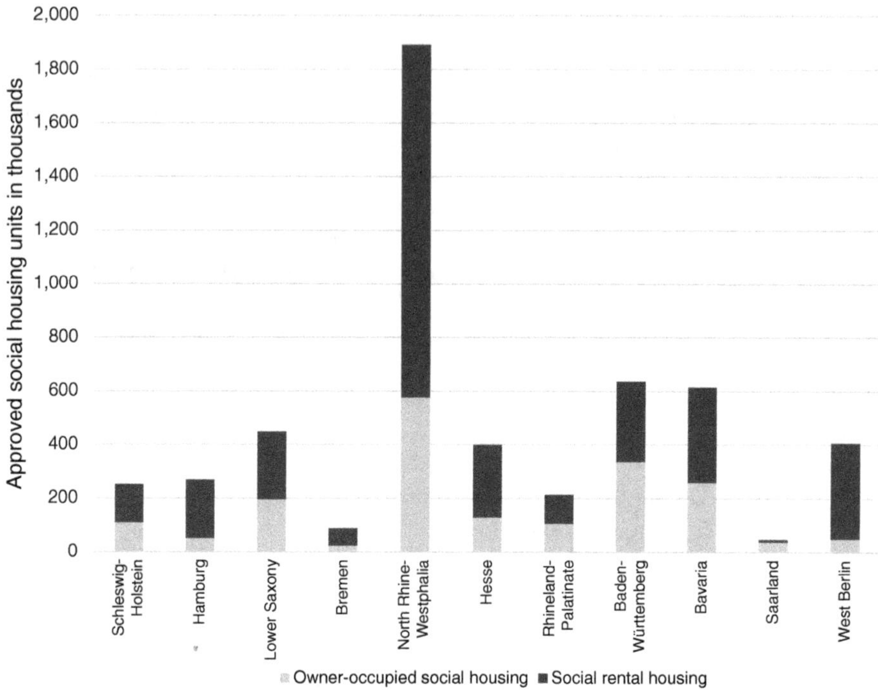

FIGURE 3.2 Social housing units approved for construction with government subsidies in the German *Länder*, 1957–1988

Note: Data for Saarland starts in 1962. *Data source:* Own calculations based on Federal Statistics Office, *Bewilligungen im sozialen Wohnungsbau* (Fachserie 5/2, 1976–1989; Fachserie E/4, 1962–1975; Reihe 4, 1957–1961; *Bundesbaublatt*, annual social housing reports.

CREATING SACRED COWS? TAX SUBSIDIES FOR RENTAL HOUSING AND HOMEOWNERSHIP

Social housing programs were not the only measures the Adenauer government used to increase the country's housing supply. It also deployed a battery of tax policies to channel capital and investment into housing, which finance minister Franz Etzel (CDU) considered a "macroeconomic necessity."[68] These tax policies, like social housing programs, were not designed to stimulate domestic demand along American lines but instead were aimed at repairing the fundamentals of the housing market and the manufacturing-based economy. As Henry Wallich (1955, 110) noted: "According to the Finance Ministry's view the important effect of a deficit-creating tax cut is not the increase in purchasing power of consumers, as one would say in the United States. It is the greater incentive given to producers who now can keep a larger fraction of their income." Importantly, German

[68] "Warum werden die Steuerverstecke weiter geduldet?" (June 18, 1958), *Der Spiegel*.

manufacturing industries demanded housing tax incentives to help improve the labor shortages and working conditions of their employees. In contrast to postwar American tax subsidies that stimulated *demand for owner-occupied homes* and associated domestic demand, their German counterparts stimulated the housing *supply of both rental and owner-occupied homes* with sensitivity to reviving industrial and manufacturing sectors vital to economic growth.

With these tax subsidies, the Adenauer government aimed to steer capital toward financing the construction of new housing. The finance ministry noted that the "urgency of supporting housing ... make strong tax incentives necessary to steer private capital into housing."[69] To achieve this, the Adenauer government strengthened the so-called paragraph 7b tax break – the paragraph was originally written into the tax code by the Economic Council (*Wirtschaftsrat*) in 1949 – which quickly became one of Germany's most important postwar tax subsidies. Given the severity of housing shortages, the tax measure subsidized builders of new rental housing *and* owner-occupied homes alike. German manufacturing industries demanded the expansion of the tax break to alleviate housing and labor shortages in industrial regions and improve conditions for employees.[70]

As was the case with social housing programs, the Adenauer government soon reformed the tax subsidy to shift its benefits in favor of individual homeowners over rental housing developers. After a tax reform in 1953, individuals could claim the tax break for purchasing owner-occupied single-family houses (previously, only those who *built* new houses could claim the tax break). In another reform in 1958, the tax break was extended to subsidize those purchasing two-family homes. According to a government report, these reforms aimed to support homeowners unable to *build* their own homes but able to *buy* houses with government support.[71] Although the 7b tax subsidy would grow into Germany's largest tax subsidy and housing program decades later, it was relatively limited in the postwar years, amounting to only DM 180 million in 1955, a share of just 4 percent of total government spending on housing (DM 5 billion) that year (Leutner 1990, 62).

Another major housing tax subsidy was a short-lived provision that helped fund social housing. The Adenauer government incentivized individuals and firms to loan interest-free money to public and limited-profit housing associations for the purpose of social housing, which they could then deduct as a business expense (the so-called paragraph 7c tax break).

[69] Bundesminister der Finanzen (November 21, 1949), *Steuervergünstigungen für den Wohnungsbau* [memorandum], BArch K B126/11676.

[70] Deutscher Industrie- und Handelstag, Ausschuß für Wirtschaftsfragen der industriellen Verbände, Gesamtverband des Groß- und Außenhandels & Hauptgemeinschaft des Deutschen Einzelhandels (November 24, 1949), *Stellungnahme zu dem Entwurf des Gesetzes zur Änderung des Einkommensteuergesetzes* [statement], BArch K B126/11676.

[71] Bundesregierung (February 8, 1979), *Bericht der Bundesregierung über Möglichkeiten zur Umstellung des §7b EStG auf ein anderes Förderungssystem* (8/2554) [report].

Given the scarcity of capital at the time, the tax break was intended to help fund social housing programs. It resulted in massive tax savings for companies and well-to-do beneficiaries amounting to DM 230 million in 1954, a share of around 5 percent of total government spending on housing (DM 5.1 billion) that year (Leutner 1990, 62). The industrial sector welcomed this provision, as it could assist the country in its "urgent necessity to support housing construction in every way possible."[72] German industries, including Daimler-Benz and Bayer, invested in housing in this way in order to enjoy massive tax benefits and help alleviate housing shortages in industrial regions.[73] When capital and housing markets improved, however, the Adenauer government first reduced the tax benefit in the mid-1950s and then eliminated it in 1961 (Kramper 2008, 117), particularly as it benefited already profitable companies.[74]

While not as sizable as social housing programs, these tax breaks subsidized building new rental and owner-occupied housing, channeling capital into housing to address the housing crisis with sensitivity to the needs of the manufacturing- and export-oriented economy.

REBUILDING HOUSING CAPITAL: PRIVILEGING SAVINGS AND INVESTMENT OVER CONSUMPTION

In the early years of the Federal Republic, after the country had experienced war and the currency reform of 1948, the capital market remained dysfunctional. As a result, private capital – desperately needed to finance new housing construction – was scarce. To mobilize private capital, in the early 1950s, policymakers subsidized both investors and household savings to attract funds into "investments of macroeconomic and national political importance" such as housing.[75] These measures supported Germany's growth regime in three principal ways. First, they channeled funding into housing, supporting the construction of new rental and owner-occupied homes, which alleviated housing-related labor shortages in industrial regions. Second, since these programs helped mobilize funding for social housing, they also contributed to keeping rents and wages low. Third, they incentivized households to save instead of consuming, restraining inflationary pressures and domestic demand that would have been detrimental to Germany's export-savings regime (Mertens 2015).

72 Deutscher Industrie- und Handelstag, Ausschuß für Wirtschaftsfragen der industriellen Verbände, Gesamtverband des Groß- und Außenhandels & Hauptgemeinschaft des Deutschen Einzelhandels (January 20, 1950), *Zweite Stellungnahme zu dem Entwurf des Gesetzes zur Änderung des Einkommensteuergesetzes* [statement], BArch K B126/11676.

73 Klabunde, E. (November 7, 1950), *Die Wohnungsbaukrise: Man kann den Wohnungsbau retten* [radio broadcast], Nordwestdeutscher Rundfunk, PA-DBT 4000 I/26.

74 "Die Bauland-Fresser" (March 3, 1955), *Der Spiegel.*

75 Bundesregierung (July 10, 1952), *Entwurf eines Gesetzes zur Förderung des Kapitalmarkts durch steuerliche Begünstigung festverzinslicher Wertpapiere* (Drs. 3596) [draft law].

An important area of political action was to subsidize household savings in building societies (*Bausparkassen*) that specialized in financing owner-occupied homes. Indeed, the German central bank had complained in 1950 that "there is only a very moderate supply of capital resulting from savings."[76] Erhard's economics ministry agreed and suggested that households' real-wage gains should be channeled into savings to strengthen the capital market.[77] As a Bundestag committee report stated: "There is too much unnecessary consumption and perhaps not enough savings."[78] As a result, in 1952, the Adenauer government adopted savings subsidy schemes in building societies (*Wohnungsbauprämie*).[79] For the CDU, it was win-win. These programs encouraged household savings, and they channeled savings into the kind of housing the CDU preferred: *Owner-occupied* housing. The subsidy grew almost twentyfold from DM 27 million in 1953 to DM 485 million in 1966 (Leutner 1990, 62).

Another subsidy that the Adenauer government took over from the Economic Council was a tax deduction allowing individuals to deduct savings accounts contributions in building societies from their taxable income (Mertens 2015, 265). This tax subsidy was one of the country's largest housing tax breaks from the 1950s until the late 1960s, amounting to DM 1 billion in 1966, placing it among the top three tax breaks that year (next to tax subsidies on pension contributions and life insurance contributions).[80]

In stark contrast to American depression-era housing programs, German housing policies did *not* make it any easier for homeowners to take out mortgage loans. On the contrary, the German primary mortgage market remained restrictive and conservative, requiring high down payments from households to qualify for a mortgage. One reason was the German economic policy priority of increasing household savings rather than mortgage indebtedness. Until the 1970s, German homeowners were typically required to pay down around 25–35 percent of the house value (Kofner 2004). They could then take out a first mortgage but only up to 60 percent of the house value, for example from a local *Sparkasse*.[81] A low loan value allowed banks to shield themselves from the risk of financial losses resulting from declining house prices and mortgage defaults. Households then frequently took out a second mortgage from a *Bausparkasse* or a social housing loan to finance the remaining costs

76 Benning, B. (May 25, 1950), *On the Problems of Capital Market Interest* [memorandum], Bank Deutscher Länder, Bundesbank Archive B330/9614.

77 Wissenschaftlicher Beirat beim Bundeswirtschaftsministerium (December 10, 1950), *Maßnahmen zur Entwicklung des Kapitalmarktes* [report], DBHA B330/9614

78 Brönner, J. (1952), *Wohnungsbau-Prämiengesetz, Bericht des Ausschusses für Wiederaufbau und Wohnungswesen* [report], PA-DBT 4000 I/268.

79 Households could use these savings schemes to save for a down payment on a home; after a multiyear savings period, they qualified for an affordable mortgage.

80 Bundesregierung (1967), *1. Subventionsbericht*, 54.

81 When extending a first mortgage, banks were legally required to limit the loan amount to no more than 60 percent of the property value (Köpfler 1996, 628).

(Kofner 2004, 72). In Germany, financial risk on mortgages was mitigated by high down payments and fixed interest rate periods of only up to 10 years. In America, the state guaranteed the risk on mortgage debt through public agencies, which allowed banks to offer more consumer-friendly and affordable mortgages with a fixed interest rate for 30 years and lower down payments.

The German government also *temporarily* supported the country's housing bond market to channel investments into housing. Before elaborating on these post-WWII measures, it is instructive to provide a short refresher on Germany's housing bond market in comparison to America's. The German housing bond market was – and still is – based on covered bonds (*Pfandbriefe*) that have attracted institutional investors to housing, which in turn has "tended to increase the supply of mortgage funds" (Jones and Grebler 1961, 104). Germany's well-developed covered bond market had its origins in late-eighteenth-century Prussia (Wandschneider 2014, 2015). At the time, German *Landschaften* – credit cooperatives that loaned farm mortgages to members of the cooperative – issued bonds (*Pfandbriefe*) to finance farm lending. From the mid-nineteenth century, private mortgage banks (*Hypothekenbanken*) adapted their model for residential mortgage lending to finance the growth of urban centers, and by 1900, urban mortgage banks had outgrown the rural *Landschaften* (i.e., the mortgage volume of mortgage banks was three times that of *Landschaften* by 1900) (Kohl 2017, 95). Mortgage banks issued covered bonds to finance their activities, with strict regulations that allowed them to lend only 60 percent of a property's value and that classified these bonds as "senior" debt with preferential treatment in the case of default. Mortgage banks operated nationally and issued covered bonds almost exclusively backed by *rental* properties.[82] They did so because, as Kohl (2017, 95–96) shows, (1) rental buildings allowed them to extend fewer mortgages at higher value and lower administrative cost and (2) mortgage banks had fewer local branches, meaning they did not mainly rely on local knowledge but instead on financing standardized urban rental buildings instead of nonstandardized single-family homes. Ultimately, the conservative and low-risk nature of German covered bonds has made them "a cornerstone of the German financial system" (Kofner 2014, 259) and export-savings regime (Mertens 2015).

While German covered bonds have not usually relied on direct government support – unlike American mortgage-backed securities – the Adenauer government temporarily subsidized covered bonds with tax incentives to help finance social housing after WWII. Even capital market policies were thus

[82] By the late nineteenth and early twentieth centuries, local deposit-based institutions (*Sparkassen*) and later building societies (*Bausparkassen*) had become major mortgage lenders, including to individual homeowners. The mission of *Sparkassen*, however, went well beyond financing homeownership: They also financed personal loans, small business loans, small agricultural loans, and municipal projects (Kohl 2017, 98–99).

a tool to keep rents and wages low.[83] Adenauer's capital market reform of 1952 exempted from taxation investor profits on "social covered bonds" (*Sozialpfandbriefe*) as well as debt obligations issued by local communities if these bonds and obligations served the purpose of financing social housing.[84] As Wilhelm Biber, a top mortgage banker at the time, noted, mobilizing private capital through social covered bonds had the effect of lowering credit costs for social housing, which in turn allowed securing low rents and limiting direct public expenditure.[85] Indeed, the housing ministry was concerned that higher credit costs for the housing sector would result in higher rents, which would create "wage pressures on industries, hurting the export strength of the German economy."[86]

The Adenauer government stopped the issuance of popular social housing bonds already in 1954 as the economy and the capital market improved. These bonds had been controversial in that they mostly benefited richer investors, while the Bank of German States (Bank Deutscher Länder), the predecessor of the Bundesbank, criticized their distorting effects of privileging housing over other investments, such as industry debt obligations or stocks.[87] But the short-lived social housing bonds helped revive capital markets and produced injections of capital into housing, making cheap funding available for building social housing. Indeed, the outstanding covered bond volume increased from DM 10 billion in 1958 to DM 48 billion in 1970 (compared to DM 174 billion in outstanding mortgage debt in 1970).[88]

As noted, the hawkish German central bank criticized social housing bonds, yet it too had previously provided direct and targeted support for the housing bond market, underlining the macroeconomic importance of housing at the time. In today's light, the central bank's actions are ironic in that the central bank experimented with policies that it today despises – that is, interventionist bond-buying programs in capital markets. Sources from the Bundesbank

[83] Biber, W. (1955), "Der Übergang zum freien Wertpapiermarkt," *Der Langfristige Kredit* 6(1), 2.

[84] Until the 1952 reform, the federal government had imposed fixed and relatively low interest rates on debt obligations and covered bonds. On the one hand, low interest rates secured affordable credit for debtors, such as builders of housing. On the other hand, they offered low returns for investors, which meant that investors stayed away from these investments. The 1952 reform provided capital market subsidies – and started lifting some interest-rate controls – with the aim of drawing investments back into these low-interest instruments, not least to finance housing construction.

[85] Biber, W. (1954), "Verzicht auf Kapitalmarktförderung unzweckmäßig," *Der Langfristige Kredit* 5(18), 161.

[86] Knoblauch, A. (January 8, 1951), *Der Wohnungswirtschaftliche Beirat beim Bundesministerium für Wohnungsbau* [memorandum], Bonn, PA-DBT 4000 I/26.

[87] Bank Deutscher Länder (1954), *Geschäftsbericht für das Jahr 1953*, 21.

[88] Zahlenspiegel der Kreditwirtschaft (1960), *Der Langfristige Kredit* 11, 103; Bundesbank (December 1973), *Monatsbericht: Statistischer Teil* [report], 52; Bundesbank (2025), *Hypothekarkredite an inländische Unternehmen und Privatpersonen* [historical statistical series: BBBK3.Q.PQ3013].

archive reveal that, in the early 1950s, the Bank of German States bought covered bonds to support capital markets. These were unusual *expansionary* measures in an otherwise *restrictive* monetary policy context brought about by the Korean War's inflationary pressures and Germany's balance-of-payment crisis.[89] In 1950, the Bank of German States circulated a memorandum saying that it wanted to increase the liquidity, confidence, and prices of certain covered bonds (*Kursstützung*) that had lost value after the country's 1948 currency reform.[90] The Allied Bank Commission – a body established by the western Allies in 1948 with powers to oversee monetary policy and veto some of the bank's decisions – cautioned that this "might well endanger the currency."[91] Even so, the bank decided to go ahead and buy housing-related covered bonds and communal debt obligations in the amount of DM 6 million between 1950 and 1951.[92] To be sure, this number was marginal, as the total outstanding amount of such bonds was DM 450 million at the time.[93] However, the point was to "feel along the market for future interventions"[94] and potentially coordinate future actions with the finance ministry to support capital markets.[95] However, the bank quickly changed course. It acknowledged that, if the overall goal of monetary policy ought to be restrictive, then asset purchases in the open market would contradict that goal, as these interventions would be expansionary and "threaten the stability of the currency in irresponsible ways."[96] In 1953, the bank's chair, Karl Bernard, rebuffed a

89 See the Bank of German States' annual reports for the years 1950 and 1951, where it outlines the bank's monetary policy objectives of restraining credit to stimulate exports and restrain domestic demand. The central bank also increased interest rates from 4 percent to 6 percent in 1950–1951.

90 For savings and securities, the 1948 currency reform replaced the Reichsmark (RM) with the Deutsche Mark (DM) at an exchange rate of 1:10. The Bank of German States discussed purchasing a maximum amount of DM 100 million in covered bonds previously denoted in RM or up to 15 percent of all RM-covered bonds in the open market; see Schmidt, W. (July 21, 1950), *Grundzüge der Interventionspolitik* [memorandum], DBHA B330/3284.

91 Allied Bank Commission (July 10, 1950), *Letter to the President of the Board of Directors, Bank Deutscher Länder*, DBHA B330/3284. The commission was abolished in 1951.

92 Council of the Bank of German States (July 27–28, 1950), *66. Sitzung: Offenmarktpolitik – Kurspflege* [minutes of meeting], DBHA B330-ZBR(1950); also see Bank of German States (February 27, 1951), *Interventionstätigkeit der Landeszentralbanken* [report], DBHA B331-BW/468. The bank had deliberated buying more covered bonds, but there was not enough demand from the mortgage and covered bond banks, with which the Bank of German States consulted before buying these assets.

93 Güssefeld, W. *Kurspflege alter Pfandbriefe und Kommunalobligationen* [memorandum] (July 21, 1950), DBHA B330/3284.

94 Bank of German States (January 17, 1951), *Memorandum*, DBHA B330/3284.

95 Bundesminister der Finanzen (July 28, 1950), *Kurspflege durch Ankauf festverzinslicher Wertpapiere auf dem offenen Markt* [correspondence], DBHA B330/3284.

96 Schmidt, W. (November 30, 1951), *Bemerkungen zu den einzelnen Punkten auf der Tagesordnung "Förderung des Kapitalmarkts"* [minutes of meeting], Sitzung des Gremiums Scharrenberg am 10. November 1951, DBHA B330/3284.

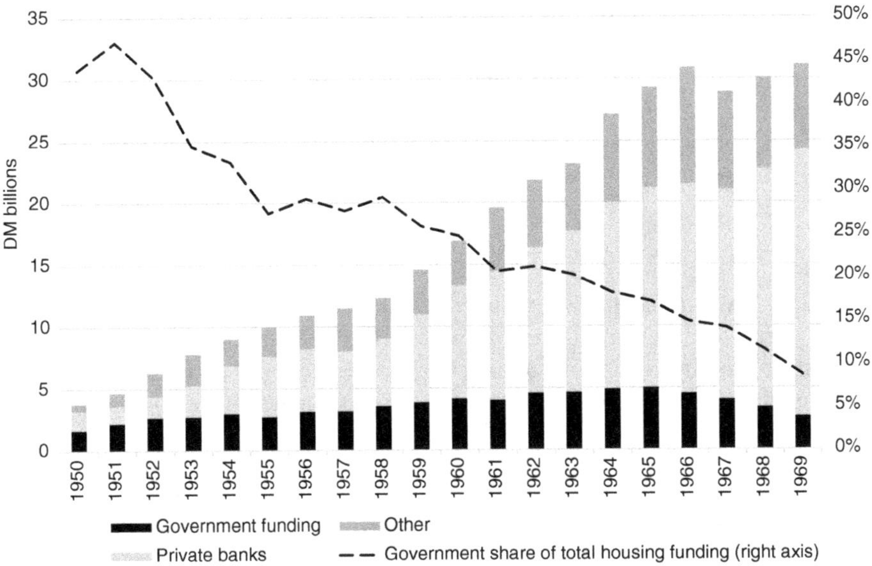

FIGURE 3.3 Sources of German housing finance funding, 1950–1969
Notes: "Private banks" include mortgage banks (*Hypothekenbanken*), *Sparkassen*, building societies (*Bausparkassen*), and life insurance companies. "Government funding" predominantly includes direct loans through social housing and other housing construction programs. "Other" includes private household funding. *Data source: Bundesbaublatt* annual housing finance reports.

request by housing minister Preusker (FDP) to intervene deeper in the covered bond market to support housing lending, as the bank considered the covered bond market to have recovered by then.[97] The bank thus decided against future interventions in the covered bond market, and it voted to slowly sell its covered bond holdings in 1958.[98] Much like the US Fed did in the 1930s, the Bundesbank engaged in modest unconventional measures to support the struggling housing bond market.

In sum, housing-related programs in the capital market channeled private capital into housing for the construction of rental and owner-occupied housing (see Figure 3.3). These actions supported the German growth regime by encouraging savings over consumption and limiting access to easy credit, and they also directed capital toward social housing programs that predominantly built low-cost rental housing, which in turn helped to limit inflationary wage demands. More generally, these policies helped rebuild the country's housing

97 Bernard, K. (December 24, 1953), *An den Bundesminister für Wohnungsbau: Anlage der sog. Pensionfonds des Zentralbanksystems in Pfandbriefen* [correspondence], DBHA B330/3284.

98 Bundesbank (April 24, 1958), *22nd Council Meeting – Open Market Decisions*, DBHA B330/140/1.

finance market and ultimately allowed the German state to retreat from providing *direct* housing loans to builders. While the government's share of mortgage funding was close to 50 percent in 1951, it gradually decreased to around 10 percent by the late 1960s as the private capital market recovered (i.e., the building societies, mortgage banks, and *Sparkassen* increased their mortgage funding share again).

GERMANY'S HOUSING AND EXPORT MIRACLES

In 1949, few would have predicted a German economic miracle just a decade later. By the late 1950s, however, the West German economy was the fastest-growing economy in the world, with robust growth rates of an average of 7.6 percent per annum, full employment, and strong real-wage growth (Herrigel 1996, 147).[99] The country's industries recovered quickly, and its export world market share increased from 2 percent in the late 1940s to 10 percent in 1970 (Lindlar and Holftreich 1997, 217), as exports grew by 20 percent per year on average between 1950 and 1973 (Eichengreen 2008, 25). The share of exports as a percentage of GDP increased from 4 percent to 17 percent in just twelve years, from 1948 to 1960 (Giersch et al. 1992, 91). Indeed, all major components of aggregate demand expanded from 1950 to 1960: Exports grew at the fastest rate (13.5 percent per year) followed by private investment (9.4 percent), government expenditure (8 percent), and private consumption (7.8 percent) (Giersch et al. 1992, 63). Macroeconomic policy was decidedly export- and investment-oriented – as opposed to privileging domestic demand – and strengthened the institutional foundation of the country's manufacturing-based, export-oriented growth regime in the long term (Kreile 1977).

The largely untold story in accounts of Germany's economic miracle is how the country's housing miracle contributed to it (for a notable exception, see Vonyo 2018). Until the mid-1960s, the country built more new homes per capita than any other advanced economy. Per 1,000 residents, Germany produced an average of 10.4 housing units per year from 1955 to 1961, whereas the United States produced 7.9 units, France 6.3 units, and the United Kingdom 5.9 units.[100] The German housing miracle related to the export miracle in that new housing helped rebuild the fundamentals of the export-oriented industrial economy. Specifically, housing programs

[99] Barry Eichengreen (2008, 17 and 264) estimates that Germany's real GDP grew by an average of 5 percent per year from 1950–1973, with only one short recession in 1966/67, while unemployment was less than 2 percent in the 1960s. German real wages rose by an average of 4.9 percent per year from 1950 to 1972, which is slightly below an average 5 percent productivity increase in the same period (Kreile 1977, 786).

[100] Korch, R. (1966), "Der Wohnungsbau der Bundesrepublik im Vergleich mit dem Ausland," *Der Langfristige Kredit* 17, 104.

strengthened manufacturing industries – faced with housing-related labor shortages – by allowing unemployed workers in rural areas to move to industrial regions to fill vacant jobs. Housing programs thus played a key part in boosting labor mobility by overcoming housing shortages. As Andrew Shonfield (1965, 283) noted, these programs "led to a vast output of new housing, which may in turn fairly be given part of the credit for the remarkable mobility of German labour during the 1950s."

Building housing allowed German industries, which survived the war with surprisingly few damages, to ramp up production. Even after the Allied powers lifted controls on industrial production – which had held it back in the occupation years alongside transportation bottlenecks and material shortages – production levels in 1950 remained below their prewar peak (Vonyo 2018, 90–91). As Tamas Vonyo (2018, 52) argues, "capacity utilisation within industry remained limited ... [and] resulted from the wartime destruction of urban housing." A primary factor holding back industrial production was thus housing-related labor shortages, despite high unemployment in rural areas. Urban industrial employment and output grew along with the number of new housing units in the 1950s. By 1955, German industry had reached full capacity and manufacturing output was 60 percent above its prewar levels (Vonyo 2018, 90). Volkswagen, for example, rapidly ramped up production from just 20,000 cars in 1948 to 100,000 in 1951 and half a million in 1958, achieving this with little investment in new production capacities and instead relying on labor growth up until 1957 (Vonyo 2018, 114).

As German production increased, it met growing external demand. During the 1950s, export manufacturing in Germany grew twice as fast as in Italy and the Netherlands, and ten times as fast as in the UK (Vonyo 2018, 130). Germany's export boom occurred in a fortuitous context: External demand from booming postwar economies in Europe and the United States; international free-trade institutions reducing trade frictions between countries, including the European Economic Community; an undervalued exchange rate in the Bretton Woods fixed exchange rate regime supported by the hawkish Bundesbank;[101] cost competitiveness through wage restraint (Eichengreen 2008; Hall 2021);[102] and low inflation despite high rates of growth and employment.[103] By the late 1950s, Germany had regained

101 Martin Höpner (2019) shows that the Bundesbank did not readjust its currency through revaluations of the Deutsche Mark, with the notable exceptions of minor revaluations in 1961 and 1969 between 1950 and 1970.

102 According to Giersch et al. (1992, 72), German real unit labor costs fell by an average of 0.9 percent per year from 1950 to 1960. Eichengreen (1994, 63) also shows that Germany's unit labor costs from 1948 until the late 1950s were more competitive than those of the Netherlands, the UK, Italy, Belgium, and France.

103 Höpner (2019, 9) estimates that Germany's inflation rate was an average of 1.4 percent per year from 1950 to 1973, which is well below the United States' average of 2.6 percent and much lower than the UK's 4.6 percent.

the status as an export champion that Germany had acquired in the early twentieth century (Abelshauser 2011).

As argued throughout this chapter, housing programs directly supported Germany's export-oriented growth regime by keeping housing costs, wages, and inflation down. As Erhard's remarks remind us, the lower the cost of living – whether achieved through wage restraint, low housing costs, or both – the better the chances for export-led success. During the 1950s, the country produced 5.2 million new homes, roughly half of which were rent-controlled social housing. According to an economist at the time, "[l]ow-cost rental housing became a major factor in keeping down the cost of living and consequently pressures for wage increases leading to the familiar wage-cost-price spirals" (Wertheimer 1958, 344). These programs thus had a price-deflating effect on the cost of living compared to what housing costs would have been in a fully private market.

Germany's powerful unions tied their wage demands to the rent level in the economy. Through social housing and rent controls, rental costs for households remained remarkably low, barely budging from a share of only 8.3 percent total household expenditure in 1949 (Führer 1995, 413) to just over 13 percent in 1968 (Zündorf 2006, 301). Low housing costs partly explain why labor unions showed wage restraint throughout the 1960s. As Michael Kreile (1977, 777) notes: "[L]abor unions exercised remarkable restraint, if not docility, in their wage policy. This attitude reflected a high degree of 'inflation-consciousness' as well as a concern for export performance. Class conflict was suspended in exchange for the dividends of growth." Indeed, rental prices grew at a slower rate than real wages until the early 1960s.[104]

While private consumption was an important driver of Germany's postwar economic growth, the larger macroeconomic policy priority was to promote exports and savings. Indeed, even Erhard called for the "courage to consume" goods like refrigerators to raise the standard of living (Logemann 2012, 41). However, German policymakers viewed American-style, unrestrained consumption as inflationary and detrimental to export-led prosperity. As Jan Logemann (2012, 42) summarizes, "the goal of expanding private consumption was sidelined whenever other economic goals – such as the need for capital buildup or an overarching emphasis on strengthening German exports – appeared to be threatened." In the 1950s, Germany stands out in its relatively low level of private consumption (59 percent of GDP) compared to the demand-led United Kingdom (67 percent of GDP) and the United States (65 percent of GDP) (Logemann 2012, 23). As an economist observed at the time (Opie 1960, 1023): "German consumption levels are very low by European standards ... It is this very low average propensity to consume which

[104] The Bundesbank's housing cost index shows an average housing cost increase of 2.3 percent from 1950 until 1959, which was well below the annual increase in nominal wages of industrial workers by over 6% per year during that time. See Bundesbank (1960), *Geschäftsbericht 1959*, 5.

is clearly of supreme importance in explaining the ability of the German economy to invest such a high proportion of its resources, and consequently to grow at such a fast rate." In addition, German consumption as a share of GDP *declined* from 59 percent in 1952 to 57 percent in 1960 (Logemann 2012, 23).

Rather than promoting private consumption, German policymakers incentivized household savings, including through postwar housing programs. They developed a "comprehensive system of promoting saving" (Strumpel 1975, 213), including subsidies on savings in building societies, which contributed to a thirtyfold increase in building society savings between 1950 and 1970.[105] The German net financial savings rate of aggregate disposable income increased from just 5.2 percent in the mid-1950s to 9.5 percent by the mid-1960s, much higher than America's rate, which increased from only 3.3 percent to 3.9 percent during the same period (Strumpel 1975, 211). Survey evidence suggests that, throughout the 1960s, high German savings can be explained by households' persistent economic pessimism and perceived economic insecurity (despite years of sustained increasing real incomes); a feeling of economic "saturation"; and a propensity to save before buying consumer goods or housing (Strumpel 1975).

GROWING FRICTIONS: HOUSING PROGRAMS MEET COST EXPLOSIONS

Despite the economic miracle, a housing shortage of 500,000 homes persisted in 1963, prompting policymakers to continue stimulating housing *supply* well into the 1960s.[106] A booming economy and demographic changes had produced ongoing shortages in industrial regions. As a result, continuing housing programs to increase supply was the logical policy response, as it had been in the past. At the same time, the improved economic and housing conditions also allowed German policymakers to partially liberalize strict rent controls, loosening their grip on the housing market. However, housing programs started to create unforeseen macroeconomic problems for the export-oriented growth regime. Labor shortages and construction capacity issues led to rising construction costs, a "virus which is infecting the entire economy," as Adenauer put it.[107] Despite housing programs adding fuel to an inflationary environment, the Adenauer government considered them a necessary evil to remedy the remaining housing shortages.

105 Savings in building societies grew from just under DM 1 billion in 1952 to DM 31 billion in 1969 (out of DM 160 billion total savings in the country). See "Zahlenspiegel der Kapitalwirtschaft" (1954), *Der Langfristige Kredit* 5(3), 24; "Zahlenspiegel der Kreditwirtschaft" (1969), *Der Langfristige Kredit* 20(11), 311.

106 Lücke, P. (1964), "Die Bauwirtschaft im Wohnungsmarkt- und Städtebau," *Bundesbaublatt*, 13(7), 332.

107 Adenauer, K. (October 9, 1962), *Regierungserklärung, Speech in the 4th Bundestag, 39th session*, 1634.

The favorable economic context allowed the Adenauer government to start the long-promised process of liberalizing rent freezes on prewar buildings, a promise Erhard had made to property owners a decade earlier but could not deliver at the time due to concerns about price stability in the economy. The goal of liberalizing rents was to stimulate private housing investment and repairs while transitioning the state-dominated rental market into the social market economy (von Beyme 1999, 130). A 1960 law granted the *Länder* the authority to implement rental liberalizations in stages from 1963 onward (cp. Führer 1995, 295–297). The SPD voted against the measure, and unions protested, threatening higher wage demands to offset higher rents (Zündorf 2006, 298–302). For example, the metalworkers' union IG-Metall criticized the move: "Despite apartment shortage, Bonn wants to liberalize housing" (cited in Schmidt-Hoepke 1962, 296). Shortly after rents were liberalized in 1964, even some Christian Democrats, particularly in the CDU-led economics ministry, raised concerns about how rising rents could threaten price stability and produce wage-cost spirals in the economy (Führer 2015, 257–258).[108] As a result, the later Erhard and Kiesinger governments repeatedly delayed completing the liberalization process, moving its conclusion from 1966 to 1971. By 1968, a typical household still paid only 13 percent of household income in rent, but this was up from 8–9 percent in 1958 (Zündorf 2006, 301).

More broadly, liberalizing German rental prices did not create an American-style rental market with few renter protections. As Chapter 5 will show, rent freezes gave way to a system with strong tenant protections against evictions (*Kündigungsschutz*), rent subsidies for low-income households (*Wohngeld*), and flexible rent controls that limited how much landlords could increase tenants' rents based on local rental levels (*Vergleichsmiete*).

As shortages persisted, stimulating housing supply remained a policy priority. However, new construction could not keep up with strong housing demand, which was creating inflationary pressures.[109] Strong housing demand was largely due to population growth, from 51 million in 1950 to 61 million in 1969. Population growth resulted from the continued influx of people from former eastern territories and East Germany until the construction of the Berlin Wall. In addition, guest workers from southern Europe and Turkey filled labor shortages in industries. At the same time, economic growth and high employment rates led to labor shortages in construction and inflationary pressures (Giersch et al. 1992). Despite 163,000 guest workers taking jobs in construction by 1962, the sector reached full capacity with more orders than it could complete. In 1962, 800,000 orders were either incomplete or had not even started, causing housing construction delays.[110]

[108] Chancellor Erhard corresponded with the property organization Haus & Grund in 1964, stating that stable prices and wages were his highest economic priority, including in the housing industry (Führer 2015, 258).

[109] Lücke, P. (1963), "Licht und Schatten," *Bundesbaublatt*, 12(1), 6.

[110] "Bericht aus Bonn" (1963), *Bundesbaublatt*, 12(1), 4.

In response to the overheating of the construction sector, the Adenauer government introduced a two-year-long stop of all nonhousing construction between 1962 and 1964. The measure was aimed at safeguarding housing construction and deflating construction prices, which increased by 42 percent between 1958 and 1963.[111] From 1962 to 1964, for the first time in the postwar period, the government also suspended the important 7b tax break for rental housing, while retaining it for owner-occupied housing. The suspension was a sign that longstanding housing programs were no longer untouchable in the context of improving housing supply. The Bundesbank welcomed the suspension, considering the tax subsidy "mistaken at a time when the demand for building work far exceeds the capacity of the building trade and prices in that trade are accordingly rising at quite an alarming pace."[112]

In the eyes of Germany's influential economic elites, housing programs suddenly started to pose problems for the export-oriented growth regime, which relied on stable prices. These programs were increasingly seen as driving up prices in times of improved housing supply, limited construction capacity, and land development restrictions.[113] The Bundesbank advocated for limiting "excessive demand" in housing construction by scaling down housing programs."[114] According to the central bank, such programs, especially social housing programs, would soon reach the point where they could be scaled back again. It warned that otherwise "housing demand would expand – even beyond the point of statistically estimated 'housing shortages.'"[115] The Bundesbank specifically criticized interest-rate subsidies on mortgages as part of social housing programs, as they interfered with the Bundesbank's authority to set interest rates.[116] In 1965, *Der Spiegel* also started to criticize social housing programs, arguing that they would shift capital away from productive industries in times of "saturated" housing supply.[117]

For the time being, however, the Adenauer government maintained social housing programs as it prioritized addressing the remaining housing shortages over dealing with what they considered temporary inflationary effects

[111] "Grunddaten zur Wohnungs- und Bauwirtschaft" (1963), *Bundesbaublatt*, 12(12).

[112] Bundesbank (1963), *Report for the Year 1962*, 8.

[113] Sachverständigenrat Wirtschaft (1965), *Jahresgutachten 1964/65*, 85.

[114] Bundesbank (1963), *Geschäftsbericht 1962*, 22.

[115] Bundesbank (1965), *Geschäftsbericht 1964*, 8; Bundesbank (1967), *Geschäftsbericht 1966*, 75. The Bundesbank also mentioned that housing programs depress the housing costs for many households despite rising real wages; this allows households to look for larger and better homes, driving housing demand even when housing shortages have been overcome.

[116] Bundesbank, *Geschäftsbericht 1962*, 8.

[117] "Notopfer Bonn" (December 11, 1966), *Der Spiegel*.

produced by capacity limits and scarce land.[118] Even at a reduced rate to limit demand, social housing programs remained relatively strong, averaging 240,000 new units per year during the 1960s, totaling 1.7 million rental units and 700,000 owner-occupied units.

Center-right political forces predictably did not give up on their idea of pushing homeownership to address the remaining housing shortages. Much to their dismay, the country's homeownership rate had increased to only 34 percent by the mid-1960s, a number 30 percent lower than that in the United States at the time (see Figure 1.1). When Erhard (CDU-FDP, 1963–1966) became chancellor in 1963, he continued the homeownership push. In 1964, his government continued the 7b tax break but restricted it to homeowners *only*. Previously, individuals constructing both owner-occupied and multi-family homes could claim the tax break. Although the reform was barely noticed at the time, it created the "homeownership tax allowance" (still paragraph 7b in the income tax code) that would grow into the country's largest tax subsidy decades later. While the rental sector still enjoyed many other important tax benefits,[119] the reform began to shift the tax policy equilibrium slowly in favor of homeownership, albeit it did little to boost homeownership rates at the time.

The Erhard government made another attempt to shift more social housing funding toward homeowners, but it failed once again. In a 1965 social housing reform, the coalition again tried to mandate that the federal states distribute most social housing funding to owner-occupied housing. To achieve this, it introduced a formal housing ranking for distributing funding, placing single-family homes and condominiums at the top of the ranking. Moreover, the federal government introduced a new program for middle- and higher-income families to receive homeownership benefits as part of social housing programs.[120] One goal was to incentivize families who had previously exceeded the income limits for social housing to attain homeownership, thereby freeing rental units for those in need of affordable rental housing (Leutner 1990, 138). The federal states, however, remained committed to supporting their regional growth regimes by allocating most funding to the rental sector.[121]

[118] Land prices increased by around 70 percent between 1962 and 1967. See Fey, W. (1968), "Tendenzen und Merkmale des Wohnungsbaues," *Bundesbaublatt* 17(5), 214.

[119] The limited-profit housing associations retained their tax benefits through the limited-profit housing association law (*Wohnungsgemeinnützigkeitsgesetz*).

[120] The so-called second way of social housing subsidies focused on middle- and higher-income homeowners, allowing them to exceed the income limits of social housing programs by up to 30 percent and to receive annuity subsidies to help them meet their monthly mortgage and interest payments.

[121] Social housing subsidies changed from the early 1960s, as direct social housing loans were reduced and replaced by interest-rate and annuity subsidies on private mortgage loans; see Klein, A. (1970), "Wohnungsbaufinanzierung," *Bundesbaublatt* 19(5), 207.

When Germany experienced its first postwar recession in 1966/67, which led to Chancellor Erhard's downfall, the new coalition of CDU and SPD briefly tried the American approach of countercyclical demand-side policy. For the first time in postwar Germany, the country had Social Democrats serving as economics minister (Karl Schiller, SPD) and housing minister (Lauritz Lauritzen, SPD) under the government led by Chancellor Kurt Georg Kiesinger (CDU-SPD, 1966–1969). To revive the economy and to address the remaining shortage of roughly 500,000 homes in the mid-1960s,[122] the new government increased social housing funds in 1967.[123] The Keynesian approach seemed to work for the domestic economy, including for the housing market, while the Vietnam War helped stimulate German exports.

However, the uncharacteristic German Keynesian period proved relatively short-lived. When stubborn inflation, oil shocks, and recessions haunted the global economy from the mid-1970s until the early 1980s, German policymakers shifted back to stricter fiscal and monetary policy (cp. Scharpf 1991; Allen 1989). Housing also lost its untouchable status during this time, as the macroeconomic frictions between housing programs and the export-oriented growth regime intensified when housing shortages were no longer a national problem. This tension will be discussed in more detail in Chapter 5.

CONCLUSION

Like their American counterparts, postwar German governments adopted a variety of housing programs, including tax subsidies and credit programs (as summarized in Table 3.1). As a result, both countries' governments dominated large parts of their respective housing markets in the immediate postwar period. Yet their macroeconomic objectives differed profoundly. In the United States, demand-side housing programs made housing finance a national champion able to stimulate the core feature of the American postwar economy: Domestic demand. German supply-side housing programs were necessary to overcome wartime housing shortages, but they were also designed to help rebuild Germany's national champions in manufacturing, driving export-oriented growth (Kreile 1977, 783). In Germany, stimulating housing was not a long-term growth strategy; rather, it served the macroeconomic objectives of improving industrial production and keeping the cost of living down.

Germany's export and housing miracles are closely related. Scholars have predominantly emphasized how strict monetary policy (Hall and Franzese 1998) and strong welfare institutions (Manow 2020) produced wage

122 Fey, W. (1969), "Die Wohngelegenheiten in der Bundesrepublik," *Bundesbaublatt*, 18(1), 13.

123 Sachverständigenrat Wirtschaft (1968), *Jahresgutachten 1967/68*, 29–30; Lauritzen, L. (1977), "Ziele, Ergebnisse und Wandel der Wohnungsbaupolitik in den letzten 10 Jahren," *Bundesbaublatt*, 26(12), 521.

TABLE 3.1 *German housing finance programs adopted or reformed between 1949 and 1969*

Tax/credit	Program	Years active	Description and changes
Tax	Tax allowance for owner-occupied buildings ("paragraph 7b" of income tax code)	1949–2006	Initially a tax subsidy for new owner-occupied and rental homes; suspended 1962–1964 for rental housing; limited to homeowners after 1964
Tax	Tax deduction for social housing loans ("paragraph 7c" of income tax code)	1949–1961	Tax deduction for individuals and companies providing social housing funding for rental and owner-occupied homes
Tax	Tax subsidy for savings schemes in building societies	1949–1995	Tax deduction allowing individuals to deduct savings account contributions in building societies
Tax	Tax subsidy for social covered bonds (*Sozialpfandbriefe*)	1953–1954	Tax-free returns on social covered bonds that funded social housing programs
Tax	Property tax reductions	1950–1990	Reduced property taxes for rental and owner-occupied homes financed by social housing funds
Tax	Tax exemption for limited-profit housing companies (*Wohnungsgemeinnützigkeit*)	1949–1990	Tax-exempt status of limited-profit housing associations that built rental (and some owner-occupied) housing
Direct subsidy	Subsidy for savings in building societies (*Wohnungsbauprämie*)	1952–	Direct subsidy for savings contributions in building societies (*Bausparen*)
Credit	Social housing programs (*sozialer Wohnungsbau*)	1950–2006	Subsidized loans and/or interest rate subsidies for new rental and owner-occupied buildings as specified in the Housing Laws of 1950 and 1956
Central bank	Covered bond purchase program	1950–1958	Covered bonds bought and held by the Bundesbank to support segments of the covered bond market

restraint and an undervalued exchange rate, facilitating cost competitiveness and export-oriented growth (Eichengreen 2008; Hall 2021; Höpner 2019). However, this is not the whole story. Germany's postwar housing programs were another, yet unrecognized, factor contributing to export-driven growth. These programs deflated domestic costs, boosted industrial productivity, and encouraged household savings over private consumption (Mertens 2015; Logemann 2012). Remarkably, around half of all new homes built after the war were rent-controlled social housing units, providing low-cost housing for industrial workers and stabilizing the cost of living for decades. Housing, in short, was a key component of Germany's reemerging export-oriented coordinated market economy (Hall and Soskice 2001).

Despite the rhetoric of the Christian Democrats and their political attempts to create higher levels of homeownership, Germany became known as a nation of renters (Voigtländer 2009; Kohl 2017). One underappreciated reason was the nature of the German growth regime: While generous subsidies were available for both homeownership and rental markets, *Länder* with dense industrial centers allocated more social housing funding toward low-cost rental housing, supporting their regional economies based on manufacturing exports.[124] By contrast, only rural areas used a higher proportion of funding for creating homeownership. These decisions aligned with the interests of Germany's powerful unions, mortgage banks, housing associations, and industrial employers but were opposed by conservative social groups and by property owners.

The regionalized character of German housing programs stands in stark contrast to their centralized American counterparts, even though both countries have federal political systems. The German *Länder* had tremendous autonomy in implementing federal housing programs, tailoring them to their regional economic contexts. The result was the creation of millions of affordable rental homes across the country. In contrast, American housing programs established a centralized, national, and standardized mortgage market, resulting in millions of affordable owner-occupied homes with little regional government influence. While both countries deployed the infrastructural power

[124] Other factors contributing to Germany's lower homeownership rate compared to that of the United States include America's higher household income, its mass production of cost-effective prefabricated single-family homes, lower mortgage down payments and better mortgage terms, looser building codes, and cheaper land and construction costs. In general, the construction of homes remained relatively expensive in postwar Germany, as influential building trades and local authorities preferred traditional building materials and methods based on solid masonry over prefabricated ones seen as inferior (Logemann 2012, 154; Diefendorf 1993, 141; Kohl 2017, 161). Moreover, prewar urban legacies of dense German cities made it pragmatic to rebuild cities and industrial regions primarily with multifamily rental homes, owing to preexisting street layouts and underground infrastructure, property and ownership issues, as well as rebuilding apartment buildings whose walls were still standing (Kohl 2017). Even so, there were powerful political and social forces – ranging from the Christian Democrats and conservative religious groups to architects and urban planners – advocating for less dense cities and more homeownership-based suburban neighborhoods (*Siedlungen*) (Diefendorf 1993).

of the state to channel private investment into housing, they did so differently. The American state primarily *absorbed risk* in the mortgage market through government guarantees to lure private investments into housing. The German state, in contrast, primarily offered *subsidized co-funding* for housing construction to attract private investment, without altering the conservative nature of the country's mortgage market.

In Germany, housing programs were organized around keeping prices and wages low partly to support the competitiveness of the economy's industrial core. As Chapter 4 will show, American policymakers continued to utilize state power to stimulate housing investments and economic growth in response to post-Keynesian challenges.

4

Financializing the American Economy and Housing Market

"Home-equity loans have become the cocaine of the financial world," Pulitzer Prize-winning columnist Jack Anderson and Joseph Spear wrote in 1987.[1] Hyperbole aside, they were right then and now: Middle-class Americans have treated their houses like credit cards, partly out of necessity and partly "to keep up with the Joneses." This trend can be traced to the economic dislocations of the 1970s. As crippling inflation led to wage stagnation, Americans borrowed money against their homes to buy cars, boats, and other consumer goods, to finance home improvements and vacations, to start small businesses, and to pay for medical bills or their children's education. A home became far more than just a place to live. It was "equity" that households could extract to defend their falling standard of living. The practice resulted from a quiet financial revolution. Borrowing against one's house to finance consumption was an unfamiliar idea to most Americans as late as 1970. It became familiar, almost a reflex, because of how American policymakers financialized the US housing market and demand-led growth regime in response to postindustrial and post-Keynesian economic challenges. This chapter tells that story.

High inflation posed major challenges to the American economy and housing market from the late 1960s until the early 1980s. Concerned about the impact on mortgage lending, which was a core engine of America's postdepression economy, policymakers expanded housing programs into new areas of the mortgage market. In doing so, they discovered new avenues of housing-based growth: Household borrowing against homes to finance spending. Housing programs no longer solely stimulated the economy through *credit-financed housing construction* – the main channel until the mid-1970s – but also increasingly through leveraging home equity and

[1] Anderson, J., and Spear, J. (September 7, 1987), "Home-equity loans buyer beware," *Washington Post*.

mortgage-financed consumption. In short, political actions turned American homes into credit cards, partly to counteract the effects of deindustrialization and stagnating wages.

Politicians addressed the first serious postdepression crisis in the US mortgage market with a series of bipartisan political actions to stimulate mortgage lending and housing-based growth. These actions were also attempts to save and reshape the country's government-sponsored housing model that policymakers had built in the depression era. From the late 1960s to the 1980s, the housing finance market struggled under the weight of high interest rates; in response, policymakers expanded housing programs. First, they created a government-backed market for mortgage-backed securities managed by the quasi-public agencies Fannie Mae, Freddie Mac, and Ginnie Mae. These actions aimed at attracting capital into housing for the purpose of expanding mortgage lending at affordable rates. Second, policymakers expanded tax privileges for owner-occupied housing, including for home equity borrowing, to promote housing-based growth and credit-financed consumer spending. Third, policymakers expanded housing programs to stimulate economic activity in marginalized communities that had previously been excluded from the country's government-sponsored housing model at the center of its demand-led growth regime.

The housing programs of this period shaped the American political economy well into the future. For one, these programs laid the foundation for the dramatic growth of the government-sponsored enterprises (GSEs) – Fannie, Freddie, and Ginnie – that would soon *dominate* the American mortgage market. However, the GSEs relied on government support for their survival and functioning, trapping policymakers into supporting these agencies for decades to come. Their enormous size and central positioning in America's housing market also turned them into powerful lobbyists ready to defend the regulatory privileges and government subsidies from which they benefit. For another, these housing programs enabled homeowners to leverage their homes for consumer spending. Boosting property values – or avoiding harm to them – thus became even more important macroeconomic and electoral concerns for policymakers than before.

HOW CRACKS IN AMERICA'S POSTWAR GROWTH REGIME SPARKED A HOUSING REVOLUTION

Credit-financed construction of new suburban homes and associated consumer spending to fill these homes was a key engine of US postwar economic growth until the late 1960s. Central to this housing-based growth machine were government programs run by the Federal Housing Administration (FHA) and the Veterans Administration (VA) that insured mortgages against default in the primary mortgage market. The postwar American demand-led growth regime was also based on mass industrial production, high wage growth, and welfare state expansion. At that time, financial markets were tightly regulated and shielded from globalization. Until the mid-1960s, inflation and unemployment remained low and growth relatively high. However, a series of economic shocks exposed some cracks in the foundation of America's "golden age" of capitalism. The first wave of economic challenges began in the mid-1960s when increased global trade competition, paired with strong wage growth, squeezed the profits of US companies. Concurrently, inflation began to rise, owing to several factors: Rising wages, social spending for President Johnson's "Great Society" programs, military expenditure for the Vietnam War (Levy 2020; Krippner 2011), and an accommodative Fed not acting aggressively enough to curb inflation (Bordo 2017). As a result, economic growth started to slow, while unemployment and budget deficits began to rise. With the first recession in almost ten years looming on the horizon, the postwar economic boom was coming to an end, signaling turbulent times ahead.[2]

In many ways, housing lay at the heart of these challenges. In 1966, the American mortgage market experienced a "credit crunch," a term referring to high interest rates that choked off credit and mortgage lending. Rising inflation and interest rates had put significant pressure on the savings and loan associations (S&Ls) – America's most important mortgage providers at the time – and threatened their abilities to lend. One problem was that the S&Ls had lent long-term mortgages with *low* interest rates (i.e., 30-year fixed-rate mortgages) but had to pay depositors *high* short-term interest rates, leading to "maturity mismatches" (Boleat 1984; Schwartz 2012). In addition, the S&Ls were legally limited in how much interest they could pay on deposits due to a provision called "Regulation Q," which led depositors to seek higher returns elsewhere (Green and Wachter 2010).[3] Ironically, Regulation Q was initially designed to shield S&Ls from competition with commercial banks by allowing the S&Ls to pay marginally higher interest on deposits than commercial banks. However, during times of high inflation and high market interest rates that exceeded interest-rate ceilings, Regulation Q became a chokehold on the S&Ls. Tightened mortgage credit soon affected the entire economy. As Greta Krippner (2011, 62) writes, "an acute recession in the construction and housing industries quickly dampened activity in other

[2] After decades of trade surpluses in the postwar period, the United States also entered a prolonged period of trade deficits starting in 1971 that has, with few exceptions, lasted to this day.

[3] Regulation Q was originally established as part of the New Deal financial regulations, setting interest-rate ceilings on bank deposits to prevent speculative behavior and excessive competition by banks. With the capping of interest rates on deposits, banks did not need to worry about financing high interest rates paid to depositors. As Greta Krippner (2011, 61–62) shows, Regulation Q was a tool for macroeconomic steering. When the US economy was running hot, creating inflationary pressures, and market interest rates rose above Regulation Q ceilings, investors withdrew funds from depository institutions, drying up mortgage lending and slowing housing and economic activity. When market interest rates fell below Regulation Q ceilings, the economy would expand again with housing as one of its main drivers of growth.

sectors, restraining the broader economy." Indeed, mortgage markets dried up, and housing starts fell from 1.6 million in 1963 to 1.2 million in 1966, the lowest level since 1946 (see Figure 2.2).

In response, policymakers sought to defend and reorganize America's demand-led growth regime by *expanding* housing programs in new areas of the mortgage market. To ensure a steady flow of affordable mortgage credit, politicians attracted new capital into housing by using the infrastructural power of the American state (Krippner 2011; Hyman 2011; Schelkle 2012; Quinn 2019; Schwartz 2020). Specifically, they crafted a government-sponsored housing bond market, gradually replacing the deposit-based housing finance market centered on the S&L industry. In the old model, the S&Ls were the main source of both mortgage *funding* and mortgage *origination* in the country. In the new model, the GSEs became the primary source of mortgage *funding*, while mortgage banks became the largest *originators*. The GSEs were tasked with buying government-insured FHA and VA loans, as well as uninsured "conforming" loans, which the GSEs bundled together in mortgage-backed securities (MBS) to be sold to investors (Jacobides 2002; Hyman 2011, 233). While the process of financializing America's housing market started in the late 1960s, it was not until the late 1980s that government-sponsored mortgage-backed securities overtook deposits as the most important source of mortgage funding. Throughout this period, policymakers expanded housing programs, leading to meaningful changes that slowly financialized the American housing finance market.

The Johnson administration's Housing and Urban Development Act of 1968 marked the beginning of the state-driven financialization of the US mortgage market. In a first step, the act "privatized" Fannie Mae, a public agency that had supported the secondary mortgage market since 1938 (see Chapter 2). Despite its new status as a privately owned enterprise, Fannie retained many government privileges: The implicit backing of the US government, preferential tax treatment, presidential appointments of its board members, and a congressional charter (Koppell 2003). The long-term goal of the reform, including Fannie's reorganization, was to improve mortgage liquidity and credit availability of low-cost mortgages.[4] As Sarah Quinn (2019) highlights, the trick was both to "privatize" Fannie without completely severing its ties to the federal government and to stimulate mortgage lending without further straining the federal deficit after the costly Vietnam War and "Great Society" programs. According to the Council of Economic Advisers in 1969, the strategy of taking Fannie off the government's balance sheet worked: "[I]t

[4] The Johnson administration's Participation Sales Act of 1966 had already experimented with "participation certificates," which were debt instruments pooling together government-backed mortgages that could be traded in capital markets. The goal of these precursors to mortgage-backed securities (MBS) was to provide funding for the housing sector without straining the budget (Quinn 2019, 189).

is now free of the budgetary constraints that had sometimes limited the role of the old Government enterprise in the mortgage market."[5] This part of the bill passed Congress without great controversy and paved the way for the remarkable growth of Fannie Mae, which had until then been a relatively marginal actor in America's mortgage market.

In a second step, the act authorized and encouraged the creation of government-sponsored mortgage-backed securities in the secondary mortgage market. It empowered Fannie to issue mortgage-backed securities, provided the underlying mortgages were backed by the FHA or VA. The goal was to "provide a greater degree of liquidity to the mortgage investment market and an additional means of financing its operations."[6] To achieve that goal, the Johnson administration also created a new, fully public agency, the Government National Mortgage Association (GNMA), known as Ginnie Mae. It tasked Ginnie with guaranteeing the principal and interest payments on mortgage-backed securities issued by Fannie Mae or private issuers, provided the underlying mortgages were backed by the FHA or the VA. Ginnie's guarantee program was designed to attract investors to the mortgage-backed securities market by offering a government guarantee on these securities in exchange for a fee. Since FHA and VA mortgages were already government-insured, Ginnie's guarantee on mortgage bonds essentially provided a double guarantee by the federal government (Quinn 2019, 193). As Senator Wallace Bennett (Republican, Utah) articulated, "[t]he bill clearly pledges the full faith and credit of the United States to the payment of any amounts due under this guaranty."[7] The hope was that the power of the state could lure capital into housing, thereby stabilizing and expanding mortgage and housing activities.

However, the goal was not to establish a government-*dominated* mortgage-backed securities market – although that became the unintended consequence decades later. Instead, both Democrats and Republicans in Congress hoped that the private sector would emulate the GSEs' practice of issuing such securities (Quinn 2019, 180). The US Senate Committee on Banking and Currency wrote in a 1968 report that "if such [mortgage-backed] securities become well enough established so that many private issuers are issuing them, they could constitute a significant factor in attracting investment funds to the field of mortgage investment."[8] Interest groups, particularly realtors

5 Council of Economic Advisers (1969), *Annual Report*, 45.

6 Housing and Urban Development Act of 1968, Title VIII, Section 804. Ginnie Mae guaranteed its first MBS in 1970; Freddie Mac and Fannie Mae issued their first MBS in 1971 and 1981, respectively. Ginnie Mae is self-financed, collecting fees on its MBS insurance from the issuers of MBS.

7 Bennett, W. (May 15, 1968), *Remarks in the US Senate, Congressional Record 114(12)*, 15236.

8 US Senate Committee on Banking and Currency (May 15, 1968), *Housing and Urban Development Act of 1968: Report to Accompany S. 3497 (No. 1123)*, 79.

and mortgage bankers, expressed their support for the provisions to counter illiquidity, which had hurt their industries.[9]

Shortly thereafter, the administration of President Richard M. Nixon (1969–1974), which faced another credit crunch and a recession driven by rising inflation in 1969–1970, responded by strengthening housing programs to stimulate home lending and housing-based growth.[10] At the time, low housing market activity was a "major reason for the dampening in the rise of aggregate demand."[11] As a result, Nixon, with the help of the Democrat-controlled Congress, signed the Emergency Home Finance Act of 1970. The act created the Federal Home Loan Mortgage Corporation, known as Freddie Mac, another government-sponsored agency, to aid the reeling S&L industry and compete with Fannie Mae in the secondary mortgage market.[12] The goal of the bill was to provide capital for the S&L market and, in the words of the chairman of the Senate banking committee, John Sparkman (Democrat, Alabama), "to get as much money in the home mortgage market as we can. Trying to stimulate it all we can."[13] The 1970 act also authorized Fannie and Freddie to securitize "conforming mortgages" – low-risk mortgages that met certain criteria, such as loan sizes set by the federal government, but did not have government insurance by the FHA or VA. From then on, Freddie started issuing government-sponsored mortgage-backed securities that guaranteed principal and interest payments to investors in exchange for a fee.[14] Nixon's actions thus seamlessly followed Johnson's in expanding government support for housing finance.

Between 1968 and 1971, the government-sponsored-mortgage trio – Fannie, Ginnie, and Freddie – successfully alleviated liquidity pressures in the American mortgage market by helping the S&Ls and other banks to obtain mortgage funding. The strategy worked: Housing starts increased from 1.2 million in 1966 to 2.1 million in 1971 (see Figure 2.2). The Council of Economic Advisers praised the efforts of the GSEs, as they "stepped up their

[9] Members of NAREB proposed to "reconstitute FNMA as an independent corporate instrumentality of the United States and authorize it to deal in conventional loans as well as FHA-insured and VA-guaranteed mortgages," which would attract considerable investment in the housing finance market. The Mortgage Bankers Association also suggested a more prominent role for Fannie Mae to make mortgage bonds "a more marketable, shiftable asset to give it more liquidity." See US Senate (June 12–28, 1967), *Mortgage Credit: Hearings before the Senate Committee on Banking and Currency* (testimonies by P. Jackson and O. Jones), 83 and 175.

[10] President Nixon, a Republican, also issued the first national peacetime rent control measure by executive order in August 1971 as part of his administration's anti-inflationary wage-price freezes. The measure expired in early 1973.

[11] Council of Economic Advisers (1970), *Annual Report*, 41.

[12] Freddie Mac was initially owned by the S&L industry until it was privatized in 1989 (while retaining its status as a government-sponsored enterprise).

[13] US Senate (March 2–6, 1970), *Secondary Mortgage Market and Mortgage Credit: Hearings before the Senate Committee on Banking and Currency* (testimony of J. Sparkman), 200.

[14] Fannie issued its first MBS in 1981; until then, it continued to act as a "portfolio lender," supporting the mortgage market by buying mortgages from banks and holding them on its balance sheet, rather than packaging and selling them as securities.

support of the mortgage market substantially."[15] Similarly, the Fed recognized that "[a]n increase in credit from Federally sponsored agencies provided a partial offset to the reduced participation of the thrift [S&L] institutions."[16] By 1973, Fannie had become the largest debt-issuing institution in the US capital market (Hyman 2011, 232). Although the GSEs' overall mortgage market share was still below 10 percent at that time – since the mortgage-backed securities market had not yet fully taken off – the federal government had crafted and sponsored a new market that would ultimately dominate the US housing finance landscape. Through the popularization of mortgage-backed securities, American housing became known as a tradable and attractive asset to domestic and, later, global investors (Gotham 2006; Schwartz 2009).

"PROSTITUTING" THE FED

In their relentless efforts to support the struggling housing finance market, policymakers even *bullied* the Fed to directly assist the housing sector in the late 1960s. While the Fed is nominally independent of elected politicians, the reality is more nuanced (Binder and Spindel 2017). For the Fed, providing targeted support for specific sectors is highly unusual, as it violates the principle of economic neutrality. However, there were precedents for such actions, such as when the Fed bought small amounts in Home Owners' Loan Corporation bonds during the depression to help finance efforts to stop the foreclosure crisis. In this instance, policymakers demanded that the Fed financially support Fannie Mae to improve mortgage lending and sustain housing-based growth.

In 1966, the Johnson administration, along with the Democrat-controlled Congress, amended the Federal Reserve Act to authorize the Fed to buy and sell bonds of *all* government-sponsored agencies, including Fannie Mae. The Fed could engage in these transactions as long as these bonds were "a direct obligation of, or fully guaranteed as to principal and interest by, any agency of the United States."[17] The reform aimed to stabilize mortgage rates and revive a weak housing market during periods of tight monetary policy. Congress, in particular, viewed high mortgage rates as a drag on the economy. The House Committee on Banking and Currency diagnosed that "the greatest immediate injury to the average citizen lies in the drying up of the mortgage market and the threat to the building industry ... Unless substantial relief is granted to the housing market, the impending devastation in homebuilding and related industries could trigger a general recession throughout the economy."[18] In

[15] Council of Economic Advisers (1970), *Annual Report*, 39.

[16] Federal Reserve Board (1973), *Annual Report*, 57.

[17] *Interest Adjustment Act of 1966* (1966), Pub. L. No. 89–597, 80 Stat. 823.

[18] House Committee on Banking and Currency (July 28, 1966), *Temporary Interest Rate Controls: Report to Accompany H.R. 14026 (No. 1777)*, 5–6.

short, policymakers demanded that the Fed purchase Fannie bonds, which would enable Fannie to raise additional funds to promote mortgage lending.

The Fed initially refused to play along. On the one hand, it welcomed its new authority to intervene in capital markets, which would, in the words of vice-chair James Robertson, "increase the potential flexibility of open market transactions" (quoted in Haltom and Sharp 2014, 2). On the other hand, the Fed also cautioned against using this authority solely to channel funds into the mortgage market. In addition, the Fed warned that large-scale purchases of housing bonds would also exert downward pressures on mortgage rates at a time when the Fed was *increasing* interest rates to combat inflation. Such actions would also favor the housing market over other sectors and would signal inconsistent monetary policy.

After two years of inaction by the Fed, Congress was furious and openly criticized the Fed for not having done enough to support housing. The Democrats, in particular, voiced their disgruntlement. Congressman Henry Reuss (Democrat, Wisconsin) noted that Fed officials "have seen fit not to lift a finger to come to the aid of this important segment of the economy." He emphasized that the Fed would be obliged to act because housing is a "favorite object of the national policy."[19] Similarly, Senator William Proxmire (Democrat, Wisconsin) even threatened to strip away the Fed's independence: "You recognize, I take it, that the Federal Reserve Board is a creature of the Congress? ... [that] the Congress can recreate it, abolish it, and so forth? ... What would Congress have to do to indicate that it wishes the Board to change its policy and give greater support to the housing market?"[20] Congress was prepared to take further legislative action and discussed amendments that could have forced the Fed to buy Fannie bonds.

The Johnson administration took a middle-ground position between Congress and the Fed, favoring a solution that granted the Fed the authority of housing interventions at its discretion. The Fed and the White House identified two main problems with the congressional proposals. First, the amendments would privilege housing over other sectors. As Fed chair William Martin stated, forcing the Fed to support housing would be "prostituting – and I use that word deliberately – the functions of the central bank when you pick out any segment of the economy and use the central bank to create credit to finance it."[21] Second,

[19] US House of Representatives (June 25–27, 1968), *To Extend for One Year the Authority for ... Open Market Operations in Agency Issues: Hearings before the House Committee on Banking and Currency on H.R. 16092* (testimony of H. Reuss), 126–127.

[20] US Senate (April 3, 1968), *Purchase of Treasury Securities and Interest on Savings: Hearing before the Senate Committee on Banking and Currency on S. 2923 and S. 3133* (testimony of W. Proxmire), 24.

[21] US House of Representatives (June 25–27, 1968), *To Extend for One Year the Authority for ... Open Market Operations in Agency Issues: Hearings before the House Committee on Banking and Currency on H.R. 16092* (testimony of W. Martin), 121.

then-Under Secretary of the Treasury Joseph Barr noted that responsibilities in the housing sector lay with Congress, not the Fed, and advised that "when the Congress wants to do something in the social area or any other area that it approach the allocation of funds head on through the appropriation process."[22] In other words, if Congress wanted to stimulate housing, it should pass spending legislation rather than delegating that responsibility to the central bank. The Fed's and the Treasury's arguments convinced other members of Congress. As Thomas Gettys (Democrat, South Carolina) remarked, "although I am very zealous about helping the housing industry ... we might neglect the rest of the economy."[23] Ultimately, efforts to persuade members of Congress were successful, and the Fed was given the authority to intervene in housing at its own discretion.

Even so, Congress maintained political pressure, and the Fed ultimately yielded. In 1971, the central bank started building "a modest portfolio of agency issues," partly to please Congress.[24] According to Fed minutes, the newly appointed Fed chair, Arthur Burns, held the view that "there was sentiment in Congress for the System to take steps that would be useful for housing ... if the System declined to use the tools Congress had provided, other less desirable legislation might be enacted in the hope of benefiting housing."[25] Yet the Fed's measures had relatively modest macroeconomic effects. As a staff economist expressed, "such operations might be of marginal benefit to housing but probably would not represent a major aid."[26] By 1977, the Fed held USD 3.5 billion in Fannie Mae bonds (Haltom and Sharp 2014), a share of around 10 percent of outstanding Fannie Mae debt that year.[27] As the Fed directly supported housing in this period, it reinforced the country's government-sponsored housing model.

In sum, politicians went to great lengths to promote housing-based growth, even in areas in which they had little formal authority. Although by the early 2000s the Fed had gradually reduced its modest – albeit involuntary – support for housing to zero, these central bank actions created the institutional authority and precedent for future housing interventions (see Chapter 6).

22 US House of Representatives (June 25–27, 1968), *To Extend for One Year the Authority for ... Open Market Operations in Agency Issues: Hearings before the House Committee on Banking and Currency on H.R. 16092* (testimony of J. Barr), 121.

23 US House of Representatives (June 25–27, 1968), *To Extend for One Year the Authority for ... Open Market Operations in Agency Issues: Hearings before the House Committee on Banking and Currency on H.R. 16092* (testimony of T. Gettys), 156.

24 Federal Open Market Committee (FOMC) (August 24, 1971), *Memorandum of Discussion*, 110.

25 FOMC (April 6, 1971), *Memorandum of Discussion*, 38.

26 FOMC (August 24, 1971), *Memorandum of Discussion*, 108.

27 The Fed also held agency debt of other federal or federally sponsored agencies such as the FHLB, Federal Farm Credit Banks, Ginnie Mae, and the Federal Land Banks. See Federal Reserve Bank of New York (1978), *The Market for Agency Securities*, www.newyorkfed.org/medialibrary/media/research/quarterly_review/1978v3/v3n1article2.pdf.

HOW THE 1970S TRANSFORMED AMERICA'S DEMAND-LED GROWTH REGIME AND HOUSING MARKET

The inflation-related credit crunches of the late 1960s were just a taste of what was to come. During the 1970s, a wave of economic shocks distressed the American demand-led growth regime. The oil shocks of 1973 and 1979, in particular, triggered skyrocketing inflation and interest rates, which not only contributed to major recessions but also prompted irreversible political and economic actions that remade American and global capitalism. However, the first economic shock of the 1970s preceded the oil crises. The postwar Bretton Woods global monetary system, which had pegged global currencies to the US dollar (itself tied to gold), collapsed when President Nixon abandoned the system in 1971. Rising US inflation – and the fact that "too many dollars were abroad" due to the US trade deficit, military spending, and foreign investments (Levy 2020, 552) – placed speculative pressure on what was widely considered an overvalued US dollar (Bordo 2017; Eichengreen 2011, ch. 3). The subsequent oil shocks hit the US economy even harder. The first oil shock in 1973 drove up prices and interest rates after the Organization of the Petroleum Exporting Countries (OPEC) imposed an oil embargo on the United States and other Western nations perceived as supporting Israel in response to the Yom Kippur War (Hansen 2023, 39–40). Throughout the 1970s and early 1980s, the US economy grappled with stagflation, high interest rates, and high unemployment. The apex of these inflationary developments was the second oil shock in 1979 following the Iranian Revolution. In response, the Fed under chairman Paul Volcker raised interest rates to an unprecedented level of 19 percent in 1980. While these measures eventually brought inflation under control, the 1970s "change[d] the global economy forever" (Hansen 2023, 35),[28] including America's demand-led growth regime and the role of housing within it.

As the housing sector is sensitive to interest rates, there were massive swings in housing activity throughout the 1970s. The first oil shock in 1973 not only brought about high inflation and interest rates but also led to a recession in 1973–1974. Housing contributed to the US economy's weakness, as it was slammed by mortgage rates reaching a postwar high of 10

[28] Annual unemployment rates climbed from 3.5 percent in 1969 to a peak of 10 percent in 1982 and then fell to around 5 percent by the end of the decade. Annual inflation rates increased from 1.6 percent in 1965 to 5.8 percent in 1970, 11 percent after the first oil shock in 1974, and 13.5 percent after the second oil shock in 1980; they then declined to 2–5 percent by the late 1980s. In response, annual interest rates rose from 2 to 3 percent in the early 1960s to 8 percent in the late 1960s, to over 10 percent in 1974, and briefly to a peak of 19 percent in 1980–1981, and then fell again to 7–9 percent toward the end of the decade. Real annual economic growth, similarly, did not regain its 1966 peak of 6.6 percent until 1984. The economy went into recession in 1970, 1974–1975, and 1981–1982. Data from FRED (2024), https://fred.stlouisfed.org.

percent. Housing starts halved from an all-time high of 2.4 million in 1972 to a trough of 1.2 million in 1975 (see Figure 2.2). Despite high interest rates, the country did not experience a credit crunch as it had a few years earlier. Although the structural economic problems of the S&Ls continued (i.e., interest-rate ceilings and maturity mismatches), Fannie Mae, Freddie Mac, and Ginnie Mae were able to offset the S&Ls' weakness by supplying additional mortgage credit. Increasingly, mortgage availability was no longer the primary issue; rather, it was the *price* of mortgages that held back lending (Krippner 2011, 82).

Policymakers responded once again by expanding housing programs, as a weak housing market threatened ripple effects throughout the economy. As the *New York Times* reported in 1973: "The decline is plunging some builders into bankruptcy and has cost thousands of construction workers their jobs. Its ripple effect is moving through the economy, from sales of lampshades to lawn mowers."[29] Like Johnson and Nixon before him, President Gerald Ford expanded the role of the GSEs in the mortgage market to cushion the sector's downturn. President Ford's Housing and Community Development Act of 1974 enabled the GSEs to purchase larger amounts of mortgage debt from banks as part of the bill's larger effort to provide "some needed help for the housing sector" and "significant assistance to the mortgage market."[30] As a result, the GSEs increased their mortgage purchases from banks from USD 10 billion in 1973 to over USD 15 billion in 1974.[31] Fannie's portfolio holdings surged from USD 4.4 billion in 1966 to USD 30 billion in 1974, representing six percent of outstanding residential mortgage debt in the latter year.[32] Together with falling interest rates, these measures helped produce a strong rebound in housing activity and demand, driving new housing starts above two million in 1978. The surge in housing activity also contributed to "bolstering spending" and increased "furniture and appliance sales."[33] More generally, the Fed presciently noted that the growing GSE mortgage-backed securities market would ultimately "make the residential mortgage market less dependent

[29] "Housing boom turns to bust and threatens a crisis" (December 31, 1973), *New York Times*.

[30] Ford, G. R. (August 22, 1974), *Statement on the Housing and Community Development Act of 1974*, The American Presidency Project, www.presidency.ucsb.edu/node/256200. The 1974 act also helped middle-class homeowners by reducing down-payment requirements for FHA mortgages and raising the limits of federal mortgage insurance. However, instead of boosting affordable rental housing programs, the act established the country's first national voucher program for low-income households ("Section 8 vouchers"). The program remained underfunded, as the federal government issued only around 2 million vouchers from 1975 to 2008 (A. Schwartz 2010, 181).

[31] Council of Economic Advisers (1975), *Annual Report*, 72.

[32] Federal National Mortgage Association (1975), *Background and History*, 7–8, https://fcic-static.law.stanford.edu/cdn_media/fcic-docs/1975-00-00%20FNMA%20--%20History.pdf.

[33] Council of Economic Advisers (1977), *Annual Report*, 37.

on thrift [S&L] institutions' deposit flows."[34] Despite these developments, the S&Ls still had a market share of 43 percent in outstanding mortgage debt by the late 1970s, compared to the GSEs' share of 16 percent.[35]

The oil shock of 1979 prompted efforts to limit inflation, which drove up interest rates to over 17 percent by early 1980 and resulted in another recession. The housing market was hit hard once again, with housing starts decreasing from a peak of 2 million in 1978 to 1.1 million in 1981 (see Figure 2.2). Moreover, the S&Ls experienced significant outflows of funds, as market interest rates soared well above the capped interest rates that the S&Ls were permitted to pay to depositors.

During this time, the administration of President Jimmy Carter initiated a deregulatory process to liberalize the S&Ls, a process that the Reagan administration would later complete. However, as I detail in what follows, financial deregulations paradoxically expanded the state's role in the housing finance market. Carter's Depository Institutions Deregulation and Monetary Control Act of 1980 phased out interest-rate ceilings on consumer deposits and granted S&Ls broader authority in their investment and banking activities (Fergus 2018, ch. 1). In successive steps, the Carter administration and Congress also allowed the S&Ls to offer adjustable-rate mortgages to shield the S&Ls from interest-rate risk. The goal was to halt the outflow of funds from the S&Ls, encourage savings, and counter the persistent problem of maturity mismatches, thereby supporting the S&Ls' lending activities which remained central to the housing finance market. Consequently, the S&Ls began to compete more directly with mortgage banks. According to the Council of Economic Advisers, these actions created a new "regulatory environment [that] should help to stabilize their deposit flow and hence the supply of mortgage funds."[36] The removal of interest-rate ceilings meant that credit was no longer rationed or restrained, but instead flowed freely based on price mechanisms (Krippner 2011, 83).

More fundamentally, the economic challenges of the 1970s and the political responses to them transformed the American demand-led growth regime into one "dominated by credit" (Krippner 2017, 7). As firms adjusted to profit squeezes and lower productivity, wage growth stagnated. Countercyclical fiscal measures adopted by the Nixon, Ford, and, to some degree, Carter administrations did not have the intended effect of lowering unemployment; instead, they contributed to rising fiscal deficits and inflation. By the late 1970s, policymakers had moved away from Keynesian demand management, focusing instead on curtailing government spending and welfare state growth to limit inflation.

While housing activity fluctuated dramatically during the inflationary 1970s, it became central to America's post-Keynesian shift toward financialization.

[34] Federal Reserve Board (1978), *Annual Report*, 43.

[35] Council of Economic Advisers (1999), *Annual Report*, 417.

[36] Council of Economic Advisers (1981), *Annual Report*, 113.

Dwindling profitability, economic uncertainty, and high interest rates deterred industrial investments and drew capital into more profitable financial, stock, and real estate markets (Gourevitch 1986; Krippner 2011; Levy 2020). One notable development was the increased role of credit in the economy, primarily driven by the growth of mortgage debt. As Òscar Jordà and colleagues (2016b, 117) estimate, US mortgage lending as a share of total bank lending increased from 39 percent in 1928 to 55 percent in 1970, and ultimately to 70 percent in 2007. By comparison, German mortgage lending as a share of total bank lending remained relatively stable over the past century: 49 percent in 1928, 42 percent in 1970, and 51 percent in 2007.

Another significant development was the shift from manufacturing to service-sector employment in real estate, insurance, and finance, particularly in the south and west, which experienced strong population growth. As Jonathan Levy (2020, 567–568) observes about the city of Houston, Texas: "Rather than ever-rising unionized male breadwinning wages, fresh incomes were often generated from the appreciation of real estate values ... The centrality of real estate, commercial and residential, meant high levels of debt, in the form of mortgages." What was true of Houston soon applied to much of the country. Given the investment potential in real estate, employment in the sector increased from 780,000 workers in 1972 to 1.2 million in 1986, at least half of whom were women.[37] A related development was that, as noted, households began borrowing against their homes to finance consumption, cover medical expenses, or smooth income losses during times of declining wages, pensions, and welfare programs (Rajan 2010; Atkinson 2019; Wiedemann 2021). Rising house prices, mortgage debt, and consumption became central elements of America's financializing demand-led growth regime.

STIMULATING DEMAND, RESTRICTING SUPPLY: TURNING HOMES INTO CREDIT CARDS

While national policymakers continued to stimulate mortgage lending and housing demand, local politicians started restricting housing supply in the 1970s (Glaeser and Gyourko 2018). Before then, building regulations had been relatively lax, allowing "pro-growth" local and national politicians to undertake large-scale developments such as mega-projects (e.g., convention centers, airports, transit projects, or stadiums), housing developments, urban redevelopment, and suburban expansion (Altshuler and Luberoff 2004). However, from the 1970s onward, land use restrictions made housing construction more difficult. While expensive homes in suburban areas were still welcome, building multifamily homes in suburbs (and in many urban neighborhoods) faced significant obstacles (Glaeser 2011; Einstein et al. 2020).

[37] Personick, V. (1987), *Projections 2000: Industry Output and Employment through the End of the Century*, US Bureau of Labor Statistics, 43, www.bls.gov/opub/mlr/1987/09/art4full.pdf.

The tightening of land use restrictions was driven by local interests opposing new developments. So-called NIMBYs ("not in my backyard") and neighborhood defenders – motivated by self-interest and community concerns, respectively (Einstein et al. 2020, 34) – opposed development on grounds of environmental protection, historic preservation, and concerns over racialized or poor newcomers (Frieden 1979; Altshuler and Luberoff 2004; Dougherty 2020). Some of these anti-growth demands were sensible, such as efforts to protect San Francisco Bay or Napa Valley from overdevelopment. However, as Bernard Frieden (1979, 5) noted, the no-growth movement soon adopted an attitude of "general hostility toward homebuilding for the average family, using the rhetoric of environmental protection in order to look after the narrow interests of people who got to the suburbs first." Whether aiming to protect their home values, schools or parks, perceived quality of life, or racial compositions of neighborhoods, organized local voters were instrumental in pressuring local officials in zoning boards to preserve the physical and social nature of their communities (Einstein et al. 2020; Trounstine 2018; Taylor 2019, 256; McCabe 2016). The combination of federal demand-side housing credit programs – FHA, VA, GSE, and tax programs that stimulated housing demand – with stricter local supply restrictions led to a substantial rise in house prices starting in the 1970s. "Rising prices squeezing first-time home buyers" was the impact of these developments, as the *New York Times* wrote on its front page on June 26, 1977.[38]

Subsidizing housing demand at the national level while restricting supply at the local level was not a coordinated strategy of national and local policymakers to boost housing values. However, the combination of these actions created the conditions for a new kind of growth based on rising property values. During the dire economic times of the 1970s, American households faced inflation that eroded their savings and salaries. For homeowners, rising house prices meant accumulating wealth, as house price growth exceeded inflation, particularly in western states (Grebler and Mittelbach 1979, 21–23).[39] The rising cost of living added financial incentives to protect the value of homes as a "hedge against inflation."[40] Existing homeowners could protect their most valuable asset by blocking new developments, thus minimizing the risk of adverse effects on their homes and neighborhoods (Fischel 2001; Hankinson 2018; Marble and Nall 2021; McCabe 2016). Conor Dougherty (2020, 86) describes these local dynamics as a vicious cycle: "[T]he more home prices went up, the further people had to stretch to buy a home, the more motivated new homeowners became to protect their investment, the more home prices

[38] Lindsey, R. (June 26, 1977), "Rising Prices Squeezing First-Time Home Buyers," *New York Times*.

[39] Inflation also meant that homeowners' mortgage debt devalued, which reduced their debt burden and increased their relative wealth and purchasing power (Germain and Schwartz 2017, 776).

[40] Federal Reserve Board (1978), *Annual Report*, 5.

went up." Rising house prices also meant that expected future house price gains became integral to the homebuying process, leading to speculative behavior in some regional housing markets, particularly in California (Grebler and Mittelbach 1979, 4–5). A 1977 survey underlines the investment motives of homebuyers in California, revealing that recent homebuyers viewed their home as "(1) an inflation hedge, (2) an opportunity to capture larger income-tax benefits, and (3) 'the best investment for my money'" (Grebler and Mittelbach 1979, 86).

Rising house prices facilitated a lasting phenomenon at the core of America's demand-led growth regime: The use of homes as cash generators for consumer spending. Homeowners could, of course, cash in by selling their homes at a profit. However, as house prices increased, housing also became valuable collateral against which homeowners could borrow – either via home equity loans or mortgage refinancing – to finance household spending (Hyman 2011, ch. 7; Fligstein and Goldstein 2015; Kohl 2021). Home equity loans are bank loans that are secured by the property of the borrower. Refinancing means that homeowners replace their existing mortgage, either with a larger mortgage and/or a mortgage with a lower mortgage rate, particularly if the equity in their home has increased. This extra cash extracted from properties can be spent on consumer goods or used to pay off other consumer debt.

The shift toward using homes as credit cards began in the 1970s. As an economist observed in 1971, "most families probably [did] not view housing equity as being available for anything – it just sits there and grows indefinitely or until the house is sold."[41] By 1976, however, the Fed had noticed a significant change: Mortgage borrowing exceeded the purchase value of new and existing homes by USD 15 billion, indicating the "withdrawal of homeowners' equity in existing residences."[42] By 1978, the Fed further elaborated that "[f]amilies sought mortgage credit not only to finance the purchase of homes but also to fund other expenditures and to add to their holdings of financial assets."[43] Two years later, in 1980, the Fed completed the picture, noting that "[t]he strong demand for housing, both as shelter and as an investment, and an evident desire to maintain past spending levels in the face of declining real disposable income kept borrowing by the household sector at an historically high level during 1979."[44]

Households, banks, and the Fed *discovered* what economists would later call "credit effects" – the phenomenon where rising house prices translate into credit-financed consumer spending, such as for maintaining living standards

[41] Juster, T. (June 1971), "Discussion." In Federal Reserve Bank of Boston, *Consumer Spending and Monetary Policy: The Linkages* (Conference Series no. 5), 184.

[42] Federal Reserve Board (1976), *Annual Report*, 61.

[43] Federal Reserve Board (1978), *Annual Report*, 33.

[44] Federal Reserve Board (1980), *Annual Report*, 45.

and consumption levels during times of stagnating or even falling real wages and social welfare (Atkinson 2019). An economist at the Fed concluded that "[t]he rates of consumption expenditures recorded since mid-1975 may not have been attained in the absence of the unprecedented rates of borrowing against home equity."[45] In short, by the mid-1970s, borrowing against homes had become a core component of America's consumption- and credit-led growth regime. An official from the Department of Housing and Urban Development (HUD) said in 1978: "A home has become more than just a shelter – it has become the new form of investment to a higher and higher proportion of Americans."[46]

While homeowners could celebrate rising house prices, they also faced higher property taxes. But not for long. As Isaac Martin (2008) highlights, homeowners successfully mobilized and revolted against high property taxes. They convinced policymakers – first in California through Proposition 13 in 1978, then in other parts of the country – to limit local property tax increases and restore tax privileges through artificially low housing value assessments.[47] Warren Buffett criticized the perverse long-term economic consequences of Proposition 13, disclosing that in 2003, he paid only around USD 2,000 (or 0.06 percent) in property tax on his California home worth USD 4 million, which he had purchased in the 1970s.[48]

Meanwhile, racialized minorities remained at the periphery of America's government-sponsored housing model. Stricter zoning and higher home values posed significant barriers for minorities to enter white middle-class suburbs or neighborhoods (Taylor 2019). In 1976, President Carter did not view this as an issue. On the contrary, he stated: "I'm not going to use the Federal Government's authority deliberately to circumvent the natural inclination of people to live in ethnically homogeneous neighborhoods."[49] Despite civil-rights-era legislation aimed at ending racial discrimination in housing, Black and other minority households still faced significant hurdles in climbing the suburban property ladder. These obstacles included rising prices, local zoning, predatory lending, and continued discriminatory practices in real estate (King and Smith 2011, ch. 5). Although suburbs *slowly* diversified (Nicolaides and Wiese 2017), many Black households instead became homeowners in urban working-class areas. As Chapter 2 outlined, however, the story for many of them ended in

[45] Seiders, D. (1978), *Mortgage Borrowings Against Equity in Existing Homes*, Staff Economic Studies of the Board of Governors of the Federal Reserve System, 26.

[46] "Rise in home prices apparently slows" (November 13, 1979), *New York Times*.

[47] Proposition 13, still in place today, specifies that property taxes are limited to 1 percent of the property value assessed at the time of sale and that, subsequently, property value assessments could rise no more than 2 percent per year. As a result, if property prices increased by more than 2 percent annually, homeowners – particularly those having purchased their homes decades ago – could reap massive tax savings over time.

[48] Buffett, W. (November 3, 2003), "Warren Buffett's response to the Journal," *Wall Street Journal*.

[49] Lydon, C. (April 7, 1976), "Carter defends all-white areas," *New York Times*.

foreclosure partly due to predatory lending practices, including in federally sponsored credit programs (Taylor 2019; Krippner 2017).[50] By 1980, the Black homeownership rate was only 45 percent, compared to nearly 70 percent for white households.[51] In addition, Black-owned homes were frequently valued much below white-owned homes. As a result, most Black households were denied an opportunity that most white households had discovered for themselves: Using rising home values as financial leverage to maintain living standards, finance consumption, and access welfare services.

REAGAN'S HOUSING PARADOX: DEREGULATION PAIRED WITH POLICY EXPANSION

When the presidential administration of Ronald Reagan took office in 1981, the American economy was about to enter another deep recession. Following the second oil shock of 1979, inflation continued to be a problem in the early 1980s, prompting the Fed to raise interest rates to 19 percent. Reagan's economic agenda for limiting inflation and regenerating growth is well known: Tax cuts for businesses and households, deregulation of industry and finance, assaults on the power of labor unions, and cuts in welfare spending – all aimed at removing governmental barriers from "free markets." Housing was central to Reagan's economic program. On the one hand, the diminished role of labor unions made affordable housing programs even more vulnerable to retrenchment (Dreier 2000). On the other hand, Reagan viewed the stimulation of private housing and homeownership as a growth strategy to spark an economic rebound. To achieve this, he prioritized mortgage deregulation and tax incentives to stimulate housing investment. Paradoxically, these measures led to an expanded role for the American state in the housing market.

The housing market remained severely depressed in the early 1980s, weakening the wider US economy, which was highly dependent on housing-based growth. Sky-high interest rates, rising unemployment, and an ongoing recession crushed the housing market. Housing starts plummeted from about 2 million in 1978 to about one million by 1981 (see Figure 2.2). After a decade of strong growth, house prices started trending down nationwide (Poterba 1991, 147). Although President Carter had initiated the liberalization of the S&Ls, capital continued to flee the S&Ls for higher-return investments, threatening the country's supply of mortgage credit. In a sign of

[50] Federal homeownership programs for low-income and minority households were cut in the late 1980s in response to the perceived failures of the program, which had borrowers facing foreclosure, partly due to predatory lending practices and insufficient government oversight.

[51] Choi, J., McCargo, A., Neal, M., Goodman, L., and Young, C. (October 2019), *Explaining the Black–White Homeownership Gap: A Closer Look at Disparities across Local Markets*, The Urban Institute.

frustration over the housing plight, Iowa homebuilders started mailing toothpicks to the incoming President Reagan, symbolizing the industry's dire state.

From the start, Reagan recognized the critical role of housing as an economic stimulant. Shortly after taking office in 1981, he scheduled a meeting with the housing industry as an "'outreach' effort to one of the most important industry sectors," as the "President has pledged to give housing a high priority in his Administration."[52] Around the same time, he established a housing commission – consisting of experts, economists, and industry leaders – symbolically located across from the White House and tasked with issuing a set of housing policy recommendations. These included further deregulating the S&Ls, providing tax incentives for mortgage and housing investments, and strengthening the secondary mortgage market, with the broader goals of attracting capital into housing, stabilizing the mortgage market, and lowering mortgage rates.[53] The administration also developed an internal "HELP for Housing" plan, which explored "ways to achieve an effective 'countercyclical stimulant' for the economy: a program to get housing production going and create jobs."[54] Despite these efforts, the housing lobby grew impatient and publicly criticized President Reagan in early 1982, claiming that the industry had "unfairly borne the brunt of destructively high interest rates." This criticism prompted Reagan to respond in a private meeting with industry representatives that "there is no anti-housing bias in this Administration."[55]

In a first major step to address the housing problem and stimulate the economy through increased mortgage lending, the Reagan administration further deregulated the S&Ls. The Garn-St Germain Depository Institution Act of 1982 widened the authorities of S&Ls, allowing them to make broader investments in financial markets and offering them more flexibility in issuing riskier adjustable-rate residential mortgages. The stated objective of the bill was to "revitalize the housing industry by strengthening the financial stability of home mortgage lending institutions and ensuring the availability of home mortgage loans."[56] In Reagan's words, the act would offer "help for housing, more jobs, and new growth for the economy."[57]

52 Dole, E. (March 10, 1981), *Meeting with the Construction, Housing, and Construction Finance Representatives* [memorandum], White House, RRPL, Elizabeth Dole Files, Box 117.

53 Fairbanks, S. (June 1, 1982), *Report of the President's Commission on Housing: Memorandum for Elizabeth H. Dole*, White House, RRPL, Dole Files, Box 45; President's Commission on Housing (January 1982), *Financing the Housing Needs of the 1980s: A Preliminary Report on Housing Finance*, www.huduser.gov/portal//Publications/pdf/HUD-2307.pdf.

54 Fairbanks, S. (February 16, 1982), *HELP for Housing: Memorandum for Martin Anderson, Ed Gray*, White House, Martin Anderson Files, Box 18, Folder 6.

55 "An open letter to President Reagan and members of Congress" (March 3, 1982), *Washington Post*; *Meeting with Housing Industry Representatives* [meeting transcript] (March 19, 1982), White House, RRPL, Dole Files, Box 121.

56 Garn–St Germain Depository Institutions Act of 1982, Pub. L. No. 97-320, 96 Stat. 1469 (1982).

57 Reagan, R. (October 15, 1982), *Remarks on Signing the Garn-St Germain Depository Institutions Act of 1982*, The American Presidency Project, www.presidency.ucsb.edu/node/244729.

The S&Ls supported the bill. Due to high interest rates, S&L representatives lamented their inability to offer their preferred product – long-term, fixed-rate mortgages, which they had helped to champion in the depression era – and instead offered variable-rate mortgages.[58] As a result, adjustable-rate mortgages became more common, peaking at 60 percent of all new mortgage originations in 1988 (Green and Wachter 2010, 429; Fergus 2018). Fannie and Freddie also began to offer variable-rate mortgages, although their main business remained in fixed-rate mortgages.[59]

In a second step, Reagan reformed the secondary mortgage market to stimulate private investment in mortgage bonds. The Secondary Mortgage Market Enhancement Act of 1984 removed legal restrictions for private banks and investors specialized in trading and investing in mortgage-backed securities. The act was intended to introduce private competition with the GSEs, which was expected to exert a downward impact on mortgage rates by increasing "the number of participants channeling investor capital to the homebuyer."[60] At the time, the GSEs dominated the growing mortgage-backed securities market, with a market share of close to 90 percent. Reagan's Council of Economic Advisers criticized the strong government involvement in the secondary mortgage market, arguing that it might have "stunted the growth of privately issued" mortgage-backed securities,[61] while noting that "the government is expected to absorb the loss" incurred by the GSEs.[62] However, these reforms were ultimately unsuccessful in stimulating private market activity, owing to the many privileges the GSEs enjoyed over private banks, such as preferential tax treatment and their government-sponsored status, which allowed them to borrow funds more cheaply than private banks.

At the same time, capital inflows from abroad significantly reinforced America's demand-led growth regime and housing-based growth. High interest rates, a strong dollar, and liberalized capital markets attracted foreign capital in the post-Bretton-Woods monetary order (Levy 2020; Krippner 2011). The US dollar's status as a global reserve currency drew capital inflows into US Treasury bonds, especially after the "Volcker shock" of high interest rates in the late 1970s and early 1980s (Eichengreen 2011, ch. 3). These capital

[58] US Senate (April 7, 1981), *Federal Role in Conventional Home Financing: Hearing before the US Senate Committee on Banking, Housing, and Urban Affairs* (testimony of J. Pohlman), 35–36.

[59] Starting in 1981, Fannie and Freddie bought some conforming, adjustable-rate mortgages. There was some underspecified leeway as to what constituted a conforming mortgage. In general, Fannie mortgages had to adhere to certain loan size limits and to loan-to-value ratios of roughly 80 percent.

[60] US Senate Committee on Banking, Housing, and Urban Development (November 2, 1983), *The Secondary Mortgage Market Enhancement Act of 1983: Report to Accompany S. 2040 (No. 98-293)*, 2.

[61] Council of Economic Advisers (1984), *Annual Report*, 182.

[62] Council of Economic Advisers (1986), *Annual Report*, 195.

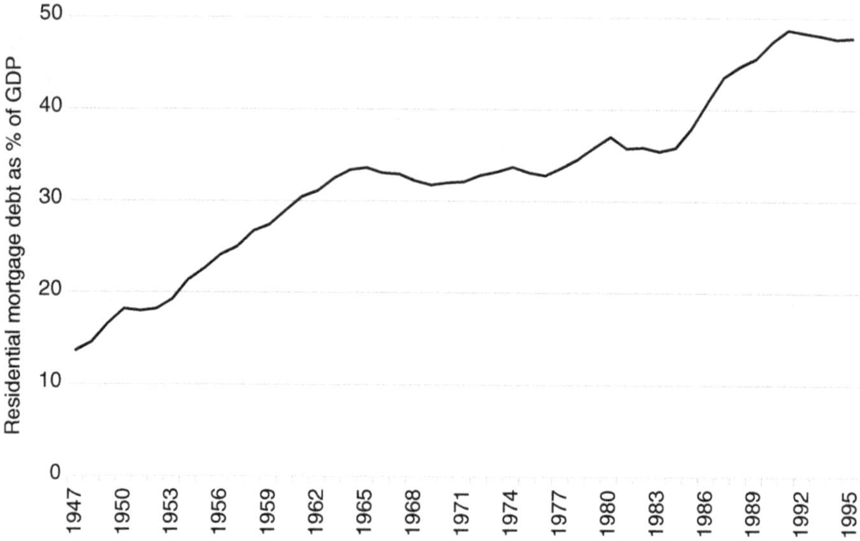

FIGURE 4.1 US residential mortgage debt as a percentage of GDP, 1947–1995
Notes: Residential mortgage debt includes both owner-occupied and multifamily mortgage debt. *Data sources:* Own calculations based on FRED (series: GDP) and Federal Reserve Flow of Funds (series: ASHMA; ASMRMA).

inflows made credit easily available for households and the US government.[63] For the housing sector, capital inflows stimulated activity by lowering the cost of mortgage credit, which in turn boosted housing demand and asset prices, contributing to credit and wealth effects (Eichengreen 2011, 116; Warnock and Warnock 2009). As a result, as Figure 4.1 illustrates, residential mortgage debt grew from roughly 32 percent of GDP (USD 343 billion) in 1970 to 46 percent (USD 2.6 trillion) in 1989. Moreover, in the absence of cross-border capital controls, foreign direct investment into US real estate surged from USD 2.3 billion in 1973 to USD 42.2 billion in 1989 (in constant 2000 dollars; see Gotham 2006, 245). Instead of increasing household savings, as Reagan had promised, consumers turned to credit markets to finance consumption by leveraging home equity, contributing to a lasting "debt-financed consumption boom" starting in the 1980s (Krippner 2011, 104).

Reagan's housing policy actions produced a paradoxical outcome: They expanded the government's role in the mortgage market even as they aimed to reduce it. The withdrawal of the state from the S&L industry contributed to the *expansion* of the American state's role in the broader mortgage market

[63] Such capital inflows allowed Reagan to run persistent budget deficits, which Peter Gourevitch (1986, 211) called a form of "right-wing military Keynesianism" (also see Warnock and Warnock 2009).

(see Figures 4.2 and 4.3). As the Reagan administration further deregulated the S&L industries, the government-sponsored agencies – Fannie, Freddie, and Ginnie – assumed an increasing share of the mortgage market. Until the late 1960s and early 1970s, the American state primarily supported the mortgage market by *guaranteeing* large volumes of mortgage debt through the FHA and the VA (see Figure 2.1). From the 1970s, the American state also incrementally became the most important *source* of mortgage funding through the GSEs.

By 1989, the GSEs had accumulated a total of USD 960 billion in outstanding mortgage debt, increasing their mortgage market share from close to 20 percent in 1980 to roughly 40 percent in 1990. As the GSEs became the dominant players in supplying mortgages in America, the S&Ls remained on shaky ground and soon required a massive industry-wide bailout. In short, rather than reducing the state's role in the housing market, Reagan's policies inadvertently *increased* it.

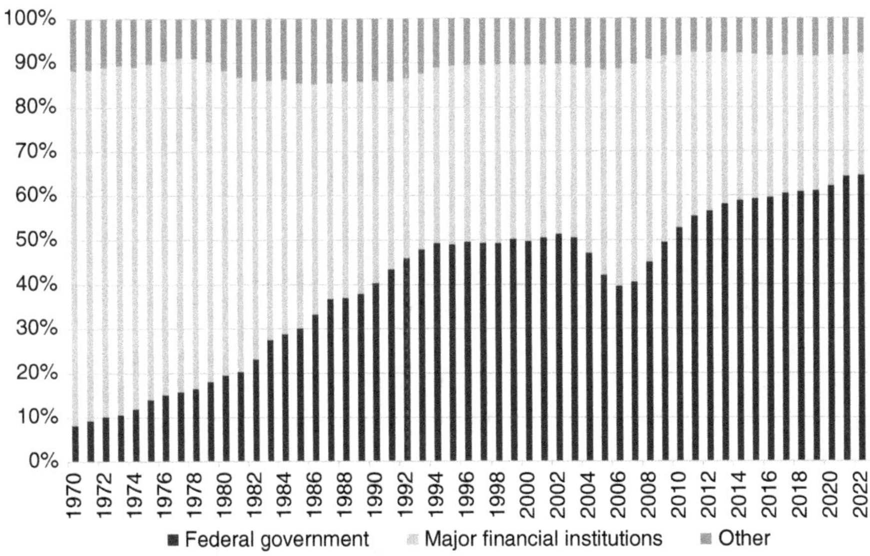

FIGURE 4.2 Sources of mortgage funding in the United States (as percentages of total mortgage funding), 1970–2022
Notes: Sources of mortgage funding are for both single-family and multifamily home mortgages. "Federal government" includes public or quasi-public agencies, such as the FHA, VA, Fannie Mae, Freddie Mac, Ginnie Mae, FHLB, and Federal Farmers' Home Administration (for home mortgages only, not farm debt). "Major financial institutions" include depository institutions, private mortgage conduits, and life insurance companies. "Other" includes credit unions, state and local governments, pension funds, real estate investment trusts, households, and nonfinancial firms. *Data source:* Federal Reserve Flow of Funds, Financial Accounts of the United States (Z.1).

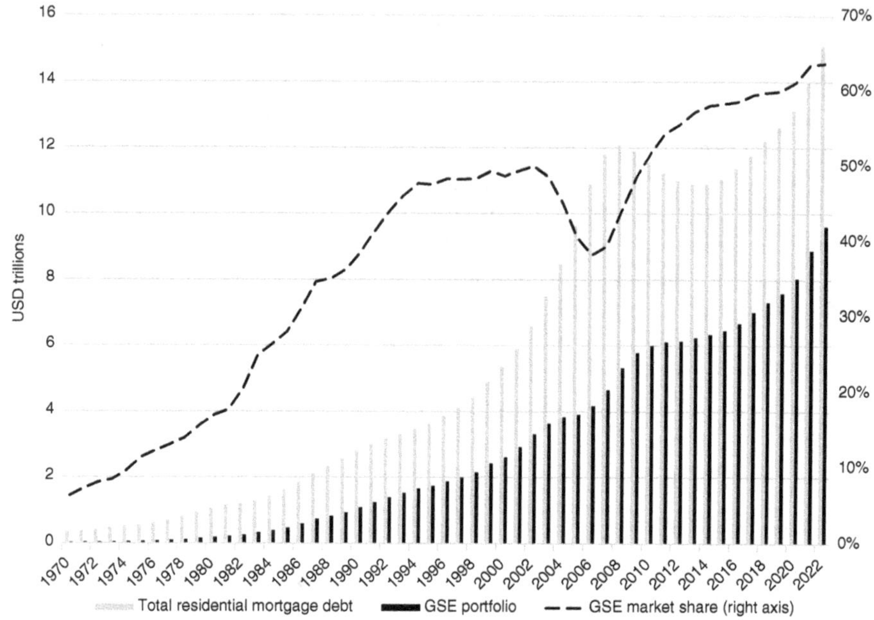

FIGURE 4.3 Government-sponsored enterprises' share of the US residential mortgage market, 1970–2022
Note: Includes data for all residential mortgage debt guaranteed by Fannie Mae, Freddie Mac, and Ginnie Mae. *Data source:* Federal Reserve Flow of Funds, Financial Accounts of the United States (Z.1).

TOUCHING AMERICA'S THIRD RAIL: TAX REFORMS AND THE MORTGAGE INTEREST DEDUCTION

A parallel development to the American state's growing footprint in the mortgage market was the unabated growth of a key housing tax program: The mortgage interest deduction (MID). Despite its rising cost and its questionable effect on promoting homeownership, the Reagan administration not only preserved the MID during major tax reforms but also strengthened it. The concern was that eliminating the deduction could hurt a struggling housing market and, by extension, the American economy. Once again, the MID had proven that it had become a key pillar of the American demand-led growth and welfare regimes (Howard 1997, 93).

The persistence of the MID is remarkable given its mixed track record. First and foremost, the subsidy was one the largest items in the income tax code, costing the taxpayer USD 25 billion in 1990 alone – a share of almost 10 percent of all tax expenditures paid to individuals that year.[64] Moreover, contrary to

[64] Joint Committee on Taxation (February 28, 1989), *Estimates of Tax Expenditures for Fiscal Years 1990–1994*, www.jct.gov/publications/1989/jcs-4-89/.

popular belief, the deduction does little to increase homeownership (Glaeser and Shapiro 2003; Hilber and Turner 2014). Despite the MID's substantial growth between the 1960s and 1980s, the homeownership rate remained at 64 percent between 1970 and 1990 (Kohl 2017). In addition, the MID is skewed toward high-income households. For example, Austin Drukker and colleagues (2021, 23) calculated that, in 1988, the richest 20 percent of households by income received an average of around USD 1,300 in tax benefits from the MID (in 2015 dollars), while the bottom 40 percent received hardly any benefit. Finally, the MID was market-distorting: It encouraged investments in owner-occupied housing while sidelining rental housing, leading to larger mortgages and homes with adverse effects on the environment (Glaeser 2011).

However, what the MID effectively supported was the rise in house prices through increasing demand. Economists agree that the elimination of the subsidy would lead to lower property values compared to prices with the subsidy in place (Poterba and Sinai 2011; Sommer and Sullivan 2018). It is precisely this potential for harming house prices that policymakers feared most during tax reform debates, as it could undermine housing-based growth and household wealth.

Reagan was well aware of previous failures to reform the MID, efforts that had burned prominent presidential candidates before him. During the 1976 presidential campaign, then-candidate Jimmy Carter proposed eliminating the MID and the property tax deduction as part of broader tax reform efforts aimed at reducing overall tax rates. He stated that, "in general, I would say, along with the elimination of other tax incentives, those [the MID and property tax deductions] would be among those that I would like to do away with."[65] Presidential candidate Senator Henry Jackson (Democrat, Washington) attacked Carter's proposal, arguing that it would harm the housing industry.[66] Similarly, President Ford attacked Carter's plans, particularly in light of what he described as "a disappointing year in the housing industry."[67] Ford expressed hope for a recovery in 1976 and emphasized the importance of the housing sector to the US economy. His campaign materials highlighted this belief:

> The housing, construction and building industries are an integral part of our national economy. Their economic success is of critical importance to the Nation's economic well-being. President Ford has made a strong commitment to assist the recovery of the housing industry ... decisive actions regarding the housing and construction industries were made in order to encourage economic recovery for those industries and the Nation.[68]

[65] Chapman, W. (February 27, 1976), "3 rivals attack Carter," *Washington Post*.

[66] Wicker, T. (March 5, 1976), "Now It's 'Stop Carter'," *New York Times*.

[67] Ford, G. R. (January 19, 1976), *Address Before a Joint Session of the Congress Reporting on the State of the Union*, The American Presidency Project, www.presidency.ucsb.edu/node/257493.

[68] The President Ford Committee (1976), *What President Ford Is Doing about Housing & Construction Industries* [campaign materials], Jimmy Carter Presidential Library, www.jimmycarterlibrary.gov/digital_library/campaign/564806/82/76C_564806_82_10.pdf.

For Ford, housing finance was a national champion essential to the country's economic health. Reforming the MID was thus out of the question. Carter quickly backtracked and, upon taking office in 1977, he declared the MID off limits. In the words of a Carter Treasury official, "[d]on't expect to see us remove the mortgage interest deduction."[69]

Despite previous warnings, President Reagan caused an uproar when he suggested that the MID *could* be reformed as part of his planned tax reform. Rising deficits in the early 1980s elevated tax reform to the top of the political agenda. The growing deficit itself was partly due to Reagan's unfunded 1981 tax cuts, which reduced tax rates for households and businesses without curbing spending. In his 1984 State of the Union address, Reagan called for "historic reform" to reduce tax rates, close loopholes, broaden the tax base, and decrease the deficit.[70] To kick off his reelection campaign, he tasked the US Treasury with drafting a report to be released just *after* the election. According to a former Treasury official, the Treasury viewed the report as just another study:

> So you have this request from the President to do the study. But it was largely a request – despite what people say *ex post* – to do just another study. Well, we will go study it! So a lot of people internally said: "let's just not do much or give him a three page summary." But I was flattered and said that this was an opportunity to put on paper some really comprehensive thinking about what's going on ... So to a large extent, the story was that, essentially, the study was a way to defer the tax issue until after the election. No one necessarily expects anything to come out of the study ... The President and the White House decided that they didn't really want to know what was going on in the Treasury, because they didn't want to be in a state of denial. This is a campaign, so part of the reason for pushing it in the State of the Union was to take the tax issue out of the presidential race.[71]

Accordingly, the Treasury began drafting what became known as "Treasury I" – a 700-page, two-volume tax reform plan.[72]

Reagan's strategy of deferring the issue until after the election failed, as rumors about the future of the MID started to circulate. At a roundtable event with the housing industry in Texas, a panelist asked Reagan whether "increased taxation on homeownership is being considered, such as doing away with interest deductibility on home mortgages." Reagan responded vaguely, suggesting that even the MID *could* be reconsidered if it helped lower overall tax rates: "Some of the things in the tax that you're talking about – deduction of interest on home mortgages and all – I have told them I want them to look

[69] "Mortgage tax break said safe" (March 25, 1977), *Washington Post*.

[70] Reagan, R. (January 25, 1984), *Address Before a Joint Session of the Congress on the State of the Union*, The American Presidency Project, www.presidency.ucsb.edu/node/261634.

[71] Former Treasury official I (author interview, Washington, DC, July 9, 2014).

[72] US Department of the Treasury (November 1984), *Tax Reform for Fairness, Simplicity and Economic Growth*, vols. I and II.

in the area of simplification at everything, but study everything that can be done."[73] A month later, he felt the need to clarify his stance in front of the National Association of Realtors (NAR) and stated:

> I know some of you've heard questions raised about whether there might be some plan to do away with the home mortgage interest deduction, which has played such an important role in helping Americans fulfill their dream of homeownership. I'm afraid that story was just another example of someone trying to read into my remarks things that weren't there. At that time, I was trying to emphasize that the Treasury Department's study of ways to simplify and reform the tax code, which I consider a real priority, is supposed to look at every aspect of the tax structure. However, in saying that, I also stressed that I strongly agreed with the home mortgage interest deduction, which is so vital to millions of hard-working Americans. And in case there's still any doubt, I want you to know we will preserve that part of the American dream.[74]

Reagan's remark to the realtors effectively took the MID out of tax reform discussions, ensuring its safety once again. Interestingly, archival records show that this passage on the MID was not part of Reagan's original speech but was inserted later.[75] A person familiar with the speech draft mentioned that the NAR convention was a good platform to clarify Reagan's tax policy preference on the MID.[76]

Declaring the MID off limits upset Treasury officials, who were the most vocal and longstanding critics of the deduction. After all, Reagan had tasked them with designing a technocratic reform proposal that was neutral in terms of revenue, investment, and distribution (Birnbaum and Murray 1988, 246). As Charles McLure, a key Treasury official at that time, and George Zodrow lamented: "This promise guaranteed that the so-called 'playing field' would not be level" (McLure and Zodrow 1987, 46). Much to the dismay of Treasury officials, they were forced to retain the deduction as part of what would become Reagan's 1985 tax reform plan.

The Tax Reform Act of 1986, which was the last comprehensive US tax reform in recent memory, was a pivotal moment for the housing market. The reform reduced tax rates and broadened the tax base, phasing out interest deductions on consumer credit, such as on credit cards and auto loans, to finance lower tax rates and increase household savings (Maki 2001). However,

[73] Reagan, R. (April 12, 1984), *Remarks During a Roundtable Discussion with Housing Industry Representatives*, Arlington, Texas, www.reaganlibrary.gov/archives/speech/remarks-during-roundtable-discussion-housing-industry-representatives-arlington.

[74] Reagan, R. (May 10, 1984), *Remarks at the Midyear Meeting of the National Association of Realtors*, Washington, DC, www.reaganlibrary.gov/archives/speech/remarks-midyear-meeting-national-association-realtors.

[75] White House Office of Speechwriting (May 8, 1984), *Presidential Remarks: Address National Association of Realtors Convention* [draft speech], RRPL, Speech Drafts, Box 153, Folder 2.

[76] Former White House official II (author interview, phone, August 8, 2014).

the reform preserved all housing tax breaks: The MID, the property tax deduction, and the capital gains exclusion (Fergus 2018).

ENTRENCHING TAX BREAKS: INTEREST GROUP POWER OR ECONOMIC CONSIDERATIONS?

Why did Reagan, like Carter before him, make a U-turn on the MID? It would be reasonable to assume that interest groups forced the change, given that Reagan clarified his stance on the deduction in front of the realtors (Birnbaum and Murray 1988; McLure and Zodrow, 1987; McLure 1986; Ventry 2010; Howard 1997). Indeed, the housing lobby – comprised of realtors, mortgage bankers, homebuilders, and the S&Ls – pressured the Reagan administration. However, evidence from archival presidential files and interviews with former White House officials suggests that Reagan had already formed a strong preference in favor of the MID in the early years of his presidency. In 1982, Reagan's housing commission recommended "continuing the current tax deduction for mortgage interest and property taxes," particularly in the context of a reeling housing market in the early 1980s.[77] Rather than succumbing to interest group pressure, Reagan ultimately declared the MID sacrosanct due to its role in stimulating mortgage credit, housing market activity, household wealth, and economic growth.

If Reagan understood the fundamental importance of the MID to the American growth regime, why did he say that everything in the tax code was subject to discussion just before the Tax Reform Act of 1986? The Reagan administration strategically declared all tax deductions to be on the table to shield itself from interest groups. If housing had received special treatment early on, other interest groups would also try "to get the president to declare their tax breaks off limits" (Birnbaum and Murray 1988, 57). However, there is no evidence that the Reagan administration actually planned on eliminating the MID. "It was his [Reagan's] sense that it would be discussed," a former senior White House official said, "but that didn't mean that he would necessarily give in on something like that." The official continued:

> We were in the process of just coming out of one of the worst economic crises that the nation had faced up to that time. Part of this was the fact that home building and home purchasing was an important part of the economic growth ... And a part of that economic growth had to do with something that is pretty fundamental to conservative principles – and that is allowing people to own their own homes, to own their own property. So it was a dual purpose: one, out of fairness to the middle class and, secondly, to preserve this idea of homeownership as a part of economic growth.[78]

[77] Fairbanks, S. (June 1, 1982), *Report of the President's Commission on Housing: Memorandum for Elizabeth H. Dole*, White House, RRPL, Dole Files, Box 45.

[78] Former White House official III (author interview, Washington, DC, September 3, 2014).

For the Reagan White House, the MID promoted economic growth as much as it embodied the more intuitively obvious conservative value of support for property ownership (Béland and Wadden 2007). The official also mentioned that the decision to retain the MID had little to do with interest group pressure: "The main driver was that the President wanted to protect something that was important economically and for the middle class ... With Ronald Reagan, I don't think the lobbyists had the final say. I think it was his own concepts of what was the right thing to do."[79] A second former Reagan White House official echoed this view, stating: "There are certain deductions that are so central to the economy and, of course, to people across the spectrum, so that we want to make sure to maintain them. I think the mortgage deduction was considered one of those." The official added that: "You can't throw out something like that [the deduction] – they didn't want to mess around with the economy. The economy was so bad in 1982 and we worked really hard to get this expansion moving. We didn't want to do anything that would unsettle people or destroy confidence, create instability in the market place and uncertainty."[80] Interest groups thus had little influence because they were pushing at an open door. They promoted what the administration already wanted: Housing-based growth.

Reagan was also aware that a broad-based coalition of policymakers from both parties strongly favored the MID, given the centrality of housing to the economy. Congressional hearings in the run-up to the Tax Reform of 1986 revealed Congress' key concerns: Falling house prices and housing wealth in individual districts and their effects on the wider economy. For example, when Congress debated flat tax proposals that were intended to eliminate all tax deductions, including the MID, policymakers were worried about the potential impact on housing activity and economic growth. In 1982, Robert Hall and Alvin Rabushka, who proposed a flat tax so simple that a tax return could fit on a postcard-sized form,[81] noted in a written statement to Congress that eliminating the MID "would tend to draw wealth out of housing and into plant and equipment, which might reduce housing values temporarily."[82] A report by the Joint Committee on Taxation to the Senate Finance Committee in 1982 also warned that "[e]liminating the deduction for mortgage interest would significantly increase the tax liability of most homeowners as well as reducing the market value of most homes."[83] Falling house prices, however, was not what members of Congress wanted to hear mentioned. During a hearing, Senator Max Baucus (Democrat, Montana) repeatedly asked Robert

[79] Former White House official III (author interview, Washington, DC, September 3, 2014).

[80] Former White House official II (author interview, phone, August 8, 2014).

[81] Hall, R., and Rabushka, A. (December 10, 1981), "A proposal to simplify the tax code," *Wall Street Journal*.

[82] Hall, R., and Rabushka, A. (September 30, 1982), "A simple income tax with low marginal rates." In US Senate, *Flat-Rate Tax: Hearings before the Senate Committee on Finance* [written statement], 77.

[83] Joint Committee on Taxation (September 28–29, 1982), *Analysis of Proposals Relating to Broadening the Base and Lowering the Rates of the Income Tax*, 31.

Hall "under which of the two alternatives would there be more housing?"[84] The answer was that the "housing industry would be in better shape" under proposals that retained the MID.[85] That settled the debate, and most tax proposals at the time retained the MID. Of course, falling house prices would also reduce the household wealth of homeowners, meaning that "you are going to do something to these homeowners," as a former Treasury official noted, "it's identifying losers."[86] Since homeowners' key asset – housing – was seen as crucial to economic growth, Congress refrained from touching the MID.

Unsurprisingly, the housing lobby supported the preservation of the MID. The National Association of Home Builders (NAHB) repeatedly stated that "[a]ny modification of the homeowner's mortgage interest deduction would have a devastating effect on both the housing market and the economy."[87] A representative of the American Bankers Association (ABA) echoed this sentiment, noting that "[t]he tax code can be a useful mechanism for stimulating economic growth. This is clearly seen in the positive effects of the mortgage interest deduction."[88] The White House and Congress did not need much convincing. As a senior White House official stated, "the mortgage bankers, the realtors ... they all had, I think, good arguments and that's why those arguments prevailed."[89] In other words, both policymakers and interest groups were singing from the same song sheet: A strong housing market would promote economic growth.

All key actors – the President, Congress, and the housing lobby – regarded the MID as a crucial policy for the stimulation of housing and the broader economy. Policymakers in Congress, such as Senator Howell Heflin (Democrat, Alabama), praised the preserved housing tax breaks as "important not only to those who cling to the American dream of owning their own homes but also to the real estate and homebuilding industries whose success is vital to a healthy economy."[90] Reflecting on reform debates about the MID, a former Republican House member stated that there were few incentives to reform the MID, as the deduction made buying homes cheaper, kept constituents happy, and stimulated the economy.[91] Policymakers believed that what was good for housing was good for the US economy, and they therefore entrenched housing tax breaks.

[84] US Senate (September 30, 1982), *Flat-Rate Tax: Hearings before the Senate Committee on Finance* (testimony of M. Baucus), 106.

[85] US Senate (September 30, 1982), *Flat-Rate Tax: Hearings before the Senate Committee on Finance* (testimony of R. Hall), 107.

[86] Former Treasury official I (author interview, Washington, DC, July 9, 2014).

[87] US Senate (August 7–9, 1984), *Major Tax Reform Options: Hearings before the Senate Committee on Finance* (testimony of P. Herder), 337.

[88] US House of Representatives (March-June 1985), *Impact of Tax Simplification on U.S. Economy: Hearings before the House Committee on Banking, Finance, and Urban Affairs* (written statement by G. Martin), 714.

[89] Former White House official III (author interview, Washington, DC, September 3, 2014).

[90] Heflin, H. (June 10, 1986), *Remarks in the US Senate, Congressional Record* 132(9), 13092.

[91] Former Member of the US House of Representatives (Republican, Arizona) (author interview, August 6, 2015).

TAX REFORM: BOON FOR HOMEOWNERS, BURDEN FOR RENTERS

A direct result of the 1986 tax reform was that American homeowners significantly increased borrowing against their homes. While credit-card and consumer debt no longer enjoyed tax benefits, mortgages still did. Banks jumped on the opportunity to aggressively advertise home equity loans. "You don't have to sell your home to get $10,000, $30,000 or even more in cash," CIT Financial advertised, "[y]ou don't even have to walk out the door."[92] Households started avoiding costlier consumer debt in favor of cheaper home equity loans to finance home improvement, consumption, educational expenses, or credit-card debt (Hyman 2011, 252). As the Fed analyzed: "The tax law change made use of mortgage credit relatively more attractive, and the active promotion by lenders of home equity lines of credit reinforced tendencies toward substitution."[93] Tax advantages, paired with rising house prices, incentivized homeowners to take out credit against their homes to an unprecedented degree.

Policymakers had not foreseen the rapid rise of home equity loans, nor did they take steps to limit their growth. Some members of Congress initially suggested restricting tax benefits on home equity loans solely for home improvement and repairs, but the provision did not garner enough support. One issue was tax reporting, as the Government Accountability Office pointed out: "Unless the interest on deductible and nondeductible mortgage financing were reported separately to the Internal Revenue Service (IRS), such distinctions would be difficult to monitor."[94] Another issue was that homeowners had other ways of claiming the MID on extracted home equity. Homeowners did not necessarily have to take out a home equity loan to receive tax advantages – they could also refinance their mortgage into a larger one with the same tax advantages. While Congress adopted a bill that required banks to properly disclose the pricing, risks, and terms of home equity loans in 1989, there was little appetite to eliminate the MID that could be used on these loans. As Congressman David Price (Democrat, North Carolina), co-sponsor of the disclosure bill, noted in front of the Consumer Bankers Association: "These loans are advantageous for many consumers. I took one out myself last year. I can tell you that the tax laws make it very attractive."[95] By 1988, households had USD 213 billion (1991 dollars) in outstanding home equity loans and another USD 91 billion in home equity lines of credit, amounting

[92] Story, L. (August 14, 2008), "Home equity frenzy was a bank ad come true," *New York Times*.

[93] Federal Reserve Board (1987), *Annual Report*, 61.

[94] US General Accounting Office (GAO) (March 25, 1993), *Tax Policy – Many Factors Contributed to the Growth in Home Equity Financing in the 1980s*, 3, www.gao.gov/assets/ggd-93-63.pdf.

[95] Nix, M. (April 11, 1988), "Congressman touts bill regulating home equity loans," *United Press International*.

to nearly 10 percent of total consumer debt.[96] Policymakers first tolerated and later encouraged the rise of yet another housing-based tool that boosted consumer spending: Tax-subsidized home equity loans.[97]

While homeowners retained tax benefits for home equity loans to finance consumer goods and welfare services, the Reagan administration retrenched public housing programs for the poor as part of its broader effort to reduce public welfare programs (Pierson 1994, ch. 4). Public housing programs were targeted due to the growing costs of their maintenance and the administration's ideological preference for private market solutions (Goetz 2013). Moreover, as Chapter 2 has shown, although unions were strong advocates for affordable rental housing from the 1930s to the 1970s, their influence in federal housing policy waned as their overall power diminished (Dreier 2000, 367).[98] Struggling to maintain membership, unions shifted their focus away from housing issues, weakening the broader coalition of low-income housing advocates. From the 1980s, no new public housing units were added, and available public housing funding was redirected toward maintenance and redevelopment of existing units.[99] Consequently, the number of public housing units *declined* from 1.4 million in 1990 to 1.3 million in 2000 (A. Schwartz 2010, 126).

In place of public housing programs came the Low-Income Housing Tax Credit (LIHTC), which the Reagan administration introduced as part of the 1986 Tax Reform Act. The LIHTC is a supply-side tax program supporting private investors in building affordable rental housing. By 2006, the program had funded 1.6 million rental units, accounting for one-sixth of all multifamily units (A. Schwartz 2010, 103). While these numbers are notable, they were insufficient to adequately house low-income Americans. The rental tax program also pales in comparison to homeownership tax subsidies, in terms of both the number of subsidized units and federal tax dollars spent. Homeowners have benefited from demand-side credit subsidies that contributed to rising property values and consumer spending, whereas low- and middle-income renters were left behind. For renters, the supply of affordable rental units shrank, while rental prices and the rental cost burden reached their highest levels in over two decades in the late 1980s.[100] As a result, the rental market remained a marginalized feature of the American political economy.

[96] GAO, *Tax Policy*, 8 and 11.

[97] In 1987, Congress limited the amount of eligible home equity loans to USD 100,000 under the Omnibus Budgetary Reconciliation Act to prevent the financing of luxury goods.

[98] Since 1984, however, the AFL-CIO's Housing Investment Trust has financed 127,839 affordable housing and healthcare units. See AFL-CIO (December, 2023), *Housing Investment Trust – Fact Sheet*, www.aflcio-hit.com/wp-content/uploads/2019/09/AFL-CIO-HIT-Factsheet-2023-Q4.pdf.

[99] The HOPE VI program, established in 1993, has helped demolish and/or redevelop distressed public housing projects into high-quality housing units.

[100] Apgar, W. C., and Brown, H. J. (1988), *The State of the Nation's Housing*, Joint Center for Housing Studies of Harvard University, 1.

FROM HOUSING DEBACLE TO GOVERNMENT-SPONSORED REVIVAL

"It is easily the biggest disaster in public finance since the Depression," the *New York Times* wrote on its front page on June 6, 1990.[101] The newspaper was referring to the S&L housing finance crisis that had been in the making for decades. Presidential administrations from Carter and Reagan to George H. W. Bush had loosened regulations on the S&L industry to address the industry's structural economic problems. However, the deregulatory approach backfired, leaving the majority of S&Ls unprofitable throughout the 1980s. Instead of resolving these "zombie banks" in the early 1980s, politicians delayed their closure, hoping that deregulation would ultimately succeed and prevent a costly taxpayer-financed bailout. Ironically, deregulation exacerbated the situation by enabling "a period of waste and corruption, excess and debauchery the likes of which the nation had not seen since the roaring twenties" (Pizzo et al. 1989, 4). Risky investments, fraud, and a lack of oversight culminated in a cascade of collapsing S&Ls toward the end of the decade. By 1987, 500 of the 3,200 S&Ls had failed and hundreds more were on the brink of collapse.

The largest banking crisis since the Great Depression was followed by the largest financial bailout in US history up to that point. Given the S&Ls' importance to the housing market, which had been crushed by high interest rates throughout the 1980s, and to savers, who had deposited funds with these institutions, the Bush administration bailed out the sector. The total cost of saving the S&Ls throughout the 1980s and early 1990s was around USD 132 billion in federal funds alone.[102] The lion's share of the funding came from the Financial Institutions Reform, Recovery and Enforcement Act of 1989. The act helped resolve around 750 bankrupt S&Ls and overhauled the industry's regulatory framework by imposing higher capital requirements on S&Ls.[103] However, these measures could not stop their demise. Gradually their market share of total outstanding mortgage debt declined, halving from 41 percent in 1980 to 21 percent in 1990.[104] At the same time, the GSEs – Fannie, Freddie, and Ginnie – stepped in and doubled their market share from 17 percent in 1980 to 38 percent in 1990 (see Figure 4.3). The GSEs were thus able to compensate for the declining activity of the S&Ls, making mortgage credit available in the wider economy.

[101] Rosenbaum, D. (June 6, 1990), "The Savings Debacle," *New York Times*.

[102] The S&Ls' deposit insurance scheme – FSLIC – had only USD 6 billion in emergency reserves in 1984; this would not have been enough to resolve unprofitable S&Ls, for which roughly USD 15 billion would have been required. As more S&Ls failed toward the end of the decade, the fund was depleted in 1986. See Federal Deposit Insurance Corporation (1997), *History of the Eighties, Lessons for the Future: An Examination of the Banking Crises of the 1980s and Early 1990s*, 39.

[103] Robinson, K. (November 22, 2013), *Savings and Loan Crisis*, Federal Reserve History, www.federalreservehistory.org/essays/savings-and-loan-crisis.

[104] Council of Economic Advisers (1999), *Annual Report*, 417.

The S&L disaster and the reeling housing market contributed significantly to an economic slowdown in 1990–1991. Various housing-related indicators illustrate the severity of the slump. Housing starts gradually declined from 1.6 million in 1987 to just one million in 1991 (see Figure 2.2). The homeownership rate *fell* from 66 percent in 1980 to 64 percent in 1990 (Kohl 2017) partly driven by rising foreclosure rates.[105] Sales of existing homes halved from a peak of 4 million in 1978 to only 2 million in 1982, and did not reach 4 million again until the mid-1990s.[106] In 1992, the Council of Economic Advisers noted that falling home prices resulted in lower household wealth and associated consumer spending, holding back the economy: "The largest asset for most households is the equity in their homes. After rising rapidly in the 1970s and 1980s, residential real estate values flattened and even fell in many areas. When consumers' expectations for a continued increase in wealth were dampened, growth of consumer spending tapered off."[107] In short, the adverse effects of a weak housing market extended beyond the sector itself, impacting the wider economy by holding back consumer spending through reduced wealth and credit effects.

To counter the housing and economic slowdown of the early 1990s, policymakers adjusted the activities of the GSEs to stimulate mortgage lending and housing activity among low-income and minority households. The George H. W. Bush administration's Federal Housing Enterprises Financial Safety and Soundness Act of 1992 tasked HUD with overseeing the GSEs' affordable housing goals, which mandated providing credit to low- and middle-income households. The increased housing goals pushed the GSEs partly into the lower-quality mortgage market (Acharya et al. 2011, ch. 2).[108] In addition, the act established a new regulator for the GSEs, the Office of Federal Housing Enterprise Oversight (OFHEO), to oversee their activities.

However, the lobbying efforts of the GSEs themselves prevented stricter housing finance regulations. Despite the obvious failures resulting from a decade of light-touch financial regulation, the new housing regulator, OFHEO, was toothless. The GSEs' successful lobby efforts helped prevent stringent regulatory oversight, caps on executive pay, and higher capital standards for the GSEs. As a NAHB representative put it: "If the system

105 Elmer, P., and Seelig, S. (1998), *The Rising Long-Term Trend of Single-Family Mortgage Foreclosure Rates* (FDIC Working Paper 98–2), Federal Deposit Insurance Corporation.

106 Perry, M. (February 2, 2009), *The Real Estate Crash of the 1980s*, American Enterprise Institute.

107 Council of Economic Advisers (1992), *Annual Report*, 27.

108 Earlier legislation had already started to formulate affordable housing goals. See, for example, Title VIII, Section 802, Housing and Urban Development Act of 1968, which stated that the Secretary of HUD could "require that a reasonable portion of FNMA's mortgage purchases be related to housing for low and moderate income families."

isn't broke, don't fix it."[109] A *Washington Post* report noted that Fannie officials were "communicating with every member of Congress who we think cares about Fannie Mae and cares about housing and telling them that this bill needs to be killed."[110] Indeed, Fannie Mae was one of the country's largest financial institutions and contributed to both Democratic and Republican congressional campaigns.[111] The GSEs successfully argued that tighter regulations would lead to higher mortgage rates for homeowners and increased fees for investors.[112] Meanwhile, politicians often ended up with high-paying jobs at the GSEs (McLean 2015). Stimulating the GSEs and fostering housing-based growth thus prevailed over financial safety.

When the administration of Bill Clinton took office in 1993, the economy had barely emerged from the recession and was still characterized by high unemployment, growing deficits, and slow economic and housing growth. For Clinton, stimulating housing could help remedy many of these symptoms. Assisted by the Fed's easing of interest rates, the administration pursued the goal of expanding homeownership among minority groups as a vehicle for economic growth. In 1995, it released its "national homeownership strategy," a one-hundred-point plan for regulators, practitioners, and homeowners. In a passage that could have been written in the 1930s or the 1970s, the document emphasized the critical role of housing in sustaining the American economy:

> Homeownership is a commitment to economic growth. Homeownership helps generate jobs and stimulate economic growth. The design, construction, and rehabilitation of homes employs local labor and uses a vast array of American-made products and services. Homebuilding has often led the economic recovery from national recessions due to its strong job multiplier effect and because increased housing starts and home sales represent renewed economic confidence.[113]

Together with consumer durables, housing had played a key role in revitalizing the economy in 1993[114] – much as it had in earlier recessions (Leamer 2015; Jordà et al. 2016b). In 1995, Clinton himself echoed this perspective in a speech reminiscent of Eccles' metaphor of housing as the "wheel within the wheel" to stimulate the economy:

[109] US House of Representatives (July 18–19, 1991), *Government-Sponsored Housing Enterprises Financial Safety and Soundness Act of 1991: Hearings before the House Committee on Banking, Finance, and Urban Affairs on H.R. 2900* (testimony of P. Barru), 78.

[110] Crenshaw, A. (September 29, 1992), "Fannie Mae flip-flops on oversight bill," *Washington Post.*

[111] Fannie contributed USD 162,000 to congressional campaigns in 1992. See Open Secrets (2024), *Total contributions: Fannie Mae*, www.opensecrets.org/ORGS/totals.php?id=D000000205&cycle=1992.

[112] Crenshaw, A. (May 30, 1991), "Fannie Mae, Freddie Mac blast Bush plan: Firms suggest regulations could raise the cost of mortgages," *Washington Post.*

[113] HUD (May 1995), *The National Homeownership Strategy: Partners in the American Dream.*

[114] Council of Economic Advisers (1994), *Annual Report*, 34.

When a family buys a home, the ripple effect is enormous. It means new homeowner consumers. They need more durable goods, like washers and dryers, refrigerators and water heaters. And if more families could buy new homes or older homes, more hammers will be pounding, more saws will be buzzing. Homebuilders and home fixers will be put to work. When we boost the number of homeowners in our country, we strengthen our economy, create jobs, build up the middle class, and build better citizens.[115]

From Franklin D. Roosevelt to Clinton, stimulating housing to promote economic growth has been a historical constant in the American political economy.

As the homeownership rate among white households was already above 70 percent, President Clinton aimed to stimulate housing-based growth and homeownership among nonwhite households, which stood at around 43 percent. A former White House official stated that:

The mood in the White House in 1993 was not: "We are in a boom!" But: "Oh god, we have a recession on our hands! What can we do to get out of it?" ... It fits with Clinton's ownership ideas, it fits with his equity ideas, because you were only able to increase the homeownership rate if you could increase it for Blacks, Latinos, minorities, and women ... It hit his equity buttons, and for Clinton that was huge. It hit the homeownership society button. And we needed something exciting going into the 1996 election. So that's where the homeownership thing came from.[116]

The strategy was an attempt to enhance partnerships between local governments, banks, realtors, homebuilders, and communities; many of these actors had denied racialized groups access to mortgage credit and housing-related services. The goal was to generate household wealth and housing-based growth among racialized communities, thereby incorporating them into America's growth regime based on credit-financed property ownership (Krippner 2017; Atkinson 2019).

To achieve this, the Clinton administration expanded the reach of the GSEs. Throughout his presidency, the administration successively increased the agencies' affordable housing goals to encourage banks to increase mortgage lending to lower-income and minority groups.[117] In a 1995 directive, the administration also revised the Community Reinvestment Act (CRA), which had required banks to extend credit to underserved communities since 1977 (Aalbers 2008; Krippner 2017).[118] Dissatisfied with the existing level of credit lending to

[115] Clinton, W. F. (June 5, 1995), *Remarks on the National Homeownership Strategy*, The American Presidency Project, www.presidency.ucsb.edu/node/220941.

[116] Former White House official I (author interview, Washington, DC, July 16, 2014).

[117] The affordable housing goals increased from 32 percent in 1993 to 40 percent in 1996 and 42 percent between 1997 and 2000; see HUD (July 2002), *Overview of the GSEs' Housing Goal Performance, 1993–2001*, www.huduser.gov/datasets/GSE/gse2001.pdf.

[118] CRA-related lending for borrowers with impaired credit ratings was not the same as the reckless subprime mortgage lending of the early 2000s. As Neil Bhutta and Daniel Ringo (2015) show, few CRA-related loans were subprime mortgages (i.e., 6 percent in 2005–2006); instead, CRA-related lending, which were often special programs developed with nonprofit organizations for

low-income communities, the administration sought to increase access to credit by subjecting banks to stricter performance-based reviews by regulators. In Clinton's words, banks would "discover new, profitable lines of business. And it doesn't cost taxpayers a dime. It can create miracles in small towns and big cities from coast to coast, miracles like mortgage or business loans for people who never thought they could own a house or business."[119] The logic was straightforward: Increased mortgage lending in low-income and minority communities would generate community and business development, consumption, and economic growth, all without increasing the budget deficit, a priority for third-way Democrats at the time. According to a 2000 Treasury report, the reformed CRA contributed to increased bank lending to low- and moderate-income households.[120] Expanding credit among low-income and minority households also reinforced an existing trend of Black households moving to the suburbs, as the number of African Americans in suburbs doubled from 6 million in 1980 to 12 million in 2000 (Wiese 2004, 255). By then, one-third of Black Americans lived in suburbs, although spatial and racial inequalities continued to exist within suburbs. More generally, the homeownership rate in 2000 stood at 71 percent among white households, 46.3 percent among Black households, 53.4 percent among Asian Americans, and 45.7 percent among Hispanics.[121]

Like other presidents before him, Clinton did little to boost rental housing. While his administration pushed the GSEs to expand their homeownership programs, their multifamily rental programs remained miniscule. In 1999, Fannie and Freddie together issued only USD 11 billion worth of multifamily mortgage-backed securities compared to USD 520 billion in single-family mortgage-backed securities.[122] The comparatively small mortgage market for rental housing – USD 330 billion in outstanding mortgage debt on rental properties compared to USD 4.3 trillion on owner-occupied properties in 1998 – can explain some of the difference.[123] However, compared to owner-occupied

households of moderate means, performed well during the crisis. In the late 1990s, high-risk subprime mortgages were still a relatively small segment of the mortgage market (FCIC 2011, 70); see Bhutta, N. and Ringo, D. (May 26, 2015), *Assessing the Community Reinvestment Act's role in the financial crisis*, FEDS Notes, www.federalreserve.gov/econresdata/notes/feds-notes/2015/assessing-the-community-reinvestment-acts-role-in-the-financial-crisis-20150526.html.

119 Clinton, W. F. (April 19, 1995), *Statement on Reform of Regulations Implementing the Community Reinvestment Act*, The American Presidency Project, www.presidency.ucsb.edu/node/220805.

120 Litan, R., Retsinas, N., Belsky, E. and Haag, S. (April 2000), *The Community Reinvestment Act after Financial Modernization: A Baseline Report*, US Department of the Treasury. Regulators assess the performance of banks in serving the credit needs of low- and moderate-income households and communities, issuing public ratings of these banks.

121 US Census Bureau (2023), *Historical Census of Housing Tables*, www2.census.gov/programs-surveys/decennial/tables/time-series/coh-ownershipbyrace/ownershipbyrace-tab.txt.

122 Federal Housing Finance Agency (May 25, 2010), *Report to Congress 2009*, 129 and 146.

123 Council of Economic Advisers (1999), *Annual Report*, 416.

housing, developing a robust affordable rental market was never a priority in America's credit- and consumption-led growth regime.

As supporting housing-based growth was one of President Clinton's main policy priorities, backers of the MID had little to fear. Some debate around the MID flared up in the mid-1990s when presidential hopeful Steven Forbes (Republican) revived the idea of a flat tax, simplified to the extent that all itemized deductions would be eliminated. Others suggested a less "pure" flat tax that would retain the MID. Yet all these proposals were quickly dismissed in Congress, and they were opposed by Clinton and the housing lobby. Policymakers in Congress were particularly concerned about the detrimental effects on economic growth and housing values. As Representative Michael Patrick Flanagan (Republican, Illinois) stated: "Real estate and housing comprise the engine that drives America's economy ... Eliminating, or further limiting, within the current Federal Tax Code, the home mortgage interest deduction will create a likelihood of a regional or national housing recession."[124] The Council of Economic Advisers also noted that the "result could be a sizable drop in housing values."[125] However, for Clinton and Congress, the priority was to stimulate housing-based growth and property values. The Taxpayer Relief Act of 1997 therefore not only preserved the MID but also expanded the capital gains exclusion on the sale of homes (Avramenko and Boyd 2013).

After the recession of the early 1990s, the financialized American growth regime was in full swing, and the American state helped support the rebound.[126] By the late 1990s, house prices were rising by an annual average of 6–7 percent, and mortgage debt had surged from 32 percent of GDP in 1970 to 56 percent by 1999 (see Figure 4.1). In the same period, outstanding residential mortgage debt increased more than tenfold: From USD 343 billion in 1970 to USD 5 *trillion* in 1999, with roughly half guaranteed by the GSEs (see Figure 4.3). Despite household wages stagnating or declining in real terms, private consumption as a share of the economy rose from 60 percent in 1970 to 65 percent in 1999 (see Figure 1.2). A key reason was that rising home values allowed homeowners to extract equity by refinancing mortgages or taking out home equity loans, which amounted to USD 420 billion in outstanding debt by 1997.[127]

124 Flanagan, P. (May 15, 1995), *Remarks in the House of Representatives, Congressional Record* 141(80), E1034.

125 Council of Economic Advisers (1996), *Annual Report*, 94.

126 Following the 1990–1991 recession, economic growth picked up and remained between 3 and 5 percent. Unemployment fell from 7–8 percent in the early 1990s to just 4 percent by 1999. Inflation remained relatively low, between 2 and 3 percent, while interest rates remained between 3 and 6 percent for most of the decade. Economic indicators from FRED, https://fred.stlo.uisfed.org.

127 Canner, G., Durkin, T., and Luckett, C. (April 1998), *Recent developments in home equity lending*, Federal Reserve Bulletin, 242, www.federalreserve.gov/pubs/bulletin/1998/199804lead.pdf.

TABLE 4.1 *American housing finance programs adopted or reformed between 1968 and 2000*

Type of program	Name of program/ agency	Years active	Description and changes
Tax	Mortgage interest deduction	1913–	The Tax Reform Act of 1986 kept the mortgage interest deduction but eliminated other personal interest deductions
Credit	Federal Savings and Loan Insurance Corporation (FSLIC)	1934–1989	The federal government bailed out the S&L sector and dissolved the insolvent FSLIC with the Financial Institutions Reform, Recovery and Enforcement Act of 1989
Credit	Federal National Mortgage Association (Fannie Mae)	1938–	The Housing and Urban Development Act of 1968 "privatized" Fannie, making it a government-sponsored enterprise tasked with issuing MBS
Credit	Government National Mortgage Association (Ginnie Mae)	1968–	Public agency created by the Housing and Urban Development Act of 1968 to provide insurance on MBS that consist of FHA/VA mortgages
Credit	Federal Home Loan Mortgage Corporation (Freddie Mac)	1970–	GSE created by Emergency Home Finance Act of 1970; tasked with issuing MBS and initially supporting the S&L industry
Credit	Section 235 homeownership program	1968–1987	Program terminated due to predatory lending, fraud, and mismanagement
Credit	Community Reinvestment Act	1977–	Increased bank and mortgage lending in low-income communities; expanded by executive action in 1995
Credit	GSE affordable housing goals	1968–	Requires GSEs to finance mortgages of lower-income households; expanded by the Federal Housing Enterprises Financial Safety and Soundness Act of 1992; expanded again by the Clinton administration
Central bank	GSE bond buying program	1966–2000	A 1966 change to the Federal Reserve Act allowed the Fed to buy GSE bonds; the Fed held GSE bonds between 1971 and 2000

CONCLUSION

When America's growth regime and housing market experienced post-Keynesian challenges, US policymakers expanded housing programs to reinforce housing-based growth (see Table 4.1). These transformative actions not only cemented the status of housing finance as a national champion but also profoundly shaped future political actions in the American political economy. Policymakers established a market for mortgage-backed securities, which has relied on government support for its functioning and survival. The quasi-public agencies – Fannie, Freddie, and Ginnie – not only rose to the center of the US mortgage market but also became powerful lobbyists themselves, defending the very system from which they benefited. Moreover, policymakers had even stronger incentives to protect homeowners' property values, as rising home prices meant leverage for consumer spending in the post-1970s context of declining wages and public welfare. In America's increasingly credit-dominated economy, property ownership was a form of "economic citizenship" – the "rights over economic resources that are conferred by membership in a given society" (Krippner 2017, 7) – granting owners privileged access to credit as wages stagnated and welfare programs declined. As a result, political actions that could have disrupted housing values, such as reforming the MID, were seen as direct attacks on America's demand-led economy and the wealth and welfare of existing homeowners at the center of the model.

By the late 1990s, America's credit- and consumption-driven growth regime depended increasingly on a virtuous circle of expanding house prices, credit, and consumption, which could sustain prosperity for many years. As Raghuram Rajan (2010, 31) notes: "Politicians love to have banks expand housing credit, for credit achieves many goals at the same time. It pushes up house prices, making households feel wealthier, and allows them to finance more consumption. It creates more profits and jobs in the financial sector as well as in real estate brokerage and housing construction." However, this growth strategy was risky and eventually turned vicious. The risks to housing-based, credit-led growth became brutally clear in 2008, when falling house prices and foreclosures unleashed a wave of negative cascade effects that reverberated throughout the American and global economy. In contrast, German policymakers not only avoided the path of housing financialization but even *withdrew* government support for housing in response to post-Keynesian challenges. Chapter 5 details why.

5

Path Shifting of German Housing Programs

By the mid-1970s, for the first time since 1914, Germany's housing market was no longer suffering large-scale national supply shortages. Despite some regional shortages in metropolitan and industrial hotspots, politicians soon started celebrating a "housing situation ... as good as never before. At no point in time could renters and homebuyers choose from such a differentiated and extensive supply as today."[1] At the same time, Germany's postwar economic miracle of sustained and strong economic growth came to an end. From the mid-1970s to the early 1980s, the country experienced economic recessions, rising unemployment, stubborn inflation, and increasing public debt. The sufficient housing supply also meant that demand for new homes plummeted compared to earlier periods, leading to a prolonged construction slump that reinforced the country's economic problems. As Chapter 4 has shown, American policymakers met such post-Keynesian challenges with additional demand-side housing programs that turned American homes into credit cards for consumer spending. In contrast, German policymakers began *withdrawing* housing programs in this period, particularly in the rental market. This chapter explains why.

While Germany's postwar housing programs *complemented* its export-oriented growth regime by establishing low-cost housing that helped to keep wages low and alleviate labor shortages, these programs reached a tipping point by the mid-1970s. From then on, policymakers increasingly perceived such programs as *contradicting* the growth regime. In times of sufficient housing supply, high inflation, and rising deficits, policymakers and economic elites began viewing these programs as structural economic problems rather than solutions. They criticized them for increasing deficits, diverting capital away

[1] Schneider, O. (November 27, 1986), *Remarks in the 10th Bundestag, 250th session*, 19523.

from manufacturing, and creating inflation in the country's export-oriented economy – which needed low inflation to thrive. These macroeconomic frictions between housing programs and the manufacturing-based, export-oriented economy started undermining the political support for these programs. As a result, policymakers reduced rental housing programs to a minimum by the late 1980s, marking the end of the postwar era of state dominance in German housing.

At the same time, however, German policymakers strengthened homeownership support, even though the country's economic elites and industries viewed such support as incongruent with the export-oriented growth regime. Like US President Reagan's 1986 tax reform, Chancellor Helmut Kohl's tax reform in the same year strengthened Germany's largest homeownership tax program. But unlike American politicians, German policymakers did not consider homeownership programs as a permanent housing-based growth strategy. They also did not financialize German homes or turn them into credit cards for consumer spending. Rather, they expanded homeownership programs to promote wealth creation, retirement planning, and family support. The decision to strengthen homeownership programs was remarkable given that key economic actors of the German growth regime – the Bundesbank, the Council of Economic Experts, and manufacturing firms – criticized these programs as poor macroeconomic policy contradicting the needs of the economy. For the time being, however, German politicians prioritized political factors and ignored macroeconomic critiques.

FADING ECONOMIC AND HOUSING MIRACLES

Germany's miracle years of strong economic growth came to an end in the 1970s.[2] The oil shocks of the mid-1970s and early 1980s exacerbated rising inflation and wage demands while also lowering demand for German products abroad (Hansen 2023). As a result, the German economy experienced two economic recessions, one in 1974–1975 and another in 1981–1982, resulting in growing unemployment and fiscal deficits.[3] The social-liberal government

[2] Germany's economic growth averaged 2.2% per year from 1973 to 1980, a number slightly higher than in the US (2.1%) and the UK (0.9%). From 1980 to 1989, it averaged 1.9% per year, which was lower than in the US (3%) and the UK (2.7%). See Giersch et al. (1992, 4).

[3] Inflation had risen from 2% in 1970 to 8% by the mid-1970s, well below the double-digit rates in France, the US, and the UK during the same period. German inflation dropped back to 2% before the second oil shock of 1979, spiked to 8% in the early 1980s, and returned to 2% by the mid-1980s. The Schmidt government – and even partly the Bundesbank – were on a relatively expansionary course from 1974 to 1980, which stimulated domestic demand but ultimately also contributed to rising inflation in the late 1970s (Giersch et al. 1992, 190). As a result, Germany experienced an unusual current account deficit between 1979 and 1981 (Giersch et al. 1992, 13). See Bundesbank (October 12, 2012), *Inflation – Lessons Learned from History*, www.bundesbank.de/en/tasks/topics/inflation-lessons-learnt-from-history-666006.

led by Chancellor Helmut Schmidt (SPD-FDP, 1974–1982) responded to the first recession of 1974–1975 with countercyclical measures to boost aggregate demand, mirroring the Kiesinger government's (CDU-SPD, 1966–1969) response to the 1966–1967 recession. However, this time the recovery was slow, and unemployment remained high (Scharpf 1991, 141). By the time of the second recession in the early 1980s, the Schmidt government had changed course and adopted a more traditional German-style approach of tight fiscal policy to limit public debt (Allen 1989; Giersch et al. 1992, 192; Manow 2020; Bökenkamp 2010, 118; Abelshauer 2011; Manow and Seils 2000). While the Bundesbank brought inflation under control with tight monetary policy during both recessions – with new monetary autonomy it had gained under floating exchange rates after the collapse of the Bretton Woods monetary system in 1973 (Mertens 2015, 222; Krampf 2019; Höpner 2019) – unemployment kept rising along with budget deficits.[4]

Despite this economic turbulence, the German economy adjusted relatively well to the post-Keynesian era. Instead of pursuing the American approach of financializing its economy to stimulate growth through private credit and consumption, German policymakers reinforced the manufacturing-based, export-oriented growth regime (Abelshauser 2011, 305; Germann 2014, 708; Kohl and Spielau 2022; Streeck 2009).[5] This adaptation came without great difficulty, as the German economy had – with the above-mentioned Keynesian exceptions – already lived by the principles that were now promoted in the dawning monetarist era: Price stability, wage restraint, austerity, and integration in world markets (Gourevitch 1986, 205; Hall 1986, 237). As Julian Germann (2014, 712) notes about the 1970s, "[i]n Germany, the fight against inflation had served to maintain the comparative advantage of the export economy and thus commanded the support of dominant capital as well as the associated trade unions." Economic growth still averaged around 2 percent per year and exports remained competitive throughout the 1970s and 1980s, making the German economy look like "an island of stability" (Kreile 1977, 775).[6] During this period, the share of exports as a percentage of GDP increased from 15 percent in 1970 to 22 percent in 1989, compensating for the declining wage share of the economy.[7]

4 Unemployment rose from 1.2% in 1973 to 4.7% in 1975 and over 9% in the mid-1980s. Public debt more than doubled from only 20% of GDP in the early 1970s to 42% in the late 1980s. See Federal Statistics Office (Destatis) (2024), *Konjunkturindikatoren: Arbeitslosenquote*; Bundesbank (1997), *Monatsbericht März 1997*, 18.

5 Abelshauser (2011, 311) shows that manufacturing constituted 41% of Germany's GDP in 1980 compared to 33% in the US.

6 Real unit labor costs decreased by an average of 0.5% per year from 1974 to 1980 and then decreased by an annual average of 1% from 1980 to 1989 (Giersch et al 1992, 211).

7 Germany's wage share of the economy decreased from around 72% of GDP in the mid-1970s to around 67% in the late 1980s (Baccaro and Pontusson 2016, 185). Private consumption as a share of GDP averaged 56% between 1970 and 1989 (compared to 62% in the US; see Figure 1.2).

In the mid-1970s, for the first time in 60 years, the housing market was approaching a balance of demand and supply, with the aggregate number of households matching the number of available housing units (Kramper 2008, 471).[8] While regional imbalances persisted – shortages in industrial areas and vacancies in deprived regions – policymakers began celebrating a balanced housing market. At the peak of the construction boom in 1973, new housing construction reached an all-time high of more than 700,000 units, which significantly improved the country's housing supply (see Figure 3.1). Yet the boom crashed against the rocks of rising inflation and interest rates, spurred by global oil shocks. The sector's emerging structural crisis was compounded by the fact that housing supply no longer needed to increase as rapidly as in previous years. The halt in guest worker migration reduced housing demand – unemployment, rather than labor shortages, became the issue. In addition, population growth slowed, partly due to falling fertility rates. The result was that demand for new housing plummeted from the mid-1970s, leading to gradually decreasing construction.[9] The following sections of this chapter detail how German policymakers dealt with these structural economic changes in the country's housing market.

THE DOG THAT DID NOT BARK: THE NONFINANCIALIZATION OF GERMAN HOUSING

When the German economy experienced post-Keynesian challenges, including a drop in housing demand, policymakers did not financialize housing (van Gunten and Navot 2018). Unlike their American counterparts, German policymakers did not deregulate or liberalize mortgages markets to stimulate mortgage lending, attract capital to housing, or generate private consumption through wealth or credit effects. They also did not establish American-style government guarantees in the secondary mortgage market to channel more capital into housing. With the notable exception of Chancellor Kohl's temporary mortgage interest deductions – which I discuss later in this chapter and also in Chapter 7 – German policymakers eschewed a path of housing financialization. Rather, they strengthened a conservative, stability-oriented housing finance system with strong complementarities to the German export-oriented growth regime.

While the German home lending system did undergo significant changes from the 1970s onward, it retained its stable and conservative nature. In the

[8] The Council of Economic Experts estimated a surplus of 200,000 housing units in 1975. See Sachverständigenrat für Wirtschaft (1975), *Jahresgutachten 1975/1976*, 198.

[9] As Axel Börsch-Supan (1994, 122) reminds us, population growth does not translate perfectly into housing demand, as demand can also rise with decreasing household size, produced by the growing number of single households of elderly or unmarried people. Germany's average household size decreased from 2.7 people 1970 to 2.3 in 1991. See Bundesinstitut für Bevölkerungsforschung (2022), *Zahl der Privathaushalte und durchschnittliche Haushaltsgröße in Deutschland (1871–2022)*, www.bib.bund.de/Permalink.html?cms_permaid=1217882.

primary mortgage market, private actors, rather than the government, drove the most important changes. Beginning in the 1970s, when inflation and rising interest rates strained the housing finance market, commercial banks collaborated with mortgage banks to offer mortgage products "out of one hand" for consumers (Köpfler 1996, 631).[10] Consumers no longer needed to take out two mortgages to finance a home; they could increasingly obtain financing from a single bank, which typically covered up to 70–80 percent of the home value and was paired with a 20–30 percent down payment (Kofner 2004, 65). As commercial banks entered the field of primary mortgages, their share of mortgage lending increased relative to other financial institutions (Wijburg and Aalbers 2017).[11] Despite these structural changes, the German mortgage market retained its deposit-based, conservative structure characterized by high down payments, long durations of mortgage terms of between twenty-five and thirty years, and a fixed interest rate for five to ten years (Voigtländer 2014; Kofner 2004; Wiedemann 2021).

In contrast to American policymakers, German politicians did not reduce down payments for homebuyers to stimulate mortgage lending. When Christian Democrats proposed a modest down-payment subsidy for the lower middle class in the mid-1970s – a small interest-free loan to support down payments – the proposal was quickly shut down. The governing Social Democrats considered the proposal too costly for both the federal and state governments. Even parts of the property lobby opposed the proposal: The German Association for People's Settlement Homes (Deutsches Volksheimstättenwerk) viewed it as too administratively burdensome, while the *Bausparkassen* considered it too "far-reaching" to grant homeowners a right to such a subsidized loan.[12] Rather, German banks focused on private solutions to attract mortgage borrowers.

Unlike American politicians, German policymakers also did not offer government support to stimulate the country's secondary mortgage market of covered bonds (*Pfandbriefe*). When the German covered bond market faced rising inflation and interest rates during the 1970s, mortgage banks developed private solutions by shortening the duration of covered bonds. Historically, covered bonds matured after thirty to forty years and had fixed interest rates. However, during the inflationary 1970s, investors preferred short-term investments with higher returns.[13] As a result, mortgage banks shortened

[10] "Baufinanzierung aus einer Hand – Ohne Ärger ans Geld" (April 23, 1971), *Die Zeit*.

[11] The market share of commercial banks in mortgage lending increased from only 5% in 1970 to over 10% in 1985, compared to 17% for *Bausparkassen*, 30% for *Sparkassen*, and 12% for *Hypothekenbanken* in 1985. "Wohnungsbaufinanzierung wiederentdeckt" (1999), *Der Langfristige Kredit*, 50(10), 4.

[12] Batz, H., (April 10, 1975), *Remarks in the 7th Bundestag, 162nd session*, 11369.

[13] Owning a long-term bond with a fixed interest rate becomes less attractive in times of high inflation, as market interest rates can exceed interest rates on these bonds, thus leading to a lower price of the bond.

the duration of covered bonds to below ten years and increased the interest earned on them (Köpfler 1996, 633; Sattler 2019, 203–205).

This is not to suggest that German policymakers did not intervene in mortgage banking at all – they did. From 1974, the Schmidt government allowed mortgage banks both to expand their business activities abroad and to assume a greater role in issuing government debt obligations (Sattler 2019, 190). This intervention was necessary as the era of large-scale postwar rental constructions, funded by mortgage banks, had come to an end. Mortgage banks then shifted their focus to other areas of finance, increasingly lending to the government, commercial real estate, and homeowners.[14] However, the conservative nature of the covered bond remained relatively unchanged. In fact, mortgage banks preferred it that way, as their chief lobbyist warned of "luring the population into over-indebtedness" in 1978 (quoted in Sattler 2019, 195).

Finally, it is difficult to find any evidence of housing-related wealth or credit effects in Germany (Mertens 2015, 325). Chapter 4 detailed how the US Federal Reserve discovered such effects in the 1970s, as American homeowners increasingly capitalized on rising property values by taking out debt against their homes for consumer spending. Yet the Bundesbank found no similar effects in Germany despite rising house prices during the 1970s. German banks did not offer home equity loans, nor did policymakers push for such instruments. In other words, even when German homeowners experienced rising house prices, they had little way of capitalizing these gains except by selling their homes. Even then, comparatively high transaction costs – such as notary costs, land registry fees, and property transfer taxes – made selling property in Germany less attractive compared to the United States. In fact, economists have found that German households tend to increase *savings* for down payments – rather than spending – when house prices rise (Geiger et al. 2016; Muellbauer 2018, 25). This may partly explain why the German savings rate kept climbing from around 11 percent of disposable household income in 1968 to around 13 percent throughout the 1970s and 1980s (Mertens 2015, 139 and 163), while the US savings rate was only around 8 percent in the late 1980s.

Although Germany experienced a major housing downturn during the 1970s and 1980s, it avoided a full-blown housing-related *financial* crisis such as the American S&L crisis of the 1980s. As John Muellbauer (1992, 544) observed, the conservative housing finance structure is why "Germany is much less prone to speculative fever in its housing markets." Rather, Germany experienced more contained *sectoral* construction crises driven by plummeting demand. Moreover, the conservative and stability-oriented

[14] In 1988, the Kohl government further broadened the mortgage banks' authority to issue second mortgages (*nachrangige Hypotheken*) to homeowners and rental investors (Sattler 2019, 216–217).

German mortgage market has shown a great deal of complementarity with the export-oriented growth regime (Mertens 2015). High savings and restrictive mortgage credit limit domestic demand, which in turn benefits export-oriented industries through lower inflation. Yet, as the next sections of this chapter show, not all housing policy efforts were congruent with Germany's growth regime in this period.

TIPPING POINTS: HOUSING PROGRAMS BETWEEN COMPLEMENTARITIES AND CONTRADICTIONS

Even though housing shortages had been continuously reduced in the postwar decades, they were not yet fully remedied by the late 1960s. As a result, German policymakers continued to strengthen social housing programs as supply-side tools to stimulate new housing construction, despite intensifying inflationary pressures in the construction sector that had started in the early 1960s. As noted in Chapter 3, in the immediate postwar period, such programs had produced massive macroeconomic benefits for Germany's industrial, export-oriented economy by helping to reduce housing and labor shortages and keeping wages and the cost of living down. However, 1973 marked a turning point. As supply shortages waned, policymakers and economic elites no longer viewed housing programs as solutions to macroeconomic problems but increasingly as macroeconomic problems themselves, adding inflationary pressure to an overheating housing sector in an export-oriented economy that required low inflation to thrive.

Like previous postwar German governments, the social-liberal government led by Chancellor Willy Brandt (SPD-FDP, 1969–1974) strengthened social housing programs to address the remaining housing shortages (Kramper 2008, 448). By the late 1960s, the housing shortage had shrunk to about half a million homes but still affected 1.5 million people who lived in poor housing conditions, such as in temporary housing structures or dilapidated buildings.[15] Strong labor migration of guest workers created additional housing demand in metropolitan areas.[16] As then housing minister Lauritz Lauritzen (SPD) noted: "[I]n the cities and metropolitan regions ... there is always the need for new housing because of internal migration and the immigration of foreign workers, which needs to be met."[17] In response, limited-profit housing associations and labor unions demanded more social housing to counter "speculative rent increases" (quoted in Kramper 2008, 447). The Brandt government strengthened social housing programs by adding regional, social, and modernization components to them.[18] The regional component provided additional funding for economically depressed regions with housing shortages, the social

[15] "Wohnungsfragen im Bundestag" (1970), *Bundesbaublatt*, 19(5), 250.

[16] The net migration surplus was 547,000 in 1970, 382,000 in 1971, 283,000 in 1972, and 352,000 in 1973. See Destatis (2024), *Wanderungen*.

[17] Lauritzen, L. (May 5, 1971), *Remarks in the 6th Bundestag, 118th session*, 6901.

[18] Lauritzen, L. (1971), "Das Wohnungsbauänderungsgesetz," *Bundesbaublatt*, 20(5), 211–214.

program targeted low-income households,[19] and the modernization program provided funding for renovating the existing and aging housing stock. The overall goal was to increase the number of new social housing units to above 200,000 per year – half of what had been subsidized in earlier decades but still high given skyrocketing construction prices (and high by today's standard of less than 30,000 new social housing units per year).[20] In total, the Brandt government subsidized 540,000 new social housing units between 1970 and 1972, including 168,000 owner-occupied units.

Brandt also tightened rent controls to keep down the cost of living and appease labor unions' wage demands. After previous CDU-led governments had successively liberalized rent controls throughout the 1960s, the Brandt government tightened rent controls to curb rising housing costs in expensive, high-demand regions (Leutner 1990, 331). A 1971 law prohibited landlords from canceling rental contracts for the purpose of re-renting homes to generate higher rents, strengthening renters' protections against evictions. It also prohibited landlords from increasing rents much above the local rental price index.[21] Labor unions and renter associations supported these measures; they had even demanded freezing rental prices.[22] In short, policymakers adopted these measures in the spirit of earlier generations of postwar German housing policy: To deflate housing costs for households and to increase supply. Until 1973, it was business as usual.

However, the German housing market reached a tipping point in 1973. While booming housing construction in the early 1970s helped to reduce the remaining housing shortages, it also produced skyrocketing construction and land prices due to labor shortages, capacity problems, scarce land, and wage increases in construction. Even though the Bundesbank increased interest rates in 1972, builders, investors, and households continued to rush into the property market to anticipate even higher prices and interest rates in the future. Property became known as concrete gold (*Betongold*), a way to hedge against inflation (Köpfler 1996, 632).[23] To tame inflation, from mid-1973 until early 1974, the Brandt government temporarily *suspended* the

[19] The social program included DM 150 million per year in federal funding to complement existing social housing programs and an additional DM 250 million per year to secure affordable rental housing for low-income households. The Brandt government increased the household income limit for these social housing programs by 40 percent to target households that would not qualify for social housing but that also could not afford to rent or buy in the private market.

[20] In the 1970s, the Brandt government also strengthened the "housing assistance program," originally adopted in 1965. It offered direct financial assistance to low-income renters (*Wohngeld*) and homeowners (*Lastenzuschuss*) struggling to pay their rent or mortgages. In 1979, the program benefited 1.5 million individuals (predominantly renters). See Statistisches Bundesamt (1982), *Wirtschaft und Statistik 8/1981*, 555.

[21] The Schmidt government then made these measures permanent in its 1974 rental protection reform.

[22] "Stimmen zur Mietenfrage" (1970), *Bundesbaublatt*, 19(8), 347.

[23] Sachverständigenrat für Wirtschaft (1971), *Jahresgutachten 1971/1972*, 22.

homeownership tax allowance (i.e., paragraph 7b of the tax code) to reduce housing demand and construction (Borgaes and Koopmann 1978, 394). Despite these deflationary measures, Germany built over 700,000 homes in 1973, a record that remains unbroken.

During the housing boom of the early 1970s, economic elites increasingly viewed housing programs as a macroeconomic problem, fueling inflationary land and construction prices (cp. Kramper 2008, 449; Führer 2015, 334). The Bundesbank diagnosed that the housing sector had "for years cultivated the inflation bacillus through strong excess demand."[24] It identified housing programs, including social housing programs, as factors that contributed to this excess demand.[25] The Council of Economic Experts criticized housing tax programs for contributing to "inflationary demand" and argued that resources allocated to housing could have been more productively utilized in other areas of the economy.[26] The Council also warned that rising construction and housing costs could undermine public trust in the functioning of the country's market economy.[27]

Like in the United States, exploding property prices at the time were also driven by strict land-use policy. In both countries, making land available for new housing was met with political difficulties, albeit different ones. From the 1970s, as described in Chapter 4, local US politicians in charge of zoning and land-use regulation increasingly catered to the interests of homeowners and other NIMBYs who opposed new housing development. In Germany, the land-use system involves all levels of government in an interlocked fashion: The federal government provides the general legal framework and planning goals, the *Länder* designate areas of possible development and set regional planning goals, and local communities make decisions about selling land to developers subject to review by higher levels of government (Von Einem 1982; Light 1999). While NIMBYs also protested new housing developments in Germany, the larger political obstacle was local governments' concerns about costs. They feared that property tax revenue from new homes would not be enough to offset the associated costs of building infrastructure, such as streets, schools, hospitals, and parks (Biedenkopf and Miegel 1978, 99–100). In the United States, by contrast, such costs are often privatized (McKenzie 1994). Due to these supply-side factors paired with strong housing demand, from 1962 to 1972, nominal land prices in Germany increased by an average of 100 to 200 percent in smaller towns and 300 percent in large cities, even by 700 percent in Hamburg and 2,900 percent in Munich's inner city – a development that all German parties bemoaned as resulting from "speculative behavior" of making profits on land merely by hoarding (Führer 2015, 58–60 and 85). Yet German parties could not agree on how to tax such profits.

[24] Bundesbank (1973), *Monatsbericht: Dezember 1973*, 5.
[25] Bundesbank (1972), *Geschäftsbericht 1971*, 6.
[26] Sachverständigenrat für Wirtschaft (1975), *Jahresgutachten 1975/1976*, 7.
[27] Sachverständigenrat für Wirtschaft (1970), *Jahresgutachten 1970/1971*, 30.

Germany's housing boom of the early 1970s turned into a bust when the country experienced a recession in 1974, partly produced by the first oil shock a year earlier. Early during the housing downturn, the new social-liberal Schmidt government (SPD-FDP, 1974–1982), believing it could manage the economy through planning, adopted stimulus programs in the amount of DM 13 billion to counter the 1974–1975 recession and soften the blow for the housing market. The programs provided some temporary funding for urban renewal and modernization projects to mitigate the construction crisis.[28] As one of these measures, in 1975, the Schmidt government temporarily offered subsidized mortgages for savers in building societies (*Bausparzwischenfinanzierung*) to stimulate owner-occupied home construction (DM 300 million).[29] However, these measures could not stop plummeting construction: New home construction nearly halved from 715,000 units built in 1973 to just 390,000 in 1976. Similarly, the number of newly approved social housing units dropped from 200,000 in 1971 to roughly 110,000 in 1977, partly because the construction of social housing became much costlier.[30]

The mid-1970s thus marked a turning point for German housing programs. Despite the problems in the construction sector, between 1970 and 1976, the government still helped build 1.1 million new social housing units (out of a total of 3.85 million new homes), providing low-cost housing for hundreds of thousands of households. However, influential economic elites started to criticize the role of housing programs in fueling inflation and fiscal deficits at a time when housing shortages were no longer a national issue (Biedenkopf and Miegel 1978, 12). Postwar housing programs were increasingly seen not as complementary but as contradictory to the needs of the German economy. As the next section shows, policymakers gradually turned their backs on large-scale rental housing programs in favor of homeownership initiatives.

BEYOND SHORTAGES: THE SPD'S FRAUGHT HOMEOWNERSHIP PUSH

The housing market remained the "problem child" (*Sorgenkind*) of the German economy throughout the latter half of the 1970s and the early 1980s.[31] Inflation drove up construction costs and interest rates. The improved

[28] In 1975, the DGB demanded a new five-year social housing construction program (Kramper 2008, 478). Yet a housing surplus paired with budget constraints made it politically difficult to expand large-scale rental housing programs.

[29] Bundesbank (1976), *Geschäftsbericht 1975*, 21; also see Gaul, C.-M. (2008), *Konjunkturprogramme in der Geschichte der Bundesrepublik Deutschland* (WD 5-3010-009/09), Wissenschaftlicher Dienst, Bundestag.

[30] Stadler, O. (1975), "Die Situation der Wohnungswirtschaft," *Der Langfristige Kredit* 25(19), 604–605.

[31] "Wohnungs- und Städtebau als Schwerpunktaufgabe" (1977), *Bundesbaublatt*, 26(1), 1.

housing supply, paired with a stagnant population, meant that the country's construction sector could no longer sustain the high levels of housing construction seen during the postwar years. As a result, housing construction was in freefall. Chancellor Schmidt did not ignore the continued construction debacle, especially given growing unemployment in the sector, and thus adopted additional temporary stimulus measures to slow down the decline of housing construction. Moreover, as producing large-scale rental housing was no longer viable with sufficient housing supply, the Social Democrats turned to subsidizing homeownership. The push toward supporting homeownership, however, created its own set of frictions with the country's growth regime, which this section will detail.

As the longstanding priority of establishing sufficient housing supply was within sight, the Schmidt government attempted to transform social housing programs into vehicles to promote homeownership. In a 1976 reform, the government improved homeownership funding as part of social housing programs and, after long legislative battles with the Bundesrat (Germany's upper parliamentary house), convinced the *Länder* to give preference to owner-occupied units over rental units wherever possible.[32] The Social Democrats thus took a cue from the Christian Democrats, who had for decades made similar attempts to boost homeownership through social housing programs.

For the Social Democrats, promoting homeownership became good middle-class politics of wealth creation and family support, as the macroeconomic need for building new housing declined. They believed the goal of adequate housing for the working and lower-middle classes was largely complete. They also made "filtering" arguments, suggesting that homeownership for the rich would free up high-quality rental units for the poor. According to a Social Democrat in the Bundestag, the social housing programs' historical rental focus reflected "what the housing needs were in past years and decades." However, now that housing shortages had been remedied, it was considered a good time to privilege homeownership.[33] The Christian Democrats were quick to declare victory: "That this was possible is due to the CDU/CSU, which consistently took this position... Our goal is not just a home for everyone, but each their own home."[34] Out of 550,000 total social housing units built between 1977 and 1981, the majority (315,000 units) were owner-occupied homes, as Figure 5.1 shows. Even so, the aggregate number of social housing

[32] The reform also lowered the down-payment requirement for lower-middle-class homeowners to 10 percent (see *Gesetz zur Förderung von Wohnungseigentum und Wohnbesitz im sozialen Wohnungsbau*). The Bundesrat succeeded in keeping social housing funding quotas for the proportion of homeowner and rental units relatively flexible, as they argued that "inflexible" quotas would contradict their regional economic needs: Some states did not have much demand for owner-occupied housing and should thus retain the flexibility to fund rental housing.

[33] Waltemathe, E. (April 10, 1975), *Remarks in the 7th Bundestag, 162nd session*, 11362.

[34] Jahn, F. A. (April 10, 1975), *Remarks in the 7th Bundestag, 162nd session*, 11345–11346.

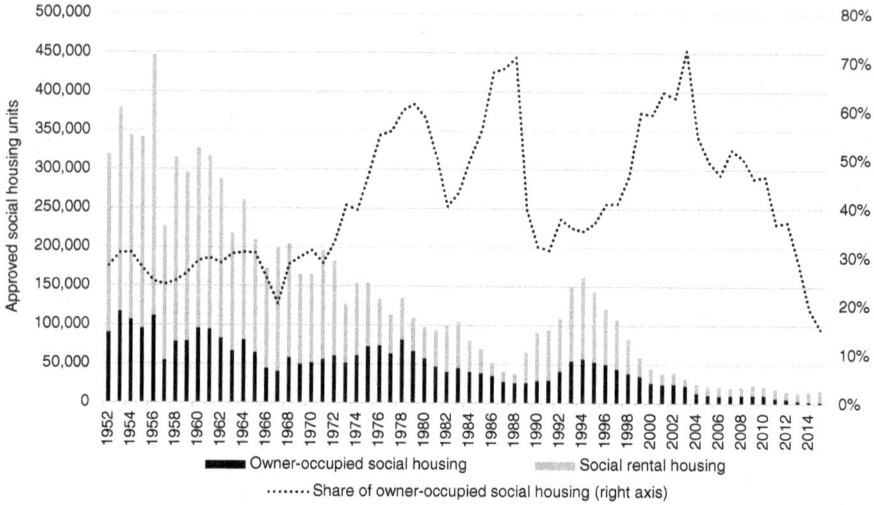

FIGURE 5.1 Rental and owner-occupied housing units approved for construction as part of social housing programs in Germany, 1950–2015
Data sources: Annual social housing reports in *Bundesbaublatt* through 2003; German Federal Statistics Office (annual social housing funding statistics) between 2004 and 2006; Bundesregierung, *Sozialer Wohnungsbau in Deutschland – Entwicklung, Bestand, Perspektive* (BT-18/8855) between 2007 and 2015.

units gradually declined in the context of falling housing demand, dropping to below 100,000 units in 1980 for the first time in postwar history.

In the tax area, the Schmidt government also strengthened subsidies for homeowners despite growing fiscal pressures to consolidate the budget. As noted in Chapter 3, the homeownership tax allowance (i.e., paragraph 7b in the tax code) had existed since 1949 to increase the country's housing supply. Once that goal was achieved, the Schmidt government transformed it from a *supply-side* policy subsidizing new home construction into a *demand-side* policy that also supported the purchase of older homes. The shift came with a 1977 reform that extended the tax allowance to include the purchase of *older* homes; previously, it had applied only to building or purchasing new homes. The reform aimed to appeal to urban constituents and to spur investment in the existing housing stock that often needed renovations (Borgaes and Koopman 1978, 395; Führer 2015, 219).[35] Many people in urban areas had not benefited from the tax break because they could not afford to build or buy new homes in metropolitan areas, where land was scarce and expensive. To accompany the expanded homeownership tax allowance for older homes, the Schmidt government also allowed for property transfer tax exemptions – at the

[35] Bundesregierung (February 8, 1979), *Bericht der Bundesregierung über Möglichkeiten zur Umstellung des §7b EStG auf ein anderes Förderungssystem* (8/2554) [report].

time set at 7 percent – for homeowners purchasing older homes.[36] Property transfer taxes were already exempt for many homeowners buying or building new homes, especially if they were financed with social housing funds.[37] The Council of Economic Experts called the reformed homeownership tax allowance "questionable" and proposed ways to scale it down to limit fiscal deficits that had exploded in the 1970s. More fundamentally, the council did *not* consider the homeownership tax allowance as key "expenditures that generate economic growth" nor as a program to "remedy structural economic weakness to make possible more production and employment."[38] On the contrary, the council considered these to be poor macroeconomic policy choices.

In 1977 and 1978, the Schmidt government initiated two more stimulus packages amounting to roughly DM 30 billion to promote economic recovery. The program provided funding for urban renewal, home modernization, and homeownership (Bökenkamp 2010, 112–117; Manow and Seils 2000). While the program helped stabilize housing construction in 1977, it also contributed to rising housing construction prices, which increased by 40 percent between 1976 and 1981, partly owing to persistent capacity problems in the construction sector.[39] Once again, the Council of Economic Experts criticized the government's role in stimulating housing for being inflationary and sending the "wrong signals"; it argued that price increases in the construction sector could have been slowed with less publicly supported construction.[40]

Against the opposition of the country's economic elites, the Schmidt government made homeownership programs even more generous in response to the 1980–1981 recession. At that point, Schmidt faced exploding fiscal deficits and public debt, making it difficult to justify large-scale stimulus.[41] While his government did not adopt another major stimulus package, it expanded the homeownership tax allowance (i.e., paragraph 7b in the tax code) by adding a subsidy for homeowners with children in 1981.[42] The Council of Economic Experts criticized this family-oriented initiative as part of the homeownership tax allowance for

36 Bundesregierung (February 2, 1979), *Grunderwerbsteuerbericht* (8/2555) [report], Bundestag.

37 Property transfer tax exemptions were eliminated in 1983, with the tax set at 2 percent that year and increasing to 3.5 percent by the late 1990s. From the mid-2000s, the *Länder* gained authority to set their own transfer tax rates.

38 Sachverständigenrat für Wirtschaft (1980), *Jahresgutachten 1980/1981*, 155–159.

39 "Vierteljahresdaten" (1983), *Bundesbaublatt*, 35(2), 117.

40 Sachverständigenrat für Wirtschaft (1979), *Jahresgutachten 1979/1980*, 49.

41 In a minor reform in 1980 (*Wohnungsbauänderungsgesetz*), the Schmidt government liberalized the social housing rental sector by allowing rental investors to prematurely pay back their public loans, at which time their rental property would not have to adhere to social housing standards any longer.

42 Homeowners received a tax credit per child and year after the first child for as long as they could claim the 7b tax break (*Zweites Gesetz zur Verbesserung der Haushaltsstruktur 1981*).

increasing budget deficits and for adding complexity to the tax system.[43] Parts of the German industry labeled the expansion "superfluous," as owner-occupied housing was booming regardless of the subsidy.[44] Yet the Schmidt government felt that a child subsidy was necessary, as families with children often could not afford to buy or build houses, particularly given mortgage rates of over 10 percent at the time. From then on, homeowners with children could combine the regular homeownership tax allowance (i.e., paragraph 7b) with a new child tax credit, resulting in higher tax benefits for families with children. Together, the homeownership tax allowance and the new child allowance amounted to DM 5 billion in 1982, making it one of Germany's largest tax subsidies.[45]

In sum, even against the warnings of influential economic elites, the Social Democrats strengthened homeownership programs in the late 1970s and early 1980s. The country's much-improved housing supply facilitated the SPD's homeownership push, a move the CDU celebrated (Jaedicke and Wollmann 1991). As sufficient rental housing supply meant that the amount an average household paid on rent *fell* from 12.3 percent of disposable income in 1970 to 11.8 percent in 1981 (Führer 2015, 325), the social-liberal Schmidt government prioritized homeownership. In doing so, it pursued a wide range of goals, including promoting homeownership as a tool for family support, urban development, wealth creation, and retirement planning, while also stabilizing the reeling construction sector. For the time being, both the Social Democrats and the Christian Democrats ignored the warnings of economic elites about the inflationary *demand*-side effects of homeownership programs.

KOHL'S HOUSING PROGRAMS: HOMEOWNERSHIP IDEOLOGY MEETS GROWTH REGIME

When Chancellor Helmut Kohl took office in 1982, he entered with an economic agenda focused on austerity and supply-side policies. However, he started his term by temporarily experimenting with a *demand-side* approach of stimulating homeownership and housing markets through countercyclical fiscal measures. Kohl even established a temporary mortgage interest deduction to halt the steady decline in construction. For the Kohl government, stimulating homeownership offered two potential benefits: It could help the reeling construction industry and realize the CDU's ideological goal of raising homeownership. For a brief period, it seemed as if Germany could take an American demand-side housing turn. However,

[43] Sachverständigenrat für Wirtschaft (1980), *Jahresgutachten 1980/1981*, 159.

[44] Engelmann, R. (August 20, 1981), *Schreiben an DIHT Geschäftsstelle* [correspondence], Industrie- und Handelskammer Aschaffenburg, RWWA-181-1223-2; Deutscher Industrie- und Handelstag (DIHT) (November 13, 1981), *Kein Konzept gegen wohnungspolitische Krise* [press release], RWWA-181-1223-2.

[45] Bundesregierung (September 6, 1983), 9. *Subventionsbericht*, 238.

German policymakers allowed these programs, including the mortgage interest deduction, to expire just a few years later. The reason was that they considered these demand-side measures as *temporary* tools to soften the sectoral demand shock in the construction sector; they did not consider housing measures as permanent economic growth strategies. On the contrary, they understood they could not reverse the structural changes of falling housing demand and construction. As a report commissioned by German government noted, "housing programs for new construction are not suitable as a stimulative tool to overcome structural unemployment in the medium-term."[46] Moreover, the Bundesbank and the Council of Economic Experts harshly criticized Kohl's housing stimulus, which they viewed as counteracting the priorities of the low-inflation, cost-suppressing German growth regime.

The Kohl government (CDU-FDP, 1982–1998) came to office with grand plans of reining in government spending and reducing government debt. However, one of Kohl's first actions was to adopt a temporary housing *stimulus* program from 1982 to 1987, including generous homeownership support to stabilize employment in the reeling construction industry, which was suffering from high interest rates and the economic recession (Zohlnhöfer 2001; Muellbauer 1992, 541).[47] In 1982, the country had produced the lowest number of new housing units annually up to that point, amounting to only 350,000 new units that year (Bökenkamp 2010, 214; Manow and Seils 2000). As part of the stimulus package, the Kohl government adopted a temporary mortgage interest deduction between 1982 and 1987. The SPD opposed the deduction and advocated for a stronger focus on the rental market. In addition, Kohl also temporarily offered subsidized mortgages for savers in building societies (*Bausparzwischenfinanzierung*).[48] For the German export-oriented growth regime, such American-style temporary housing programs, aimed at stabilizing the reeling housing sector, were unusually demand-oriented (Zohlnhöfer 2001, 79).

For this reason, Kohl's temporary housing programs were subject to criticism for counteracting the priorities of the German growth regime. The Council of Economic Experts repeatedly found fault with these programs for (1) setting

[46] GEWOS-Kommission (1985, September), *Perspektiven der Wohnungsfinanzierung*, Ricardi Verlag, Frankfurt, 15, PA-DBT 4000 X/225.

[47] Schneider, O. (1982), "Wohnungsbau im Vordergrund," *Bundesbaublatt*, 30(11), 753.

[48] In an attempt to stimulate rental housing construction, the Kohl government also somewhat liberalized rent controls. Even after the reform, however, renters continued to enjoy strong rent controls: Landlords could increase rents by a maximum of 30 percent in three years and only up to the local rent (*ortsübliche Vergleichsmiete*), but the measure did raise the reference point for local rents (Führer 2015, 344–345). The German Tenants' Association (Deutscher Mieterbund) and the SPD opposed the Kohl rental reform that passed in December 1982. The latter cynically called it "Kohl's Christmas gift: 30 percent higher rents!" See SPD (December 12, 1982), *Zeitung am Sonntag* [campaign newspaper].

the wrong "price signals," (2) creating artificial demand, (3) channeling capital away from manufacturing, and (4) pushing up construction prices. It even called the existing battery of housing finance subsidies a "misery" for Germany's market economy.[49] The Bundesbank supported the Council's critique, arguing that past housing programs had contributed to an oversupply of housing, postponed inevitable structural adjustments in the housing sector, and contributed to "distorted prices" in the economy.[50] In short, the Council and Bundesbank considered these programs poor economic policy choices that did not serve the macroeconomic needs of the German economy. German industries also urged the Kohl government not to make the mortgage interest deduction permanent and to reduce housing-related tax subsidies to retain tax neutrality.[51] They also expressed the view that housing-based growth was not a viable growth strategy, as "urgently needed investments to stimulate growth are not primarily needed in housing construction, but rather to enhance the productivity and competitiveness of future-oriented jobs."[52] Finally, a 1983 report by the economics ministry emphasized the distorting role of housing programs in that "interventionist measures steered capital into the housing sector and thereby withdrew capital from other sectors," which would produce an inefficient allocation of resources and hurt the broader economy.[53] More generally, stimulating domestic demand via costly housing programs also contradicted Kohl's own priority of reducing fiscal deficits and public debt to boost competitiveness (Wullkopf 1982).

Temporary homeownership programs have often become permanent in the United States, illustrating the adage that nothing is so permanent as a temporary government program. In contrast, German policymakers eliminated the temporary mortgage interest deduction after just five years. The timing is striking, as it happened during the country's postwar construction trough, with only 250,000 units produced in 1986. In addition, the program was designed to create 100,000 jobs, yet the sector actually lost 50,000 jobs from 1982 to 1985.[54] Eliminating the US mortgage interest deduction might be near impossible in the best of economic times, but it is even more inconceivable during a housing downturn, as Chapter 6 will show. The reason why German policymakers provided only temporary sectoral support was to alleviate the demand shock to housing construction. They did

[49] Sachverständigenrat für Wirtschaft (1982), *Jahresgutachten 1982/1983*, 230.

[50] Bundesbank (1986), *Geschäftsbericht 1985*, 9; Bundesbank (1983), *Geschäftsbericht 1982*, 49.

[51] DIHT (December 23, 1983), *Schreiben an den Bundesminister für Finanzen* [correspondence], Bonn, RWWA-181-1226-3. If anything, German industries instead preferred housing programs to be implemented outside the tax code.

[52] Sabathil, G. (December 23, 1982), *Wohnungspolitik als Beschäftigungspolitik* [report], DIHT, RWWA-181-1223-1.

[53] Wissenschaftlicher Beirat des Bundeswirtschaftsministeriums (January 22–23, 1982), *Probleme der Wohnungswirtschaft* [report], Bonn, RWWA-181-1223-1.

[54] "Der Wohnungsmarkt ist gesättigt" (March 10, 1985), *Der Spiegel*.

not, however, institutionalize countercyclical tools as permanent measures, which they believed would only postpone structural changes in the economy. "Subsidized housing," a top housing ministry official wrote in *Die Zeit*, "has no macroeconomic policy [*wachstumspolitische*] priority" and could even "hinder growth" by channeling private capital and fiscal resources away from more growth-generating industries.[55] As housing minister Oscar Schneider (CSU) told *Der Spiegel* in 1985: "I cannot build just to employ masons. I can only build homes if there is demand for housing."[56] The realization was that temporary housing programs could not reverse the structural trend of declining housing demand and that reductions in the capacities of the construction industry were inevitable. American policymakers, in contrast, have viewed the mortgage interest deduction as part of a *permanent* and long-term growth strategy.

The expiration of Kohl's *temporary* housing programs sparked a broader debate about *permanent* ones, resulting in a major housing tax overhaul in 1986. Much like Reagan's 1986 tax reform, the German reform also strengthened the country's most important homeownership benefit: The longstanding homeownership tax allowance (paragraph 7b in the tax code).[57] The CDU provided at least two reasons for their continued support of the tax subsidy, even in the context of a balanced housing market.[58] None of these reasons, however, included stimulating the economy. The first reason was to raise the homeownership rate. The Kohl government's goal was to raise the country's homeownership rate from 39 to 50 percent (Stimpel 1990, 62). The second was to create wealth and old-age security, particularly for families with children.

[55] Pfeiffer, U. (October 22, 1982), "Ein Faß ohne Boden," *Die Zeit*.

[56] "Der Wohnungsmarkt ist gesättigt" (March 10, 1985), *Der Spiegel*.

[57] On an important technical note, the tax reform switched the country's way of taxing housing from the *investment good* to the *consumption good* model. Before 1987, the country's investment good model meant that homeowners had to pay tax on imputed rental income – the rental income a homeowner generates by living in one's own home (*Nutzungswertbesteuerung*) – and allowed them to claim a negligible mortgage interest deduction as an investment expense, although only up to the amount of the imputed rental income. In this context, the mortgage interest deduction was not considered a tax break (with the notable exception of offering a temporarily extended mortgage interest deduction from 1982 to 1987 as a separate housing program). In 1987, the country switched to the consumption good model by eliminating the tax on imputed rent and scrapping the negligible mortgage interest deduction. All major parties agreed that the consumption good model is preferable, given the administrative difficulties of measuring imputed rental income and the associated practice of under-taxing imputed rent that had rendered the tax inefficient. Indeed, the imputed rental income was based on 1964 property values (while the 1964 baseline was increased by 40 percent by the early 1980s, the baseline was still very much undervaluing property values) (Fecht 1983). Policymakers also viewed the tax on imputed rent as punitive because it would place debt-free elderly homeowners under unnecessary financial pressure. See Finanzauschuss (March 17, 1986), *Beschlußempfehlung und Bericht* (Drs. 10/5208) [report].

[58] Bundesminister der Finanzen (February 12, 1985), *Referentenentwurf eines Gesetzes zur Neuregelung der steuerlichen Förderung des selbstgenutzten Wohneigentums* [draft law], PA-DBT 4000 X/225.

As the parliamentary state secretary in the finance ministry Hansjörg Häfele (CDU) argued, homeownership would be the "fourth pillar of retirement and life savings – next to the general pension schemes, company pensions, and private savings … . At the same time, we want to strengthen families by focusing on instruments that especially support families."[59] Importantly, the CDU emphasized that the tax subsidy was not primarily meant to stimulate the economy. A CDU Bundestag member said that "the goal of this legislation is not to stimulate new construction of homes for macroeconomic reasons. The primary goal is to help as many families as possible to own their own homes."[60] In short, the CDU proposed to continue the homeownership tax allowance for political reasons but not for macroeconomic ones (Haas 2020).

However, Kohl's planned retention of the homeownership tax allowance presented several *macroeconomic problems*. The SPD was not against subsidizing homeownership altogether, as it too considered homeownership subsidies to be sound family and wealth policy. However, the SPD criticized the regressive nature of the homeownership tax allowance, which privileged high- over middle-income households. The Social Democrats therefore proposed a tax *credit* – not a deduction – that benefited every household equally.[61] Bundestag member Gunter Huonker (SPD) called the existing homeownership tax allowance "a perversion of justice."[62] Moreover, the SPD took issue with the subsidy's demand-side support for households that bought older homes – as opposed to subsidizing only newly built homes – which the party considered "macroeconomic waste."[63] They argued that such a policy would contribute to "price inflation" in the market for older homes.[64] The irony is that it was the center-left Schmidt government that had first allowed the subsidy to be used for buying older homes in 1977. Even the FDP, the CDU's coalition partner at the time, raised concerns about the policy's possible "price-inflating" effect for properties.[65]

German manufacturing industries opposed subsidizing homeownership through the tax code. In 1984, the Deutscher Industrie- und Handelstag (DIHT) called for a reduction in homeownership programs and social

59 Häfele, H. (September 12, 1985), *Remarks in the 10th Bundestag, 156th session*, 11666.

60 Daniels, H. (February 26, 1986), *Remarks in the 59th session of the committee for housing and urban development, 10th Bundestag*, PA-DBT 4000 X/225.

61 Müntefering, F. (SPD) (February 26, 1986), *Remarks in the 59th session of the committee for housing and urban development, 10th Bundestag*, PA-DBT 4000 X/225. The SPD-led North Rhine-Westphalia also proposed such a tax incentive.

62 Huonker, G. (March 29, 1985), *Remarks in the 10th Bundestag, 130th session*, 9646.

63 Reschke, O. (January 4, 1984), *Wohnunsgbauförderung ohne Grund und Boden*, SPD-Pressedienst, https://library.fes.de/spdpd/1984/840104.pdf.

64 Reschke, O. (February 26, 1986), *Remarks in the 59th session of the committee for housing and urban development, 10th Bundestag*, PA-DBT 4000 X/225.

65 Grünbeck, J. (January 29, 1986), *Remarks in the 56th session of the committee for housing and urban development, 10th Bundestag*, PA-DBT 4000 X/225.

housing programs (although they were generally less critical of the former compared to the latter), arguing that housing markets were balanced and large-scale shortages a thing of the past. They also warned that housing programs would lead to capital misallocations and steer capital into housing and away from industries.[66] In a 1985 statement, the group expressed concern that homeownership subsidies would limit labor mobility: "[S]trengthening homeownership programs raises psychological barriers to being willing to move across the country."[67] They were instead open to tax subsidies supporting the renovation of existing housing. The German Taxpayers' Federation (Bund der Steuerzahler) also opposed tax subsidies for homeownership, stating that "good housing market conditions and low expected long-term housing demand makes government policy to construct new housing unnecessary."[68] Similarly, the German Tenants' Association (Deutscher Mieterbund) opposed homeownership subsidies, lamenting the retreat of state support for the rental market. They argued that supporting homeownership, particularly the purchase of older apartments, would make the rental market more expensive and generate "housing speculation."[69] The German financial press warned of exploding fiscal costs and that the subsidy could "shoot up prices."[70] Of course, the property lobby – such as construction firms, realtors, *Bausparkassen*, property owners – all welcomed the tax subsidy.

Despite these macroeconomic concerns, the Kohl government strengthened homeownership tax support with its 1986 tax reform. The homeownership tax allowance survived, just under a different label (changing from "paragraph 7b" to "paragraph 10e" in the tax code).[71] During Reagan's tax reform of 1986, US policymakers were concerned that reforming homeowner tax breaks could deflate house prices and housing demand, threatening the country's demand-led growth regime. In Germany, policymakers retained the subsidy for different reasons: Family and wealth policy (Haas 2020). In passing the tax reforms, the Kohl government ignored the SPD's distributive concerns, which the CDU dismissed as being guided by envy,[72] and it also disregarded the macroeconomic concerns of influential German industrial leaders and economists

66 DIHT (June 1984), *Leitlinien für die künftige Wohnungspolitik* [position paper], RWWA-181-21921.

67 DIHT (October 23, 1985) *Stellungnahme zur Neuregelung der steuerrechtlichen Förderung des selbstgenutzten Wohneigentums* [statement], PA-DBT 4000 X/225.

68 Bund der Steuerzahler (October 23, 1985), *Gesetz zur Neuregelung der steuerlichen Förderung selbstgenutzten Wohneigentums: Anhörung vor dem Finanzausschuß* [hearing], 10th Bundestag, PA-DBT 4000 X/225.

69 Deutscher Mieterbund (October 23, 1985), *Stellungnahme* [statement], Cologne, PA-DBT 4000 X/225.

70 "Immer kostspieliger" (November 15, 1985), *Wirtschaftswoche*.

71 The law also allowed homeowners to claim the child allowance for every one of their children (previously, they could claim the child allowance only for every child after the first child).

72 Bundestag member II (SPD) (author interview, Berlin, May 14, 2015).

who warned that these subsidies would hurt the German growth regime. The tax break tripled in size from DM 2.2 billion in 1975 to over DM 6.2 billion in 1988, leading commentators to label the homeownership tax allowance a "sacred cow" of federal housing policy (Stimpel 1990, 62).[73] As German economic elites repeatedly criticized the tax subsidy for being incongruent with the needs of the industrial, export-oriented economy, however, political support for it was on borrowed time, as Chapter 7 will show.

Meanwhile, as the Kohl government boosted homeownership support, it slashed rental housing programs. In 1987, housing minister Schneider (CSU) proclaimed that "the time of large-scale [housing] programs is over. The race to catch up with excess demand is won. Housing policy is increasingly becoming *Ordnungspolitik* [ord-liberal politics]."[74] Indeed, between 1986 and 1988, the Kohl government supported only 10,000 to 20,000 new social rental units per year.[75]

Along those lines, the Kohl government eliminated a key tax break for the rental housing market: The tax-exempt status of limited-profit housing associations (*Wohnungsgemeinnützigkeit*). The very housing associations that had rebuilt large parts of the German housing market after the war came under intense scrutiny. The union-owned Neue Heimat – Europe's largest housing company at the time – became mired in several corruption and mismanagement scandals that were unearthed by *Der Spiegel* in the early 1980s.[76] The image and importance of limited-profit housing associations took a massive hit from which they never recovered (Kramper 2008; Jaedicke and Wollmann 1991). As a result, the limited-profit housing associations' share of building permits plummeted from 25 percent of all residential building permits in the 1960s to a mere 6 percent in 1988.[77] Moreover, the Kohl government cut other tax subsidies that were related to social housing programs, such as the property tax subsidy (*Grundsteuervergünstigung*). The property tax subsidy – used mainly by rental investors but also some homeowners if they fulfilled social housing program criteria – had doubled in size from the late 1960s until the late 1980s, amounting to DM 1.2 billion in 1986, which made it the ninth-largest tax break at that time.[78]

[73] Bundesregierung (1977), *6. Subventionsbericht*, 246; Bundesregierung (1987), *11. Subventionsbericht*, 26.

[74] Schneider, O. (1987), "Wohnungspolitik in der marktwirtschaftlichen Ordnung," *Der Langfristige Kredit*, 38(8), 247.

[75] The CDU had long criticized that many households continued to live in low-cost social housing units even once they exceeded the income limits for these units (*Fehlbelegung*).

[76] "Gut getarnt im Dickicht der Firmen – Neue Heimat: Die dunklen Geschäfte von Vietor und Genossen" (February 7, 1982), *Der Spiegel*.

[77] Fey, W. (1968), "Tendenzen und Merkmale des Wohnungsbauers 1967," *Bundesbaublatt*, 16(5), 217; Hamm, H. (1989), "Der soziale Wohnunsgbau 1988/89," *Bundesbaublatt*, 37(11), 569.

[78] Bundesregierung (1985), *10. Subventionsbericht*, 28.

Finally, Kohl also reduced savings subsidies to consolidate the budget (Börsch-Supan 1994; Mertens 2015). The Council of Economic Experts noted that savings subsidies were no longer necessary, as households would save regardless of subsidies.[79] First, the Kohl government reduced the building society tax subsidy – which allowed households to deduct savings contributions in building societies from their income – from DM 760 million in 1971 to DM 580 million in 1988 (ranked fifteenth out of the twenty largest tax subsidies that year).[80] Second, the government reduced another direct subsidy for low- and middle-income savers in building societies (*Wohnungsbauprämie*). The subsidy had peaked in 1975 at DM 1.6 billion, making it one of the largest direct subsidies in Germany. The Schmidt and Kohl governments gradually reduced the subsidy by refusing to adjust household income eligibility limits upward despite annual wage increases and inflation in the late 1970s and the 1980s (Börsch-Supan and Stahl 1991, 269; Mertens 2015). By 1988, the subsidy amounted to only DM 870 million, which still made it the sixth largest direct subsidy that year.[81]

Despite these measures, savings remained an important element of the German political economy (Mertens 2015). However, the Kohl government did not consider *subsidizing* savings in building societies as a priority in times of fiscal strain, as housing and savings markets were functioning well even without such subsidies. Instead, the policy focus shifted away from housing-based savings toward savings in "productive capital" (i.e., employee savings in industries).

As housing demand is cyclical, the conclusion that housing shortages were a thing of the past was premature. Just before the country's reunification, a confluence of factors contributed to strong housing demand that met insufficient supply: The influx of 700,000 ethnic Germans from eastern Europe (*Spätaussiedler*) between 1986 and 1989, strong economic and income growth, household preferences for larger homes, and very little social housing construction.[82] The result was large-scale housing shortages in the country's metropolitan areas. In 1988, *Der Spiegel* spoke of a "Housing Emergency in Affluent Germany," pointing out that while Germans were enjoying expensive cars and vacations to faraway places as never before, a basic necessity – housing – was becoming scarce again.[83] In 1988, the country only produced 210,000 new housing units, including a mere 37,000 social housing units, which was an all-time postwar low.

79 Sachverständigenrat für Wirtschaft (1980), *Jahresgutachten 1980/1981*, 156.

80 Bundesregierung (1973), 4. *Subventionsbericht*, 228; Bundesregierung (1987), *11. Subventionsbericht*, 27.

81 Bundesregierung, *11. Subventionsbericht*, 26.

82 Bund der Vertriebenen (2024), *Aktuelle Aussiedlerstatistik*, www.bund-der-vertriebenen.de/fakten/spaetaussiedler/aktuelle-aussiedlerstatistik.

83 "Wohnungsnot im Wohlstands-Deutschland" (December 11, 1988), *Der Spiegel*.

In response to growing housing shortages, the Kohl government reversed course and strengthened social housing programs to boost housing supply. In 1989, it introduced the so-called third way of social housing, which gave the *Länder* more flexibility in negotiating directly with investors, homeowners, and limited-profit housing associations about funding rental and owner-occupied housing. This instrument was created with the goal of increasing the housing supply and the hope that it would have "price-deflating effects" in the housing sector while being sensitive to local and regional needs. The measure also enjoyed support from the Social Democrats.[84] Even for the conservative and austerity-oriented Kohl, low-cost housing was a priority when shortages threatened to drive up the cost of living, although these measures were relatively limited in scope. Similarly, German industries bemoaned low-skill labor shortages, driven by the lack of housing, in metropolitan areas and advocated for the creation of affordable housing in those areas.[85]

By the late 1980s, the Kohl government had reduced rental programs to a minimum while strengthening homeownership support. However, the retrenchment of rental programs contributed to reemerging housing shortages by the end of the decade, which would only worsen with the country's reunification, as Chapter 7 will show.[86] In place of these rental programs, policymakers prioritized homeownership programs in the late 1970s and 1980s. Yet the homeownership rate barely budged, increasing marginally from 38 percent in 1978 to 40 percent in 1989 (Kohl 2017). Against the macroeconomic warnings of economists and industries, the homeownership tax allowance became the largest tax subsidy and housing program in the country, but it continued to create tensions with the German growth regime, resolved only by abolishing the tax program in the post-unification years.

CONCLUSION

The mid-1970s marked a turning point for German housing programs. As housing shortages were no longer a macroeconomic problem, supply-side housing programs lost their macroeconomic importance for the export-oriented growth regime. As discussed in Chapter 3, German housing programs were essential in alleviating housing and labor shortages in industrial areas and keeping living costs down. By the mid-1970s, however, most Germans lived in relatively low-cost and high-quality housing. When housing shortages ended, policymakers and economic elites increasingly viewed large-scale housing programs as macroeconomic problems that contradicted the priorities of the export-oriented

[84] Ausschuss für Raumordnung, Bauwesen und Städtebau (December 2, 1988), *Beschlußempfehlung und Bericht des 16. Ausschusses* (Drs. 11/3637) [report].

[85] DIHT (January 11, 1990), *Stellungnahme zum Wohnungsbauerleichterungsgesetz* [statement], RWWA-181-2848-3.

[86] Pfeiffer, U. (March 17, 1989), "Auf Sand gebaut: Ein Program gegen den Wohnungsmangel," *Die Zeit*.

TABLE 5.1 *German housing finance programs adopted or reformed between 1969 and 1990*

Type of program	Policy	Years active	Adoption and changes
Tax	Mortgage interest deduction for homeowners	1982–1987	Temporary program to support housing sector
Tax	Homeownership tax allowance (paragraph 7b → 10e of the tax code)	1949–2006	Suspended in 1973 and reinstated in 1974; expanded for purchases of older homes (not just newly built homes) from 1977; extra subsidy for homebuyers with children introduced from 1981; 1986 reform retained subsidy under different label ("paragraph 7b" became "paragraph 10e" of the income tax code)
Tax	Tax subsidy for savings schemes in building societies	1949–1995	Gradually reduced from mid-1970s
Tax	Tax exemption for limited-profit housing companies (*Wohnungsgemeinnützigkeit*)	1949–1990	Eliminated in 1990
Tax	Property tax reductions	1950–1990	Eliminated in 1990
Direct subsidy	Subsidy for savings in building societies (*Wohnungsbauprämie*)	1952–	Subsidy gradually reduced
Credit	Subsidized mortgages for savers in building societies (*Bausparzwischenfinanzierung*)	1975–1976 1982–1983 1989–1990	Temporary programs to support housing sector
Credit	Social housing programs (*sozialer Wohnungsbau*)	1950–2006	Strengthened in late 1960s and early 1970s but gradually reduced from mid-1970s; focused increasingly on homeownership over rental housing

economy: They increased fiscal deficits, fueled inflation in the construction sector, and channeled capital away from manufacturing. As a result, policymakers reduced rental housing programs to a minimum between the mid-1970s and the late 1980s (see Table 5.1).

Despite influential German economic elites viewing homeownership programs as incongruent with the needs of the export-oriented growth regime, policymakers retained these programs during this period. Like Reagan's 1986 tax reform, Kohl's tax reform in the same year strengthened the generous homeownership tax allowance, which became the country's largest housing program by the late 1980s. German politicians did so primarily to promote family, wealth, and retirement policy, rather than to permanently stimulate domestic demand. Indeed, these political factors overrode macroeconomic ones in this period, as politicians ignored the warnings of the Bundesbank, the Council of Economic Experts, and German industries about the detrimental effects of these programs on the export-oriented economy. As Germany was regarded as "the most internationally successful of the major economies" by the late 1980s (Streeck 1997, 237), policymakers did not yet feel a strong need to eliminate or sacrifice homeownership programs. It would take a more severe structural economic crisis to change course.

One lesson from this chapter is that growth regimes need not dictate policies. Policymakers *can* adopt programs that are not congruent with a growth regime for ideological reasons. The German homeownership tax allowance is a case in point: Economic elites and industries highlighted the various detrimental *demand-side* effects of the tax subsidy on the country's manufacturing-based, export-oriented growth regime. These effects included contributing to fiscal deficits, limiting labor mobility, and inflating construction costs, thus hurting an economy that had thrived on low costs and inflation. These tensions would be resolved only by abandoning the homeownership subsidy in the post-unification period, as Chapter 7 will show.

6

The Double Down

Nationalizing American Housing Finance

The US housing market was the epicenter of the devastating financial crash of 2007–2009. When the housing bubble burst in 2007, millions of homeowners lost their homes, while millions of others were "underwater," meaning that their mortgages were worth more than their houses. *Trillions* of dollars in household wealth vanished. The collapsing housing market took the US economy down with it: Stock markets plunged, economic growth plummeted, and unemployment doubled. European economies soon followed, as investments in toxic US mortgage debt triggered the continent's own economic crisis. Some commentators blamed America's longstanding government support for housing, arguing that it had inflated the property bubble (Wallison 2016). Barney Frank (Democrat, Massachusetts), the former chair of the House Financial Services Committee and long-time champion of these housing programs, recanted. "If I were starting a new country," he said about the mortgage interest deduction (MID) in 2011, "I would not have it."[1] Two years later, he stated that the government-sponsored enterprises (GSEs) Fannie Mae and Freddie Mac "should now be abolished."[2] Frank's Republican successors on the committee, Spencer Bachus (Alabama) and Jeb Hensarling (Texas), joined the chorus and suggested "putting the spike in Fannie and Fred" in a letter to the *Wall Street Journal*.[3]

A housing bust of this magnitude, one that almost wrecked the global economy, presented policymakers with a once-in-a-lifetime opportunity to end generous housing programs that had inflated the housing bubble. However,

[1] Prior, J. (March 31, 2011), "Barney Frank says mortgage interest tax deduction is safe," *HousingWire*.

[2] Menza, J. (May 9, 2013), "Fannie Mae should be abolished: Barney Frank," *CNBC*.

[3] Bachus, S. and Hensarling, J. (April 6, 2011), "Putting the spike in Fannie and Fred," *Wall Street Journal*.

they did the opposite and expanded housing support during and after the crash, even effectively *nationalizing* the country's housing finance market. In 2024, the American state backed 70 percent of all US single-family-home mortgage debt.[4]

Rather than retreating from housing support, US policymakers doubled down on housing programs to rescue and revive the country's demand-led growth regime during the 2008 crash. With remarkably little partisan conflict, they expanded housing support to kill two birds with one stone: Fixing the key source of the crisis and promoting economic recovery by restoring housing-based growth. Although these crisis measures were intended to be temporary, they became entrenched as politicians retained them to promote, or avoid harming, housing-based growth that they saw as essential to the demand-led economy. In short, policymakers considered housing to be the root of economic disaster and the source of recovery; it was both the disease and the cure.

To prevent the economy from spiraling downward when the housing bubble burst in 2007, policymakers adopted several housing programs aimed at stabilizing house prices, foreclosure rates, mortgage lending, and consumer spending. The first set of actions involved nationalizing the housing finance market by placing the crisis-battered GSEs Fannie Mae and Freddie Mac under government control. This was a monumental move, as these agencies handled close to half of all mortgage debt in the country – USD 5 trillion out of USD 12 trillion in 2008 (see Figure 4.3). Previously, these agencies had enjoyed the *implicit* backing of the US government; the bailout made this backing *explicit.* The second set of actions involved the Fed purchasing trillions of dollars in mortgage debt issued by Fannie and Freddie to offer emergency support for housing finance and stimulate domestic demand. The Fed hoped these actions would reduce mortgage rates, stimulate mortgage lending, increase house prices, and boost consumer spending in the wider economy. In doing so, the Fed added another major layer of support to America's government-sponsored housing model.

Earlier policy choices profoundly shaped American policymakers' decision to support housing as a way to rescue the US economy. For decades, policymakers had actively nurtured the growth of Fannie Mae and Freddie Mac, using these agencies to boost mortgage lending and housing-based growth. Bailing them out meant stabilizing the systemically important housing finance market, which was deeply interwoven with the American growth regime. In addition, the Fed could point to historical policy precedents for supporting the GSEs in stabilizing home finance markets, as seen during the Great Depression and the credit crunches of the 1960s and 70s. The Fed's substantial housing support during the 2008 crash was thus a logical next step in reinforcing the American demand-led growth regime.

4 Housing Finance Policy Center (HFPC) (November 2024), *Housing Finance at a Glance*, Urban Institute, 6.

Many of these crisis-era measures were intended to be provisional but became entrenched as politicians feared that removing them could lead to higher mortgage rates, lower house prices, and disruptions in a complex mortgage market that was central to America's demand-led economy. Despite bipartisan discomfort with the quasi-nationalized status of Fannie and Freddie, policymakers kept them under government control long after the 2008 crisis. Similarly, the Fed retained its support for housing well beyond the crisis. When considering reducing housing support, central bankers faced similar macroeconomic constraints as policymakers: Reducing support risked increasing mortgage rates, lowering house prices, and disrupting the home finance market essential to growth and prosperity.

POLICY OVERSHOOT: MORTGAGE BOOM AND PREDATORY INCLUSION

Before discussing how policymakers responded to the 2008 housing crash, it is important to analyze its origins. In the early 2000s, President George W. Bush continued the Clinton administration's deep political commitment to stimulating mortgage lending and housing markets. Both administrations aimed to mitigate racialized poverty and wealth inequality, not through redistributive social spending but through housing policy. By stimulating low-income and minority homeownership, they sought to spur economic growth and build private wealth and welfare in underprivileged communities without increasing welfare spending. More broadly, American policymakers' strong commitment to housing-based growth reflected a "rare but dysfunctional instance of bipartisan policy consensus," resulting in policy overshoot that enabled the development of a housing bubble (McCarty et al. 2013, 118).

In what it termed an "aggressive housing agenda," the George W. Bush administration (2001–2009) seamlessly continued Clinton's push to expand access to homeownership credit among minorities as a growth and welfare strategy (Atkinson 2019, 1146; Goodman and Mayer 2018). The goal was to close the homeownership gap between white and nonwhite households (see Figure 6.1), aiming to create 5.5 million new homeowners by the end of the decade, particularly among Black and Hispanic households (Thompson 2010, 77).

For the Bush administration, stimulating homeownership among minorities meant stimulating economic activity. A 2002 HUD report estimated that "meeting the President's goal to close the housing gap will involve $256 billion in economic activity in the form of construction and remodeling jobs, spending on household goods, and other benefits."[5] The same report also

[5] White House (October 15, 2002), *President Hosts Conference on Minority Homeownership* [press release], https://georgewbush-whitehouse.archives.gov/news/releases/2002/10/20021015.html

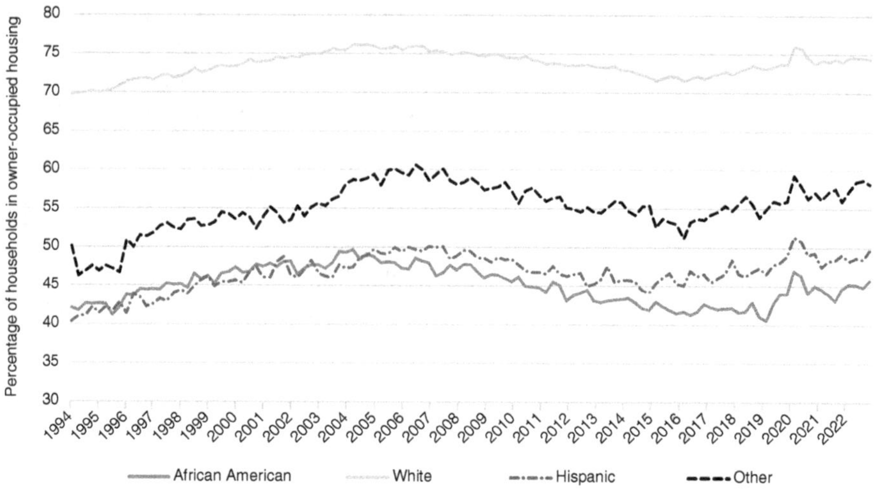

FIGURE 6.1 Racial homeownership gap in the United States, 1994–2023
Note: "Other," as defined by the US Census Bureau, includes "people who reported Asian, Native Hawaiian or Other Pacific Islander, or American Indian or Alaska Native regardless of whether they reported any other race, as well as all other combinations of two or more races." *Data source:* FRED based on US Census Bureau.

mentioned four primary macroeconomic benefits of increasing homeownership among minorities: (1) job creation in housing construction; (2) benefits to businesses specializing in home improvement or selling housing-related goods and services, (3) wealth effects from building home equity, and (4) rising home values in minority neighborhoods as a wealth-building strategy.[6] To achieve these goals, the Bush administration introduced several initiatives. In 2003, it launched the American Dream Downpayment Act, which authorized up to USD 200 million annually between 2004 and 2007 to assist low-income and minority homeowners with their down payments.[7] In 2004, the administration proposed a zero-down-payment initiative for FHA mortgages aimed at first-time, low-income, and minority buyers, although the bill did not pass Congress.[8] The third initiative involved increasing Fannie and Freddie's affordable housing goals between 2001 and 2008, requiring them to securitize

6 HUD (2002), *Economic Benefits of Increasing Minority Homeownership* [report], https://archives.hud.gov/initiatives/blueprint/econreport-101502.pdf.

7 Bush, G. W. (December 16, 2003), *Remarks by the President at Signing of the American Dream Downpayment Act*, https://georgewbush-whitehouse.archives.gov/news/releases/2003/12/20031216-9.html.

8 HUD (January 19, 2004), *Bush administration announces new HUD 'Zero Down Payment' mortgage* [press release], https://archives.hud.gov/news/2004/pr04-006.cfm.

more low-quality mortgages.[9] As a result of these efforts, the homeownership rate among Black and Hispanic households increased from 45 percent in 1999 to roughly 50 percent in the mid-2000s (see Figure 6.1). Between 2002 and 2006, 2.7 million more minority households became homeowners, with one-quarter of first-time minority buyers receiving direct support from FHA or VA programs.[10]

The problem, however, was that minority households often did not receive affordable, conventional thirty-year fixed-rate mortgages, partly due to banks' discriminatory or predatory lending practices (Faber 2013; Bayer et al. 2018). Just as racialized minorities did during the late 1960s and early 1970s (see Chapter 4), they experienced predatory inclusion as part of America's housing-based growth regime in the early 2000s. Predatory inclusion meant that even when racialized minorities qualified for a prime and conventional mortgage they disproportionately received high-cost, high-risk nonconventional loans, including subprime mortgages, or higher-cost conventional loans from high-risk lenders that targeted minority borrowers (Bayer et al. 2018).[11] Risky and high-cost subprime loans were on the rise in the 2000s, a product of decades-long mortgage liberalizations aimed at expanding housing-based growth. A 2000 HUD report had already observed "the rapid growth of subprime lending during the 1990's [*sic*] and, further, the disproportionate concentration of such lending in the nation's minority and low-income neighborhoods," which also suffered from "widespread predatory practices in the subprime market."[12] Based on 1998 data, the study found that subprime loans were five times more likely in Black neighborhoods than in white neighborhoods. As the subprime boom continued – peaking at over 20 percent of all mortgage originations in 2006, up from just 8 percent in 2003 (Financial Crisis Inquiry Commission 2011, 70) – the disproportionate targeting of minority groups for subprime loans persisted (King and Smith 2011, ch. 5). A study using 2006 data found that, when controlling for income and geographical factors, Hispanic and Black borrowers were two to three times more likely than white borrowers to have their mortgage application denied. Similarly,

[9] Between 2000 and 2007, the affordable housing goals increased from 42 percent to 55 percent. See HUD (November 2008), *Overview of the GSEs' Housing Goal Performance 2000–2007*, https://archives.huduser.gov/portal/datasets/GSE/gse2007.pdf.

[10] Weicher, J. (October 11, 2006), *Closing the Gap: The Quiet Success of the Bush Administration's Push for Minority Home Ownership*, Hudson Institute.

[11] Nonconventional loans include subprime loans, which have higher interest rates than conventional loans to take account of the higher credit risk presented by borrowers with "subprime" credit ratings. Interest-only loans, while not exclusively subprime, allow borrowers to pay only the interest on the loan for an initial period, after which they must begin to also pay the principal. Alt-A loans, neither conventional nor subprime, are typically given to borrowers with relatively good credit ratings but insufficient documentation of income, assets, and employment.

[12] HUD (January 20, 2009), *Subprime Lending Report – Unequal Burden: Income and Racial Disparities in Subprime Lending*, https://archives.hud.gov/reports/subprime/subprime.cfm.

when approved for mortgages, Hispanic and Black borrowers were 2.4 times more likely to receive a subprime loan than comparable white households (Faber 2013, 341). Finally, Bayer and colleagues (2018) analyzed 2004–2007 data and found that Black and Hispanic households were 103 percent and 78 percent more likely, respectively, to receive high-cost mortgages, even after controlling for credit scores, income, and type of mortgage. In short, minorities often ended up with higher-cost and riskier mortgages than comparable white households.

The Bush administration did foresee some dangers in its housing-based growth strategy but did not act on them. The administration's concern was not the growth of subprime mortgage debt, but the astronomical growth of the GSEs. Fannie and Freddie dominated the country's market of conventional mortgages, holding a market share of close to 50 percent, with their combined portfolios exceeding USD 3.5 trillion by 2003 (see Figure 4.3). There was widespread political agreement on the need for regulatory improvement without touching the government-sponsored nature of the GSEs. However, little consensus emerged on how to tighten GSE regulation without harming their activities, which were inextricably linked with America's housing-based growth machine. In 2003, Bush's chief economic adviser, Greg Mankiw, stated that a new regulator for Fannie and Freddie was necessary to reduce systemic risk. The new regulator would need "broad authority to set both risk-based and minimum capital standards" and "receivership powers necessary to wind down the affairs of a troubled GSE."[13] The administration was concerned about the GSEs' size, their opaque accounting practices, and the lack of proper oversight by their ineffective regulator, OFHEO, established under George H. W. Bush.

Over the next few years, the Bush administration and Republican-controlled Congress debated several GSE reform proposals (McDonald 2012, ch. 10). The reform efforts ultimately failed, as policymakers feared that tightened financial regulation could harm housing-based growth. The administration and Senate Republicans pushed for tougher regulations on the GSEs, which could have reduced the size of the GSEs and, consequently, their footprint in the mortgage market. Yet House Republicans and Democrats in both chambers favored a weaker regulatory bill that would allow the GSEs to *expand* their activities for low-income households and minorities.[14] Representative Michael Oxley (Republican, Ohio), who co-sponsored the less stringent House bill, emphasized the importance of "permitting the GSEs to continue to play

[13] White House (October 9, 2008), *Setting the Record Straight: Six Years of Unheeded Warnings for GSE Reform*, Office of the Press Secretary, https://georgewbush-whitehouse.archives.gov/news/releases/2008/10/20081009-10.html.

[14] The House passed a bipartisan regulatory bill, which would have strengthened the GSEs' regulator but also allowed for the GSEs' expansion in business activities. Yet the administration rejected the bill for insufficiently tightening regulations. See Jickling, M. (October 27, 2005), *Government-Sponsored Enterprises (GSEs): Regulatory Reform Legislation*, Congressional Research Service Report (RL32795).

their important role in the secondary mortgage market."[15] Similarly, Senate Majority Leader Harry Reid (Democrat, Nevada) opposed the Bush administration's proposals on the grounds that they would potentially reduce the activities of the GSEs, arguing that "we cannot pass legislation that could limit Americans from owning homes and *potentially harm our economy in the process*."[16] Policymakers' concerns that tightening regulations could damage housing-based growth thus prevented reform.

Fannie and Freddie themselves lobbied ferociously against tighter financial regulation in private meetings with political leaders. Despite appearing cooperative in public (Thompson 2010, 86–90), the GSEs became powerful defenders of America's government-sponsored housing model. As Representative Richard Baker (Republican, Louisiana), co-sponsor of the House bill, noted: "The lobbying ability of Fannie and Freddie is second to none in Washington ... They have not only unlimited financial resources but good personnel who maintain good relations with many members of Congress. When their interests are threatened, the response is almost army-like. They're tactical, and they're everywhere."[17] From 1999 to 2008, Fannie and Freddie spent USD 164 million on lobbying, supporting "malicious political attacks and efforts of intimidation," as a regulator recalled (Financial Crisis Inquiry Commission 2011, 41–42). The American state had created the GSEs, which then grew into political powerhouses beyond government control, further reinforcing the opposition to tighter GSE regulations (Thompson 2012).

Bush's emphasis on homeownership expansion also made attacks on homeowner tax breaks unlikely. The 2001 and 2003 Bush tax cuts, for example, lowered tax rates, particularly benefiting affluent households. In 2005, Bush prioritized overhauling the tax system and social security for his second term. He commissioned an advisory panel on federal tax reform to simplify the tax code and promote economic growth, "while recognizing the importance of homeownership and charity in American society."[18] But when the expert panel released its recommendations, it created a stir. Surprisingly, the panel recommended replacing the mortgage interest *deduction* with a less generous tax *credit* amounting to 15 percent of mortgage interest paid on the primary residency.[19] James Poterba, a member of the president's panel who supported reducing the MID, acknowledged that the proposal, if implemented, would

[15] Quoted in Schroeder, R. (May 25, 2005), "House OKs Fannie, Freddie regulator," *MarketWatch*.

[16] Quoted in "Dems rip new Fannie Mae regulatory measure" (July 28, 2005), United Press International. My emphasis.

[17] Tierney, J. (June 17, 2003), "Privileged life in peril for 2 mortgage giants," *New York Times*.

[18] Bush, G. W. (January 7, 2005), *Executive Order 13369: President's Advisory Panel on Federal Tax Reform*, The American Presidency Project, www.presidency.ucsb.edu/node/217486.

[19] The President's Advisory Panel on Federal Tax Reform (November 2005), *Simple, Fair, and Pro-Growth*, 237, https://home.treasury.gov/system/files/131/Report-Fix-Tax-System-2005.pdf.

lead to a "downward effect on prices." The housing lobby responded predictably with concerns about declining housing activity and prices, warning of "a devastating effect on the nation's housing economy."[20] Congressional leaders of both parties immediately opposed these recommendations. Representative Katherine Harris (Republican, Florida), for example, stated that limiting the MID would "stifle economic growth" (quoted in Ventry 2010, 277). President Bush himself reassured the public that the MID would remain safe, stating: "I don't think you have to worry about the mortgage deduction not being a part of the income tax law."[21] Once again, tax economists – focused on tax neutrality – were the driving force behind MID reform proposals, but politicians quashed these efforts owing to concerns about falling house prices and the associated negative economic ripple effects.

In the early 2000s, the American housing market and economy were booming, but it was a boom built on shaky ground. Residential mortgage debt more than doubled in less than a decade, from USD 5 trillion in 1999 to USD 12 trillion in 2007 (see Figure 4.3), with credit growth occurring across all segments of the mortgage market, not just subprime borrowing. Like his predecessors, President Bush did little to tame growing housing excesses. On the contrary, for Bush, the booming housing market was a key achievement – a bright spot amid the dark wreckage of the burst of the dot-com bubble, the 9/11 terrorist attacks, and the subsequent wars in Afghanistan and Iraq. As Bush remarked: "We can put light where there's darkness, and hope where there's despondency in this country. And part of it is working together as a nation to encourage folks to own their own home."[22] John Snow, then Treasury Secretary, even proclaimed that the American housing finance system would be "one of the economic wonders of the world."[23] However, the American economy's bright light – housing – was about to go dark.

FROM VIRTUOUS TO VICIOUS CIRCLE: HOUSING BOOM AND BUST

America's booming housing market reinforced the demand-led growth regime through a "virtuous circle" that would soon turn vicious. Several

[20] Quoted in Porter, E., and Leonhardt, D. (November 3, 2005), "Goodbye, my sweet deduction," *New York Times*.

[21] Bush, G. W. (February 17, 2006), *Remarks on the War on Terror and a Question-and-Answer Session*, Tampa, Florida, https://georgewbush-whitehouse.archives.gov/news/releases/2006/02/20060217-4.html.

[22] Bush, G. W. (October 15, 2002), *President hosts conference on minority homeownership* [speech], https://georgewbush-whitehouse.archives.gov/news/releases/2002/10/20021015-7.html.

[23] US Senate (October 16, 2003), *Proposals for Improving the Regulation of the Housing Government Sponsored Enterprises: Hearings before the Senate Committee on Banking, Housing, and Urban Affairs* (testimony of J. Snow), 72.

factors enabled the massive housing boom and exploding property prices during the early 2000s: Low interest rates, a proliferation of low-quality mortgages, mortgage liquidity in financial markets through foreign capital inflows, growing fiscal and off-budget mortgage subsidies, persistent land-use restrictions in expensive metropolitan areas, and overly optimistic house-price expectations among market participants. House prices increased by roughly 60 percent from 2000 to 2006 (see Figure 7.3). Rising house prices not only channeled investments into housing but also increased household wealth and home equity, which households could leverage for higher consumer spending. As Acharya and colleagues (2011, 107) note, "US mortgage equity withdrawals were the engine of world economic growth between 2000 and 2007." However, just as the US housing market could stimulate economic activity through wealth and credit effects in a virtuous cycle, a distressed housing market could have the opposite effect, inhibiting credit lending and consumer spending in a vicious circle. This is precisely what happened when the housing bubble burst in 2007.

The booming housing market initially produced a virtuous cycle that stimulated the entire economy. First, low interest rates contributed to above-average numbers of housing starts and construction, peaking at 2 million new homes in 2005 and exceeding the historical average (1960–2000) of 1.5 million homes (see Figure 2.2). Second, global and domestic investors were attracted to American mortgage-backed securities in search of yields in a low-interest environment, flooding the US mortgage market with capital, which reduced borrowing costs. Foreign investors, particularly from Asia but also from Europe, considered US mortgage-backed securities as safe and lucrative assets, increasing their holdings from USD 150 billion in 2003 to USD 770 billion in 2008.[24] Third, rising house prices and falling interest rates allowed homeowners to extract cash from their homes, resulting in higher consumer spending and aggregate demand. Homeowners took advantage of falling interest rates to refinance their mortgages at a "frenzied pace."[25] The extra cash extracted from refinancing – through reduced mortgage payments or larger mortgages – increased from USD 127 billion in 2001 to an all-time high of USD 431 billion in 2006.[26] Homeowners also took out loans against their homes, with the volume increasing from USD 185 billion in 2002 to USD 470 billion in 2007.[27] According to the Council of Economic Advisers, rising house prices "supported growth in consumer

[24] Ginnie Mae (September 2023), *Foreign Ownership of Agency MBS*, www.ginniemae.gov/newsroom/publications/Documents/foreign_ownership_agency_mbs2023.pdf.

[25] Federal Reserve Board (2001), *Annual Report*, 14.

[26] Freddie Mac (April 25, 2022), *Trends in Mortgage Refinancing Activity* [research note], www.freddiemac.com/research/insight/20220425-trends-mortgage-refinancing-activity.

[27] FRED (2024), *Revolving Home Equity Loans*, https://fred.stlouisfed.org/series/RHEACBW027SBOG.

spending" through the wealth channel.[28] Finally, the finance and real estate sectors were the main beneficiaries of the housing boom, with 1.3 million jobs added across construction, real estate, mortgage brokerage, and contracting from 2001 to 2006.[29]

However, the virtuous cycle soon turned vicious. As early as 2005, the Fed acknowledged risks relating to the pace of house-price growth, noting that "some observers believe that home values have moved above levels that can be supported by fundamentals and that some realignment is warranted."[30] When the Fed slowly raised interest rates between 2004 and 2006, the refinancing boom ended, leading banks to focus on originating risky subprime mortgages to satisfy investor appetite for mortgage bonds (Fligstein 2021). By 2006, the share of subprime originations climbed to over 20 percent of all mortgage originations that year, up from roughly 10 percent in the early 2000s, while the market share of FHA and VA loans dropped from roughly 20 percent to around 5 percent during the same period.[31] In 2006 alone, banks originated USD 600 billion worth of subprime mortgages (Financial Crisis Inquiry Commission 2011, 70). As the Fed continued to increase interest rates, borrowers with adjustable-rate and subprime mortgages faced higher mortgage costs. The bubble eventually burst when mortgage delinquencies rose to unsustainable levels. In 2007, one-fifth of all subprime mortgage were delinquent.[32] The picture for the overall mortgage market was not much better, with delinquencies rising from 5 percent in 2003 to 9 percent in 2009.[33] The foreclosure crisis began in the subprime sector and quickly spread to the prime sector as well, where over-leveraged middle- and upper-class households could no longer repay their mortgages (Adelino et al. 2018). In general, households had taken on excessive amounts of debt for increasingly expensive homes, while banks ignored underwriting standards, relying on expectations of future house-price appreciations. Mortgage defaults led to a massive wave of home foreclosures, with a total of 9 million homes foreclosed between 2006 and 2013 (Reid et al. 2017, 469).

As racialized minorities disproportionately held high-cost, high-risk mortgages, they bore the brunt of the foreclosure crisis (Bayer et al. 2016; King and Smith 2011, ch. 5). While only 12 percent of white homeowners who

[28] Council of Economic Advisers (2007), *Annual Report*, 30.

[29] Byun, K. (December 2010), "The U.S. housing bubble and bust: Impacts on employment," *Monthly Labor Review*.

[30] Federal Reserve Board (2005), *Annual Report*, 4.

[31] Ferreira, F. (January 4, 2018), *Mortgage lending and housing markets*, NBER Reporter, National Bureau of Economic Research.

[32] Federal Reserve Board (2007), *Annual Report*, 10.

[33] Calculated Risk Blog (February 10, 2022), *MBA: "Mortgage Delinquencies Decrease in the Fourth Quarter of 2021,"* www.calculatedriskblog.com/2022/02/mba-mortgage-delinquencies-decrease-in.html.

bought their homes between 2004 and 2008 were seriously delinquent or experienced foreclosure, the numbers were significantly higher for minority households: 28 percent of Black homeowners, 31 percent of Hispanic homeowners, and 15 percent of Asian American homeowners by 2013 (Reid et al. 2017, 479). Research by Bayer and colleagues (2016) using 2004–2009 data shows that Black and Hispanic households were up to three percentage points more likely to experience foreclosure compared to white households with similar credit scores. Minority neighborhoods were especially affected, suffering greater declines in house prices (Raymond et al. 2016). The Black homeownership rate correspondingly dropped from 50 percent before the crisis to just 41 percent in 2016 (see Figure 6.1). Black households therefore incurred greater relative losses in household wealth during the Great Recession, losing 48 percent household wealth compared to 26 percent among white households and 44 percent among Hispanic households (McKernan et al. 2014, 244). One consequence of the financial crisis was a *widening* of the racial homeownership gap between white and Black homeowners, a gap that increased from 27 percent in 1960 to 30 percent in 2017.[34] Over the past 60 years, America's government-sponsored housing model has oscillated between racial exclusion and predatory inclusion without narrowing the homeownership gap.

Given the centrality of housing to the broader financial system in the American economy, the housing crash quickly generated widespread financial turmoil. The problem was that mortgages rarely stayed on a bank's balance sheet; they were instead bundled together by private banks or the GSEs and sold off to investors. When a critical mass of homeowners defaulted on their mortgage payments, the GSEs and private banks struggled to pay domestic and global investors holding mortgage-backed securities their promised returns (Morgan and Reisenbichler 2022; Fligstein 2021). While the GSEs had long dominated the mortgage-backed securities market, investment banks gained significant ground between 2004 and 2006. In the context of a booming housing market, private banks tapped the growing unconventional mortgage market of subprime mortgages, a segment of the mortgage market that the GSEs were not allowed to touch. By 2005, investment banks were issuing the majority of mortgage-backed securities, reaching a peak of 59 percent in 2006, up from around 20 percent in the late 1990s and early 2000s and outperforming the GSEs for the first time ever (see Figure 6.2).

The GSEs came under competitive pressure from private banks and began investing more in low-quality mortgages – although not as aggressively as private banks – leading to a competitive "race to the bottom" (Acharya et al. 2011, ch. 3; Nelson and Katzenstein 2014). Financial actors massively mispriced the risk of mortgage-backed securities, often rating them as safely as

[34] Urban Institute (2024), *Reducing the racial homeownership gap*, www.urban.org/policy-centers/housing-finance-policy-center/projects/reducing-racial-homeownership-gap.

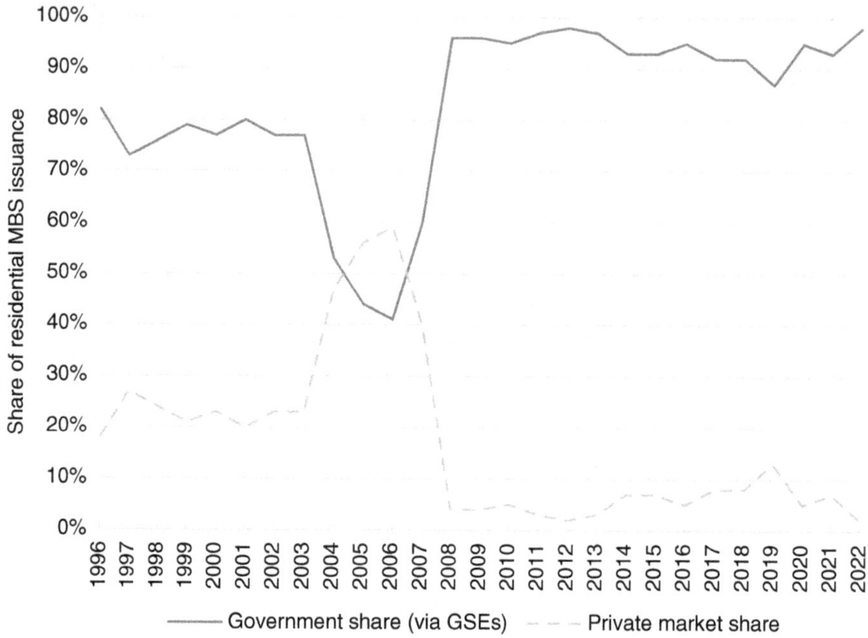

FIGURE 6.2 Share of mortgage-backed securities issued by the American state compared to the private market, 1996–2022
Data source: Securities Industry and Financial Markets Association (series: US MBS Securities).

US Treasuries (Thompson 2009), an assumption that was flawed and, in many ways, ignorant (Tett 2019). When millions of homeowners defaulted on their mortgages, the housing finance system could not absorb the catastrophic losses and the system came crashing down.

The macroeconomic consequences of the housing crash were immense. The economy entered a deep recession from late 2007 until mid-2009, with unemployment peaking at 10 percent in 2009. House prices were in freefall, wiping out USD 7 trillion in household wealth.[35] Nearly one-quarter of all mortgage borrowers were underwater in 2009, with more than USD 800 billion in negative home equity that year.[36] Housing starts plummeted to just 500,000 in 2009, and residential investment declined from 7 percent of GDP in 2006 to 2 percent in 2010.[37] Mortgage defaults and

[35] Council of Economic Advisers (2012), *Annual Report*, 110.

[36] Calculated Risk Blog (February 23, 2010), *Q4 Report: 11.3 Million U.S. Properties with Negative Equity*, www.calculatedriskblog.com/2010/02/q4-report-113-million-us-properties.html.

[37] FRED (2024), *Shares of Gross Domestic Product: Private Residential Fixed Investment*, https://fred.stlouisfed.org/series/A011RE1Q156NBEA.

home foreclosures remained high even after the financial crisis. The rate of mortgage delinquencies peaked at 10 percent in 2010, up from 4–5 percent in 2006, and only gradually declined to pre-crisis levels in 2016. The foreclosure peak of 1.2 million homes was reached in 2010, gradually falling to 336,000 in 2016.[38]

The housing crash also had severely negative ripple effects on aggregate demand. Just as rising house prices stimulated the US economy, falling house prices had dramatic negative effects on America's consumption- and credit-led economy (Mian and Sufi 2014). The Council of Economic Advisers estimated that "a $100 billion decline in the value of the housing stock would reduce the long-run level of annual consumption by between $4 billion and $8 billion."[39] When house prices fell, households' home equity decreased, and many homeowners ended up underwater. As a result, many households were forced to cut back spending and focus on paying off existing debt, as they could no longer refinance or take out debt via home equity loans to finance consumer spending. This process of deleveraging lowers consumption and aggregate demand in the economy. As the Council of Economic Advisers noted: "The macroeconomic effects of the downturn in housing and the credit market disruptions may occur through several channels, including the direct effect on residential investment, the reduction of wealth on personal consumption, and tighter lending standards on business investment."[40] Restoring mortgage market stability, housing wealth, and consumer spending was therefore an economic priority for policymakers.

SAVING THE GOVERNMENT FROM ITSELF

In response to the financial crisis, American policymakers doubled down on government support for housing by rescuing the home lending market. Their goal was to immediately stabilize the mortgage market, house prices, and household wealth, which would restore consumer lending and household spending – the key elements of America's credit-led and consumption-based growth regime. At the center of political action were the mortgage giants Fannie Mae and Freddie Mac. Although these GSEs had always enjoyed the *implicit* backing of the US government, the crisis made this backing explicit. Policymakers nationalized the battered companies to stabilize the housing market and economy: They were "too big to fail."

[38] Sobrevinas, A. (March 16, 2017), "A decade later, CoreLogic looks back at the foreclosure crisis," *Mortgage Professional*, www.mpamag.com/us/news/general/a-decade-later-corelogic-looks-back-at-the-foreclosure-crisis/62938; Calculated Risk Blog, *MBA: "Mortgage Delinquencies Decrease in the Fourth Quarter of 2021,"* www.calculatedriskblog.com/2022/02/mba-mortgage-delinquencies-decrease-in.html.

[39] Council of Economic Advisers (2008), *Annual Report*, 74.

[40] Council of Economic Advisers (2008), *Annual Report*, 52.

When Fannie and Freddie faced bankruptcy, the Bush administration decided to intervene and support the two mortgage giants. The rationale was to stabilize the American mortgage market, which is deeply interwoven with the broader American political economy. By 2007, the GSEs had become massive entities at the center of the US mortgage market, guaranteeing close to USD 5 *trillion* in mortgage debt (see Figure 4.3). Policymakers had allowed – and even encouraged – the mortgage giants to grow to these astronomical dimensions, making them a classic case of "too big to fail." The crisis made it increasingly difficult for the GSEs to pay investors their guaranteed principal and interest on the underlying mortgages, as the GSEs had incurred massive losses from holding and issuing low-quality mortgage-backed securities. In a bipartisan effort, the Bush administration and the Democratic Congress adopted the Housing and Economic Recovery Act of 2008 (McCarty et al. 2013, 80). The act gave the US Treasury the authority to extend emergency lending to Fannie and Freddie and to seize control of the GSEs through a new regulator, the Federal Housing Finance Agency (FHFA). Then Treasury Secretary Henry Paulson memorably stated that this new authority should calm investors: "If you have got a bazooka and people know you have got it, you may not have to take it out."[41] However, it was paradoxical, as Adam Tooze (2018, 173) notes, that a "conservative, free-market administration led by businessmen was proposing unlimited state spending to nationalize a large part of the housing finance system."

Just three months later, the Bush Treasury used its authority to place Fannie and Freddie in "conservatorship," as the previous actions had been insufficient to restore market confidence in the GSEs. Conservatorship is a form of quasi-nationalization, where the US government began collecting the profits, choosing the leadership, and conserving the assets of the two firms. It also included largely unexercised warrants on 79.9 percent ownership in each firm, a number chosen to keep the GSEs off the government's balance sheet. The bailout of Fannie and Freddie was one of the largest in the country's history, amounting to USD 191.6 billion. "When Paulson pulled the trigger," a former FHFA regulator recalled in an interview, "the FHFA went into the enterprises ... It's very dramatic. It's very law and order. For Fannie and Freddie, it was humiliating."[42] Both Republicans and Democrats agreed that the GSEs were too systemically important to fail. In Paulson's words: "Fannie Mae and Freddie Mac are so large and so interwoven in our financial system that a failure of either of them would cause great turmoil in our financial markets here at home and around the globe."[43]

[41] US Senate (July 15, 2008). *Recent Developments in U.S. Financial Markets and Regulatory Responses to Them* (S. Hrg. 110-1008): *Hearing before the Senate Banking, Housing, and Urban Affairs Committee* (testimony of H. Paulson), 19.

[42] Former FHFA official (author interview, Washington, DC, July 25, 2014).

[43] Paulson, H. (September 7, 2008), *Statement on Treasury and Federal Housing Finance Agency Action to Protect Financial Markets and Taxpayers*, https://home.treasury.gov/news/press-releases/hp1129.

Conservatorship allowed mortgage securitization to continue and stabilized the level of liquidity in the mortgage market, enabling households to refinance or acquire mortgages (Frame et al. 2015). In short, nationalizing the GSEs saved the home lending market that was central to the American economy.

The GSEs not only were important institutions domestically but also attracted sizable foreign capital that helped fund American mortgages. Indeed, the American demand-led growth regime has relied on foreign capital inflows to finance household debt, with the GSEs serving as a vehicle for this purpose. International investors, particularly China, owned large amounts of GSE mortgage-backed securities, assuming that these were "safe assets" backed by the US government (Thompson 2010; Schwartz 2009; Bardhan and Jaffee 2007). In 2008, foreign investors held over 16 percent of GSE mortgage-backed securities, with the majority owned by state and private institutions in China, Taiwan, and Japan.[44] These foreign capital inflows flooded the American mortgage market with cash, which reduced borrowing costs for consumers, stimulated housing markets, and generated household consumption (Ansell et al. 2018; Schwartz and Blyth 2022). If the US government had allowed the corporations to fail, the US would have risked losing creditworthiness, impairing global capital flows, and further crashing the economy. Conservatorship thus stabilized not only domestic housing credit and wealth but also the flow of global capital that helped fund American mortgages.

Unsurprisingly, the housing lobby supported the bipartisan consensus in favor of bailing out Fannie and Freddie. The influential National Association of Realtors (NAR) first backed the Housing and Economic Recovery Act "to help the housing and mortgage industries and boost the U.S. economy."[45] When the GSEs faced potential bankruptcy, the NAR also supported bipartisan efforts to bail them out. However, policymakers needed little convincing: They were inclined to bail out the GSEs regardless, given their significant macroeconomic role. Lobby interests and party ideology were secondary considerations (Tooze 2018, 172–173).

The plan was to place the GSEs into conservatorship for a few months until a long-term solution could be found. But there is nothing as permanent as the provisional. The central role of the GSEs in the housing sector – integral to America's demand-led growth regime – made their quasi-nationalized status semi-permanent. As the Council of Economic Advisers noted, "while conservatorship can provide necessary stability over a period of months, a long-term plan to reestablish the link between mortgage lenders and financial markets is critical to the future of the mortgage market."[46] That plan, however,

[44] Ginnie Mae (September 2023), *Foreign Ownership of Agency MBS*.

[45] "NAR statement on President signing housing bill" (August 6, 2008), *The Fillmore Gazette*, www.fillmoregazette.com/real-estate/nar-statement-president-signing-housing-bill.

[46] Council of Economic Advisers (2009), *Annual Report*, 93.

never materialized. While other bailed-out financial firms, such as American International Group, were gradually released back to the private market soon after the financial crisis, it took policymakers years to even begin discussing possible ways to end the GSEs' nationalization.

HELP FOR HOMEOWNERS, LITTLE SUPPORT FOR RENTERS

Policymakers not only bailed out the GSEs to rescue the housing finance market but also provided direct support to distressed homeowners. The rationale was that offering homeowners debt reductions and refinancing help could prevent foreclosure while stabilizing house prices, mortgage lending, and consumer spending – key factors in preventing the Great Recession from becoming another Great Depression. Given homeowners' central position in America's economy based on credit and consumption (Krippner 2017), millions of homeowners received government support, while distressed renters received little or no assistance.

In terms of fiscal policy, the Bush administration introduced temporary tax relief for distressed homeowners. From 2008 to 2017 (with later extensions through 2020), the Mortgage Forgiveness Debt Relief Act allowed homeowners a tax exclusion on income generated through debt forgiveness or cancelled debt after foreclosure, costing the US Treasury an estimated USD 1.3 billion through 2017.[47] In addition, as part of the Housing and Economic Recovery Act of 2008, the Bush administration introduced a first-time homebuyer tax credit of USD 7,500. Around 2.3 million homeowners benefited from this provision, which cost around USD 16 billion from 2008 to 2010 (Baker 2012).

In the mortgage market, the administration of President Barack Obama (2009–2017) launched programs that helped distressed homeowners restructure and refinance their mortgages.[48] The Making Home Affordable Program consisted of two core components. First, the Home Affordable Modification Program (HAMP) was designed to restructure home loans by reducing interest and/or principal payments on mortgages. The US Treasury allocated roughly USD 45.6 billion from the Troubled Asset Relief

[47] Joint Committee on Taxation (October 5, 2007), *Estimated Revenue Effects of … Mortgage Debt Forgiveness Act of 2007*, www.jct.gov/publications.html?func=startdown&id=1366.

[48] An ineffective predecessor of these programs was the 2007–2008 *FHAsecure* program that allowed homeowners with adjustable-rate mortgages to refinance their mortgage into a fixed-rate FHA mortgage. But only a miniscule number of homeowners were able to make use of the program. In its place came the Hope for Homeowners program, part of the Housing and Economic Recovery Act of 2008, which authorized the FHA to insure up to USD 300 billion in newly refinanced mortgages of distressed borrowers from 2008 to 2011. The Obama administration integrated some of these programs into its Making Homes Affordable initiative.

Program (TARP), passed in 2008, mainly for this program. Second, the Home Affordable Refinance Program (HARP) allowed underwater homeowners to refinance their mortgages at lower rates if these mortgages were guaranteed by the GSEs. By 2018, when both programs had concluded, 1.7 million homeowners had restructured their mortgages through HAMP, and 3.5 million underwater homeowners had refinanced their mortgages through HARP.[49] The Council of Economic Advisers explained that restoring consumer spending in this way was important:

> Households that have refinanced their mortgages at the lower rates have obtained considerable savings. These savings have effects similar to tax cuts, improving households' financial positions and encouraging spending on other goods. With the help of the Home Affordable Refinance Program, approximately 3 million borrowers have refinanced, putting more than $6 billion of purchasing power at an annual rate into the hands of households.[50]

Supporting homeowners and their properties was thus intended to help turn around the economy through wealth and credit effects, and it was also a way to support their most important assets on which the American public–private welfare regime rested (Schelkle 2012; Atkinson 2019; Hacker 2002).

Of course, homeowners were not the only ones hit by the crisis. Many renters – predominantly racialized minorities – struggled with their rent payments and faced the prospect of eviction (Desmond 2016). Yet renters received far less in government support than homeowners during the crisis. One study found that 2.9 million renters received eviction filings in 2011, a number comparable to the peak of homeowners' foreclosure filings in 2010 (Gromis et al. 2022). The Housing and Economic Recovery Act of 2008 established a National Housing Trust Fund to support affordable rental housing for low-income households. But the fund was suspended immediately after its creation, as the GSEs – tasked with financing the fund – were placed into conservatorship the same year. The GSEs' new regulator, the FHFA, temporarily suspended the fund until 2016.[51] More generally, there is an interesting dynamic between owner-oriented housing groups and low-income housing advocates. Powerful housing groups, such as

[49] Making Home Affordable also included the Hardest Hit Fund, a program to prevent foreclosures in very distressed areas (USD 10 billion). HAMP and HARP data from US Treasury (2023), *Home Affordable Modification Program (HAMP) Summary*, https://home.treasury.gov/system/files/256/129_HAMP_Modification_Performance_Summary_Mar2023_v1.0.pdf. Also see FHFA (2019), *Refinance Report*, www.fhfa.gov/sites/default/files/2023-03/Feb19_Refi.pdf.

[50] Council of Economic Advisers (2010), *Annual Report*, 61.

[51] In 2016, the Fund allocated USD 174 million to low-income projects, a number that would gradually increase to USD 740 million in 2022; National Low Income Housing Coalition (2024), *National Housing Trust Fund (HTF) Allocations for 2024: $214 million*, https://nlihc.org/explore-issues/projects-campaigns/national-housing-trust-fund/allocations.

those representing realtors or homebuilders, do not want to be seen as opposing low-income housing. As a representative from the National Low Income Housing Coalition (NLIHC) explained:

> They don't want to be perceived as being in opposition to what we do, because we have a cachet of authenticity ... They all like to be seen as supporting us. They all give us money. And major banks give us money. It's sort of: "saving their souls." They don't give us *tons* of money, but they give us money, they support us. So we have very cordial relationships with everybody.[52]

However, their support masks a more pernicious aim: Lobby groups can buy off the little resistance from low-income housing advocates with relatively small amounts of cash.

Despite helping millions of homeowners, the Obama-era homeowner support programs were controversial – not for what they achieved but for what they did *not* achieve. Beyond the messy rollout,[53] some critics argued that these programs were not bold enough to stop the foreclosure crisis and adequately assist distressed homeowners (Mian and Sufi 2014). They contend that a more effective macroeconomic policy would have been to help more homeowners, which could have prevented the negative ripple effects of foreclosure and falling home values on household spending and aggregate demand.

While these critics have a point, it is telling that there was no similar debate about insufficient government support for renters. In the demand-led American growth regime, the economic well-being of homeowners and their home values is a national objective inextricably linked to the overall health of the economy. The minimal prominence of rental housing support during the Great Recession is a reminder of the marginalized role of renters in the American political economy.

THE FED'S HOUSING BAZOOKA

In addition to the actions of elected officials, the Fed also provided direct support to the housing market early in the financial crisis. While the Fed had provided direct housing support in the past, such as during the Great Depression and the credit crunches of the 1960s and 70s (see Chapters 2 and 4), the scale of the Fed's emergency housing support during the 2008 crisis was unmatched. The Fed soon held over one *trillion* dollars in housing bonds on its balance sheet, which helped stabilize and stimulate mortgage lending and house prices. The Fed's housing support became the latest addition to America's policy toolkit to support home lending.

52 NLIHC representative (author interview, Washington, DC, August 5, 2014).

53 The HAMP rollout was messy in that homeowners were required to submit extensive documentation and banks often mishandled processing homeowner applications for HAMP modifications; HUD official (author interview, Washington, DC, August 1, 2014).

The Fed's housing programs were part of larger central bank actions to stimulate the economy during the crisis. When the central bank had lowered interest rates to zero and exhausted conventional options, the Fed turned to "quantitative easing." This meant that the central bank purchased massive amounts of assets – primarily US Treasuries and GSE mortgage-backed securities – to flood financial markets with cash, thereby making credit readily available, lowering borrowing costs, and raising asset prices (Jacobs and King 2021; Wessel 2009). Housing was a major component of these important central bank programs. The macroeconomic aim was clear: Purchasing mortgage-backed securities on a massive scale would lower mortgage rates for consumers (and yields on mortgage-backed securities for investors).[54] The Fed's logic was that, if mortgage rates fell, housing demand would increase, boosting house prices and mortgage lending, which in turn would stimulate consumption via wealth and credit effects. In short, the Fed targeted housing as a monetary transmission strategy to stimulate the core elements of the American growth regime: Credit, demand, and consumption (cp. Mishkin 2007).

The Fed's initial idea behind purchasing GSE mortgage-backed securities and GSE agency debt was to achieve two objectives: Providing emergency support for housing and stimulating the wider economy. As the Fed noted, these actions were intended to "support the mortgage and housing markets and the economy more broadly."[55] First, these actions provided emergency assistance for the housing sector. Buying GSE agency debt helped the struggling GSEs by injecting funds into their operations. In addition, buying mortgage-backed securities from banks removed these distressed securities from their balance sheets.

Second, the Fed's interventions aimed to stimulate the wider economy by lowering mortgage rates, which central bankers hoped would stimulate housing demand, raise house prices, and boost private investment and consumption. Fed economists viewed depressed house prices and housing wealth as factors impairing consumer lending and spending. The Fed diagnosed that "[t]he deteriorating job market, along with the sizable losses of equity and housing wealth and the tightening of credit conditions, has depressed consumer sentiment and

[54] One mechanism for lowering mortgage rates is the signaling channel, suggesting that a central bank's housing bond purchases signal strong commitment to mortgage markets, which then drives down the risk and yields of these bonds. Another is the portfolio-rebalancing channel, suggesting that asset classes are imperfect substitutes in an investor's portfolio – owing to market frictions and regulatory constraints – such that a central bank's large-scale asset purchases of housing bonds reduce the supply and increase the demand of these bonds in the open market, which then raises their prices and lowers their yields. As the yields of housing bonds and mortgage rates are linked – that is, mortgages are often securitized – mortgage rates tend to fall along with the yields on housing bonds (Krishnamurthy and Vissing-Jorgensen 2011; Hancock and Passmore 2015).

[55] Federal Reserve Board (2008), *Annual Report*, 5.

spending."[56] The solution was straightforward: By purchasing large amounts of housing bonds, the central bank could help lower mortgage rates. In an internal memorandum, staff economists noted that "lower mortgage rates could prevent house prices from declining as much as otherwise, thereby minimizing the fall in private wealth and supporting consumption. Also, a wave of refinancing activity would raise disposable income for homeowners."[57] By lowering mortgage rates and boosting housing demand and prices, Fed economists believed they could stimulate consumer spending via wealth and credit effects. Such programs would also allow new buyers to enter the housing ladder at historically low mortgage rates.[58]

In late 2008, the Fed initiated its first round of housing bond purchases to improve both the housing sector and the economy. The Fed bought USD 500 billion in GSE mortgage-backed securities and USD 100 billion in GSE agency debt. By early 2009, it had raised these amounts to USD 1.25 trillion for MBS and USD 200 billion for agency debt. According to the Fed, these actions were designed to lower mortgage rates and improve mortgage availability, "which in turn should support housing markets and foster improved conditions in financial markets more generally."[59] In an interview, a former senior Fed official explained:

> So there was precedent for buying Fannie and Freddie securities even before they were under conservatorship in 2008. By purchasing mortgage-backed securities, the Fed was trying to influence the flow of credit and faith in the housing markets. We were authorized to buy those securities and we bought them before. I saw that the problems with the mortgage markets were a real impediment to easing monetary policy and the transmission of easing monetary policy. It was an important channel for monetary policy – important in and of itself and because it was the area causing problems. So if you could stabilize the housing market, it would help stabilize the financial system. I think the Federal Reserve had identified the weakness in the housing market, and the lack of a bounce back in the housing market as one of the primary factors holding back the economic recovery.[60]

A staff economist echoed this view, noting that the Fed bought mortgage-backed securities because the mortgage market was suffering and was the key source of the crisis, with perceived transmission effects into the wider economy.[61]

[56] Federal Reserve (February 24, 2009), *Monetary Policy Report to Congress*, www.federalreserve.gov/monetarypolicy/files/20090224_mprfullreport.pdf.

[57] Gagnon, J., and Holscher, M. (December 5, 2008), *Purchases of Agency MBS and Debt* [memorandum], Federal Reserve Board, Freedom of Information Act (FOIA) No. 2014-26.

[58] Dudley, W., and Madigan, B. (November 26, 2008), *Current status of program to purchase GSE debt and Agency MBS securities* [memorandum], Federal Reserve Board, FOIA 2014–26; Gagnon and Holscher, *Purchases of Agency MBS and Debt*.

[59] Federal Reserve (November 28, 2008), *Federal Reserve announces it will initiate a program to purchase the direct obligations of housing-related government-sponsored enterprises and mortgage-backed securities backed by Fannie Mae, Freddie Mac, and Ginnie Mae* [press release], www.federalreserve.gov/newsevents/pressreleases/monetary20081125b.htm.

[60] Former Fed official (author interview, Washington, DC, July 10, 2014).

[61] Fed staff economist (author interview, Washington, DC, September 10, 2014).

While the majority at the Fed viewed these measures as important tools to stimulate the economy, others criticized their market-distorting effects. By purchasing housing bonds, the central bank privileges housing over other sectors by channeling capital into housing and artificially reducing mortgage rates. In an internal memo, staff economists noted that market distortions would be a necessary evil: "This policy tool would tend to skew credit allocation toward one sector of the economy – something that ... would be unusual from a historical standpoint. Nonetheless, some distortion of credit allocation may be an acceptable price to achieve the Federal Reserve's dual mandate of maximum employment and price stability."[62] In an interview, the senior Fed official noted that:

> There was discomfort, for sure, with the idea that the Federal Reserve was allocating credit to particular a sector: housing. Some of the Reserve Bank Presidents, in particular, worried that this would set a precedent and Congress would come to us for other things. I didn't see it as that big of a threat. I saw it making policy more effective.[63]

Charles Plosser, then president of the Philadelphia Fed, voiced concern that these programs would invite pressure from politicians and interest groups: "We will get pressure from various interest groups to retain certain assets. We will certainly, in all likelihood, get calls from consumers, builders, and Congressmen if we start to sell mortgage-backed securities out of our portfolio in order to reduce its size. We will hear fears that the mortgage rates may rise."[64] Richard Fisher, president of the Dallas Fed, stated "I don't believe that we should be in the business of financing housing. I think that is a matter for the Treasury and for other authorities, and I would like to get out of that business as quickly as possible."[65] He went so far as to call the practice of buying housing bonds "social engineering."[66] Jeffrey Lacker, president of the Richmond Fed, warned that the Fed's housing programs would distort credit allocations and perpetuate "this really corrosive political economy in our country of tapping government resources to subsidize the housing market."[67] In an opinion piece, he elaborated that "[i]t is as if the Fed has provided off-budget funding for home-mortgage borrowers."[68]

Despite these dissenting voices, the majority within the Fed viewed housing as the key impediment holding back the US economy, paving the way for additional housing bond purchases later on. For the time being, the Fed kept its housing bond portfolio at around USD 1 trillion until 2012

62 Gagnon and Holscher, *Purchases of Agency MBS and Debt.*
63 Former Fed official (author interview, Washington, DC, July 10, 2014).
64 FOMC (January 27–28, 2009), meeting transcript.
65 FOMC (January 26–27, 2010), meeting transcript.
66 FOMC (April 26–27, 2011), meeting transcript.
67 FOMC (September 20–21, 2011), meeting transcript.
68 Lacker, J., and Weinberg, J. (October 7, 2014), "The Fed's mortgage favoritism," *Wall Street Journal.*

(see Figure 8.2).[69] Fundamentally, the Fed joined federal policymakers in *directly* supporting the country's home lending market, providing massive monetary policy support for America's national champion – housing finance – that no other economic sector has enjoyed (Jacobs and King 2021).

A NATIONALIZED HOUSING FINANCE MARKET: THE NEW NORMAL?

The conservatorship, or quasi-nationalization, of the GSEs was initially intended as a short-term crisis measure. However, when the worst of the crisis was over, policymakers opted to keep them in conservatorship. Reforming the nationalized status quo could have hurt housing by increasing mortgage costs and creating disruptions in a highly complex housing finance system, thereby damaging a sector essential to America's demand-led growth regime. Although both parties and even the housing lobby felt uneasy about the state of quasi-nationalization, they recognized that reducing the government's role in housing finance has one key consequence: "any GSE reform, no matter where it lands, will likely drive up mortgage rates."[70] Starting from a point of conservatorship means that reform would inevitably reduce government involvement and increase private market participation. As private markets would assume more risk, mortgage rates would rise (Parrott and Zandi 2015, 5), leading to lower house prices, decreased household wealth, and reduced credit and spending. In contrast to the sweeping Dodd-Frank financial reforms that took on the powerful banking industry, comprehensive housing finance reform stalled owing to the fear of increasing mortgage costs, harming housing wealth, and slowing economic growth.[71]

As a result of a fragile postcrisis housing market, the Obama administration and Congress initially refrained from even debating housing finance reform until 2012. Housing remained a drag on the economy, contributing to the slow-moving return to economic growth that averaged only around 2 percent per year from 2010 to 2013, with unemployment still at 8 percent in 2012. Growth in other sectors, such as health and manufacturing, could not fully compensate for the weakness in housing. Despite low mortgage rates, housing demand remained subdued because of high unemployment, market uncertainty, and low levels of investor and consumer confidence. As a result, housing starts remained well below one million per year from 2010 to 2013 (see Figure 2.2), partly also because of high vacancy rates. House prices also

[69] In 2010, the Fed introduced a second round of quantitative easing that included the purchase of USD 600 billion in Treasury bonds, with the goal of bringing down long-term interest rates more generally, not just mortgage rates.

[70] Garrison, T. (April 28, 2014), "GSE reform will drive up mortgage rates," *HousingWire.*

[71] Former member of the US House of Representatives (Republican, Arizona) (author interview, August 6, 2015).

remained depressed until 2012, preventing households from recovering the USD 7 *trillion* in household wealth lost during the crisis. At the same time, 10 million homeowners (or 20 percent of all mortgaged properties) were still underwater in early 2013, forcing households to deleverage – that is, to reduce debt burdens by selling off distressed properties or by increasing household savings and reducing spending (Mian and Sufi 2014).[72] Meanwhile, banks tightened mortgage credit for moderate-income households, slowing mortgage lending. The Council of Economic Advisers repeatedly highlighted that wealth effects were inhibited, noting that "a massive loss of wealth during the financial crisis … continues to constrain consumption."[73] As a result, housing finance reform was on the back burner.

It was not until 2013, when the housing market began to show more signs of life and the economy continued to improve, that Congress entertained the idea of housing finance reform, albeit half-heartedly.[74] The reform proposals discussed ranged from fully privatizing the GSEs to replacing the GSEs with many smaller private firms that would still enjoy government support.[75] Concerns about potential adverse economic effects, such as higher mortgage costs or disruptions in the mortgage market that could negatively impact housing markets and the broader economy, contributed to stalling the reform process.

The 2013 Protecting American Taxpayers and Homeowners (PATH) Act, proposed by House Republicans, suggested the privatization of Fannie and Freddie. This proposal would have marked a significant retreat of the American state from the mortgage market and deviated from the longstanding path of America's government-supported housing model. However, it was immediately dismissed by the Obama White House, along with Democrats and moderate Republicans in Congress, who viewed it as a threat to mortgage affordability and the availability of the thirty-year fixed-rate mortgage.[76] Privatization would have required banks to bear more mortgage risks, as they could no longer offload their mortgages to the GSEs. Such a change could have driven up mortgage rates and limited banks' ability to offer the popular

72 Calculated Risk Blog (June 12, 2013), *CoreLogic: Negative Equity Decreases in Q1 2013, 9.7 Million Properties Still with Negative Equity*, www.calculatedriskblog.com/2013/06/corelogic-negative-equity-decreases-in.html.

73 Council of Economic Advisers (2012), *Annual Report*, 21.

74 In 2011, the Obama administration laid out some broad options for future housing finance reform as mandated by the Dodd-Frank Act, but without spending much political capital to implement these options. See US Treasury and HUD (2011), *Reforming America's Housing Finance Market*, https://archives.hud.gov/news/2011/housingfinmarketreform.pdf.

75 Layton, D. (July 6, 2022), *When Will Government Control of Freddie Mac and Fannie Mae End?* (Part 1), NYU Furman Center, https://furmancenter.org/thestoop/entry/when-will-government-control-of-freddie-mac-and-fannie-mae-end.

76 Policy staffer for House Majority Leader Eric Cantor (Republican, Virginia) (author interview, phone, August 25, 2014).

thirty-year fixed-rate mortgage. Joseph Murin, former president of Ginnie Mae, cautioned about reducing the government's role in housing finance:

> The assumption that, even with time, private markets would simply pick up the role of the GSEs and Ginnie may or may not be accurate. But what if it *is* wrong? The economic chaos would be astronomical, and simply picking up the pieces of the infrastructure we had just replaced would be no mean feat ... Mortgage lending would become much riskier for banks and non-bank lenders ... The cost of a mortgage would likely go up.[77]

Another option, recapitalizing and releasing the mortgage giants to their pre-crisis status, was also rejected by the Obama administration, as it would "willfully [recreate] the very system that helped do this nation so much harm."[78] The inability and unwillingness to reform the housing finance system led Obama White House economists to describe it as the "key unfinished piece of business from the financial crisis."[79]

A set of bipartisan bills, among them the Johnson-Crapo and Corker-Warner bills, showed more promise as they suggested retaining a key role of the federal government but increasing some private market participation. In simple terms, the idea was to replace the GSEs with multiple small private firms that would compete with one another in issuing and trading mortgage-backed securities. A new public entity – the Federal Mortgage Insurance Corporation, modeled after the Federal Deposit Insurance Corporation – would support these firms by offering government insurance on mortgage-backed securities. In this model, investors would still be guaranteed payments from mortgage-backed securities for a fee, but investors would also take first losses in the case of large-scale mortgage defaults. However, an Obama Treasury official expressed in an interview that "[t]here was the overall concern that this would wind up being too expensive [for homeowners] relative to where things are now."[80] An internal memorandum from Freddie Mac indicated that "[t]here is no question that ... mortgage rates would increase under the bill."[81] As house prices and mortgage lending recovered, the urgency for reform diminished.[82] The proposals also struck a difficult balance: They involved too much government intervention for free-market Republicans and insufficient promotion of affordable homeownership for progressive Democrats. For instance, Senator Elizabeth Warren (Democrat,

[77] Murin, J. (May 26, 2015). "Caution: GSE reform could have serious unintended consequences," *HousingWire*.

[78] Cited in Lane, B. (October 29, 2015), "Stegman doubles down: White House will not recapitalize Fannie, Freddie," *HousingWire*.

[79] Furman, J., and Stock, J. (April 24, 2014), "The moment is right for housing reform," *Wall Street Journal*.

[80] Former Treasury official II (author interview, Washington, DC, August 1, 2014).

[81] Timiraos, N. (April 25, 2014), "Fannie, Freddie say overhaul would boost mortgage rates," *Wall Street Journal*.

[82] Ginnie Mae official (author interview, Washington, DC, March 8, 2016).

Massachusetts) said that "[i]t is harder to get a Freddie or Fannie mortgage than at any time in history. [Johnson-Crapo] would cut the pool of qualified borrowers by 20 percent. Think about that, one in five families who would be eligible today would not be."[83] Consequently, the proposals failed to garner sufficient support.[84] Beyond these political issues, a former Freddie Mac official also mentioned in an interview that, while these reform proposals were sound in principle, they likely would not have worked in practice. The technical challenge of incentivizing private market actors to create firms akin to the GSEs would require large amounts of capital, and the transition from the old to the new system could have caused severe market disruptions, threatening the still fragile economy recovery.[85]

In 2018, Representatives Jeb Hensarling (Republican, Texas) and John Delaney (Democrat, Maryland) introduced another bipartisan bill, which would have retained strong government guarantees through Ginnie Mae, a fully public agency, while privatizing the GSEs. It was surprising that Hensarling, one of the most vocal free-market Republicans, sponsored a bill with strong government involvement. He admitted that the bill "does not necessarily represent my preferred policy, or optimal policy."[86] Just a few years earlier, Hensarling had pushed the PATH Act, which would have completely privatized the GSEs. His shift illustrated the perceived importance of housing to the economy, convincing even the most free-market Republicans that the American state is essential in housing finance. However, the bill stalled because it was expected to drive up mortgage costs, and by that point, housing finance reform had lost momentum in Congress.

The housing lobby fiercely opposed the complete privatization of the GSEs and instead supported proposals that retained a strong role for the government. Early on, in 2013, the NAR condemned the Republican PATH Act:

> any new secondary market entity replacing the enterprises must have an explicit government guarantee to ensure the availability of affordable credit products for all creditworthy individuals and families … . A federal guarantee is essential to ensure borrowers have access to affordable mortgage credit. Without government backing, creditworthy consumers will pay much higher mortgage interest rates and mortgages may at times not be readily available.[87]

[83] Cited in Garrison, T. (May 15, 2014), "Johnson-Crapo reform bill voted to Senate floor," *HousingWire*.

[84] Policy staffer for House Majority Leader Eric Cantor (Republican, Virginia) (author interview, phone, August 25, 2014).

[85] Former Freddie Mac official (author interview, phone, July 19, 2022).

[86] US House of Representatives (September 6, 2018), *A Failure to Act: How A Decade Without GSE Reform Has Once Again Put Taxpayers at Risk* (No. 115-115): *Hearing before the House Committee on Financial Services* (testimony of J. Hensarling), 2.

[87] US Senate (October 29, 2013), *Housing Finance Reform: Essentials of a Functioning Housing Finance System for Consumers* (S. Hrg. 113-146): *Hearing before the Senate Committee on Banking, Housing, and Urban Affairs* (written statement of G. Thomas), 89.

The mortgage bankers and homebuilders echoed the sentiment, agreeing that any reform should retain a significant role for the government in ensuring the availability of low-cost mortgages for borrowers and a steady flow of mortgage credit. The Mortgage Bankers Association (MBA) warned that "[w]ithout this Government backstop, the mortgage market would be smaller and mortgage credit would be more expensive,"[88] while the National Association of Home Builders (NAHB) insisted that the "Government role must be maintained to avoid future interruptions in the flow of credit to mortgage borrowers ... such a system would entail lower housing credit costs than one that relied exclusively on private players."[89] Even without these demands, it is unlikely that the PATH Act would have secured congressional support. In 2020, the housing lobby endorsed housing finance reform that would gradually release the GSEs from conservatorship while retaining explicit government guarantees on mortgage debt via the GSEs.[90] In principle, many policymakers of both parties agreed with these calls for reform. In practice, however, politicians' concerns that reforms could produce higher mortgage costs, create market disruptions, and hinder economic growth "locked in" the quasi-nationalized status quo of the American mortgage market. In previous decades, policymakers had built a housing finance model dominated by the American state; they feared that replacing or even reforming it could disrupt the housing finance system that had become so essential to the American economy.

As legislative reform proved nearly impossible, regulators and policymakers opted for internal administrative reforms to the existing GSEs. For example, the GSEs reduced their massive investment portfolios and mitigated their exposure to credit risk through "credit-risk-transfer programs," which are complicated financial instruments that have allowed the GSEs to sell off credit risk to investors since 2013.[91] However, these changes are relatively minor, and major reforms still require congressional approval. As Figure 6.3 shows, America's housing sector continues to enjoy the vast majority of federal credit guarantees when compared to commercial or student loans.

[88] US Senate (October 31, 2013), *Housing Finance Reform: Essential Elements of a Government Guarantee for Mortgage-Backed Securities* (S. Hrg. 113–167): *Hearing before the Senate Committee on Banking, Housing, and Urban Affairs* (testimony of D. Stevens), 104.

[89] US Senate (November 7, 2013), *Housing Finance Reform: Essential Elements to Provide Affordable Options for Housing* (S. Hrg. 113–175): *Hearing before the Senate Committee on Banking, Housing, and Urban Affairs* (testimony of R. Judson), 37.

[90] ABA, MBA, NAHB, and NAR (December 14, 2020), *Housing and Mortgage Industries' Views Regarding the Status of the GSE Conservatorships* [joint letter], Washington, DC, www.aba.com/advocacy/policy-analysis/joint-letter-to-treasury-on-gse-conservatorships.

[91] Wachter, S. (December 2018), "Credit risk transfer, informed markets, and securitization," *Federal Reserve Bank of New York Economic Policy Review* 24(3); Layton, D. (July 6, 2020), *Demystifying GSE Credit Risk Transfer: Special Interests and Politicization*, Industry Perspectives, Joint Center for Housing Studies.

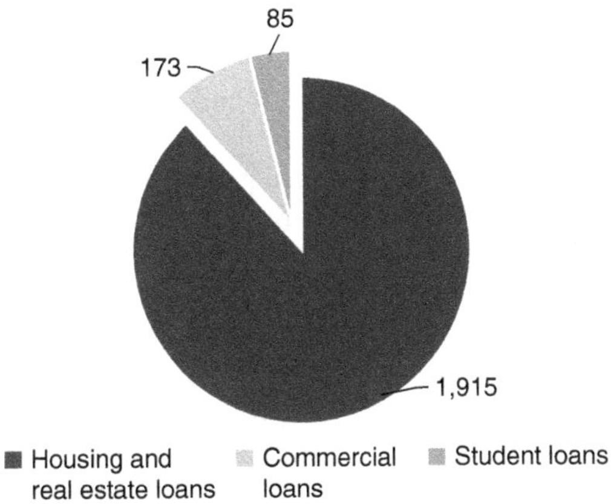

FIGURE 6.3 Federal credit commitments and obligations in 2023, USD billions
Data source: Congressional Budget Office (CBO) Estimates of the Cost of Federal Credit Programs in 2023.

The nationalization of America's housing finance market, described as a form of "comradely capitalism" by *The Economist*, was here to stay.[92]

TRAPPING THE FED: MAKING MORTGAGE SUPPORT PERMANENT

When the worst of the crisis was over, elected officials chose to make the quasi-nationalization of the GSEs semi-permanent, even though the measure had originally been designed to be temporary. The Fed faced a similar decision about whether to reduce its holdings of GSE mortgage-backed securities, which had directly supported the country's housing finance market throughout the crisis. As an independent institution, the Fed presumably faced fewer political constraints in reducing support for the US housing market. However, the Fed, too, doubled down on its housing support, aiming to lower mortgage rates to stimulate housing, consumption, and above all economic growth. For the central bank, stimulating housing shifted from being an extraordinary crisis measure to a *permanent tool* for achieving economic growth and reinforcing the American demand-led growth regime. Alongside the country's housing tax breaks and government guarantees in primary and secondary mortgage markets, the Fed institutionalized a new layer of *permanent* government support for mortgages: Large-scale housing bond-buying programs. The Fed's support was the logical next step in the expansion of

[92] "Comradely capitalism: How America accidentally nationalised its mortgage market" (August 20, 2016), *The Economist*.

America's government-supported housing model essential to the country's demand-led growth regime.

In 2012, the Fed initiated another round of housing bond-buying, stating it would continue to do so "until the outlook for the labor market has improved substantially."[93] At this point, the Fed's housing support was no longer addressing an acute crisis; instead, it had been repurposed to foster economic recovery. This round of bond-buying included monthly purchases of USD 40 billion in mortgage-backed securities issued by the GSEs, as well as USD 45 billion in US Treasuries. The goal was to "put downward pressure on longer-term interest rates, support mortgage markets, and help to make broader financial conditions more accommodative."[94] When questioned about why the Fed did not exclusively expand its balance sheet with US Treasuries – an alternative strategy considered less risky and more sector-neutral by some regional central bankers – a staff economist explained that purchasing MBS was part of an ongoing effort to revive the housing sector, which was holding back the economic recovery.[95] As a result, the Fed's balance-sheet holdings of GSE mortgage-backed-securities increased from USD 1.1 trillion in 2010 to USD 1.7 trillion in 2014 (see Figure 8.2).

Some Fed officials remained concerned that housing would be privileged over other sectors, but the majority believed that the weak housing market was holding back the country's economic recovery. According to the Federal Open Market Committee (FOMC) minutes: "MBS purchases could be preferable because they would more directly support the housing sector, which remains weak but has shown some signs of improvement of late. One participant, however, objected that purchases of MBS, when compared to purchases of longer-term Treasury securities, would likely result in higher interest rates for many borrowers in other sectors."[96] The San Francisco Fed explained that housing bond purchases were intended to "stimulate the economy … by pushing down residential mortgage interest rates. Lower mortgage rates encourage home purchases and mortgage refinancing. … When mortgage rates are lower, payments are lower and house prices tend to rise. *Homeowners are better off and may spend more.*"[97] Some members of the Fed thus believed that housing asset purchases would actively stimulate not only the housing market but also consumer spending through wealth and credit effects resulting from lower mortgage rates and higher house prices.

Expanding the Fed's balance sheet to support housing market activity was one thing; reducing the Fed's bloated balance sheet was another, and nobody

93 Federal Reserve Board (2013), *Annual Report*, 35.

94 FOMC (October 24, 2012), "Federal Reserve issues FOMC statement," press release.

95 Fed staff economist (author interview, Washington, DC, September 10, 2014).

96 FOMC (September 12–13, 2012), minutes of meeting, 8.

97 Bauer, M. (May 21, 2012), "Fed asset buying and private borrowing rates," *FRBSF Economic Letter* (no. 16), 4. My emphasis.

quite knew how to do it. As the US economy and housing market kept recovering – with unemployment dropping and house prices rising again in 2013 and 2014 – the monetary policy debate shifted toward balance-sheet consolidation. Under outgoing chair Ben Bernanke, the Fed announced the end of its balance-sheet *expansion* with the tapering of asset purchases in December 2013, a policy continued by the incoming chair Janet Yellen. Tapering meant that the Fed largely *retained* its balance-sheet holdings until 2018, amounting to USD 1.8 *trillion* in mortgage-backed securities and USD 2.5 trillion in Treasury bonds (see Figure 8.2). However, even mentioning the idea of tapering caused a "taper tantrum" among investors in June 2013, making the process of scaling back the Fed's balance sheet a delicate task.

As the economy and housing market continued to recover, in 2017, the Fed began reducing its balance-sheet holdings, but not nearly to pre-crisis levels. By 2019, the Fed's holdings of mortgage-backed securities were still USD 1.4 trillion. While policymakers had to bully the Fed into buying housing bonds in the late 1960s and 1970s, as Chapter 4 described, this time was different – the Fed did not need any convincing. Despite some criticism from Republicans,[98] it embraced supporting housing as a *permanent* tool to manage and stimulate America's demand-led growth regime. However, as Acharya and colleagues (2011, 101) note, "the more that the Fed gets caught up in the rest of the federal government's expansion into mortgage finance, the more likely it is that its future monetary policy will *not* be independent."

To put it another way, America's growth regime trapped not only elected officials but even the world's most powerful central bank into supporting housing.

THE TRUMP SHOCK: DISRUPTING THE BIPARTISAN HOUSING-BASED GROWTH CONSENSUS?

President Donald Trump's first term (2017–2021) disrupted American politics in more than one policy area. Positions once inconceivable in the United States – such as withdrawing from NATO or disputing fair democratic elections – became reality. When it came to housing, however, Trump met his match. The pro-business Trump administration took issue with the outsized role of the US government in the housing finance market, leading to attempts to reform housing tax breaks and the GSEs. Yet macroeconomic imperatives thwarted these efforts, as they had so many times before, and America's government-sponsored housing finance model remained largely intact.

As previous chapters have detailed, there is a long history of failed attempts to reform the MID. After the Great Recession, for example, President Obama

[98] In 2015, Republicans proposed a bill, known as Audit the Fed, to curb the Fed's independence by granting oversight authority to the Government Accountability Office (Binder and Spindel 2017).

attempted to curb the MID for the wealthiest households as part of the administration's annual budgets but did not expend much political capital on the effort.[99] Suzanne Mettler (2010, 811) suggests that Obama's hesitancy was due to "the political power possessed by the organized groups that benefit from such provisions, starting with the real estate lobby." Indeed, the housing lobby emphasized the damage a reform could do to the housing market's recovery when these discussions arose in 2012. As the mortgage bankers argued: "We need the housing market to recover … for the broader U.S. economy to get back on track."[100] Politicians, including influential Democrats in Congress, such as Representative Nancy Pelosi (California) and Senator Charles Schumer (New York), were already in favor of preserving the MID. Senator Ron Wyden (Democrat, Oregon) noted that taking away the deduction from the "housing sector [that] is so fragile" could result in serious economic harm (quoted in Benson and Tomkin 2010). Shaun Donovan, then HUD Secretary, conceded that "[a]nything that would change the system substantially now [could create] a real risk of stopping the momentum that we have in the housing market."[101] It was once again policymakers' macroeconomic imperative of avoiding disruptions to the housing market that prevented reform, not just the housing lobby.

Nonetheless, President Trump made headlines when he attacked the MID in 2017. By the mid-2010s, the economic and housing context had significantly improved. House prices exceeded their pre-crisis level in 2016. After a long period of household deleveraging that had begun in 2007, outstanding mortgage debt significantly rose again for the first time in 2015. As vacancies dwindled, housing starts trended upwards from a trough of only 550,000 in 2008 to 1.2 million in 2016, although they remained below the historical averages of 1.5 million (see Figure 2.2). In early 2016 the number of underwater homeowners also decreased from 11 million in 2011 to 4 million (8% of all mortgage holders), while housing wealth reached its pre-crisis level of USD 14 trillion in the same year.[102] The Council of Economic Experts found that wealth effects had returned by 2014, noting that "[s]trong gains in aggregate household net

[99] President Obama's National Commission on Fiscal Responsibility and Reform recommended capping the mortgage amount to USD 500,000 for principal residences and eliminating the MID on home equity loans and second homes. See National Commission on Fiscal Responsibility and Reform (December 2010), *The Moment of Truth*, www.ssa.gov/history/reports/ObamaFiscal/TheMomentofTruth12_1_2010.pdf.

[100] Panchuk, K. A. (October 10, 2012), "MBA ready to defend mortgage interest deduction," *HousingWire*.

[101] Dennis, B. (September 28, 2012) "Hands off homeowners' tax break, HUD chief says," *Washington Post*.

[102] Calculated Risk Blog (June 9, 2016), *CoreLogic: 268,000 US homeowners regained equity in the first quarter of 2016*, www.calculatedriskblog.com/2016/06/corelogic-268000-us-homeowners-regained.html; Housing Finance Policy Center (November 2024), *Housing Finance at a Glance*.

worth – both an increase in assets and a decline in the debt burden – have supported aggregate consumer spending."[103] By 2017, housing-based growth was recovering well but was not yet the engine of growth it had once been.

It was in this context that Trump's Tax Cuts and Jobs Act of 2017 targeted the MID, but the deduction survived with some temporary limitations. The centrality of housing to the American growth regime narrowed the parameters within which Trump and House Republicans could enact reform. As a result, the reform neither eliminated nor permanently reduced the MID. Eliminating the MID was never seriously on the table. While Democrats opposed Republican tax reform proposals altogether, even some Republicans – particularly in high-tax, high-cost states such as California, New Jersey, and New York – did not want to inflict potential damage on the housing market.[104] Representative Peter King (Republican, New York) noted that the "mortgage interest deduction and the property tax deduction are essential to stabilizing our housing market and safeguarding home values."[105] Senate Finance Committee Chair Orrin Hatch (Republican, Utah) thus said "there's some room to do something there, but not much room."[106]

Given these constraints, the Trump administration managed to *temporarily curb* the MID, capping it at USD 750,000 in home value (previously one million), but only until the end of 2025.[107] The reform also temporarily capped the state and local tax (SALT) deduction at USD 10,000 (previously unlimited), which includes local property taxes.[108] Capping the SALT deduction meant that owners of expensive homes received fewer tax subsidies. Ironically, President Trump, a real estate mogul, reduced some of America's most cherished real estate tax breaks against the resistance of the housing lobby, which predicted a 10 percent decline in house prices.[109] These reforms can be interpreted both as a political attack on coastal Democrat-leaning states, where house prices and property taxes are high, and as a move to finance corporate tax cuts (Slemrod 2018). The episode demonstrates that

[103] Council of Economic Advisers (2014), *Annual Report*, 57.

[104] Senate Republicans wanted to retain the MID, while House Republicans were the driving force behind capping the MID.

[105] Quoted in Congressional Office of Congressman Brad Sherman (July 28, 2017), *Congressman Sherman Introduces Resolution to Preserve the Dream of Homeownership*, https://sherman.house.gov/media-center/press-releases/congressman-sherman-introduces-resolution-to-preserve-the-dream-of.

[106] Ota, A. (December 6, 2016), *Battle Lines Form Over Popular Mortgage Interest Reduction*, Roll Call https://rollcall.com/2016/12/06/battle-lines-form-over-popular-mortgage-interest-deduction/.

[107] The reform also temporarily limited the use of the MID on home equity loans for home improvement only.

[108] The tax reform also doubled the standard deduction for both singles and married couples, providing fewer incentives for many households to itemize deductions such as the MID.

[109] Mendenhall, E. (November 20, 2017), *Association's Strong Opposition to 'The Tax Cuts and Jobs Act'* [letter to the US Senate], https://narfocus.com/billdatabase/clientfiles/172/2/3045.pdf.

the power of housing interest groups is often overstated, as they could not prevent these changes from the pro-business Trump administration who they helped elect.[110] Despite these changes, which the second Trump administration and the Republican-controlled Congress might make permanent, the MID continues to be one of the largest subsidies in the tax code.

The Trump administration ran up against the imperatives of the American growth regime again when it tried to privatize the housing finance system. In 2019, Trump proposed reforms combining the privatization of the GSEs with strong government guarantees to support them.[111] The plan faced familiar challenges that had stymied previous reform efforts: Projected increases in mortgage costs and falling house prices, which would undermine housing-based growth.[112] Once again, Congress was unwilling to revisit GSE reform. Trump then attempted to privatize the GSEs through administrative actions but ultimately failed. Despite some executive actions, such as allowing the GSEs to retain their earnings and build capital reserves, the Trump administration ran out of time during its first term and would have needed congressional action for more comprehensive changes to the GSEs. These ideologically driven attempts to reform and privatize the housing finance system failed: A critical mass of policymakers viewed rising borrowing costs and falling house prices, as well as the risk of disrupting a complex housing finance system, as detrimental to America's housing-based growth regime to which their electoral prospects were tied. While President Joe Biden (2021–2025) showed little interest in legislative GSE reform and retained the quasi-nationalized status quo of the GSEs with minimal changes, the implications of the second Trump administration and the Republican-controlled Congress for the GSEs remain uncertain at the time of writing.

CONCLUSION

In response to the Great Recession, US policymakers doubled down on government support for housing to rescue and reinforce America's housing market and demand-led growth regime (see Table 6.1). One of the most far-reaching rescue actions was the *nationalization* of the country's housing finance market through the seizure of mortgage giants Fannie Mae and Freddie Mac. Another significant set of rescue actions involved the Fed's direct housing support, which included purchasing large amounts of mortgage-backed securities

110 Wilhelm, C. (August 4, 2017), "Trump administration weighs slashing mortgage deduction," *Politico*.

111 US Treasury (September 2019), *Housing Reform Plan*, https://home.treasury.gov/system/files/136/HUD-Housing-Finance-Reform-Plan-September-2019.pdf.

112 Jan, T., and Merle, R. (September 10, 2019), "Trump's housing finance plan will make mortgages more expensive," *Washington Post*.

TABLE 6.1 *American housing finance programs adopted or reformed between 2000 and 2024*

Type of program	Name of program/agency	Years active	Implementation and modifications
Tax	Mortgage interest deduction	1913–	Tax Cuts and Jobs Act of 2017 temporarily reduced deduction (until 2025)
Tax	Property tax deduction	1913–	Tax Cuts and Jobs Act of 2017 temporarily limited state and local tax deduction (SALT), including for property taxes (until 2025)
Tax	Mortgage Forgiveness Debt Relief Act	2008–2020	In response to 2008 crisis, allowed homeowners a tax exclusion on income generated through debt forgiveness or cancelled debt after foreclosure; replaced by a modified provision in 2020, extended through 2025
Credit/direct subsidy	American Dream Downpayment Initiative	2003–2007	Assisted low-income and minority households with down payments for buying homes
Credit	GSE affordable housing goals	1968–	In the 2000s the Bush administration expanded affordable housing goals
Credit	Fannie Mae conservatorship	2008–	The Treasury placed Fannie Mae in conservatorship under authority granted by Housing and Economic Recovery Act of 2008
Credit	Freddie Mac conservatorship	2008–	The Treasury placed Freddie Mac in conservatorship in 2008
Credit	Making Home Affordable Program	2009–2016 (some initiatives until 2018)	The Home Affordable Modification Program restructured distressed home loans; the Home Affordable Refinance Program refinanced underwater mortgages
Central bank	GSE bond buying program (i.e., quantitative easing)	2008–	The Fed's large-scale GSE bond and mortgage-backed securities buying program, initially in response to the 2008 crisis

issued by Fannie Mae and Freddie Mac. These crisis-era measures were initially designed to be temporary but quickly became entrenched. Policymakers and central bankers faced similar macroeconomic constraints: Withdrawing support from housing could undermine housing-based growth essential to the demand-led economy. Consequently, a quasi-nationalized mortgage market and a highly interventionist central bank became the new postcrisis normal in the American political economy. To some, the vast expansion of housing programs might seem paradoxical in the "land of free markets." Instead, as this book has argued, it was the logical culmination of a century-long process of cumulative political actions to stimulate housing and reinforce America's demand-led growth regime.

The contrast with Germany is striking. During the Great Recession, American policymakers boosted housing *demand* even though housing vacancies had increased from around 11 percent in the early 2000s to almost 15 percent of the entire US housing stock in 2009, and well over 20 percent in such states as Florida and Arizona (Baker 2018). When Germany experienced its own housing crisis in the 2000s, including large-scale vacancies, politicians took the opposite approach, *reducing* government support for housing. This will be the topic of Chapter 7.

7

The Double Back

Retrenching German Housing Programs

After experiencing a post-unification housing boom that left Germany's eastern regions with one million too many homes, the housing market came crashing down in the late 1990s and early 2000s. Symbolic of this decline was the demise of one of the country's largest construction firms and employers, Holzmann AG. In 1999, the company narrowly avoided bankruptcy with a bailout orchestrated by Deutsche Bank and the government under Chancellor Gerhard Schröder. As German banks were initially reluctant to come to the rescue, both the German and international press had associated Holzmann's near-collapse with the demise of the German model of coordinated capitalism: "Many Germans, who credit the system for the country's postwar economic rebirth, see the failure of banks to support Holzmann as a breakdown of what has come to be known as 'Rhineland' capitalism."[1] Just three years later, in 2002, the company declared bankruptcy and failed. While the German model did not fall apart, the story captures the doom and gloom about the reeling post-unification economy. From the mid-1990s to the early 2000s, Germany was one of the slowest-growing economies in Europe. "The sick man of the euro," as *The Economist* called the country,[2] exhibited several structural economic problems: High nonwage labor costs, losses in export competitiveness, and exploding fiscal deficits that put Germany in the embarrassing position of violating the eurozone's Maastricht criteria that the country itself had helped to enshrine. Although often overlooked, the country's dismal housing performance was a key part of Germany's economic woes.

American and German policymakers responded in strikingly different ways to their respective housing and economic crises in the 2000s. As discussed in

[1] Schmid, J. (November 24, 1999), "Germany fails in effort to keep builder afloat," *New York Times*; also see Baron, S. (November 26, 1999), "Rhineland capitalism's last hurrah," *Wall Street Journal*.

[2] "The sick man of the euro" (June 3, 1999), *The Economist*.

Chapter 6, American policymakers doubled down on housing programs to stabilize private demand, credit, and consumption – even though excesses in these areas had contributed to the financial crisis of 2008–2009. In contrast, German policymakers responded to their own housing and economic crisis by *doubling back* and eliminating longstanding federal social housing programs and homeownership programs to revive the export-oriented economy. The contrast between the two countries could not be starker. While American policymakers formed a bipartisan consensus, viewing housing programs as essential for rescuing and stimulating the US economy, the German political consensus regarded housing programs as structural economic problems. In Germany, housing programs were sacrificed in the name of reviving the reeling export-led growth regime.

Parts of the country's economic and housing woes of the late 1990s and early 2000s were related to reunification. When the Federal Republic of Germany absorbed the former German Democratic Republic (GDR), the unified country experienced significant housing shortages due to population movements of eastern newcomers to the west and the poor housing conditions left by the GDR in eastern housing markets (Von Beyme 1999, 142; Conradi and Zöpel 1994). In response, the Kohl government adopted temporary yet massive housing programs for both homeownership and rental investors to stimulate investment, growth, and employment in the east. Kohl's housing stimulus – including a mortgage interest deduction – was a textbook case of an American-style housing-based growth strategy that brought about a short-lived property and construction boom in eastern Germany. However, the boom was built on shaky ground and led to massive overinvestment. By the late 1990s, the construction industry had collapsed, as the Holzmann example illustrates, and eastern Germany had a surplus of over one million housing units. Kohl's American housing approach failed. While other rich democracies – especially the United States – saw booming housing markets from the late 1990s until the financial crisis of 2008–2009, German house prices fell or stagnated during this period.

At the same time that the country experienced a housing downturn, the German growth regime was also threatened by increasing fiscal deficits and losses in export competitiveness. It was in this context that German policymakers pulled the plug on housing programs. Longstanding housing programs – already under considerable pressure from the mid-1970s (see Chapter 5) – became structural economic problems in the eyes of policymakers. The Social Democrats under Chancellor Gerhard Schröder led the charge, blaming these policies for having contributed to a fiscal crisis and capital misallocations in the economy resulting in massive housing oversupply in eastern Germany. They also identified a trade-off between housing programs and the export-led growth regime, arguing that these programs would shift private capital and government funds away from education, research, and technology essential to the German export model.

The Christian Democrats – who had long supported homeownership programs for ideological reasons – eventually agreed that sacrificing housing programs was necessary to revive the country's growth regime. Housing policy retrenchment was thus part of a broad-based consensus on austerity measures and structural economic reforms, including the Hartz labor market and welfare state reforms (named after former Volkswagen executive Peter Hartz, who chaired the commission that developed the 2003–2005 reforms).

REUNIFICATION AND THE RETURN OF HOUSING SHORTAGES

The reunification of the former German Democratic Republic and the Federal Republic of Germany in 1990 was one of the most celebrated political events in German history. Yet it also posed huge economic challenges to the country's growth regime and housing market. Joining a relatively uncompetitive command economy with one of the world's most competitive economies was an unprecedented experiment. Indeed, the task is still not complete even 35 years later, as economic output, household income, and wealth have not yet fully converged. The challenge was to integrate what had been the East German economy into the West German export-oriented *Modell Deutschland*. The chosen strategy was to transfer western Germany's economic and political institutions to eastern Germany and invest heavily in eastern infrastructure and housing. Policymakers hoped that these efforts would strengthen economic fundamentals in the east (*Standortqualität*). In addition, the eastern economy underwent shock therapy managed by the Treuhand – a government agency responsible for restructuring the GDR's state-owned firms – that privatized some profitable eastern firms and closed others in the face of new competitive realities (Böick 2018).

The decade after reunification was a wrenching period of adjustment for the new all-German economy (Baccaro and Höpner 2022). After an initial unification boom, partly driven by eastern consumer demand for western products (consumer demand that was itself financed by transfer payments), the country entered a recession in 1993. When foreign demand for German products declined amidst a global economic slump, consumer demand could not offset the decline in exports.[3] An important reason for the country's weakening export strength was the post-unification currency reform. The reform converted wages of the weaker East German Mark at a ratio of one-to-one with the stronger West German Mark to maximize eastern households' purchasing power. As a result, eastern unit labor costs became high relative to western ones, given the vastly different productivity levels between the two regions. Until the mid-1990s, unit labor costs

[3] Bundesbank (1993), *Geschäftsbericht*, 19–21.

increased because wage demands outpaced productivity gains in the west and were "wholly unrelated" to productivity gains in the east (Manger and Sattler 2020, 653).[4] One result was rising unemployment: 19 percent in the east compared to 10 percent in the west by the late 1990s. Eastern Germany's industrial sector, with a few exceptions, collapsed, and the weak services sector could not absorb the unemployment shock (Manow and Seils 2000, 286–288). Another result was a loss of export competitiveness, reflected in an unusually long period of current account deficits from 1991 to 2001 (Manger and Sattler 2020, 653; Carlin and Soskice 2009, 69). Germany's export share of the economy even declined from 24 percent to 20 percent between 1991 and 1993 (see Figure 1.3).

The challenge of integrating two very different housing markets was no easier. In the west, reunification exacerbated the housing shortages that had already emerged in the late 1980s. Population movements from eastern to western Germany and the influx of two million *Spätaussiedler* (ethnic, mostly Russian-speaking, Germans able to migrate after the fall of the iron curtain) from eastern Europe by the late 1990s created housing demand that exceeded supply in both east and west.[5] Even though the eastern housing market was characterized by 400,000 housing vacancies in 1990, these vacant homes were in uninhabitable condition, as the GDR had neglected renovating thousands of pre-WWII apartment buildings and instead focused on building new Soviet-style housing that nearly one-quarter of East Germans had called home (Kofner 2004, 194–195; Conradi and Zöpel 1994).[6] Consequently, there was a shortage of homes for at least 470,000 households in the east at the time of reunification.[7] The eastern housing stock required extensive renovation and new construction to meet the standard of the west. Moreover, in 1993, the homeownership rate in the east was only around 25 percent compared to 43 percent in the west.[8] As a result, homeownership support for eastern households was on the political agenda, particularly because western German (and some international) investors had bought much of the eastern property market while eastern

[4] Germany's real exchange rate increased by 20% within five years of reunification, making exports more expensive and therefore less competitive (Manger and Sattler 2020, 653–656).

[5] Bund der Vertriebenen (2024), *Aktuelle Aussiedlerstatistik*, www.bund-der-vertriebenen.de/fakten/spaetaussiedler/aktuelle-aussiedlerstatistik.

[6] Pfeifer, U., Simons, H., and Porsch, L. (November 2000), *Bericht der Kommission: Wohnungswirtschaftlicher Strukturwandel in den neuen Bundesländern* [report], PA-DBT 4000 XIV/289; Hinrichs, W. (July 1992), *Wohnungsversorgung in der ehemaligen DDR* (P92-105), AG Sozialberichterstattung Wissenschaftszentrum Berlin (WZB).

[7] Bartholmai, B. (1991), "Perspektiven des Wohnunsgbaus und der Wohnungsbaufinanzierung in den neuen Bundesländern," *Der Langfristige Kredit*, 6, 4.

[8] Henger, R., and Voigtländer, M. (October 2, 2015), *Vereint in regionalen Unterschieden – Der deutsche Wohnungsmarkt 25 Jahre nach der Wiedervereinigung*, IW policy paper 31, Institut der deutschen Wirtschaft, Cologne.

Germans themselves did not have the necessary capital to buy their own property (Pfeiffer and Ammann 1994, 14).

In short, housing supply shortages returned to the newly unified German political economy, prompting a short-lived renaissance of large-scale housing programs in both the east and west of the country. Chancellor Kohl viewed housing as an opportunity to generate investment, growth, employment, and prosperity in eastern Germany, an American-style housing-based growth strategy that would, however, soon turn into a full-blown housing disaster.

FROM LOCOMOTIVE TO DEBACLE: A POST-UNIFICATION HOUSING BOOM BUILT ON SAND

"The housing industry," Chancellor Kohl said in 1993, "is eastern Germany's economic motor."[9] Such a statement from a federal chancellor is rare in a country that prides itself on being an export champion. But it was not accidental that the eastern housing market was booming at that time. In response to unification-related housing challenges, Kohl adopted a range of *temporary* housing programs to stimulate housing, investment, and economic growth in the east, partly to offset the region's industrial decline. It was an American-style approach, even including a temporary mortgage interest deduction, which would soon fail.

The traditional German response to housing shortages has been the increased production of affordable housing through social housing programs, and this time was no different. Even though the Kohl government had previously decided that building social rental housing was no longer the task of the federal government, the emerging post-unification housing shortages in both eastern and western Germany led the government to change course. Social housing programs experienced a short-lived renaissance, with the federal government and *Länder* subsidizing 162,000 units in 1994 alone (up from just 37,000 in 1988), including 56,000 units in the east and 106,000 units in the west. In both east and west, most social housing units approved between 1991 and 1998 were rentals (see Figure 7.1). Boosting social rental housing reveals a general truth about postwar German social housing programs: Regardless of federal policymakers' ideological preferences, the *Länder* have primarily based their social housing funding decisions on the overall housing situation, economic needs, and urban structures of their regions. When housing shortages were acute, they prioritized rental units, while homeownership became the priority when housing supply was sufficient.[10] In a 1994 social

[9] Kohl, H. (November 8, 1993), *Das Baugewerbe – Motor des Aufschwungs in Ostdeutschland* (Bulletin 96–93), speech delivered at the Baugewerbetag 1993 (Construction Industry Day 1993), Bonn.

[10] Housing ministry official in North Rhine-Westphalia (author interview, phone, December 22, 2015).

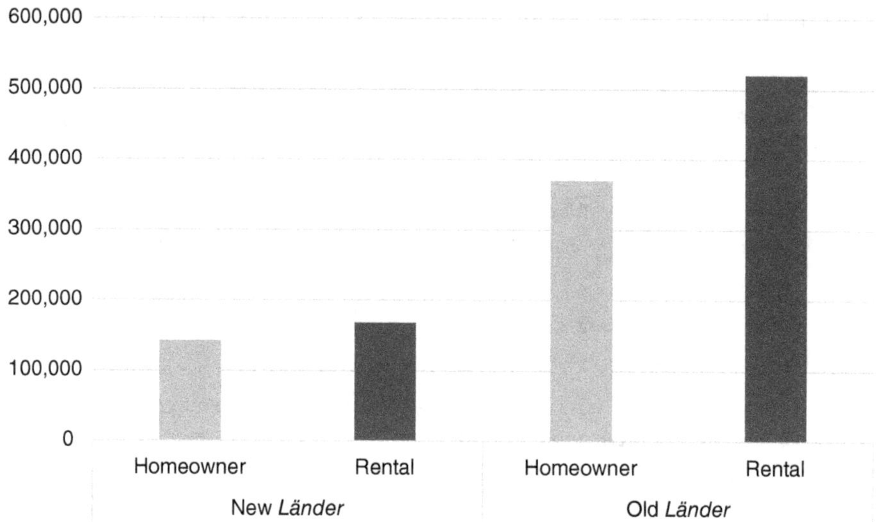

FIGURE 7.1 Newly approved social housing units in the new and old German *Länder*, 1991–2004
Data source: annual social housing reports in *Bundesbaublatt*.

housing reform, the Kohl government strengthened social housing programs by expanding income limits for potential homeowners (especially for families with children), focusing on the modernization of housing stock (particularly in eastern Germany), and extending the relatively new "third way of subsidies" mentioned in Chapter 5. Relatedly, the Kohl government created housing programs funded by the Kreditanstalt für Wiederaufbau (KfW), a government-owned development bank (Mertens 2015). The bank provided subsidized loans for modernizing existing rental housing, which facilitated 65 percent of eastern housing renovations after 1990, and it also established some small-scale homeownership programs.[11]

To alleviate housing shortages and stimulate housing investment, the Kohl government also expanded existing homeownership programs. Until reunification, households could only use the homeownership tax allowance (paragraph 10e in the tax code) once in their lifetime. However, the Kohl coalition allowed western German households to use the tax break (through the *Steueränderungsgesetz* 1991) a second time if they bought a home in eastern Germany, and it also expanded benefits for households with children.

However, the Kohl government did not stop there: It adopted sizable *temporary* housing programs, amounting to an American-style housing-based

[11] KfW (2024), *Aufbau Ost*, www.kfw.de/Über-die-KfW/Förderauftrag-und-Geschichte/Geschichte-der-KfW/KfW-Themen/Aufbau-Ost/.

growth strategy for eastern Germany. This included a temporary mortgage interest deduction from 1992 to 1994 (*Steueränderungsgesetz* 1992), a measure typically found in the American toolbox of stimulating housing demand. As part of this legislation, the Kohl government also included temporary but substantial tax subsidies for both building new rental homes and renovating old ones, with special provisions for housing investment in the east.

These provisional housing programs – particularly the temporary mortgage interest deduction – drew criticisms for being misplaced in Germany's growth regime. The Council of Economic Experts argued that "interest-rate subsidies make it more difficult for the Bundesbank to fulfill its mandate of securing price stability,"[12] as such subsidies would prevent "the expected credit-restraining effect" of high interest rates.[13] The Council instead advocated for programs that "*lower* house prices that are currently too high."[14] Once again, the country's economic elites preferred policies with price-deflating effects over those with price-inflating effects. The Bundesbank also opposed subsidizing mortgage debt. When mortgage debt skyrocketed in the UK in the 1990s, the Bundesbank noted that when "speculative bubbles burst and objects lost their value, this led to overleveraged households and lower consumer spending, which exacerbated recessionary tendencies." It also identified the cause of these speculative booms and busts: Mortgage liberalizations and "inflationary rises in house prices fueling demand."[15] Even though mortgage indebtedness in Germany remained lower than in the United States in the early 1990s, the potential effects of speculative housing bubbles and rising mortgage indebtedness that the Bundesbank was concerned about would soon become a reality, unleashed by the Kohl housing programs. Finally, German industries warned that an expansion of housing programs – including the mortgage interest deduction – would inflate construction prices and contribute to budget deficits.[16]

Kohl's temporary housing stimulus worked as intended – actually, too well – and produced a boom in housing investment, mortgage debt, and construction in eastern Germany, driven by an inflow of capital from the west (Michelsen and Weiß 2010, 398). In the late 1990s, as Figure 7.2 shows, the level of mortgage indebtedness as a share of the economy even began to exceed that of the United States for the first time in the twentieth century. Initially, the booming German housing market was a bright spot amidst a

[12] Sachverständigenrat für Wirtschaft (1991), *Jahresgutachten 1991/1992*, 179.

[13] Sachverständigenrat für Wirtschaft (1992), *Jahresgutachten 1992/1993*, 130.

[14] Sachverständigenrat für Wirtschaft (1991), *Jahresgutachten 1991/1992*, 221. My emphasis.

[15] Bundesbank (1993, April), *Monatsbericht*, 30.

[16] DIHT (October 1991), *Neues wohnungspolitisches Konzept der Bundesregierung* [statement], RWWA-181-2827-2. They instead advocated for further liberalizing rental prices and land-use regulations.

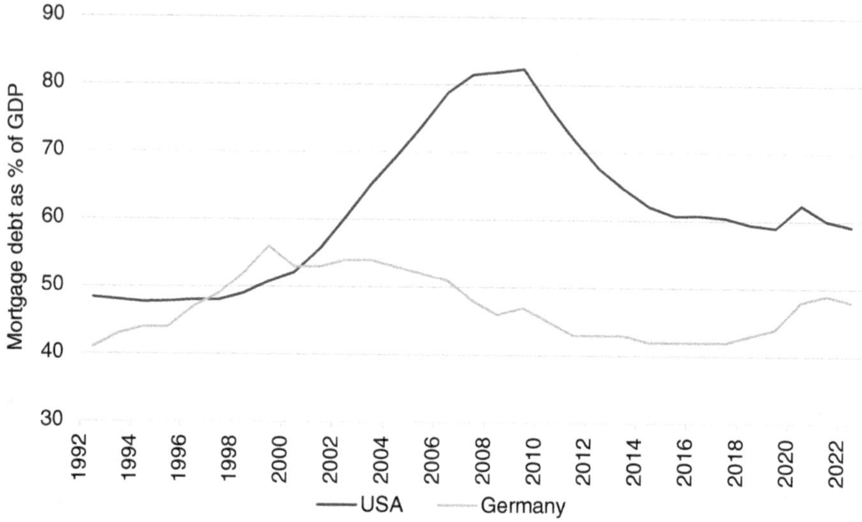

FIGURE 7.2 Mortgage debt as a percentage of GDP in the United States and Germany, 1992–2022
Data sources: Federal Reserve Flow of Funds for the United States; EMF Hypostat for Germany.

prolonged period of low economic growth and rising fiscal deficits that had started with the 1993 recession.

However, the housing situation soon deteriorated. While the number of newly built homes reached levels last seen in the 1970s, peaking at 600,000 completions in 1995, housing construction subsequently declined (with western Germany's peak in 1994 and eastern Germany's in 1997; see Figure 3.1). Policymakers had not fully realized that Kohl's housing stimulus had contributed to massive overinvestment in eastern property markets. It was a housing boom "built on sand," as *Die Zeit* reported.[17]

Still in the middle of the eastern construction boom, the Kohl government expanded the existing homeownership tax allowance in late 1995, partly to boost eastern homeownership and to anticipate slower housing investment and construction after the expiration of temporary housing programs. Before the reform, the homeownership tax allowance (paragraph 10e in the tax code) had privileged higher-income households, who could deduct a larger amount from their tax bills than lower- or middle-income households, often from eastern Germany.[18] In view of this, the Social Democrats proposed reforming the tax allowance into a tax *credit* that would

[17] Schmid, K. P. (October 17, 1997), "Auf Sand gebaut," *Die Zeit.*

[18] In the same year, the KfW development bank also started a modestly sized homeownership loan program, which grew to EUR 3 billion in annual credit volume in 2000. It is still in place today and amounted to EUR 4.2 billion new loans made to homeowners in 2023. See KfW (December 31, 2023), *Förderreport 2023*, 4; KfW (December 31, 2001), *Geschäftsbericht 2001*, 42.

benefit all beneficiaries equally regardless of income, a reform the SPD had pushed from the mid-1980s. While the Kohl government initially defended the status-oriented, regressive nature of the homeownership allowance, it ultimately relented: From 1996, the new homeownership tax allowance (now called the *Eigenheimzulage* under the *Eigenheimzulagengesetz* 1996) benefited all recipients equally. An SPD Bundestag member stated that the bill was also intended to help transfer ownership from former state-owned GDR housing into private hands.[19] A CDU Bundestag member mentioned that the core idea was to find a solution that did not legally privilege the new federal states with special measures but that still provided them with benefits that the pre-reform homeownership tax allowance could not.[20] Finally, the bill also included an environmental component: Homeowners building environmentally friendly homes or modernizing homes received an additional tax credit (the so-called ecological component). The SPD and Greens successfully pushed for this component to reduce energy consumption and emissions.

However, the expanded homeownership subsidy remained incongruent with the country's growth regime. The Association of German Cities (Deutscher Städtetag) warned that the subsidy would contribute to costly suburbanization and population movements away from cities, hurting the country's regional economies.[21] The subsidy also did little to boost homeownership in eastern Germany, which increased only moderately from 24 percent in 1994 to 29 percent by the end of the decade.[22] The German Tenants' Association (Deutscher Mieterbund) criticized the subsidy for promoting the purchase of older homes without creating any new housing, saying that it would artificially inflate urban house prices.[23] Moreover, the subsidy helped fuel massive housing overproduction and overinvestment in ways that were not recognized at the time, and it contributed to exploding fiscal deficits (Michelsen and Weiß 2010).

The construction boom in eastern Germany, fueled by generous government subsidies, burst in 1997–1998 and left the region with a massive oversupply of housing. Instead of the "blühende Landschaften" (loosely translated as "thriving economic landscapes") that Kohl had promised former East Germans after unification, they faced large-scale vacancies that would take a decade to overcome. The eastern housing bust also meant that the all-German construction sector was in freefall, as the number

19 Bundestag member II (SPD) (author interview, May 14, 2015).

20 Bundestag member III (CDU) (author interview, Berlin, June 22, 2015).

21 Deutscher Städtetag (September 18, 1995), *Stellungnahme: Entwurf eines Gesetzes zur steuerlichen Wohneigentumsförderung* [statement], Bonn, PA-DBT 4000 XIII/53.

22 Henger and Voigtländer, *Vereint in regionalen Unterschieden*, 14.

23 Deutscher Mieterbund (September 27, 1995), *Stellungnahme: Entwurf eines Gesetzes zur steuerlichen Wohneigentumsförderung* [statement], PA-DBT 4000 XIII/53.

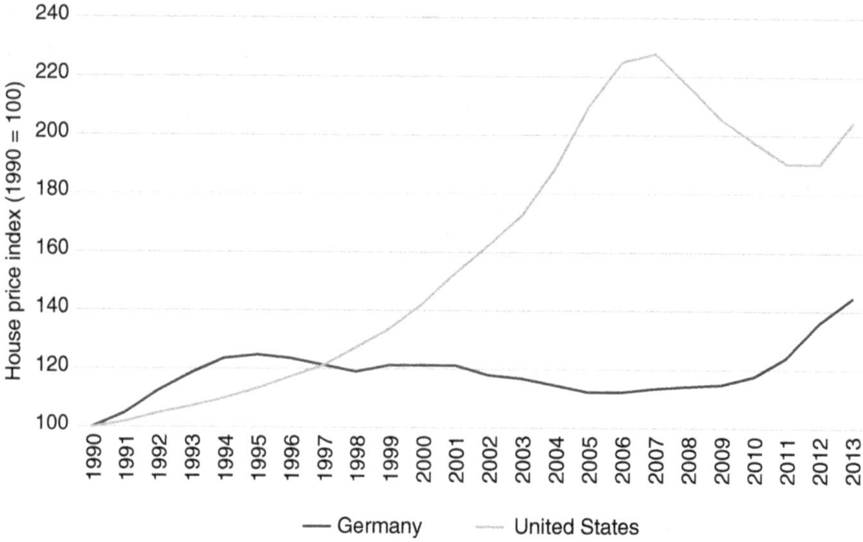

FIGURE 7.3 House price developments in the United States and Germany, 1990–2013
Data source: Jordà-Schularick-Taylor Macrohistory Database (2016a).

of newly constructed homes gradually declined after the mid-1990s construction peak (Carlin and Soskice 2009). As Figures 7.2 and 7.3 show, the result was that German house prices and mortgage debt levels fell or stagnated from the mid-1990s to the mid-2000s (Knoll et al. 2017; Lindenthal and Eichholtz 2012; Muellbauer 2018; van Gunten and Navot 2018).

Despite the colossal failure of the Kohl-era housing programs, the *Eigenheimzulage* remained the country's largest housing program. However, the contradictions between this program and the growth regime became increasingly apparent and politicized as the country's economy was on its knees in the early 2000s – a tension that would ultimately be resolved by abandoning the policy.

HOW HOUSING MADE THE "SICK MAN OF EUROPE" EVEN SICKER

A decade after unification, the euphoria of the historic moment had vanished and what had been the economic motor of Europe became known as the sick man of Europe (Manow and Seils 2000). It was a perfect storm. The German state entered a fiscal crisis due to the ongoing costs associated with reunification as well as rising unemployment and welfare costs.

The country's key export industries were no longer the employment engine they once were, partly because of rising nonwage labor costs that helped fund the social insurance system (Streeck and Trampusch 2005). German firms responded by outsourcing production to eastern Europe (Tooze 2018, 95), further exacerbating unemployment and the fiscal crisis.[24] Finally, the adoption of the euro in 1999 was initially a difficult adjustment for the German economy: As the nominal interest rates of high-inflation countries converged with those of low-inflation Germany, the real interest rate of Germany increased, capital fled Germany for southern Europe, and the Bundesbank was unable to cut interest rates to stimulate the economy (Matthijs and Blyth 2015). Once an object of envy in the capitals of other European countries, the German economy became an object of pity, as it entered a prolonged period of low growth, increasing deficits, and high unemployment (Baccaro and Höpner 2022).[25]

The depressed German housing market reinforced these structural economic problems. The housing construction boom in eastern Germany had added more housing units than needed, resulting in one million vacant homes (i.e., 13 percent of the entire housing stock) in eastern inner cities in 2000 (Michelsen and Weiß 2010, 399–401). While the problem of housing vacancies was less severe in the country's west, the construction crisis had consequences for the entire country: Housing prices fell, rental prices stagnated and in many regions fell, and the construction industry went into a deep and protracted crisis symbolized by the demise of Holzmann (Carlin and Soskice 2009).[26] Germany became the only major European economy in which house prices *decreased* – by a total of 4.3 percent – between 1999 and 2005, while house prices in the overall euro area increased by 45 percent

[24] After an unusual decade of current account deficits from 1991 to 2001, Germany began running uninterrupted current account surpluses again from 2002. Germany's export share as a percentage of GDP kept increasing from 31% in 2000 to 38% in 2005. German unit labor costs increased at an average of 0.6% per quarter between 2000 and 2004 (eurozone average: 1.7%), which meant that Germany slowly regained cost competitiveness compared to other eurozone countries, even though Germany's effective real exchange rate increased moderately from 2001 to 2004 (Manger and Sattler 2020, 655; Baccaro and Höpner 2022; OECD (2024), *Productivity and Unit Labour Costs*, https://data-explorer.oecd.org/).

[25] Economic growth averaged only 1.2% per year from 1998 to 2005, with recessions in 2002 and 2003. Public debt as a percentage of GDP increased from 39% in 1991 to 59% in 1998 and 67% in 2005. The unemployment rate was 12% in 1998 and remained that high until 2006. See OECD (2024), *Quarterly Real GDP Growth*, https://data-explorer.oecd.org/; Destatis (2024), *Registrierte Arbeitslose und Arbeitslosenquote nach Gebietsstand*, www.destatis.de/DE/Home/_inhalt.html; IMF (2024), *General Government Debt*, www.imf.org/external/datamapper/datasets/GDD.

[26] Between 2000 and 2012, average rental burden remained at around 28–29% of western German household income and 25–27% of eastern German household income. See 19th Bundestag (January 17, 2018), *Plenary protocol, 6th session* (written response by R. Schwarzelühr-Sutter), 501.

during those years.[27] At the same time, the construction sector lost 800,000 jobs in just a few years from 1995 to 2004.[28] The dire housing situation thus contributed significantly to the economic gloom in Germany. Moreover, nationwide unemployment remained high, hovering between 10 and 12 percent in the late 1990s and early 2000s, paired with relatively low net migration surpluses of only roughly 140,000 people per year from 1998 to 2006, further limited housing demand.[29] Demographic predictions were also dire, projecting a population *decline* of around 10 million people by the year 2050, which led policymakers to believe that the days of housing shortages were over.[30] Indeed, housing construction numbers plummeted to 270,000 in 2003 for the entire country (recall that housing construction had peaked in 1973 with over 700,000 units). The Council of Economic Experts considered the oversupply of housing – partly produced by "excessive subsidies" – a major structural economic problem at the time.[31] The silver lining of the housing surplus was that renters could choose high-quality apartments at relatively low prices.

While scholars have emphasized how the country's first center-left government of Social Democrats and Greens under Chancellor Schröder responded to the country's structural economic problems with the Hartz labor market and welfare state reforms, much less has been written about how it dealt with the other German economic crisis: Housing.

THE LONG GOODBYE FROM SOCIAL HOUSING PROGRAMS

When the red–green Schröder government (SPD–Greens, 1998–2005) entered office, the housing market was depressed. It was, as then housing minister Franz Müntefering (SPD) called it, a product of "building beyond need," particularly in the country's east.[32] Policymakers said their long goodbye to social housing programs – once the country's main tool to secure affordable housing for the masses – in times of oversupply and pessimistic demographic projections. As housing supply *surpluses* became the problem, the center-left government viewed large-scale rental housing programs as causing structural economic problems in the housing market and the economy. Social housing reform was thus part of the Schröder coalition's strategy to cure the German economy.

In 2001, the red–green government passed a social housing reform (*Wohnraumförderungsgesetz*), which significantly limited the scope of

[27] Sachverständigenrat für Wirtschaft (2006), *Jahresgutachten 2006–2007*, 200.

[28] Höh, H. (2006), *Strukturwandel im Baugewerbe*, Statistisches Bundesamt, Wiesbaden, 815.

[29] Destatis, *Wanderungen zwischen Deutschland und dem Ausland von 1950 bis 2023*, www.destatis.de/DE/Home/_inhalt.html.

[30] Statistisches Bundesamt (November 2006), *Bevölkerung Deutschlands bis 2050*, Wiesbaden, 5.

[31] Sachverständigenrat für Wirtschaft (2002), *Jahresgutachten 2002–2003*, 211.

[32] Quoted in "Politikbereiche vernetzen" (March 1999), *Bundesbaublatt*, 48(3), 12.

these programs. The law succeeded the landmark Second Housing Law that had guided social housing policy since 1956. While the historical goal of Germany's social housing programs had been to establish sufficient housing supply for the masses, the reform narrowed the scope to modernizing the existing housing stock and targeting low-income groups and regions in need of housing support. As housing supply in the country was sufficient, building new rental housing was no longer a priority; instead, social housing programs subsidized more owner-occupied units than rental units in the early 2000s, although the aggregate number of social housing units was negligible. In 2002, only 40,000 new social housing units were approved, including 25,000 owner-occupied units. Such low numbers hardly make a dent in the homeownership rate, which remained at 42 percent in the mid-2000s (Kohl 2017). Social housing was relegated to being a limited and narrow policy tool.

Interest groups had mixed feelings about the creeping decline of social housing. Left-leaning interest groups tried to save social housing programs, including the German Tenants' Association (Deutscher Mieterbund),[33] the limited-profit housing associations (Bundesverband deutscher Wohnungs- und Immobilienunternehmen, GdW),[34] and the Association of German Cities (Deutscher Städtetag), whose main argument was that housing shortages still existed in metropolitan areas.[35] However, these groups also conceded that bringing back the old days of large-scale social housing would be politically difficult given the increased cost of building.[36]

These interest groups were unable to stop the demise of social housing programs, which were considered to have caused supply-side problems in the housing market and the wider economy. The Council of Economic Experts recommended the retrenchment of social housing programs to consolidate the budget in times of sufficient housing supply.[37] In addition, the Council repeatedly pointed out that "excessive" government subsidies were partly responsible for "worrying allocative effects," such as the oversupply of housing in the east.[38] An influential report commissioned by the housing ministry also mentioned that these programs were contributing to "capital misallocations," meaning that capital was artificially channeled into housing.[39] Right-leaning housing interest groups also opposed social housing programs.

[33] Deutscher Mieterbund (May 16, 2001), *Stellungnahme zum Entwurf eines Gesetzes zur Reform des Wohnungsbaurechts* [statement], Berlin, PA-DBT 4000 XIV/289.

[34] GdW (May 16, 2001), *Stellungnahme: Reform des Wohnungsbaurechts* [statement], Berlin, PA-DBT 4000 XIV/289.

[35] Representative of Deutscher Städtetag I (author interview, phone, December 11, 2015); representative of Deutscher Städtetag II (author interview, phone, December 11, 2015).

[36] Representative of GdW (author interview, phone, January 18, 2016).

[37] Sachverständigenrat für Wirtschaft (2003), *Jahresgutachten 2003–2004*, 290.

[38] Sachverständigenrat für Wirtschaft (2000), *Jahresgutachten 2000–2001*, 123.

[39] Pfeifer, Simons, and Porsch, *Bericht der Kommission*, 30.

The building societies viewed social housing programs as the "worst waste of money," producing housing surpluses beyond need, and urged for the privatization of social housing (Egner et al. 2004, 180). Similarly, the association representing property owners (Haus & Grund) argued that the programs would distort markets.[40]

Another reason for the decline of social housing programs was that they exemplified the complicated workings of the country's system of federalism: Concurrent jurisdiction, co-financing, and decisions at the state level that often did not match federal objectives. Policymakers of all stripes agreed that the complicated federalist setup required an overhaul, as it was holding back much-needed economic reforms to revive the German growth regime. As Fritz Scharpf (2008, 512) remarks, reforming federalism was intended to do just that:

> Given the economic heterogeneity of German regions, and the separation between federal legislation and Länder administration, however, national policy could not be sufficiently targeted to the needs of specific regions, whereas Länder competence was insufficient to achieve the concerted effects which smaller nation states could design for their more specialised economies. It made sense, therefore, for ambitious Land governments to seek broad legislative authority over the "regional aspects" of all economically significant policy domains.

Yet federalism reform needed two-thirds majorities in both houses of the German parliament and thus required widespread political support. For now, it would have to wait for a new government with large majorities in both the Bundestag and the Bundesrat.

In the context of housing oversupply, the Schröder government even adopted costly demolition programs to *reduce* the housing stock in both eastern and western Germany. The urban renewal program (*Stadtumbau Ost*) was designed to demolish 350,000 homes, mostly prefabricated (*Plattenbau*) homes that had been built as part of the GDR's housing push from the mid-1970s to the late 1980s that had created around 2 million such homes to address its housing shortages (Michelsen and Weiß 2010, 395). The urban renewal program cost the federal government and *Länder* roughly EUR 2.5 billion between 2002 and 2009.[41] Its western equivalent (*Stadtumbau West*) followed in 2004, providing funds for urban renewal and housing demolitions. The irony is that, a decade earlier, the Kohl government had spent billions to stimulate the construction and modernization of homes to increase housing supply.

Around the same time, German municipalities also reduced their social housing stock by privatizing social housing units to consolidate their

[40] Representative of Haus & Grund (author interview, phone, January 14, 2016).

[41] Liebmann, H. (2005), "Stadtumbau Ost: Kommt die Aufwertung zu kurz?" *Bundesbaublatt* 54(2), 16.

budgets (Wijburg and Aalbers 2017). In 2000, around 9 million people lived in 3.4 million social housing units operated by public or municipal housing associations.[42] Against the warnings of housing experts, the fiscal crisis led many municipalities to privatize social housing units. Local politicians assumed that housing markets would remain affordable even without social housing programs in the context of housing surpluses and a stagnant population. Such privatization was supported by the Council of Economic Experts with the aim of achieving balanced budgets.[43] Unlike the large-scale privatizations in the United Kingdom – such as Margaret Thatcher's "right to buy" program, which offered tenants the option of buying the social housing units they lived in (Wood 2018) – German rental units largely went to investors. For example, in 2006, the eastern city of Dresden sold all its 48,000 rental units in a EUR 1.7 billion deal to the investment firm Fortress to consolidate the city's budget.[44] Other cities across the country – from Nuremberg and Berlin to Hamburg – did the same. The result was the net privatization of at least 618,000 social housing units from 1999 to 2011.[45] While these actions provided cash-starved municipalities with one-off sources of revenue, they deprived policymakers of tools for taming rents and providing low-cost housing.

For German policymakers, housing surpluses of that magnitude showed a world turned upside down. With the notable exception of the late 1970s and early 1980s, the usual problem was one of shortages, not surpluses. In what might be described as a short-sighted overreaction, the Social Democrats – the historical champions of these programs – made social housing programs leaner, narrower, and almost unrecognizable.

ON THE CHOPPING BLOCK: ATTACKING HOMEOWNERSHIP SUBSIDIES IN THE NAME OF GROWTH

The rental market was not the only housing area suffering cutbacks. When Germany's growth regime was under threat from a crisis of cost competitiveness and a fiscal crisis in the early 2000s, the Schröder government targeted homeownership programs. The coalition viewed these subsidies as detrimental to the struggling export-led growth regime, contributing to fiscal deficits, vacant inner cities, and capital misallocations. As a result, even popular homeownership subsidies ended up on the chopping block in the name of reviving the export-led economy. The retrenchment push included

42 Steinert, J. (2000), "Wohnungsprivatisierung: Es drohen irreversible Entscheidungen," *Der Langfristige Kredit*, 49(1), 23.

43 Sachverständigenrat für Wirtschaft (2007), *Jahresgutachten 2007–2008*, 258.

44 Polke-Majewski, K. (February 22, 2006), "Dresdner Coup," *Die Zeit*.

45 Held, T. (2011), "Verkäufe kommunaler Wohnungsbestände," *Informationen zur Raumentwicklung*, no. 12, 675.

the country's largest tax subsidy: The *Eigenheimzulage*, amounting to EUR 11 billion in 2004.[46] Going after the subsidy was not necessarily great politics, as opinion polls demonstrated that 71 percent of respondents supported the *Eigenheimzulage*.[47] In addition, between 1996 and 2000, the tax break had benefited 2.6 million households.[48] Even so, the SPD started attacking the subsidy, facing continued ideological opposition from the Christian Democrats for the time being.

During Schröder's first term from 1998 to 2002, the red–green coalition began efforts to reduce the *Eigenheimzulage*. In 2002, it phased out the environmental component of the homeownership tax allowance, which had provided additional subsidies for building environmentally friendly homes.[49] Instead, a 2001 executive order (*Energieeinsparverordnung – EnEv*) mandated stricter energy-saving building standards, ensuring that environmentally friendly housing could be achieved without the need for the additional subsidy.

During Schröder's second term (2002–2005), the SPD–Greens coalition took more aggressive steps against homeownership subsidies, at a time when fiscal deficits had worsened and the housing depression hit its low point. In a first attack on the tax subsidy, the coalition aimed to restrict the tax allowance to homeowners with children only. However, the bill did not pass in the Bundesrat, where the CDU and the FDP were able to block it (Egner 2014; Heinelt and Egner 2006).

The Social Democrats had actively supported the subsidy as a major tool to support homeownership from the mid-1970s; however, they increasingly made the macroeconomic argument that the homeownership tax allowance was detrimental to the export-led growth regime. First, hawkish finance minister Hans Eichel (SPD) told *Der Spiegel* that the homeownership tax allowance would be "economic nonsense" and a "gravely misdirected subsidy," especially because of overcapacities in the eastern housing markets.[50] He also criticized the subsidy's house "price-inflating" tendencies.[51] Along those lines, Stephan Hilsberg (SPD) called the tax break "pointless" and "anachronistic," because "[i]t does not make any sense – in some parts of Germany this is the daily practice – to spend public money on reducing housing and simultaneously on the construction of housing."[52] Other SPD Bundestag members echoed these

46 Bundesregierung (2006), *20. Subventionsbericht*, 103–104.

47 Bundesgeschäftsstelle Landesbausparkassen (December 2, 2003), *71-Prozent-Mehrheit für Beibehaltung der Eigenheimzulage* [press release], www.presseportal.de/pm/35604/505457.

48 Bundesamt für Bauwesen und Raumordnung (September 2002), *Bericht zur Inanspruchnahme der Eigenheimzulage in den Jahren 1996–2000* [report], Bonn, 1.

49 The coalition also tightened the income limits for eligible households in 2000.

50 "Das tut immer weh" (October 28, 2002), *Der Spiegel*.

51 Eichel, H. (September 30, 2004), *Remarks in the 15th Bundestag, 129th session*, 11696.

52 Hilsberg, S. (December 1, 2005), *Remarks in the 16th Bundestag, 5th session*, 292–293.

views. One characterized the *Eigenheimzulage* as misdirected spending, as it reinforced vacancies and depopulated city centers in the east.[53] Another stated that the problem in eastern Germany was an overheating market fueled by tax incentives, including the homeownership tax allowance, which resulted in an overblown construction sector and housing vacancies.[54] The Greens agreed, as Kerstin Andreae pointed out: "The elimination of the *Eigenheimzulage* is right. The subsidy leads to distorted allocations in the housing market. When the subsidy was introduced, there was a housing crisis. We don't have that situation any longer."[55]

Second, Social Democrats criticized the homeownership subsidy for limiting labor mobility at a time when Germany's sclerotic labor market was the target of structural economic reforms. With an unemployment rate approaching 11 percent in 2002, a Schröder cabinet member complained that the tax break reinforced a sclerotic labor market: "If you have the necessity for firms to restructure and people have to look for new jobs, and they might also have to relocate, then a high rate of ownership is a hindrance for more flexibility."[56] In spelling out the link between rigid labor markets and homeownership (cp. Börsch-Supan 1994), the proposed retrenchment of the *Eigenheimzulage* is thus also linked to the Hartz labor market reforms, which liberalized the country's employment relations system by allowing more flexible use of agency work and other atypical work arrangements for firms (Hassel and Schiller 2010; Vail 2010).

On top of these labor-market and housing-related concerns, the Social Democrats also argued that government funds would be better spent on growth-generating sectors of the German model. One parliamentarian mentioned that the idea was to shift funds from the housing sector to productive areas that are essential to Germany's high-skill growth regime, such as education and research.[57] As the CDU continued to defend the subsidy, the political left questioned the CDU's commitment to the German growth regime, a model that had traditionally relied on public commitments to education and vocational training as opposed to real estate (Thelen 2019, 302; Aizenman and Noy 2012). Kerstin Andrea (Greens) provocatively asked the CDU whether public funds should be spent on "bricks or education?"[58] Angela Merkel (CDU), then chair of the Christian Democratic parliamentary group, labeled these arguments "poisoned."[59]

Yet the SPD's views were in line with those of the country's economic elites. An influential report on the *Eigenheimzulage* recommended the policy's elimination

[53] Bundestag member V (SPD) (author interview, phone, September 25, 2015).
[54] Bundestag member I (SPD, cabinet member) (author interview, phone, May 7, 2015).
[55] Andreae, K. (December 15, 2005), *Remarks in the 16th Bundestag, 8th Session*, 442.
[56] Bundestag member I (SPD, cabinet member) (author interview, phone, May 7, 2015).
[57] Bundestag member VI (SPD) (author interview, phone, October 27, 2015).
[58] Andreae, K. (October 22, 2004), *Remarks in the 15th Bundestag, 133rd session*, 12156.
[59] "Union will am Zuschuss festhalten" (March 29, 2004), *Süddeutsche Zeitung*.

partly because of its "price-inflating" effects.[60] Given the "saturated" housing supply and large-scale vacancies, the Council of Economic Experts viewed the *Eigenheimzulage* as indefensible on both economic and social grounds, particularly in the context of stagnant population numbers.[61] More generally, the council had repeatedly recommended the reduction of fiscal and market-distorting subsidies, of which the *Eigenheimzulage* was a prime example.

In a second attempt of retrenchment and in a sign of growing bipartisanship in 2003, Peer Steinbrück (SPD) and Roland Koch (CDU), then the respective minister-presidents of North Rhine-Westphalia and Hesse, proposed to cut all subsidies in the tax code by 12 percent to balance the budget, including the *Eigenheimzulage*.[62] The proposal was perceived as fair because it targeted all subsidies equally in a broad effort to balance the budget, without singling out the homeownership tax allowance. As the country's largest tax break, the *Eigenheimzulage* was a continued source of irritation for the center-left government at a time when Germany was experiencing a "financial crisis of the state" (Streeck and Trampusch 2005, 175) and had begun violating the Maastricht criteria by generating fiscal deficits in excess of 3 percent in 2002. The Schröder government then successfully passed a budget bill based on the bipartisan proposal, reducing the homeowner subsidy, including by tightening income limits for eligibility.

The SPD–Greens coalition launched another retrenchment attempt in 2004, again emphasizing the detrimental effects of the subsidy on economic growth. Germany had just experienced two consecutive years of economic recessions in 2002 and 2003. In a draft bill, tellingly entitled "Law for the financial support of innovation through the elimination of the *Eigenheimzulage*," the coalition proposed to shift public funds spent on the homeowner tax subsidy toward innovation, research, and education to boost competitiveness and growth. As the bill reads: "The elimination of the *Eigenheimzulage* is connected with the federal government's innovation initiative. The freed-up resources will directly fund government support of research and innovation. With that, Germany will be boosted as a scientific location, economic growth will increase, and new jobs will be created."[63] Clearly, the Social Democrats were ready to sacrifice housing programs, as they did not view housing to be a key economic sector for stimulating growth. On the contrary, it was proposed that sizable homeownership subsidies be eliminated so that freed-up funds could be invested in innovative areas that would benefit the country's

[60] Färber, G. (2003), *Wirkungen der Eigenheimzulage*, Institut für Landes- und Stadtentwicklungsforschung und Bauwesen des Landes Nordrhein-Westfalen, ch. 2.

[61] Sachverständigenrat für Wirtschaft (2003), *Jahresgutachten 2003/2004*, 292.

[62] Koch, R., and Steinbrück, P. (2003), *Subventionsabbau im Konsens* [joint proposal], Wiesbaden.

[63] Bundesregierung (September 27, 2004), *Entwurf eines Gesetzes zur finanziellen Unterstützung der Innovationsoffensive durch Abschaffung der Eigenheimzulage* (Drs. 15/3781) [draft law], Berlin.

key export-oriented manufacturing firms. One might argue that this growth-model framing is but a clever rhetorical move to balance the budget without much reinvestment. Even so, it was a credible macroeconomic argument congruent with the country's growth regime – and, indeed, an argument that would be almost impossible to make in the United States given the centrality of housing to the growth regime.

The draft bill made the contradictions between the growth regime and the homeowner subsidy explicit, directly calling the subsidy a hindrance for growth. Among other factors, the bill explicated three macroeconomic reasons why the homeownership tax allowance should be eliminated: (1) it was the single largest subsidy in the tax code, increasing fiscal deficits; (2) it had outlived its original purpose of alleviating the housing supply crisis after WWII and was no longer needed in times of sufficient supply and dire demographic projections; and (3) it had price-inflating effects on construction costs and land prices. The bill concluded that it would be a "mistake to use scarce resources in areas where the market already provides sufficient supply." While the measure passed the center-left Bundestag, it was still blocked by the CDU in the Bundesrat.

Rising debt and deficits made it difficult for German politicians to invest in key areas that made the export-oriented economy competitive: Education, research and development, and technology. Schröder's economics minister Wolfgang Clement (SPD) stated that "the *Eigenheimzulage* must go" to free up investments for innovation and technology and increase the auto industry's competitiveness:

> The example of the German auto industry illustrates the far-reaching consequences of these developments for our export industries ... If we do not widen our technological advantages vis-à-vis China – or at least retain them – and do not invest in research and innovation at home, then we will be sorry about the rise of Chinese cars in 10 or 20 years.[64]

Retrenchment would thus reinforce the export-led growth regime by redirecting public funds to innovation and technology that would benefit export industries. While the CDU continued its ideological opposition to retrenchment, the party's united front soon showed cracks.

RETRENCHMENT: MACROECONOMIC CONSENSUS WINS OVER PARTY IDEOLOGY AND INTEREST GROUPS' RESISTANCE

The CDU's ideological opposition to retrenching homeownership subsidies faded in light of mounting *macroeconomic* pressures in the mid-2000s. Despite the party's continued ideological support of homeownership, it

[64] Clement, W. (October 25, 2005), *Made in Germany* [speech], Berlin, www.bundesregierung.de/breg-de/service/newsletter-und-abos/bulletin/rede-des-bundesministers-fuer-wirtschaft-und-arbeit-wolfgang-clement--795744.

became increasingly open to sacrificing the *Eigenheimzulage* to improve budget deficits, boost regional economies, and reallocate capital into growth-oriented areas. The CDU thus joined a wider macroeconomic consensus with the SPD and economic elites, who viewed the tax subsidy as detrimental to the German growth regime. It was the reverse image of the United States. There, both the main political parties and the economic elites agreed that eliminating homeownership subsidies would significantly hurt the economy. In Germany, however, homeownership subsidies were on borrowed time.

The federal states accelerated the CDU's policy U-turn, as they considered the subsidy to be hurting their regional economies. The *Länder* were co-financing 42.5 percent of the *Eigenheimzulage* while experiencing their own public finance crises, competitiveness deficiencies, and housing problems (Heinelt and Egner 2006). In the east, housing markets were still reeling from an unwinding housing construction boom that left the region with large-scale vacancies and demolitions. Investment incentives, such as the *Eigenheimzulage*, had produced "a notable stream of West German private capital into the East German housing market" (Michelsen and Weiß 2010, 398). The new federal states, including the CDU-led Saxony and Saxony-Anhalt, became increasingly open to eliminating the *Eigenheimzulage* to both reduce deficits and enhance competitiveness by redirecting spending and capital into productive sectors. In 2003, the minister-president of Saxony-Anhalt, Wolfgang Böhmer (CDU), stated that "I would not like to dispute what the homeownership allowance means for Baden-Württemberg or some other states. For the new federal states, in part with vacancy rates of up to 20 percent, we need different priorities. We would like to use that money for urban planning and not only for supporting homeownership."[65]

Indeed, the Federal Office for Building and Regional Planning found that the homeownership tax subsidy had incentivized eastern households to move away from city centers and into suburbs.[66] Partly for this reason, Böhmer signaled that the state would be open to "reducing the volume of the subsidy."[67] Similarly, Georg Milbradt (CDU), Saxony's minister-president, stated that "[w]e in Saxony do not need to support new residential construction ... We have enough of that."[68] Moreover, he said that "[i]n a situation in which city centers depopulate, there are vacancies, and the state in eastern Germany supports demolition, we can no longer afford new residential construction."[69]

65 "Haushaltsituation der Länder" (May 22, 2003), *Deutschlandfunk*.

66 Bundesamt für Bauwesen und Raumordnung, *Bericht zur Inanspruchnahme der Eigenheimzulage in den Jahren 1996–2000*.

67 Weiland, S. (March 11, 2005), "Krisengipfel im Kanzleramt: Union sagt zur Eigenheimzulage leise Servus," *Spiegel Online*.

68 Fras, D., Levine, T., and Vestring, B. (June 17, 2003), "Milbradt bricht CDU-Tabus," *Berliner Zeitung*.

69 "Milbradt für spezielle Eigenheimzulage Ost" (November 27, 2003), *Die Welt*.

The CDU-led Thuringia also signaled openness to reform. In the west, too, some CDU-led *Länder* were open to reform, such as Hamburg and Saarland.[70] They viewed the *Eigenheimzulage* as a drain on public funds in light of fiscal crises and as channeling capital into suburban housing, contributing to population movements away from cities. Interest groups representing German cities and local communities echoed that the tax subsidies were economically damaging, as they neglected local housing needs and contributed to urban sprawl, suburbanization, and vacancies in eastern (and some western) inner cities.[71] Suburbanization, in turn, would also reinforce other environmentally and economically damaging tax breaks, such as the commuter's tax break (*Pendlerpauschale*) that had provided financial aid to commuters.[72]

Christian Democrats in the Bundestag could not ignore the regional economic concerns of their own party members in the Bundesrat. As fiscal consolidation was one of the most important macroeconomic priorities for the CDU, the party began to accept the idea of sacrificing the homeownership tax allowance. Despite the struggling construction sector, the CDU increasingly advocated reforming the subsidy to balance the budget. As Otto Bernhard (CDU) nostalgically expressed: "In committee, I have made clear that it was not easy for me to let go of the subsidy ... Given the financial situation, we unfortunately don't have much room for maneuver. That is why we have to cut back completely, in order to balance the budget."[73] In other words, macroeconomic priorities of fiscal consolidation trumped ideological ones. In contrast to American policymakers, the CDU was not concerned that such actions would significantly hurt the German growth regime. As a CDU Bundestag member pinpointed in an interview: "We don't usually emphasize the demand side of economic policy in Germany, but we instead emphasize the supply side ... That's why I don't share the American view of stimulating the economy as a cure for an itch."[74] In other words, the CDU viewed the homeownership tax allowance as contributing to the country's larger *supply-side* economic problems at that time, such as increasing fiscal deficits and public debt, as well as hurting the country's regional economies.

In late 2005, the first Merkel grand coalition (CDU–SPD, 2005–2009) decided to phase out the *Eigenheimzulage* starting in 2006, solidifying the broad consensus on fiscal consolidation and structural reform to revive the economy.[75] A CDU Bundestag member stated that their party accepted

[70] "Union wankt bei Eigenheimzulage: Front der CDU/CSU-regierten Länder gegen Abschaffung der Subvention für Häuslebauer bröckelt" (November 26, 2004), *Handelsblatt*.

[71] Representative of Deutscher Städtetag I (author interview, phone, December 11, 2015).

[72] Representative of Deutscher Städtetag II (author interview, phone, December 11, 2015).

[73] Bernhard, O. (December 15, 2005), *Remarks in the 16th Bundestag, 8th session*, 438–439.

[74] Bundestag member III (CDU) (author interview, phone, June 22, 2015).

[75] Part of the reform was the elimination of the accelerated rental market depreciation deduction (*degressive Absetzung für Abnutzung, AfA*), the counterpart of the homeownership tax allowance.

the elimination as part of a larger deal that included the reduction of corporate taxes and labor costs, while continuing moderate support for homeowners through pension schemes. Indeed, soon after the retrenchment of the tax subsidy, the Merkel government adopted a subsidized homeownership pension savings scheme (*Wohnriester*) in 2008 (Mertens 2017). But the measure was only a fraction of the previous tax allowance, amounting to merely EUR 420 million in 2014.[76] The CDU member also remarked that the reform required a grand coalition, because the SPD and Greens would not have been strong enough on their own, while the CDU and FDP would not have gone against their own core constituencies of homeowners.[77] The grand coalition gave both parties enough political cover to push through such a major reform.

Strong lobby efforts could not save the subsidy either, as they could not credibly argue that eliminating it would hurt the German export-led growth regime. The housing lobby formed a "homeownership initiative" to defend the subsidy that included eighteen powerful interest groups. The initiative included groups representing building societies (Verband der Privaten Bausparkassen), property owners (Haus & Grund), and mortgage banks (Verband der Hypothekenbanken). They argued that the elimination of the subsidy would result in slowing housing demand and 220,000 lost jobs.[78] The construction industry (represented by the Zentralverband Deutsches Baugewerbe, ZDB) emphasized that 50 percent of those willing to build or buy owner-occupied homes in the near future would not be able to do so without the subsidy.[79] Similarly, the construction union – IG-BAU – lobbied for the preservation of the subsidy to save jobs in the sector.[80] The inability of such efforts to prevent retrenchment was thus not due to lack of mobilization. Rather, arguments about stimulating demand were inherently less effective or persuasive in export-led Germany than in the demand-led United States. In an interview, one SPD Bundestag member stated that housing policy did not have the same salience as labor market policy, which made it easier to retrench the subsidy.[81] One housing interest group representative added: "Even if we see house prices decline by 20 percent, then this is covered by equity [high down payments] … so that banks do not have to be concerned about this at all."[82]

[76] Bundesregierung (February 19, 2018), *Kosten und Wirkungen Wohnungspolitischer Instrumente Bezüglich Bezahlbaren Wohnraums* (Drs. 19/794) [response to parliamentary inquiry], Berlin, 16.

[77] Bundestag member III (CDU) (author interview, Berlin, June 22, 2015).

[78] Initiative Wohneigentum (April 18, 2002), *Eigenheimzulage Muss Uneingeschränkt Erhalten Bleiben* [statement], www.baulinks.de/webplugin/2002/0330.php4.

[79] ZDB (December 6, 2005), *Entwurf eines Gesetzes … zur Abschaffung der Eigenheimzulage* [statement], PA-DBT 4000 XVI/4.

[80] "IG Bau Kämpft um Eigenheimzulage" (April 7, 2004), *Taz*.

[81] Bundestag member VI (SPD) (author interview, phone, October 27, 2015).

[82] Representative of Haus & Grund (author interview, phone, January 14, 2016).

Housing is less systemically and financially important to the German economy compared to the American one. These economic realities weakened the effect of lobbying by housing interest groups.

In contrast, labor unions, renter groups, and export-oriented industries expressed their support for the elimination of the tax break to support regional economies and the wider economy. The German Tenants' Association (Deutscher Mieterbund) had long argued that the homeownership tax allowance would be inequitable and contribute to vacancies and urban sprawl. They advocated shifting housing funds toward the affordable urban rental sector, with sensitivities to regional and local housing needs (Egner et al. 2004, 161). The Association of German Cities (Deutscher Städtetag) also favored reforming the subsidy on regional economic grounds. Although the largest interest group representing rental housing companies (Bundesverband deutscher Wohnungs- und Immobilienunternehmen, GdW) was part of the "homeownership initiative," they did not feel strongly about the reform of the tax allowance, as their core focus is rental housing.[83] Outside housing, the influential export-oriented Bundesverband der Deutschen Industrie (BDI) welcomed the retrenchment of the subsidy as part of larger fiscal consolidation efforts. The union federation Deutscher Gewerkschaftsbund (DGB) initially lobbied for its preservation to support the construction industry – along with the IG-BAU – but then supported the retrenchment of the subsidy if the Merkel government agreed to adopt a smaller homeownership pension savings program (*Wohnriester*) in lieu of the tax subsidy.[84]

Policymakers did not claim that eliminating the homeownership program would directly reinforce the German model by boosting exports. However, they viewed retrenching the subsidy as a means to indirectly improve export competitiveness by suppressing domestic costs through fiscal consolidation and reallocating capital into research, development, education, and technology.[85] The retrenchment of homeownership programs was seen as *sound* macroeconomic policy for the export-led growth regime – something that was never seriously considered in the United States.

83 Representative of GdW (author interview, phone, January 18, 2016).

84 "BDI Chef fordert Subventionen zurückzufahren" (June 24, 2006), *Handelsblatt*; DGB (October 8, 2003), *Stellungnahme zum Gesetzentwurf der Bundesregierung Entwurf eines Haushaltsbegleitgesetzes 2004* [statement], https://webarchiv.bundestag.de/archive/2005/0825/parlament/gremien15/a08/Oeffentliche_Anhoerungen/27_Sitzung_ADrs_798_und_800_1_Ergaenzung.pdf; DGB (December 7, 2005), *Stellungnahme des DGB: Entwurf eines Gesetzes zur Abschaffung der Eigenheimzulage* [statement], PA-DBT 4000 XVI/4.

85 The parliamentary state secretary of the finance ministry mentioned that the savings from the subsidy would be needed for spending around 3% of GDP on research, development, and education by 2010. See Diller, K. (December 14, 2005), *Remarks in the 4th session of the budget committee, 16th Bundestag*, PA-DBT 4000 XVI/4.

Addressing some alternative explanations for retrenchment further highlights the link between Germany's export-oriented growth regime and the retrenchment of housing policy. First, the German story was not merely one of housing oversupply leading to policy retrenchment. Indeed, housing supply surpluses did not stop American policymakers from subsidizing homeownership when the crash of 2008–2009 produced massive housing oversupply in many US states, such as Arizona and Florida. The better interpretation is that German policymakers did not consider the subsidy a key macroeconomic tool for stimulating the economy. On the contrary: Had policymakers done so, they would *not* have touched the subsidy when the German economy and housing sector were hurting. Second, retrenchment was not merely due to policymakers' drive for fiscal consolidation. Indeed, politicians did not touch other major subsidies that benefited export-oriented steel and manufacturing industries, subsidizing their energy-related costs to secure international competitiveness.[86] In other words, subsidies that policymakers viewed as reinforcing the German growth regime remained in place, while others that they considered as contradictory to it were retrenched.

Finally, policymakers also eliminated federal social housing programs that supported both rental and owner-occupied housing. Fiscal austerity and affordable housing are both important – but sometimes competing – principles of Germany's export-led growth regime.[87] As affordable housing seemed within sight, policymakers emphasized fiscal austerity during this period. With large majorities in both houses of parliament, in 2006, Merkel's grand coalition reformed the country's federalist setup and, in doing so, eliminated *federal* social housing programs. The federal government transferred the authority of social housing to the *Länder*, which had already paid the greater part of social housing funding. Until 2019, the *Länder* received compensation (EUR 518 million per year) for taking over social housing; but the states could freely decide how to use these funds, including for the reduction of fiscal deficits. The eventual deal was that the federal government retained legislative authority over urban development,[88] whereas the *Länder* received power over social housing. There was little debate in the Bundestag about social housing reform and even less public debate, as social housing was a low-salience concern at a time of depressed housing markets and grim demographic projections. In short, federal social housing programs were eliminated as part of the country's federalism reform of 2006, itself adopted in the name of structural

[86] Bundesregierung (March 22, 2006), 20. *Subventionsbericht*, 20–22.

[87] Bundestag member VIII (FDP) (author interview, November 21, 2023).

[88] Urban development programs include *Stadtumbau Ost*, which focused on demolishing vacant housing units, and *Soziale Stadt*, a large-scale initiative aimed at revitalizing economically depressed and socially disadvantaged neighborhoods.

economic reform to turn around the economy by making governance processes more efficient.

By the mid-2000s, few housing programs were left for either homeowners or rental investors in comparison to earlier periods and to other countries such as the United States. One year after these major housing reforms, in 2007, German housing production had dropped to around 200,000 new housing units (down from 560,000 in 1994), including a mere 20,000 new social housing units (see Figure 3.1). Yet German politicians' austerity drive also meant that the federal government gave up on its authority to shape social housing policy and housing supply in the future – a shortsighted decision that started to bite a decade later.

THE ROLE OF HOUSING IN GERMANY'S RISE AS EUROPE'S ECONOMIC SUPERSTAR

The country's economic revival from sick man to miracle puzzled policymakers and experts alike, as it occurred around the time of the financial crisis of 2008–2009. While most other advanced economies experienced a drawn-out economic slowdown and rising unemployment during the Great Recession and the subsequent eurozone crisis, Germany's unemployment rate *decreased* from 12 percent in 2006 to 8 percent in 2011 and less than 6 percent in 2022 – a figure that had been unimaginable in 2002 and that recalled the heady miracle years of the mid-twentieth century (Reisenbichler and Morgan 2012).

Like other economies, Germany experienced a major recession in 2008, but it was short-lived and unrelated to housing; on the contrary, the housing market remained remarkably stable during the financial crisis and started to recover from its decade-long depression (Kofner 2014; Voigtländer 2014; Muellbauer 2018). Given the country's conservative housing finance structure, the global housing collapse had few direct effects on the Germany economy (except indirect ones via lower American and European demand for German exports). While Germany did experience some problems in its banking sector that required government bailouts, the recession was driven mainly by a slowdown of foreign demand for German products. During the 2008 crisis, the Merkel government considered the German covered bond market "safe enough already" (quoted in Sattler 2019, 272), explicitly excluding covered bonds from financial rescue measures for the time being.

This outcome was consistent with what we would expect given Germany's export-oriented growth regime: As house price inflation did not underpin the country's growth regime – and indeed threatened it – policymakers shied away from financializing housing (van Gunten and Navot 2018, 91). While the German home lending market did undergo important regulatory changes in the post-unification period, none of these changes touched the conservative

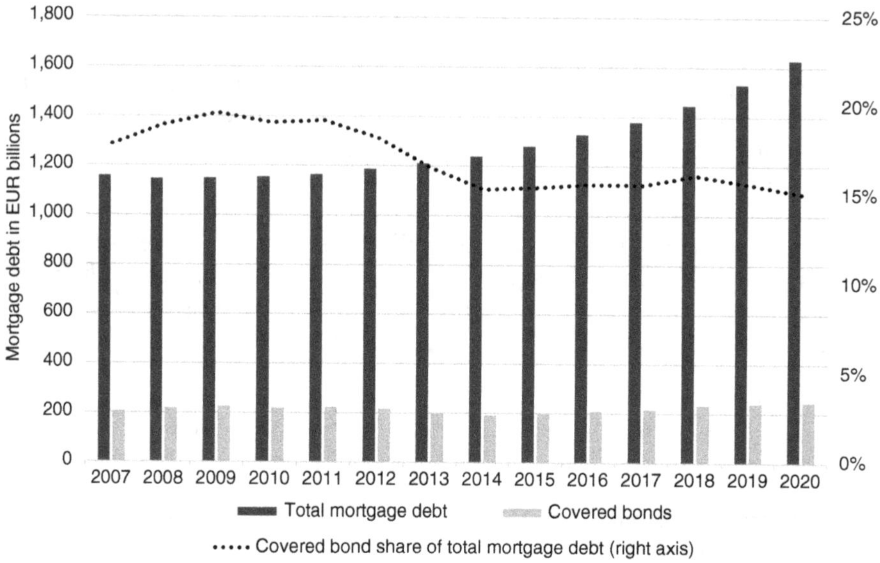

FIGURE 7.4 Housing-related covered bonds as a share of total mortgage debt in Germany, 2007–2020
Data source: EMF Hypostat.

nature of covered bonds or mortgage lending.[89] As Figure 7.4 shows, the German covered bond market – which does not rely on government guarantees – retained its status as an important source of mortgage funding in the country's primarily deposit-based mortgage system, with a share of 15–20 percent of the residential mortgage market. However, this is a much lower share compared to American government-sponsored mortgage-backed securities that dominate US mortgage funding (see Chapter 6).

Germany exported its way out of the crisis much faster than other countries when demand from emerging economies picked up again. Just before the 2008–2009 crisis began, German industries had regained competitiveness and experienced an export boom, producing strong economic growth of 3.9 percent in 2006 and 2.9 percent in 2007. Germany's export share as a percentage of GDP kept increasing from 26 percent in 1998 to 44 percent in 2008, while the share of private consumption as a percentage of GDP dropped slightly from 57 to 55 percent in the same period (see Figures 1.2 and 1.3).

[89] In the 1990s, German policymakers had authorized specialized mortgage banks to conduct unrestricted business in the EU, while these banks started offering larger covered bonds (called Jumbo covered bonds) to attract foreign buyers in an otherwise nonstandardized and fragmented European covered bond market. In 2005, the Schröder government eliminated the mortgage banks' specialization principle, allowing mortgage banks to act like universal banks, while universal banks were allowed to issue covered bonds as long as they got licensed and adhered to strict rules set by German financial regulators (Sattler 2019, 221–232 and 243–244).

The sources of Germany's export-led success and turnaround are still a matter of debate, but there is growing evidence that housing contributed to it. Most scholars agree that repressing domestic costs – whether through wage restraint, flexible business-labor relations (Reisenbichler and Morgan 2012; Dustmann et al. 2014; Manger and Sattler 2020), or government reforms (Kirkegaard 2014) – improved the competitiveness of the German export-led growth regime in the eurozone (Baccaro and Pontusson 2016; Hassel and Palier 2021; Baccaro and Höpner 2022).[90] Since eurozone countries cannot devalue their currencies to boost exports in times of crisis, the eurozone privileges economies that can enhance export competitiveness through internal devaluation – that is, by repressing domestic costs, such as wages or government spending (e.g., Baccaro and Höpner 2022; Höpner 2019; Nölke 2021). As Donato Di Carlo and Martin Höpner (2022) show, German construction was the sector with the slowest wage growth from the mid-1990s to the late 2000s (without *any* nominal wage increase from 1991 to 2006), owing to the prolonged construction slump and high unemployment in the sector, paired with transnational wage competition. The repressed housing market thus helped suppress German wages.

In addition, German economic elites identified a trade-off between housing and export strength. In its 2014/2015 annual report, the Council of Economic Experts devoted a special section to this relationship, highlighting a correlation between current account surpluses and depressed real estate prices from the 1970s to the 2010s in Germany. The council suggested that this link arose because booming real estate prices can "shift resources from sectors such as export industries to the construction sector" and attract capital inflows from abroad, which negatively affects current accounts.[91] Similarly, as Oxford economist John Muellbauer (2018, 28) notes, bricks and mortar played another role in boosting competitiveness: "Germany has gained competitive advantages in the Eurozone from its lower housing costs, which is one factor contributing to the divergences in unit labour costs between Germany and other Eurozone members" (cp. Égert and Kierzenkowski 2014). Indeed, the rental burden of an average household was around 25 percent of disposable income in the early 2000s. As this book has argued, house prices in Germany play exactly the opposite role to those in the United States. While rising house prices are largely celebrated as a positive development for the US economy in that they stimulate domestic demand, they are decried for driving up costs (and wages) in the German economy (Reisenbichler and König 2024).

After the Great Recession of 2008–2009, German housing markets started booming again, partly driven by the ultra-loose monetary policy of

[90] Germany's unit labor costs improved relative to its competitors, especially from 2003 to 2007 and from 2010 to 2011. See OECD, *Productivity and Unit Labour Costs*.

[91] Sachverständigenrat für Wirtschaft, *Jahresgutachten 2014/2015*, 235–236.

the European Central Bank (ECB). However, key actors within the German growth regime criticized the ECB's post-2008 loose monetary policy as incongruent with the German economic model (Reisenbichler 2020b). When the ECB reduced interest rates to zero and began unconventional "quantitative easing" programs – buying government and covered bonds from 2009 onward – the Bundesbank was up in arms.[92] The hawkish Bundesbank president, Axel Weber, resigned in 2011, followed by the German member of the ECB's executive board, Jürgen Stark, in the same year. Both criticized the ECB's ultra-loose approach for threatening price stability, market discipline, and financial stability. Indeed, the Bundesbank repeatedly warned that loose monetary policy would fuel the overvaluing of the German housing market. Similarly, the export-oriented Federation of German Wholesale, Foreign Trade and Services (Bundesverband Großhandel, Außenhandel, Dienstleistungen) articulated that it preferred a stable currency over ultra-loose monetary policies, viewing these policies as artificial, detached from market fundamentals, and threatening currency stability.[93] As Germans do not ordinarily put their savings in stocks, but in savings accounts or pension funds, Sigmar Gabriel (SPD), then Germany's vice-chancellor, said that "[w]hat the European Central Bank is doing now is for many savers, for little people, for workers, for pensioners, an expropriation."[94] The country's widely read tabloid, *Bild*, even called the ECB president Mario Draghi "Count Draghila" for sucking dry the savings of households.[95] In all these ways, ultra-loose monetary policy – and rising house prices – contradicted the macroeconomic priorities of the German growth regime.

This traditional German advantage – low housing prices supporting internationally competitive exports – was about to become a major disadvantage when house prices increased, as Chapter 8 will detail.

[92] For the first time since 1950, the Bundesbank purchased covered bonds again. In both periods, the goal was not to stimulate housing but to stabilize or revive the covered bond market. While covered bonds fared better than US MBS during the 2008–2009 crisis, the covered bond market was not completely immune and experienced some mild problems in early 2009. Even so, the ECB's covered bond purchases were marginal (a total of EUR 16 billion by 2012) compared to the Fed's purchase of MBS, which amounted to well over USD one trillion by the end of 2012 (see Figure 8.2). In the case of Europe, the central bank provided much less *direct* support for housing markets, partly because covered bond markets in Europe are much smaller than American MBS markets and because housing is much less of a monetary-transmission (and growth-generating) sector in all of Europe compared to the United States (Reisenbichler 2020b).

[93] Krohn, P., and Pennekamp, J. (March 12, 2015), "Der Euro im Sturzflug," *Frankfurter Allgemeine Zeitung*.

[94] Wagstyl, S., and Jones, C. (April 10, 2016), "Germany blames Mario Draghi for rise of right-wing AfD party," *Financial Times*.

[95] Esslinger, L. (October 24, 2019), "Wie gruselig war Graf Draghila wirklich? Sparer haben während Draghis Amtszeit 120 Milliarden Euro verloren," *Bild*.

CONCLUSION

In response to Germany's post-unification economic crisis of the early 2000s – which included an often-forgotten housing downturn – policymakers across the center ground eliminated longstanding federal housing programs that had supported rental investors and homeownership (see Table 7.1). While American policymakers doubled down on housing programs during the 2008–2009 crash, German policymakers did the opposite and doubled back. For German politicians, housing was not the solution to economic problems; rather, housing programs themselves were considered a structural economic problem holding back the German economy. Indeed, Chancellor Kohl's American-style experiment of post-unification housing stimulus left the country with many more homes than needed and a depressed construction sector with low capacity. German policymakers retrenched housing programs to repair the fundamentals of the export-led growth regime by reducing fiscal deficits, eliminating capital misallocations, and shifting government resources into what policymakers considered growth-generating sectors such as technology and education. Much like the Hartz labor and welfare reforms, policymakers considered these housing reforms to be sound macroeconomic policy aimed at reviving Germany's export-led growth regime.

The retrenchment of German housing programs is remarkable in that it defies the conventional wisdom about the path dependence of social programs, particularly homeownership programs that benefit the middle class and powerful interest groups (Pierson 1994, 96). Indeed, the German homeownership tax allowance had enjoyed strong popular support among voters and had a strong housing lobby behind it. The reason for its retrenchment is that policymakers perceived housing programs to be in direct opposition to the macroeconomic needs of Germany's export-oriented economy. Unlike their American counterparts, the German housing lobby could not convincingly argue that homeownership programs served the wider economic interests of the German export-led economy; in other words, the German economy did not rely on housing as an economic locomotive for stimulating private credit or consumption. As a result, the peripheral positioning of the housing lobby in Germany's export-oriented growth regime weakened the impact of their demands compared to those of the American lobby, which is at the center of the US demand-led growth regime. Even though more and more German households have relied on homeownership to supplement declining public pensions over the years, German public pensions remain much more generous than America's, a factor that gave German policymakers more leeway for shifting housing policy paths.

Policy retrenchment was the logical culmination of a decades-long political process in which policymakers had come to believe that federal housing programs rejected the economic principles and needs of the country's

TABLE 7.1 *German housing finance programs adopted or reformed between 1990 and 2024*

Type of program	Policy	Years active	Policy adoption and modifications
Tax	Mortgage interest deduction	1992–1994	Temporary policy
Tax	Homeownership tax allowance (*Eigenheimzulage*)	1949–2006	1996 reform made subsidy more progressive ("paragraph 10e" in tax code became the *Eigenheimzulage*); subsidy introduced for environmentally friendly homes (1996–2002); elimination in 2006
Tax	Tax subsidy for savings schemes in building societies	1949–1995	Eliminated in 1995
Tax / direct subsidy	Homeownership pension savings scheme (*Wohn-Riester*)	2008–	Allows subsidized savings to be used for home purchases; taxed upon withdrawal during retirement
Direct subsidy	Subsidy for savings in building societies (*Wohnungsbauprämie*)	1952–	Reduced to a marginal program
Direct subsidy	Homeownership subsidy for families with children (*Baukindergeld*)	2018–2021	Temporary policy
Credit	Social housing programs (*sozialer Wohnungsbau / soziale Wohnraumförderung*)	1950–2006	Program strengthened to cope with reunification-related housing problems in early 1990s; scope of program narrowed with 2001 reform; federal social housing programs eliminated in 2006
Credit	German development bank homeownership programs (KfW)	1995–	Small-scale subsidized loans, including programs for young families and climate-friendly homes
Central bank	Asset purchase programs	2008–	ECB purchased marginal amount of German covered bonds

growth regime. Yet it was also paradoxical. Eliminating federal social housing programs – as opposed to just reducing them – deprived the federal government of the tools required to address future housing supply shortages. Indeed, the austerity overshoot began to bite when housing shortages returned to Germany just a few years later. Ironically, the German government thus contributed to the very conditions it had historically worked to avoid: A housing-cost explosion that jeopardized affordable housing and low wages.

8

Paradoxes of American and German Housing Policy

The United States and Germany have taken radically different and counter-intuitive housing policy approaches. Free-market America has developed a government-sponsored housing model, which US policymakers gradually expanded from the Great Depression onward. The cumulative result is that American housing programs for owner-occupied residential housing are some of the most generous in wealthy democracies. For instance, the American state spends billions of tax dollars on homeowners through the mortgage interest deduction. In addition, by the end of 2024, it was directly backing USD 9 *trillion* dollars in mortgage debt through quasi-governmental agencies such as Fannie Mae and Freddie Mac. By any standard, American housing programs for homeownership have gone through the roof, providing households with relatively easy access to subsidized credit. Meanwhile, rental housing support remains a footnote in the American political economy.

In contrast, social-market Germany currently offers only marginal housing finance programs for homeownership and rental housing alike, and it restricts access to mortgage credit. Over time, German policymakers have gradually retrenched housing programs for both homeowners and rental markets – policies originally adopted to address WWII-related housing shortages – despite facing strong interest-group and constituency pressures. It is America, not Germany, that has socialized its home lending system.

This book has argued that the two countries' different economic growth regimes – demand-led in the United States and export-led in Germany – produced contrasting political dynamics that have resulted in diverging housing policy approaches. The US economy is demand-led and relies heavily on consumption and credit, and housing is *the* key sector generating such demand, credit, and consumption. Since the Great Depression, American policymakers have concluded that housing programs subsidizing mortgage debt fuel housing demand, house prices, and housing wealth, and thereby consumer lending and spending. Rising house prices are central to the functioning of this virtuous circle, where American homes effectively serve as credit cards. Consequently, protecting home values has been a longstanding policy priority in the United States. American politicians have repeatedly deployed the power of the state to absorb risk in the housing finance market, attracting private capital into housing, guaranteeing profits to financial markets, and lowering borrowing costs for consumers. Despite little agreement in other social policy areas such as healthcare, American policymakers have developed a bipartisan consensus in favor of preserving and expanding housing programs as a growth strategy to support mortgage credit and private consumption. Over time, American housing programs have become integral to the functioning of the US housing market and therefore to the American economy. Take away government support, and the systemically important housing finance system could collapse. In short, housing finance became America's unspoken national champion, a strategic sector relied upon to deliver growth, prosperity, and employment.

In contrast, the German export-oriented economy relies on *restraining* demand, consumption, and credit to secure export competitiveness through low wages and low inflation. Housing therefore plays a fundamentally different role in the German economy. After WWII, German policymakers adopted large-scale housing programs with broad-based political support, yet with a different goal: To guarantee sufficient housing supply to keep the cost of living and wages down. This approach also benefited the country's powerful export-oriented manufacturing industries. Once housing shortages ended, German policymakers did what would be the unthinkable in the United States: They retrenched housing programs, including those for homeowners, in the name of fiscal consolidation and structural reforms to boost export competitiveness. These macroeconomic imperatives overcame the pro-homeownership ideology of the German political right and made politicians more resistant to pressures from the housing lobby. Where American policymakers used state power to channel private capital into housing, German policymakers used the power of the state to channel capital *away* from housing and into manufacturing. Industrial exports, not housing finance, are Germany's national champions.

Paradoxically, however, the very policy actions intended to preserve both countries' growth regimes can also threaten them. The US housing market is one of the country's greatest economic strengths, but it can also be the source of its undoing. American property markets are key engines of economic growth, but the policies necessary to support that growth exhibit crisis tendencies, such as inflating the property market, which can create the conditions for asset-price bubbles. This is the story of housing in America: Policymakers run the risk of policy overshoot by stimulating housing-based growth. In Germany, the pursuit of austerity, low inflation, and depressed domestic demand can similarly hurt the country's export-led growth regime. Policymakers' retrenchment of longstanding housing programs deprived them of the tools to deflate housing costs, leaving politicians struggling with housing shortages that have the potential to fuel inflation and threaten competitiveness.

RISKY BUSINESS: AMERICAN HOUSING BETWEEN BOOM AND BUST

The American demand-led growth regime is founded on a paradox. On one hand, US property markets – and the housing programs that underpin them – are key engines of economic growth. Rising house prices tend to translate into higher investment activity, bank lending, and consumer spending via wealth and credit effects. On the other hand, booming property markets and asset-price bubbles – and the programs that stimulate them – can create financial turmoil when asset prices drop, as was the case during the 2008–2009 crash. With the help of the US government and the Fed, the American housing market recovered from the prolonged 2008–2009 downturn. Yet it recovered too well, as house prices skyrocketed during the last decade (see Figure 8.1). "So you really had a housing bubble," Fed chair Jerome Powell said in November 2022, "you had housing prices going up at very unsustainable levels and overheating."[1]

As Chapter 6 has shown, American policymakers' doubling down on housing programs in response to the 2008–2009 crash restored housing as an engine of the American economy. After a prolonged housing slump, the US housing market started booming again after 2012. By 2019, real house prices had surpassed their 2006 peak, allowing many households to more than recover their crash-related losses in housing wealth. The Fed identified strong wealth effects by the late 2010s again, noting that "[t]he relatively high level of aggregate household net worth also supported consumer spending."[2] Indeed, in 2019, the level of household net wealth was around seven times the value of disposable income, the highest ratio recorded since 1947. Toward the end of the decade, outstanding residential mortgage debt increased to a record level of USD 13 trillion, exceeding its pre-crisis peak of USD 12 trillion in 2008 (see Figure 4.3). Low interest rates and rising house prices also generated a refinancing boom, allowing households to either take out larger mortgages or lower their monthly mortgage payments, which in turn generated extra cash for household spending. Freddie Mac estimated that homeowners extracted USD 114 billion and USD 250 billion through cash-out refinancing in 2019 and 2021, respectively. Only the mid-2000s

[1] Powell, J. (November 30, 2022), *The Economic Outlook, Inflation, and the Labor Market* [transcript]. Brookings, Washington, DC, www.brookings.edu/wp-content/uploads/2022/11/es_20221130_powell_transcript.pdf.

[2] Federal Reserve Board (2019), *Annual Report*, 11; Federal Reserve Board (2018), *Annual Report*, 13.

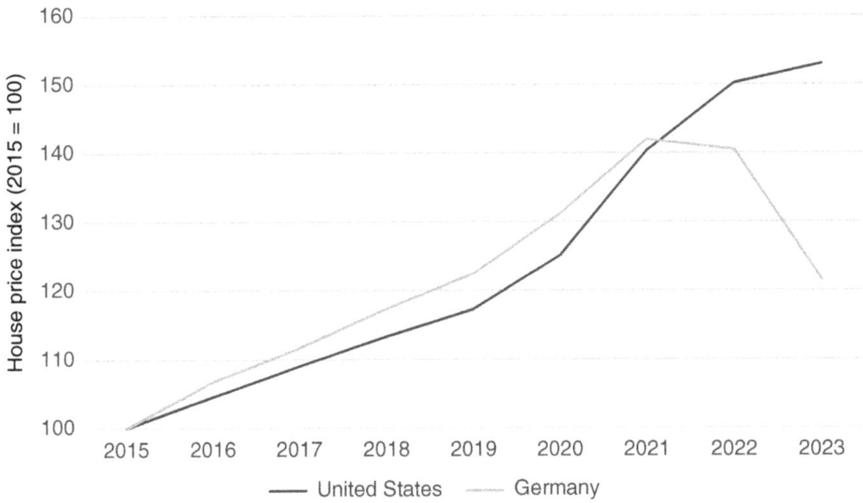

FIGURE 8.1 Real house prices in the United States and Germany, 2015–2023
Data source: OECDstat (series: "real housing prices").

saw higher levels of refinancing.[3] More generally, fixed residential investment as a share of GDP rose to 4 percent in 2019, up from its trough of 2.4 percent in 2011.[4] Housing starts trended upwards as well, reaching 1.3 million in 2019 as vacancies dwindled. This number is well above its trough of just 600,000 units in 2009 but still below the historical average of 1.5 million between 1960 and 2000 (see Figure 2.2). By the end of the 2010s, housing was a major driver of the economy again.

When the COVID pandemic hit the American economy in early 2020, policymakers' and central bankers' first instinct was to protect the housing market and, with it, the American growth regime. Experts feared that the US housing market, which had seen hefty house-price gains in the years prior, might collapse again. "Another U.S.-wide housing slump is coming," read a *Bloomberg* article in April 2020.[5] The concern was not a subprime bubble but simply that mass unemployment or a general economic downturn could result in large-scale mortgage defaults. However, the heavy-hitting spending program called the Coronavirus Aid, Relief, and Economic Security (CARES) Act passed by Congress and signed by President Trump included two key provisions that prevented this outcome. First, despite a massive, albeit brief, spike in unemployment, the federal government offered generous unemployment

[3] Freddie Mac (April 25, 2022), *Trends in Mortgage Refinancing Activity* [research note], www.freddiemac.com/research/insight/20220425-trends-mortgage-refinancing-activity.

[4] FRED (2024), *Fixed investment: Residential*, https://fred.stlouisfed.org/series/A011RE1Q156NBEA.

[5] DiMartino Booth, D. (April 10, 2020), "Another U.S.-wide housing slump is coming," *Bloomberg*.

benefits to those in need. Second, the act included a "forbearance" provision for all federally backed mortgages (i.e., FHA, VA, GSEs) – over 60 percent of all mortgages in 2020 – which allowed households to temporarily (for 6–12 months) pause or reduce mortgage payments if they were experiencing financial stress. The act also temporarily prohibited foreclosures on homeowners and evictions of renters if their homes were financed with federally backed mortgages. According to data from the Mortgage Bankers Association, the number of mortgages in forbearance peaked at around 8 percent of all mortgages in May 2020 and then gradually decreased to 0.5 percent in 2023 as the pandemic eased.[6]

Similarly, the Fed sprang into action to protect housing during the pandemic, taking its housing support to the next level compared to its earlier interventions in response to the 2008 crash. When the pandemic started, investors started selling mortgage-backed securities and US Treasuries to raise cash, resulting in liquidity problems in these markets. Despite the Fed lowering interest rates, thirty-year mortgage rates, as well as yields on mortgage-backed securities and US Treasuries, were *rising* and moving in the opposite direction to short-term interest rates. In response, the Fed expanded its existing balance-sheet holdings of US Treasuries and GSE mortgage-backed securities. By 2022, the Fed owned USD 2.7 *trillion* in mortgage-backed securities (up from USD 1.3 trillion in early 2020), which was roughly one-third of the entire MBS market. In contrast, as Figure 8.2 shows, the ECB bought very little in housing-related bonds, partly because housing is not a transmission sector to stimulate the wider economy (Reisenbichler 2020b).[7]

As a result, American mortgage rates dropped to their lowest-ever level of less than 3 percent during the height of the pandemic. The Fed's actions were not necessarily intended to stimulate the housing market but to save the American financial system and economy via housing interventions. What was considered an extraordinary crisis measure in 2008 has since become a standard monetary policy tool reinforcing the American growth regime.

There is no doubt that generous housing programs implemented by politicians and the Fed helped inflate the property market during the pandemic, as real house prices increased by 20 percent between 2020 and 2022 (see Figure 8.1). However, government actions were not the only factors. Increased household savings also translated into higher housing demand, exacerbating an insufficient supply of nearly four million missing homes in late 2020.[8] The shortage was partly due to post-2008 capacity problems

[6] Calculated Risk Blog (May 15, 2023), *MBA Survey: Share of Mortgage Loans in Forbearance Decreases to 0.51% in April*, www.calculatedriskblog.com/2023/05/mba-survey-share-of-mortgage-loans-in.html.

[7] Former ECB official (author interview, Frankfurt March 30, 2015).

[8] Freddie Mac (May 7, 2021), *Housing Supply: A Growing Deficit* [research note], www.freddiemac.com/research/insight/20210507-housing-supply.

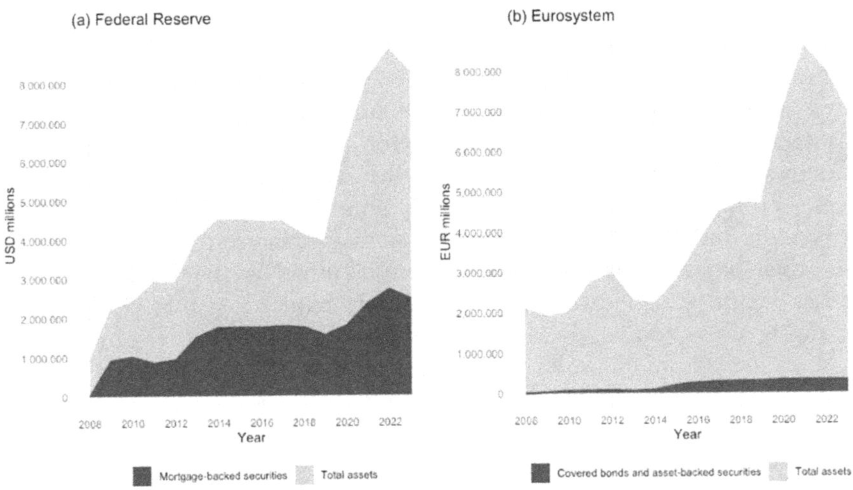

FIGURE 8.2 Housing-related bonds held by the US Federal Reserve and the European Central Bank, 2008–2022
Notes: The ECB's purchases include the covered bond purchase programs (CBPP) I, II, and III, and the asset-backed securities purchase program (ABSPP). The Fed's purchases of MBS were part of its quantitative easing programs. Note that the ECB's balance sheet was larger than the Fed's in 2008, mainly because the ECB already engaged in large-scale lending programs to eurozone banks (i.e., refinancing operations). *Data sources:* ECB (series: annual consolidated balance sheet of the Eurosystem; asset purchase programmes) and FRED (series: WSHOMCB, WALCL).

in the construction industry, labor shortages, pandemic-related material shortages, and notoriously strict zoning regulations (Glaeser and Gyourko 2018).[9]

Fed officials grew increasingly concerned about a housing bubble that could result in economic disaster. Consequently, some Fed officials advocated for reducing mortgage support to cool down the housing market. For example, Eric Rosengren of the Boston Fed stated that "[t]he mortgage market probably doesn't need as much support now," while James Bullard of the St. Louis Fed put it even more bluntly: "maybe we don't need to be in mortgage-backed securities with a booming housing market and even a threatening housing bubble here."[10] Despite these concerns, the Fed barely reduced its mortgage support, fearing disruptions in a market that is so central to the American growth regime.

Even rising inflation from early 2022 did not lead the Fed to make major corrections to its housing course. One might reasonably conclude that the

[9] Council of Economic Advisers (2020), *Annual Report*, ch. 8.

[10] Quoted in: Kiernan, P. (June 28, 2021), "Fed officials debate scaling back mortgage-bond purchases at faster clip," *Wall Street Journal.*

Fed had become subject to growth-model constraints similar to those that affect policymakers: There is never a good time to withdraw housing support, not even in times of high inflation. The inflationary environment of the 2020s – stemming from pandemic-related supply-chain disruptions, pent-up consumer demand after the pandemic, labor shortages, massive fiscal policy packages, and Russia's war on Ukraine driving up energy and commodity prices – prompted a monetary policy shift among global central banks. Both the Fed and the ECB started tightening by raising interest rates and scaling down their bloated balance sheets, a process known as quantitative tightening (see Figure 8.2). However, the Fed barely reduced its massive holdings of housing assets and still held USD 2.3 trillion in mortgage debt by the end of 2024, down from its peak of USD 2.7 trillion in 2022. Esther George, the Kansas Fed president, unhappily asked: "is that the footprint we want in the mortgage market?"[11]

American housing programs and sky-high house prices also pose problems for the American growth regime by exacerbating inequality. The cocktail of excessive demand-side housing programs and restrictive supply-side land polices has produced soaring house prices, an affordability crisis, and inequality. First, research has found that unaffordable housing makes prosperous superstar cities less attractive to skilled workers, preventing them from taking jobs there, which negatively affects productivity and economic growth (Hsieh and Moretti 2019). Second, rising house prices contribute to inequalities in wealth and access, both intergenerational and racial. Existing American homeowners are the winners of the recent house-price boom, while renters face unaffordable rental markets and aspirational buyers are priced out. Moreover, the Black–white homeownership gap, which has remained at 30 percent and virtually unchanged since 1970, means that white households have benefited from rising house prices to a much higher degree than minority households (see Figure 6.1). Finally, the recent house-price boom also exacerbated intergenerational inequality, as older homeowners have seen massive increases in their wealth while young households struggle to climb the property ladder (Dewilde and Flynn 2021).

Meanwhile, American labor unions have rediscovered the issue of housing affordability. Local union representatives called housing affordability their "biggest issue," much like union leaders did in the 1930s and 1940s (Dreier 2000; also see Chapter 2).[12] Many local unions have made housing a core issue during their strikes, as workers are unable to afford skyrocketing housing costs in metropolitan areas. This includes repeated hotel workers' strikes in Los Angeles that resulted in higher wages partly to offset rising housing

[11] Quoted in: Schneider, H. (January 23, 2023), "Fed needs mortgage-backed securities exit plan 'earlier than later,' George says," *Reuters*.

[12] Greenhouse, S. (February 16, 2024), "US unions target the housing affordability crisis as their 'biggest issue'," *The Guardian*.

costs. In 2023, also in Los Angeles, housing activists and organized labor successfully pushed for a measure to tax the sale of ultra-expensive homes (above USD 5 million) to finance affordable rental housing (Dreier 2023). However, union-led efforts for renter affordability and protections are relatively localized and have not amounted to a national housing policy agenda.

Finally, housing poses another major problem to the American growth regime: As in other countries, it is one of the economy's largest carbon emitters. Residential housing contributes 20 percent of energy-related greenhouse gas emissions. As Benjamin Goldstein and colleagues (2020, 1912) note, "[i]f considered a country," American housing emissions alone would exceed Germany's total emissions. According to the Organisation for Economic Co-operation and Development (OECD), Americans' housing-related carbon emissions are the highest per capita among advanced economies (almost 3 tons of CO_2 per capita), including emissions from the construction, heating, cooling, lighting, and powering of homes (Hoeller 2023, 9). Germany's housing emissions are roughly 2 tons of CO_2 per capita, still relatively high by OECD standards. In both countries, structural reliance on carbon-intensive sources of energy has significantly contributed to their elevated housing-related emissions. Relatedly, American housing policy has encouraged single-family homes in suburban areas, resulting in larger average living spaces for Americans than Germans. On average, Americans had 73 square meters of living space per person in the 2010s, compared to just 47 in Germany.[13] Larger homes require more energy for heating, cooling, and powering, which, paired with generally less stringent building codes, contribute to higher housing-based emissions in the United States. As a recent study of US housing notes, "even the most ambitious scenarios modelled do not meet a ... goal of zero emissions in 2050" (Berrill et al. 2022, 713).

America's most important climate-related housing policy is one that protects homeowners – and their property values – against the risk of natural disasters such as flooding. The National Flood Insurance Program has insured property owners against the risk of floods since the late 1960s. The program has incentivized households to build, rebuild, or buy homes in high-risk natural disaster areas increasingly prone to floods in the context of climate change. This is another way in which the American government subsidizes house prices by absorbing financial risk, creating overvalued home prices in high-risk areas by as much USD 237 billion (Gourevitch et al. 2023; Bittle 2023; Elliott 2021). By contrast, Germany does not have a comparable federal flood insurance program protecting homeowners.

Creating affordable and climate-friendly multifamily housing in urban areas could make the American growth regime greener by limiting sprawl, reducing long commutes, optimizing land use, and decarbonizing the housing

[13] Center for Sustainable Systems (2024), *Residential Buildings Factsheet* (Pub. No. CSS01-08), University of Michigan; Umweltbundesamt (2021), *Wohnfläche*, www.umweltbundesamt.de/daten/private-haushalte-konsum/wohnen/wohnflaeche#zahl-der-wohnungen-gestiegen.

sector (Glaeser and Kahn 2010). The Biden administration recognized the need to build affordable and climate-friendly housing but delivered very little policy action. President Biden's landmark infrastructure legislations of 2021 and 2022 included modest green housing subsidies amounting to USD 9 billion for making energy-efficient home improvements and retrofits.[14] These legislations also included tax credits for property owners installing solar panels or electric heat pumps. In May 2024, the Biden administration also increased energy-efficiency standards for homes built with the support of an FHA mortgage. However, stricter energy standards make it costlier to build homes, leading the building lobby to oppose these standards, advocating instead for voluntary measures. More generally, President Biden passed few other noteworthy housing measures for either homeowners or rental housing that the administration had originally proposed as part of its 2020 housing plan, including a zoning reform to incentivize local communities to build more multifamily instead of just single-family homes.[15]

POLICY OVERSHOOT AND THE NEW HOUSING QUESTION IN GERMANY

The German export-led growth regime is also founded on a paradox. Fiscal austerity is an important feature of the German growth regime, aimed at keeping domestic costs low and exports competitive, but it can also cripple housing programs that have successfully helped suppress the cost of living, inflation, and wages in the past. The unintended consequence is that fiscal consolidation has exacerbated housing shortages, which can in turn fuel inflation, deepen skill shortages, and threaten competitiveness. When German policymakers eliminated the country's longstanding social housing programs in the mid-2000s – the very programs that had successfully helped the German growth regime overcome housing shortages after WWII (see Chapter 3) – they ignored the fact that housing markets are cyclical. Few politicians would have predicted that Germany would experience a new housing affordability crisis just a decade later during the 2010s. When Germany's economy recovered around the time of the 2008–2009 crisis, so did its housing market: House prices skyrocketed along with housing demand, while supply dwindled. Yet the retrenchment of federal housing programs, particularly social housing programs, was a case of throwing the baby out with the bathwater. It deprived politicians of the tools to deflate housing costs – a key priority of the German growth regime – which left policymakers struggling to find solutions to the new affordability crisis.

[14] US Department of Energy (November 2, 2022), "Biden-Harris administration announces state and tribe allocations for home energy rebate program," www.energy.gov/articles/biden-harris-administration-announces-state-and-tribe-allocations-home-energy-rebate.

[15] The Biden administration somewhat tightened rent controls of units funded with Low-Income Housing Tax Credits in 2024, capping rent increases at a maximum of 10% per year.

From the early 2010s, German housing prices went through the roof. Between 2010 and 2022, house prices more than doubled in nominal terms, while rental prices increased by 60 percent for new tenants and 20 percent for existing tenants (the slower growth of rental prices for existing tenants is due to flexible rent controls).[16] Housing shortages have reemerged, especially in cities, as the growth in the number of households outpaced the construction of new housing units in metropolitan areas.[17]

Several factors explain exploding housing costs and prices in Germany. First, a prolonged period of low interest rates after the 2008–2009 crisis – produced by the ECB's ultra-accommodative monetary policy – created a Europe-wide house-price boom (Reisenbichler 2020b). In the early 2010s, domestic and global investors looking for returns discovered a goldmine in Germany, where prices were cheap compared to those of other advanced economies. Domestic buyers were encouraged by a booming economy, employment growth, and real wage increases. International buyers, such as hedge funds, considered Germany a high-flying market with tremendous profit-making opportunities, and they bought up social housing units from local governments (Wijburg and Aalbers 2017; Gabor and Kohl 2022).

Second, demographic factors were a driver. Net migration averaged 514,000 people per year between 2010 and 2023 – five times more than a decade earlier. Initially, internal European Union migration drove these numbers, as migrants fled southern European stagnation and sought economic opportunities in the continent's most successful economy. The migration crisis of 2015 and Chancellor Merkel's decision to open the border to over one million refugees from the Middle East also increased housing demand in German cities. Most recently, Russia's war on Ukraine has led to 1.1 million Ukrainian refugees entering Germany and requiring housing. As a result, Germany's population increased from 81.8 million in 2010 to almost 84 million in 2024.[18] Additionally, there is a longstanding trend of urbanization and decreasing household sizes due to an aging population and more single-person households.[19]

Third, the German construction sector does not have sufficient capacity to ramp up production after the sector's structural decline from the mid-1970s (Kohl and Spielau 2022, 478).[20] Between 2010 and 2022, they produced an

[16] Bundesbank (2024), *System of Indicators for the German Residential Property Market*, www.bundesbank.de/resource/blob/622520/009721bf2c8ff30b51a9d3669b8b92e8/472B63F073F071307366337C94F8C870/german-residential-property-market-data.pdf.

[17] Rat der Immobilienweisen (2017), *Frühjahrsgutachten Immobilienwirtschaft 2017*, Zentraler Immobilienausschuss, Berlin, 265.

[18] Destatis (2024), *Bevölkerungsstand (Basis Zensus 2011); Wanderungen zwischen Deutschland und dem Ausland von 1950 bis 2023; Gesellschaft – Ukraine*, www.destatis.de/DE/Home/_inhalt.html.

[19] Rat der Immobilienweisen (2019), *Frühjahrsgutachten 2019*, Zentraler Immobilienausschuss, Berlin, 57–58.

[20] Bundesbank (2017), *Monatsbericht Dezember 2017*, 16.

average of only 250,000 new units per year (see Figure 3.1), while 400,000 units per year were necessary to keep up with growing demand. The low, albeit rising, level of construction is a major disappointment, considering that it was once possible to build over 700,000 new housing units in 1973 in West Germany alone.

Rising house prices have been a cause for alarm for the German growth regime's most important actors. The Bundesbank repeatedly sounded the alarm about "overvalued" house prices.[21] Whether correct or not, the Bundesbank estimated that house prices in German cities were overvalued by 15 to 30 percent in 2017, posing a significant risk to financial stability. The central bank's reasoning was that an economic recession could produce credit defaults and investor flight, which could lead to collapsing prices and financial instability.[22] In 2017, Bundesbank board member Andreas Dombret remarked that "[t]he mixture of booming real estate market and low interest rates can become a dangerous cocktail for the banking and savings bank sector."[23] Similarly, the Council of Economic Experts recommended policy actions to address housing-market "excesses," warning of a boom-and-bust cycle similar to the one already experienced in eastern Germany in the 1990s.[24] To tame house prices, the Council advocated for supply-side measures to increase the housing supply, such as liberalizing land supply restrictions.[25]

Rising housing costs also posed economic problems for other key actors of the growth regime, such as labor and business. Unions argued that high housing costs would "eat up wages,"[26] adding to already existing wage inflation that was pressuring Germany's cost competitiveness.[27] Employers and industries viewed rising house prices as a business risk. In a 2019 survey of the German *Mittelstand* of small- and medium-sized companies, 24 percent of firms responded that high rents and housing shortages made it more difficult to attract skilled labor, while 20 percent mentioned that they faced rising rental costs themselves.[28] In interviews, a Bundestag member

[21] Bundesbank (2018). *Monatsbericht Februar 2018*, 54. The Bundesbank did not publish house price indices until after the financial crisis of 2008–2009; former Bundesbank board member (author interview, October 5, 2021).

[22] Bundesbank (2019), *Geschäftsbericht 2018*, 24; Bundesbank (2020), *Geschäftsbericht 2019*, 19.

[23] Quoted in "German real estate bubble?" (May 4, 2017), *Deutsche Welle*.

[24] Sachverständigenrat für Wirtschaft (2017), *Jahresgutachten 2017–2018*, 242.

[25] Sachverständigenrat für Wirtschaft (2016), *Jahresgutachten 2016–2017*, 31–32.

[26] IG Metall Berlin (February 16, 2021), *Wohnraumspekulation frisst Löhne auf*, www.igmetall-berlin.de/aktuelles/meldung/wohnraumspekulation-frisst-loehne-auf/.

[27] Schiermeyer, M. (December 30, 2017), "Hohe Mieten setzen Verdi unter Druck," *Stuttgarter Zeitung*.

[28] BVR & DZ Bank AG (June 11, 2019), *Mittelstand im Mittelpunkt* [survey], www.bvr.de/p.nsf/0/494DDCB46E8A6E01C125841D0041BF72/%24FILE/Mittelstand%20im%20Mittelpunkt%20Frühjahr%202019.pdf.

and an industry representative echoed these concerns.[29] As a result, the German business newspaper *WirtschaftsWoche* reported a "comeback" of employer-subsidized housing with the goal of attracting skilled workers.[30] As a Bundestag member pointed out, however, the problem of growing housing costs was less pronounced in rural regions (particularly in eastern Germany), where concerns about infrastructure and transportation were more pressing.[31]

Federal policymakers recognized the problem and responded, predictably, with attempts to deflate housing costs. However, the one tool that had helped them do so in the past – federal social housing programs – was no longer available.[32] Rather, the Merkel grand coalition introduced the so-called rental brake (*Mietpreisbremse*) in 2015, currently scheduled to expire in late 2025, an initiative originally driven by the Social Democrats. Germany already had a flexible rent-control system in place that limited how much landlords can increase rent for sitting tenants in a given year. The new measure gave the *Länder* the authority to impose the "rental brake" in areas they deemed "tense housing markets," meaning that new rental contracts could only be 10 percent above the local rental price index (*Mietspiegel*). The brake did not apply to housing units built after 2014 (or after landlords had modernized older apartments).[33] However, the rental brake did not slow down soaring property values. One study suggests that the rental brake was effective in limiting price increases, but only in a few select inner cities of the country, particularly in Berlin.[34] Price controls alone could not address the underlying issue of a lack of affordable housing supply (Voigtländer 2019).

In 2018, Angela Merkel hosted a housing summit to devise more solutions for the problem of unaffordable housing, yet the results were underwhelming.

[29] Bundestag member VIII (FDP) (author interview, November 21, 2023); DIHK representative (author interview, phone, September 28, 2023).

[30] The newspaper mentions that the number of employer-subsidized housing units had decreased significantly from over 450,000 the early 1980s to just under a few tens of thousands and then climbed again to over 100,000 by the early 2020s; Gerth, M. (February 10, 2021), "Konzerne ködern Mitarbeiter mit günstigen Wohnungen," *WirtschaftsWoche*.

[31] Bundestag member VII (Linke) (author interview, Berlin, September 25, 2023).

[32] As noted in Chapter 7, the federal government promised the German *Länder* annual compensation payments (from 2007 to 2019) in the amount of EUR 518 million in exchange for the *Länder* taking on social housing responsibilities after the federalism reform in 2006. The Merkel government increased these payments to EUR 1 billion in 2016 and EUR 1.5 billion between 2017 and 2019 in light of high numbers of incoming refugees.

[33] From a consumer perspective, it is problematic that renters often do not know their local rental price index, and they frequently do not want to (or know how to) initiate sanctions against their landlords. Low-income households might still not benefit from the rental brake, as landlords can choose well-to-do households given the excess demand for affordable housing; the latter households also often have much better networks that could land them an affordable apartment compared to low-income households and/or newcomers from other countries.

[34] Kholodilin, K., Mense, A., and Michelsen, C. (2018), *Mietpreisbremse ist besser als ihr Ruf, aber nicht die Lösung des Wohnungsmarktproblems*, DIW Wochenbericht 7.

The goal was to increase the housing supply by 1.5 million units between 2018 and 2021 to deflate housing costs for both renters and homeowners. To support this goal, the federal government allocated EUR 5 billion between 2018 and 2021 for the *Länder* to build 100,000 total new social housing units (recall that, after the country's 2006 federalism reform, the *Länder* had exclusive authority over social housing programs).[35] Yet these social housing funds were insufficient to make a significant impact on the larger housing market. In fact, the country's social housing stock even steadily *decreased* from 1.7 million units in 2010 to 1.1 million units in 2022, because social housing units are often transferred to the private market once the landlord no longer receives subsidies.[36] The Merkel government also reintroduced a temporary tax subsidy for private rental housing (2018–2021) to stimulate rental construction and reduce rents through increased supply. However, these subsidies likely produced the opposite effect by inflating construction and land prices due to insufficient availability of land for construction.[37]

For homeowners, the Merkel government reintroduced a temporary and small-scale homeownership subsidy for first-time buyers with children, also yielding mixed results. The so-called *Baukindergeld* subsidy, for owner-occupied properties bought or built between 2018 and 2021, aimed to make homeownership more affordable and help families climb the property ladder in times of rising house prices.[38] However, the new subsidy was a shadow of the former *Eigenheimzulage*, totaling only EUR 10 billion over its entire duration, compared to around EUR 11 billion *per year* under the old program.[39] German economists, including the Council of Economic Experts, widely criticized the new subsidy for its price-inflating and *demand-side* effects.[40] The problem was that the subsidy supported not only newly constructed homes but also existing homes, which limited its supply-side function. As a result, the Merkel government let the subsidy expire, considering it ineffective in creating affordable homeownership.

The pandemic gave an unwanted impetus to already booming German housing prices, prompting regulators to restrain house prices and mortgage lending. When the pandemic hit, the ECB further reduced interest rates, while the German government provided extensive support for businesses preserving employment. In April 2020, the Merkel government introduced a forbearance scheme that allowed mortgage borrowers to temporarily pause

[35] Bundesregierung (September 21, 2018), *Gemeinsame Wohnraumoffensive von Bund, Ländern und Kommunen* [summary of housing conference], Berlin.

[36] Bundestag (September 25, 2023), "Deutschland hat noch etwa 1,09 Millionen Sozialwohnungen," *Kurzmeldungen (hib)*, www.bundestag.de/presse/hib/kurzmeldungen-967750.

[37] Rat der Immobilienweisen (2019), *Frühjahrsgutachten 2019*, 84.

[38] Bundesrat member (CDU) (author interview, July 10, 2019).

[39] See KfW *Förderreport* for the years 2018–2022.

[40] Sachverständigenrat für Wirtschaft (2018), *Jahresgutachten 2018–19*, 373–376; Rat der Immobilienweisen (2019), *Frühjahrsgutachten 2019*, 73.

mortgage payments in case of pandemic-related financial distress. However, since there had been no unemployment shock to the economy, very few mortgage borrowers made use of this provision. On the contrary, households accumulated excess savings that they used for down payments for buying homes in a low-interest environment. In 2021 and 2022, the Financial Stability Committee (*Ausschuss für Finanzstabilität*) – consisting of representatives from the Bundesbank, the Federal Finance Ministry, and the Financial Supervisory Authority (Bundesanstalt für Finanzdienstleistungsaufsicht, BaFin) – appealed to banks to tighten their credit standards for mortgage lending. They also required banks to increase their capital buffers as risk protections.[41] Avoiding a house-price bubble and excessive mortgage lending was their macroeconomic priority.

Despite all these measures, policymakers could not stop rising housing costs in Germany. While the *average* rental burden has risen only slowly in the past two decades (between 25 and 28 percent of disposable income), with rising rents being offset by rising income, there are significant regional and temporal differences. Households in big cities and/or with new rental contracts pay significantly more as a share of their disposable income, with many paying between 40 and 50 percent in 2022 (also cp. Baldenius et al. 2020).[42]

Today's housing cost crisis in large German cities is partly the result of past policy overshoot – specifically, the elimination of longstanding housing programs. In retrospect, German politicians regretted the retrenchment of social housing programs. In an interview, a Social Democrat acknowledged that the housing market did not behave in ways expected in the years after the 2006 reform.[43] Another Social Democrat called the reform nonsense, noting that it was clear "there would be housing shortages again at some point – and that's precisely what happened."[44] Similarly, a Christian Democrat criticized the federal states for not yet internalizing their new social housing responsibilities.[45]

The persisting housing cost crisis in some regions has created a new socioeconomic fault line in Germany: Between housing insiders and outsiders. Housing insiders are, first and foremost, older homeowners whose house values have increased.[46] Relatedly, as homeownership is lower in eastern Germany compared to the west, households in western Germany have

[41] Bundesbank (2022), *Geschäftsbericht 2021*, 34.

[42] Destatis (March 31, 2023), *Haushalte wendeten 2022 durchschnittlich 27,8% ihres Einkommens für die Miete auf* [press release], www.destatis.de/DE/Presse/Pressemitteilungen/2023/03/PD23_129_12_63.html.

[43] Bundestag member IV (SPD) (author interview, Berlin, September 9, 2015).

[44] Bundestag member V (SPD) (author interview, phone, September 25, 2015).

[45] Bundestag member III (CDU) (author interview, Berlin, June 22, 2015).

[46] Housing wealth in eastern Germany – the part of the country where the housing depression was most severe – only recovered to its 2002 levels in 2012; Sachverständigenrat für Wirtschaft (2014), *Jahresgutachten 2014–15*, 386.

benefited disproportionately from the housing boom. More than thirty years after reunification, people in the east still own significantly fewer homes than their western counterparts, with a homeownership gap of 10–15 percent.[47] Similarly, in 2018 only 30 percent of people with a "migration background" – broadly defined as people who are not German citizens or are born to at least one parent who is a noncitizen – lived in their own home, compared to 54 percent of people without a migration background.[48] Growing inequalities also exist *within* the rental market. Some renters are insiders who have locked in attractive rental rates and who benefit from rent controls. Outsiders are those seeking new apartments in expensive areas – young people moving into their first apartments, families seeking larger spaces, migrants arriving in the country, the elderly seeking to downsize, and many others relocating for work or personal reasons. Even a permanent and relatively well-paid work contract might no longer be enough to qualify a person as an "insider" in Germany's political economy (Palier and Thelen 2010; Thelen 2014). Today, housing constitutes an equally important socioeconomic fault line (Baldenius et al. 2020).

The German population has shown tremendous frustration with recent house-price increases. In particular, the country's large group of renters have protested rising housing costs that pose a threat to their livelihoods. Berlin became the hotspot of "rental madness" (*Mietenwahnsinn*) protests against rising housing costs. To some degree, these protests bore fruit: The leftist Berlin state government (SPD–Left–Greens) adopted a "rent freeze" (*Mietendeckel*) on top of the federally legislated "rental brake" in 2020 (the constitutional court declared the former unconstitutional shortly thereafter). The uproar about rising housing costs also forced a Berlin-wide 2021 referendum on whether large-scale landlords and their apartments should be expropriated, including those of Deutsche Wohnen and Vonovia. The referendum passed with an astonishing majority of 56 percent. In Germany's capital – in the land of ordo-liberal principles based on private property, free enterprise, and regulated competition – most residents voted to *expropriate* from landlords. The referendum was not legally binding and did not have any legislative effect, but that is beyond the point. Most Germans care deeply about price stability in the housing sector and do not view housing as objects of speculation but instead as places to live (Führer 2015).

When the government of Chancellor Olaf Scholz took office in late 2021 (SPD–Greens–FDP coalition, 2021–2024), it continued Germany's longstanding policy

[47] In 2022, homeownership in the east was 34 percent, while it was 44 percent in the west and 41.8 percent nationwide; author's own calculations, based on 2022 census data from Destatis (2024), *Eigentumsquote*, www.destatis.de/DE/Home/_inhalt.html.

[48] Bundeszentrale für politische Bildung (March 10, 2021), *Datenreport 2021*, 40–41, www.destatis.de/DE/Service/Statistik-Campus/Datenreport/Downloads/datenreport-2021.pdf?__blob=publicationFile.

priority of trying to counteract rising housing costs, but, much like under Chancellor Merkel, the results were underwhelming. In September 2023, Chancellor Scholz hosted a housing summit, but the resulting measures were disappointing. Already before the summit, two of the largest housing lobby groups had decided not to participate. The property-owner organization Haus & Grund and the organization representing (social) landlords, GdW, boycotted the meeting, complaining about the low ambition of the Scholz government's planned housing measures. In the end, the Scholz government agreed to adopt a range of *supply-side* housing measures to bring down housing costs, but these measures were widely considered a drop in the bucket.[49] Among others, they included relatively marginal increases in social housing funds for the *Länder* and a new small-scale loan program for low- and medium-income households, with children, buying or building climate-friendly homes (*KfW Wohneigentum für Familien*).[50] However, few lower-income families could afford to buy or build a climate-friendly home, especially in expensive metropolitan areas.[51] In 2024, the Scholz government also introduced a temporary tax subsidy (to 2029) for investors building new homes (an accelerated depreciation schedule called *degressive Abschreibung für Abnutzung*, *AfA*). It also reintroduced some modest tax privileges for limited-profit housing associations that are unlikely to result in a significant revival of the limited-profit housing sector. More generally, these programs are designed to bring down housing costs by increasing supply, but they lack the ambition and magnitude necessary to create significantly more affordable housing.

The summit took place when German house prices and construction had already trended downwards. After peaking in early 2022, house prices declined (although in late 2024, real house prices were still 25 percent higher than they were in 2012), largely owing to the inflationary environment of rising energy and material costs that made building more expensive.[52] The ECB responded with interest rate hikes, which also made home financing via mortgage debt more expensive. To some degree, falling house prices were welcome news, as experts considered falling house prices an adequate "price correction" with little effect on Germany's stable housing finance system.[53] However, high building and financing costs, coupled with a sluggish economy, were holding back new construction projects. Even though house prices have corrected somewhat, housing shortages and renter unaffordability in cities remain a major challenge in the German political economy.

[49] DBG representative (author interview, Berlin, September 29, 2023).

[50] The Scholz government had the goal of building 100,000 new social housing units per year. To support this, it offered the *Länder* federal funding for social housing, increasing from EUR 2 billion in 2022 to EUR 3.5 billion by 2025. The KfW credit program amounted to EUR 305 million in total loan volume in 2023 and EUR 1 billion in 2024.

[51] German housing ministry official (author interview, May 8, 2024).

[52] OECD, *Analytical House Price Indicators*, https://data-explorer.oecd.org.

[53] "Stärkster Preisverfall bei Häusern und Wohnungen seit 60 Jahren" (February 8, 2024), *Der Spiegel*.

One thing, however, seems clear: German politicians do not regard an American-style housing-based growth strategy as the solution to their current problems. As housing minister Klara Geywitz (SPD) stated in 2022, building new owner-occupied homes would be "economic and ecological nonsense."[54] The approach is yet again the reverse of the American housing strategy of stimulating homeownership. According to Geywitz, Germany should modernize existing owner-occupied homes and build new energy- and space-efficient multifamily rental homes with consideration of growing climate pressures. Indeed, the German building sector accounts for 30 percent of Germany's greenhouse gas emissions, including emissions from powering, heating, and cooling residential and commercial real estate.[55] Like its US counterpart, the sector is not on track to achieve net-zero emissions by 2045.[56] Germany's per capita emissions from the housing sector are relatively high (1.9 tons of CO_2 per capita) compared to those of other rich democracies (Sweden, Norway, Denmark, France, Spain, and Portugal all have levels below one ton of CO_2 per capita), partly owing to the Germany's reliance on carbon-intensive energy (Hoeller 2023).

A stronger and greener German growth regime requires *both* affordable *and* climate-friendly housing, but political actions to decarbonize housing have thus far been too timid. The Scholz government's most far-reaching climate-related housing policy was the controversial "heating law" (*Gebäudeenergiegesetz* also known as *Heizungsgesetz*) in 2023, which started to phase out fossil-fuel-based heating in residential buildings by requiring most new buildings to heat with an energy mix of at least 65 percent renewable energy (the goal is to have no more fossil-fuel-based heating in residential buildings after 2045). To support that transition, the Scholz government started offering subsidies to existing homeowners of older buildings for installing electric heat pumps. Other loan programs subsidize the construction of new climate-friendly homes and the retrofitting of older homes (EUR 12 billion in total credit volume in 2023).[57] However, given the tall order of decarbonizing the country's entire housing stock within just two decades, these programs are insufficient. They also face opposition from property owners and developers fearing higher costs. Building affordable and climate-friendly housing is expensive and can only be achieved with massive state investment that German policymakers seem unwilling to provide.

[54] "Ökonomisch und ökologisch unsinnig" (April 15, 2022), *Tagesschau*.

[55] Umweltbundesamt (September 5, 2024), *Energiesparende Gebäude*, www.umweltbundesamt.de/themen/klima-energie/energiesparen/energiesparende-gebaeude#eigentuemer.

[56] Umweltbundesamt (July 5, 2024), *Berichterstattung und Monitoring durch Projektionsberichte*, www.umweltbundesamt.de/themen/klima-energie/klimaschutz-energiepolitik-in-deutschland/szenarien-fuer-die-klimaschutz-energiepolitik/integrierte-energie-treibhausgasprojektionen#Berichterstattung.

[57] KfW (December 31, 2023), *Förderreport 2023*.

HOUSING AND GROWTH REGIMES IN OTHER ADVANCED ECONOMIES

While the focus up to this point has been on the United States and Germany, the book's findings are relevant to other demand- and export-oriented economies. The demand-led United Kingdom and Canada, for example, resemble the United States in their reliance on real estate as a means of generating economic growth and prosperity. Both countries have also adopted a public policy approach that emphasizes demand-side homeownership programs stimulating house prices. Like Germany, export-oriented Austria relies much less on housing for economic growth, mirroring Germany's longstanding policy emphasis on housing affordability and limiting house-price growth. The Nordic economies of Sweden or Denmark as well as the Netherlands might be described as in-between cases. Their more "balanced" growth regimes – meaning a combination of strong exports and robust domestic demand (cp. Hassel and Palier 2021, 38; Thelen 2019; Baccaro and Hadziabdic 2023; Erixon and Pontusson 2022; Baccaro and Höpner 2022) – have allowed for the development of housing regimes that combine elements of "financialized" homeownership programs with strong affordable rental housing programs and rent controls.

The British economy is demand-led and relies on private consumption and credit for economic growth (Hay 2013). As in the United States, British housing is an engine of growth, stimulating credit and consumption through wealth and credit effects (Aron et al. 2012; Muellbauer 2018). British households, two-thirds of whom are homeowners, rely on growing property values to finance personal consumption, as they can use their homes as collateral for obtaining personal credit. Studies estimate that a house-price increase of 10 percent would result in 2–3 percent more household borrowing in the country (Cloyne et al. 2019, 2134). In 2021, British mortgage indebtedness was much higher than Germany's (71 percent vs. 48 percent of GDP), and the United Kingdom saw higher numbers of real estate transactions: 1.5 million compared to just 600,000 in Germany.[58] The British financial, insurance, and real estate industries are some of the country's most important sectors – including strong lobby groups such as UK Finance and the Home Builders Federation – constituting over 21 percent of GDP in 2022 compared to manufacturing, which accounted for just 9 percent.[59]

British public policy has privileged demand-side homeownership programs over rental housing programs since the 1970s, with the explicit goal of stimulating house prices. As Ken Gibb (2019, 16) notes, "[t]he media and indeed key politicians ... have been explicit about the need to secure and maintain rising real house prices." The UK's financialized housing-based growth strategy

58 Mortgage debt and homeownership data for this chapter are drawn from EMF (2024), *Hypostat 2024*, https://hypo.org/app/uploads/sites/3/2024/08/HYPOSTAT-2024_web.pdf.

59 Sectoral data for this chapter are drawn from OECD (2024), *Value Added By Activity*, https://data-explorer.oecd.org/.

began in the economically tumultuous 1970s (Malpass and Rowlands 2010). At that time, the post-WWII housing shortages had been overcome, leading the Conservative Party – and increasingly Labour – to privilege homeownership programs and move away from the council housing that had been built in response to postwar shortages (Harloe 1995, 289–290).[60] These efforts culminated in Margaret Thatcher's Right to Buy program, which has subsidized the privatization of more than two million public housing units from the early 1980s to today (Wood 2018; Ronald 2008), while simultaneously slashing funding for new council housing (Pierson 1994, ch. 4; Torgersen 1987). Financial deregulation reinforced these demand-side homeownership programs by stimulating and expanding mortgage lending (Oren and Blyth 2019). The financialization of the British housing market produced rising levels of mortgage indebtedness and growing real house prices from the 1970s. The result was a form of "house-price Keynesianism," meaning that rising house prices translated into higher consumer spending (Watson 2010; Crouch 2009). In short, stimulative housing programs became a permanent feature of the British demand-led growth regime, supported by an unshakable cross-party consensus (Reisenbichler and Wiedemann 2022; Hopkin and Shaw 2016).

However, rising house prices can also come crashing down, as they did during a housing bust in the 1990s and during the 2008–2009 crisis (Muellbauer 1992; 2018). In response to the latter crisis, British policymakers doubled down on demand-side homeownership programs by adopting the Help to Buy program, a set of measures that subsidized mortgages for British households to stimulate owner-occupied housing construction (Hilber and Schöni 2016).[61] They also introduced a savings subsidy for first-home buyers, now called the Lifetime Individual Savings Account. Like American crisis-era policies, Help to Buy remained in place long after the 2008–2009 crash. However, the policy likely helped fuel the country's recent house-price boom. As Christian Hilber (2023) notes: "Help to Buy ... failed to induce additional housing construction in the severely supply-constrained Greater London but also increased the price of new build houses by far more than the implicit government subsidy." In short, demand-side homeownership support is the UK's policy priority compared to affordable rental housing.

Original survey evidence that Pascal König and I collected in June 2022 confirms that German households viewed rising house prices more skeptically than their British counterparts (Reisenbichler and König 2024). In a survey of

[60] The British public housing sector was remarkably large in the mid-1970s, sheltering about one-third of households, while around half owned their own home, meaning that the private rental sector was the smallest sector (Kemeny 1981, 130). In 2021, homeownership was by far the most dominant form of tenure in England and Wales (63% of households, compared to 17% in council housing and 20% in private rental housing). See UK Office for National Statistics (2021), *Housing, England and Wales: Census 2021*.

[61] Former housing minister, UK (Conservative) (author interview, February 10, 2022).

1,352 German and British participants, we found that 50 percent of German voters viewed rising house prices as an outright negative development for the economy, while only 38 percent of British voters held such views. Similarly, 47 percent of German voters would favor government actions to *restrain* house prices compared to just 37 percent of British voters. Finally, German voters showed much higher support for affordable housing policies when compared to British voters. Around 75 percent of German voters favored renter-friendly housing policies and 71 percent supported homeownership programs, while only 65 percent of British voters supported renter-oriented policies and 60 percent supported homeownership programs.[62]

The differences between the two countries do not simply reflect the fact that there are more homeowners in the United Kingdom than in Germany. In fact, we found particularly intriguing differences between German and British voter groups. First, German and British homeowners significantly differ in their perception of house prices. While 40 percent of German homeowners considered rising property values as a negative development for the economy, only 26 percent of British homeowners felt the same way.[63] Second, German and British voter groups also differed in their preferences for restraining house prices. For example, 37 percent of German homeowners supported government interventions to restrain house prices compared to 29 percent of British homeowners. Similarly, 58 percent of German renters but only 51 percent of British renters favored restraining house prices.[64] Third, we also found striking differences between German and British homeowners regarding homeownership programs. In Germany, 75 percent of homeowners supported owner-oriented policies, while only 57 percent of British homeowners did so. There is, though, little difference between how the two countries' renters view homeownership programs: In both countries, around two-thirds of renters supported owner-oriented policies.[65] Fourth, we also found major differences between German and British renters regarding renter-friendly policy. While 85 percent of German renters supported affordable rental housing policies, only 68 percent of British renters did so.[66] On this point there is no significant difference between the two countries' homeowners, as 68 percent of German homeowners and 64 percent of British homeowners supported renter-friendly policies. Overall, German voters tend to

[62] All differences between German and British voters reported in this paragraph are statistically significant at the $p < 0.01$ level.

[63] In terms of house-price perceptions, the difference between German and British voters is statistically significant ($t = 4.1$, $p < 0.01$).

[64] Regarding policies that would restrain house prices, the difference between homeowners is statistically significant at the 0.05 level ($t = 2.2$, $p < 0.05$), while the difference for renters is significant only at the 0.1 level ($t = 1.7$, $p < 0.1$).

[65] For owner-oriented policy, the difference between homeowners is statistically significant ($t = 5.6$, $p < 0.01$), while the difference between renters is not ($t = -0.6$, $p = 0.56$).

[66] For renter-friendly policy, the difference between renters is statistically significant ($t = 4.6$, $p < 0.01$), but the difference between homeowners is not ($t = 1.4$, $p = 0.18$).

be more skeptical of rising house prices and show higher support for affordable housing programs compared with British voters.

This book provides an explanation for these differences. In the United Kingdom, rising house prices are more important to its demand-led economy, as they can help generate prosperity or maintain living standards in the absence of wage growth or generous public pensions, particularly for the large number of homeowners. In Germany, rising house prices are not part of the country's export-based growth strategy, and homeownership is less important as a form of old-age security. Voter attitudes therefore likely reflect these different socio-economic contexts.

Canada is another example of a demand-led economy that is dependent on real estate for economic growth. The finance, real estate, and insurance industries makes up roughly 20 percent of the Canadian economy (including powerful lobby groups such as the Canadian Bankers Association and the Canadian Real Estate Association), double that of the manufacturing sector. As in the United States and the United Kingdom, most Canadians own their own home (67 percent of households). Importantly, Canadian household consumption has tracked house-price developments in recent years through wealth and credit effects. As a report by the Bank of Canada noted, "as home values rise, homeowners find it easier to borrow using their home value as security." The central bank estimates that Canadian households took out equity against their homes to the tune of CAD 89 billion (USD 63 billion) in 2017 alone.[67]

Since the 1980s, Canadian governments, both left and right, have favored demand-side homeownership programs over boosting affordable rental housing supply (Bacher 1993; Walks 2016; Chisholm and Hulchanski 2019). In the realm of taxation, the federal government currently provides subsidies to first-time buyers in the form of tax-subsidized savings accounts to be used for down payments for home purchases (e.g., the First Home Savings Account and the Home Buyers' Plan). In the mortgage market, the Canadian Mortgage and Housing Corporation, a government agency akin to Fannie Mae in the United States, offers guarantees on mortgages and mortgage-backed securities (Walks 2014) as well as interest-free loans for environmentally friendly homes (e.g., Canada Greener Homes). While Canadian demand-side housing programs are more moderate in size than American ones – including stricter mortgage market regulations that have thus far prevented a major real estate crash in recent years – there are warning signs about overheating housing markets in such cities as Toronto and Vancouver. Despite these signs, Canadian federal policymakers have privileged demand-side homeownership programs while neglecting supply-side affordable rental programs to address Canada's affordability crisis.[68]

[67] Ho, A., Khan, M., Mow, M., and Peterson, B. (September 2019), *Home Equity Extraction and Household Spending in Canada*, Staff Analytical Note 27, Bank of Canada.

[68] Canadian social housing programs remained a relatively marginal element of the country's housing policy toolkit. While there was a short period between the late 1960s and the early

The Netherlands and Sweden are perhaps best described as cases in between the models of the United States and Germany, as they have developed financialized homeownership markets *and* retained large social rental markets. From the mid-1980s, Dutch and Swedish center-right, but also center-left, governments have financialized their homeownership markets (Anderson and Kurzer 2020; Cooper and Kurzer 2023). Underlying the shift to stimulating homeownership markets was a growing belief in the superiority of market-based provision of housing as opposed to state-based social housing (Boelhouwer 2002). In the Netherlands, a 2001 national housing policy memorandum mentioned a key macroeconomic benefit of this strategy: "the increase of property value and wealth" that would result in higher consumer spending (cited in van Gent 2010, 744; also cp. Bakker 1999; Zhang 2019). The Dutch central bank estimated that such wealth effects contributed between 0.3 percent and 1 percent of annual economic growth during the 1990s (Becker 2005, 1089–1090). In Sweden, similarly, the Sveriges Riksbank (2014, 18) found that rising house prices have long fueled home equity withdrawal to "finance consumption" (cp. Vestman et al. 2023; Chen 2006). In both countries, homeownership rates are comparable to those in the US, UK, and Canada, with 64 percent in Sweden and 71 percent in the Netherlands. Their levels of mortgage debt are even higher than those found in the United States, Canada, or the UK, at 87 percent of GDP in Sweden and 80 percent in the Netherlands in 2023, some of the highest household debt levels among rich democracies.

Today, the Dutch state offers American-style demand-side support for homeowners. It guarantees mortgage debt through the Dutch National Mortgage Guarantee (NHG), established in 1993 (cp. Cooper and Kurzer 2023), backing EUR 192 billion in housing loans or 24 percent of all residential mortgage debt in 2022.[69] It also offers hefty tax advantages, such as a mortgage interest deduction, already introduced in the late nineteenth century, and an exemption of property transfer taxes for first-time buyers under the age of 35. Finally, Dutch governments liberalized a previously restrictive mortgage market by encouraging the introduction of new mortgage products (e.g., interest-only mortgages) and lowering down-payment requirements (Elsinga et al. 2016), allowing households to take out mortgage debt exceeding the home value (Brounen and Eichholtz 2012; Spielberger and Voss 2024; Van Gunten and Navot 2018).

1990s in which Liberal governments strengthened social housing programs as part of larger efforts to expand the welfare state and resolve urban affordability crises, the programs became subject to austerity and structural reform efforts in light of fiscal pressures during Canada's recession and housing crash in the early 1990s. The result is that only about 3% of Canadian households live in social housing units (Suttor 2016).

[69] Nationale Hypotheek Garantie (NHG) (2022), *Jaarverslag 2022*, www.nhg.nl/media/1bgf13fd/nhg_jaarverslag2022-hr.pdf.

While the 2008–2009 crisis led to falling Dutch house prices, it did not produce a major shift away from housing financialization (Brounen and Eichholtz 2012). Modest changes included curbing the mortgage interest deduction and making mortgage lending somewhat more restrictive (Bokhorst 2019; Cooper and Kurzer 2023). Yet the Dutch government continued to subsidize homeownership with generous demand-side programs. These soon fueled rises in mortgage debt and house prices in the post-2008 period, which, together with land-use restrictions and decades-long austerity measures in social housing, have contributed to a major housing affordability crisis in recent years.

In Sweden, public policy has also increasingly privileged homeownership over affordable rental housing (Christophers 2013; Bengtsson et al. 2017). As in the United States and the Netherlands, the Swedish government offers a generous mortgage interest deduction to homeowners. While Sweden's mortgage credit system was relatively restrictive until the mid-1980s, policymakers liberalized mortgage lending by introducing new mortgage products (e.g., interest-only loans) and lower down-payment requirements, in some cases as little as 5 percent or even zero, and enabling home equity withdrawals (Sveriges Riksbank 2014, 46–47; Anderson and Kurzer 2020). These changes produced a more volatile Swedish housing market prone to boom-and-bust cycles and attendant volatility in household consumption. These cycles resulted in a major real estate crash and banking crisis in the early 1990s (Blyth 2002) and a relatively minor house-price slump in 2008. Yet the lesson politicians drew from these crises was not to de-financialize housing; on the contrary, in 2008, the Swedish government lowered the tax burden for homeowners by reducing property taxes (Christophers 2013), which added fuel to a prolonged house-price boom that ended only in 2022 on the heels of rising interest rates.[70]

However, the relatively affordable Dutch and Swedish rental markets, including large social housing segments and rent controls, are closer to the German housing model than to America's. Despite Dutch austerity measures of recent decades, in 2018, 28 percent of the country's housing stock remained rent-controlled and relatively affordable social housing units for lower- and middle-income households offered by nonprofit housing associations. By comparison, the private rental sector constituted only 12 percent of total housing units, while 60 percent of all housing units were owner-occupied.[71] As Dirk Brounen and Piet Eichholtz (2012, 138) note, 70 percent of all rental units are subject to rent controls. However, the demand for these units far outstrips supply, often resulting in a multi-year wait for households. Since

[70] In 2010, fearing financial instability, Swedish regulators somewhat tightened mortgage lending by recommending that banks require a 15% down payment on mortgages.

[71] Kullberg, J., and Ras, M. (2020), *Wonen*, Sociaal en Cultureel Planbureau, https://digitaal.scp.nl/ssn2020/wonen/#:~:text=Sinds%202009%20is%20dit%20aandeel,huishoudens%20woont%20in%20een%20corporatiewoning%20.

most social housing units are now reserved for low-income households (following a 2015 housing reform), middle-income households are pushed into the private rental market or homeownership markets that are often too expensive for them (Van Gent and Hochstenbach 2020). Today's housing shortages are the combined result of failed government policy (retrenchment of social housing and strict land-use policy), demographic developments (migration and shrinking household size), and slow construction (high construction costs and interest rates).[72] Historically, as in Germany, Dutch social housing for the masses, including middle-class households, was a response to post-WWII housing shortages when social housing encompassed 40 percent of all housing units (Aalbers et al. 2021; Van Gent and Hochstenbach 2020). At that time, "it was a macro-economic necessity to keep rents low" (Salet 1999, 550) and to keep wages and inflation in check (Brounen and Eichholtz 2012; Visser and Hemerijck 1997, 92). However, the macroeconomic need for low housing costs faded when the Dutch economy transitioned toward a knowledge economy.

In Sweden, the social housing sector is similarly large. In 2018, 39 percent of the housing stock was owner-occupied and another 23 percent "tenant-owned" apartments in housing cooperatives (owned collectively by their members and historically connected to the labor movement of the 1920s). The rental sector comprised 38 percent of the housing stock, including municipal and private rental housing.[73] Municipal housing units offer below-market rents largely for lower- and middle-income households, while private rentals tend to be more expensive than municipal units. Municipal and cooperative housing was thriving in the post-WWII period as part of the country's universal welfare state. These associations received generous government funding to solve post-WWII housing shortages, not due to wartime destruction but because of poor-quality housing stock and urbanization. The hegemonic Social Democrats formulated a goal of building one million homes between 1965 and 1974, with municipal and cooperative housing associations leading the charge supported by generous government funding (Blackwell 2021; Hall and Viden 2005; Harloe 1995, ch. 6). This effort was also part of the country's corporatist industrial model, as housing shortages in industrial areas limited labor mobility (Brunnström et al. 2021). As Gøsta Esping-Andersen (1978, 50) noted, the state's role in housing was anti-inflationary: "Viewed in its totality, government intervention in the Swedish housing sector ... has prevented the proliferation of speculative real

[72] Boelhouwer, P. (2023), *De woningcrisis in Nederland: Achtergronden en oplossingen* [report], https://monitor-koopwoningmarkt.nl/wp-content/uploads/2023/10/De-woningcrisis-in-Nederland.-Achtergronden-en-oplossingen.pdf.

[73] Lago, A. (November 2018), *Cooperative Housing in Sweden* [presentation], www.housinginternational.coop/wp-content/uploads/2019/01/Anders-Lago2c-International-experiences-with-housing-cooperatives2c-PP2c-Kiev-2018.pdf.

estate investment and high inflation rates." Social housing programs and rent controls were thus integral elements of the Swedish universal welfare state and industrial model, which was based on price stability, egalitarian wages, labor mobility, and full employment (Erixon and Pontusson 2022; Blyth 2002; Katzenstein 1985).

Starting in the 1990s, Swedish municipal and cooperative housing increasingly faced austerity measures, deregulation, and privatization efforts (Lindvall 2006; Christophers 2013; Blackwell 2021; Blackwell and Bengtsson 2023). One result was a decline in the share of municipal public housing units. Another was that spending cuts made building new housing units more expensive for municipal and cooperative housing associations, which translated into higher rents for households. Despite these measures, Sweden retained a "corporatist" system of rent controls for the entire rental market – negotiated by tenant associations, municipal housing companies, and landlords – based on an apartment's size, quality, and location (Öst and Johansson 2023; Kemeny 1995, 116). However, given the shortage of rental apartments in big cities, with hundreds of thousands of people currently on a waiting list for rent-controlled apartments and an average wait of about ten years, many young or newcomer households are driven into the more expensive and less regulated secondary sublet rental market (Listerborn 2023). In other words, the withdrawal of state support for new affordable rental housing has contributed to housing affordability crises in big cities.

More generally, the characteristics of the Dutch and Swedish "hybrid" housing regimes are compatible with this book's larger explanation centered on the different natures of growth regimes. In fact, policymakers financialized housing markets in the Netherlands and Sweden at a time when their growth regimes were undergoing significant changes, shifting away from "traditional" manufacturing. In the post-WWII period, like Germany, the Dutch and Swedish economies were manufacturing-heavy, corporatist, and export-oriented, although the Netherlands "has never been a classical industrial country" (Visser and Hemerijck 1997, 28; Katzenstein 1985; Ornston 2018).

In the Netherlands, the export-oriented manufacturing sector had severely declined by the 1990s. Several factors contributed to this decline: Increased global competition in industries such as textile machinery and shipbuilding, rising labor costs, and an appreciating real exchange rate driven by gas exports, which made industrial exports more expensive (Visser and Hemerijck 1997). While policymakers retained wage moderation as a key economic principle to boost export competitiveness, they also turned toward knowledge-intensive, high-end business services (Thelen 2019) and credit-financed housing growth that could offset plummeting industrial activity (Becker 2005; Bakker 1999). In 2022, manufacturing accounted for 13 percent of the Dutch economy, including electrical machinery, computers, pharmaceuticals, and optical and medical equipment. Finance, insurance, and real estate accounted for another

13 percent, while business services comprised an even larger 15 percent and ICT 5 percent of the economy.[74]

In Sweden, the shift away from "traditional" manufacturing toward high-tech and ICT sectors occurred between the mid-1980s and the early 1990s (Ornston 2018; Thelen 2019). As low- and medium-tech industries structurally declined due to growing global competition and the 1970s energy-price shocks, a broad-based political consensus emerged to address these structural economic problems by liberalizing financial and housing markets in the 1980s (Blyth 2002, ch. 7) and by strengthening programs to support innovation, technology and IT, and education in the 1990s (Ornston 2018, ch. 2). Today, Sweden has a much more diversified export profile than Germany, including manufactured goods such as cars and machinery, low-tech raw materials such as processed wood, and high-tech ICT-based exports in telecommunications (including services and goods from national champion Ericsson), broadcasting, and software (Thelen 2019, 296; Erixon and Pontusson 2022, 275). In 2022, manufacturing still accounted for 15 percent of the economy, while the financial, insurance, and real estate industries comprised 12 percent, business services 12 percent, and ICT 8.5 percent.

The more "balanced" production profiles of the Dutch and Swedish growth regimes compared to Germany's likely gave Dutch and Swedish policymakers more flexibility in embarking on a financialized housing path.[75] Dutch and Swedish policymakers did not view financialized housing programs as contradictory to their countries' industrial profiles and economic needs, although both countries' economic elites repeatedly cautioned policymakers about the risks of financial instability posed by financialized housing markets (cp. Bokhorst 2019, 234–235).[76] There are perhaps two related mechanisms that could account for the Dutch and Swedish moves to financialize housing. The first suggests a small-state logic, meaning that small states' economic openness to world markets makes them more vulnerable to global economic developments than large states such as Germany (Katzenstein 1985; Ornston 2018). As a result, policymakers in small states have incentives to diversify

[74] Dutch exports in goods and services have remained strong, even when accounting for "re-exports," meaning that the Dutch economy is a major hub for importing goods and re-exporting them without processing them through its ports (Baccaro and Habdiadzic 2023).

[75] Baccaro and Hadziabdic (2023) as well as Spielberger and Voss (2024) call the Dutch growth regime "balanced" for the period of 2000–2007, while Kohler and Stockhammer (2020) characterize the Dutch case as an intermediate case combining export-led and debt-driven growth (also see Engelen et al. 2010). During and after the financial crisis (2008–2013), the Dutch housing market and domestic demand plummeted, meaning that the country relied on exporting its way out of the crisis. Domestic demand picked up again when the housing market recovered after 2013 (Spielberger and Voss 2024).

[76] Former central bank economist, Netherlands (author interview, phone, April 18, 2024). The interviewee also mentioned that the financialized Dutch housing market tends to encourage investments in "unproductive" sectors of the economy, which could hurt the Dutch economy in the long run.

their economies beyond exports for economic growth and toward generating economic growth via housing-related domestic demand (for the Danish case, see Wood 2019). The second mechanism is related to the specific exporting profile of the Dutch and Swedish economies (for an excellent study on differences in export compositions, see Wierts et al. 2014). It might be that the more "knowledge-intensive" Dutch and Swedish export profiles of ICT, high-tech manufacturing, and high-end business services rely less on wage and cost competition than "traditional" German and Austrian exports of cars and machine tools (cp. Baccaro and Hadziabdic 2023; Reisenbichler 2020a, 328–329).[77] As a result, a strong housing sector – sometimes associated with inflationary tendencies that could hurt cost competitiveness – need not contradict the strength of an export sector if it specializes in knowledge-intensive products and services, where competition is less about price. As Lennart Erixon and Jonas Pontusson (2022, 289) write in the case of Sweden, "[a]s exports have shifted to more knowledge-intensive products and services, export-oriented firms have become less concerned with domestic labor costs." In turn, both countries' more diversified industrial and production profiles may have given more leeway to policymakers to pursue a broader range of macroeconomic policies. However, future empirical research will be needed to substantiate these claims.

Finally, one might look to Austria for an export-oriented country that has successfully restrained house prices and housing costs. Like Germany, Austria has an export-oriented economy with a relatively strong manufacturing sector that relies on low inflation and wage restraint (Ederer et al. 2015; Baccaro and Höpner 2022). While the finance, insurance, and real estate industries comprised 13 percent of its economy in 2022, the manufacturing sector constituted 18 percent and included machine, chemical, and car industries. Like its German neighbor, Austria is also considered a "nation of renters," with a homeownership rate of 54 percent, slightly higher than Germany's rate of just below 50 percent (the difference is partly due to the more rural character of the Austrian housing market). Austrian households are also some of the least indebted among rich democracies, with mortgage indebtedness amounting to less than 30 percent of GDP in 2023. Personal consumption, similar to Germany's, amounted to only 51 percent of GDP in 2023.[78]

[77] In 2023, 80% of Germany's total exports were goods and only 20% were services. In contrast, in 2020, the Netherlands' total exports (not counting re-exports) consisted of 53% goods and 47% services. Slightly older 2015 data for Sweden shows that the country exported 68% in goods and 32% in services as a share of total exports. See German Federal Ministry for Economic Affairs and Climate Action (July 2024), *Facts about German Foreign Trade*, Berlin; Jaarsma, M., and Rooyakkers, J. (2021), *Composition of Dutch International Trade*, Statistics Netherlands; Nordic Council of Ministers (2016), *Services and Goods Exports from the Nordics*, Copenhagen.

[78] World Bank (2024), *Households and NPISHs Final Consumption Expenditure*, https://data.worldbank.org/.

Austria has long pursued a public policy approach of keeping housing costs and house prices low, and it has done so with more success than Germany. Despite recent increases in Austrian house and rental prices, the *New York Times* hailed Vienna as a "renters' utopia" given the city's affordable housing costs compared to other major European cities such as London, Paris, and Berlin.[79] Three-quarters of Austrian rental apartments are directly rent-controlled (Thomas et al. 2020).

Much like Germany, Austria developed a comprehensive system of affordable housing programs in the post-WWII years to address postwar housing shortages and keep housing costs low. First, Austrian policymakers adopted social housing programs to help build affordable rental and owner-occupied housing for the masses.[80] As in Germany, tax-subsidized limited-profit housing associations (*gemeinnützige Bauvereinigungen*) were the main recipients of social housing funding to build affordable rental and, to a lesser degree, owner-occupied housing. Second, Austrian governments strengthened rent controls covering most rental homes in the post-WWII period, measures that were first established during WWI and are still in place today (Förster 1996). As the city of Vienna publicized in 1929, these policies were much more than just affordable housing programs; they were a "national economic necessity" (*volkswirtschaftliche Notwendigkeit*) to keep wages low to boost exports:

> Our competitiveness can only be maintained by relatively low wages ... There is only one component that can be eliminated from the worker's wages without the necessity of stepping up his productivity. That is rent. ... When rent control ends, wages must rise. Our export industry, on which the fate of this country depends, cannot ... accommodate any such wage increases. Continued rent control is therefore the highest economic priority in today's Austria. It is in the interest of the national economy (English translation partly my own and from Blau 1999, 137).[81]

In Karl Polanyi's words, "Vienna achieved one of the most spectacular triumphs of Western history," meaning that it produced a form of social capitalism partly achieved through the construction of social housing for the masses financed by taxing the rich.[82] Austria's powerful unions, organized under the umbrella of

[79] Mari, F. (May 23, 2023), "Imagine a renters' utopia. It might look like Vienna," *New York Times Magazine*.

[80] As in Germany, Austria's first social housing programs originated in the post-WWI years, at a time when major European cities suffered from overcrowded and unhygienic housing conditions for workers. During the time of "Red Vienna," when Vienna was governed by strong Social Democratic majorities, the city championed social housing programs financed by the so-called housing tax (*Wohnbausteuer*) (Förster 1996).

[81] Gemeinde Wien (1929), *Die Wohnungspolitik der Gemeinde Wien: Ein Überblick über die Tätigkeit der Stadt Wien seit dem Kriegsende zur Bekämpfung der Wohnungsnot und zur Hebung der Wohnkultur*, 2nd ed., Vienna: Gesellschafts- und Wirtschaftsmuseum Wien, 58–59.

[82] Quoted in Kuttner, R. (December 21, 2017), "The man from Red Vienna," *New York Review*.

the Austrian union federation (Österreichischer Gewerkschaftsbund, ÖGB), have long supported both rent controls and social housing programs. Most recently, the federation decried increases in housing costs and called for actions to stop housing "speculation" and expand social housing programs to make housing more affordable.[83]

Finally, like Germany, Austria established a longstanding system of restrictive mortgage lending with high down payments. The Austrian state also does not offer tax privileges for homeowners such as a mortgage interest deduction.[84] Some moderate homeownership programs exist at the state level in Austria, but those have a strong *supply-side* emphasis meaning the creation of new owner-occupied homes with the goal of deflating house prices (cp. Deutsch and Tomann 1995). Until recently, Austria's conservative mortgage system – prioritizing subsidized savings (including in *Bausparkassen*) over debt-driven housing growth – has restrained Austrian house-price growth and limited major house-price fluctuations. The country's restrictive mortgage system also means that Austrians do not leverage their homes for consumer spending.

In contrast to their German counterparts, Austrian policymakers have left many more affordable housing programs in place. While German governments have privatized large portions of the country's social housing stock, Austrian governments have done so to a much lesser degree. In addition, limited-profit housing associations remain major players in the Austrian housing market, continuing to receive tax privileges and social housing funding in exchange for building affordable rental and owner-occupied housing. By contrast, German limited-profit associations have lost significant market share due to the Kohl government's elimination of government support for these associations in 1990 (see Chapter 5), while Chancellor Merkel further weakened social housing programs. Indeed, Austrian limited-profit associations (*gemeinnützige Bauvereinigungen*), including housing cooperatives (*Genossenschaften*) and municipalities (*Gemeinden*), still own an astonishing 57 percent of all rental housing (Thomas et al. 2020, 323). Despite recent increases in housing costs, Austria's housing market has remained more affordable than Germany's. The Austrian case thus demonstrates what Germany's housing market might have looked like if policymakers had not retrenched longstanding social housing programs that had for decades reinforced the German economy through affordable housing costs.

[83] ÖGB (2023), *Programm 2023–2028: Dafür ÖGB.*

[84] Kunnert, A., and Baumgartner, J. (July 2012), *Instrumente und Wirkungen der österreichischen Wohnungspolitik*, WIFO, Austrian Institute of Economic Research.

Primary Sources

Archives

Bundesarchiv Koblenz (BArch K) – Federal Archives, Koblenz, Germany
Deutsche Bundesbank, Historisches Archiv (DBHA) – Historical Archive of the German Bundesbank, Frankfurt, Germany
Parlamentsarchiv des Deutschen Bundestags (PA-DBT) – Parliamentary Archive of the German Bundestag, Berlin, Germany
Ronald Reagan Presidential Library (RRPL), Simi Valley, CA, United States
Stiftung Rheinisch-Westfälisches Wirtschaftsarchiv zu Köln (RWWA) – Rhenish-Westphalian Economic Archive, Cologne, Germany

Interviews

Former Treasury official I (Washington, DC, July 9, 2014).
Former Fed official (Washington, DC, July 10, 2014).
Former White House official I (Washington, DC, July 16, 2014).
Former FHFA official (Washington, DC, July 25, 2014)
Former Treasury official II (Washington, DC, August 1, 2014).
HUD official (Washington, DC, August 1, 2014).
NLIHC representative (Washington, DC, August 5, 2014).
Former White House official II (phone, August 8, 2014).
Policy staffer for House Majority Leader Eric Cantor (Republican, Virginia) (phone, August 25, 2014).
Former White House official III (Washington, DC, September 3, 2014).
Fed staff economist (Washington, DC, September 10, 2014).
Former ECB official (Frankfurt, March 30, 2015).
Bundestag member I (SPD, cabinet member) (phone, May 7, 2015).
Bundestag member II (SPD) (Berlin, May 14, 2015).
Bundestag member III (CDU) (Berlin, June 22, 2015).

Former member of the US House of Representatives (Republican, Arizona) (August 6, 2015).
Bundestag member IV (SPD) (Berlin, September 9, 2015).
Bundestag member V (SPD) (phone, September 25, 2015).
Bundestag member VI (SPD) (phone, October 27, 2015).
Representative of Deutscher Städtetag I (phone, December 11, 2015).
Representative of Deutscher Städtetag II (phone, December 11, 2015).
Housing ministry official in North Rhine-Westphalia (phone, December 22, 2015).
Representative of Haus & Grund (phone, January 14, 2016).
Representative of GdW (phone, January 18, 2016).
Ginnie Mae official (Washington, DC, March 8, 2016).
Bundesrat member (CDU) (July 10, 2019).
Former Bundesbank board member (October 5, 2021).
Former British housing minister (Conservative) (February 10, 2022).
Former Freddie Mac official (phone, July 19, 2022).
Bundestag member VII (Linke) (Berlin, September 25, 2023).
DIHK representative (phone, September 28, 2023).
DBG representative (Berlin, September 29, 2023).
Bundestag member VIII (FDP) (November 21, 2023).
Former Dutch central bank economist (phone, April 18, 2024).
German housing ministry official (May 8, 2024).

References

Aalbers, M. (2008). "The financialization of home and the mortgage market crisis." *Competition and Change*, 12(2), 148–166.

Aalbers, M. (2016). *The Financialization of Housing: A Political Economy Approach*. New York: Routledge.

Aalbers, M., Hochstenbach, C., Bosma, J. and Fernandez, R. (2021). "The death and life of private landlordism: How financialized homeownership gave birth to the buy-to-let market." *Housing, Theory and Society*, 38(5), 541–563.

Abelshauser, W. (2005). *The Dynamics of German Industry: Germany's Path toward the New Economy and the American Challenge*. New York: Berghahn Books.

Abelshauser, W. (2011). *Deutsche Wirtschaftsgeschichte: Von 1945 bis zur Gegenwart*, 2nd ed. Bonn: Bundeszentrale für politische Bildung.

Abrams, C. (1946). *The Future of Housing*. New York: Harper & Brothers.

Acharya, V., Richardson, M., van Nieuwerburgh, S. and White, L. (2011). *Guaranteed to Fail: Fannie Mae, Freddie Mac, and the Debacle of Mortgage Finance*. Princeton: Princeton University Press.

Adelino, M., Schoar, A. and Severino, F. (2018). "The role of housing and mortgage markets in the financial crisis." *Annual Review of Financial Economics*, 10(1), 25–41.

Aizenman, J. and Noy, I. (2012). "Reflections on the curious contrast of public policies between Germany and the US: Real estate versus human capital." VoxEU, August 25, 2012. Retrieved March 15, 2025, from https://cepr.org/voxeu/columns/reflections-curious-contrast-public-policies-between-germany-and-us-real-estate.

Allen, C. (1989). "The underdevelopment of Keynesianism in the Federal Republic of Germany," in Hall, P. A. (ed.). *The Political Power of Economic Ideas: Keynesianism across Nations*. Princeton: Princeton University Press, pp. 263–289.

Altshuler, A. and Luberoff, D. (2004). *Mega-Projects: The Changing Politics of Urban Public Investment*. Washington, DC: Brookings Institution Press.

Amable, B. (2003). *The Diversity of Modern Capitalism*. Oxford: Oxford University Press.

Anderson, K. M. and Kurzer, P. (2020). "The politics of mortgage credit expansion in the small coordinated market economies." *West European Politics*, 43(2), 366–389.

Ansell, B. (2014). "The political economy of ownership: Housing markets and the welfare state." *American Political Science Review*, 108(2), 383–402.

Ansell, B. W. (2019). "The politics of housing." *Annual Review of Political Science*, 22(1), 165–185.

Ansell, B., Broz, L. and Flaherty, T. (2018). "Global capital markets, housing prices, and partisan fiscal policies." *Economics & Politics*, 30(3), 307–339.

Aron, J., Duca, J. V., Muellbauer, J., Murata, K. and Murph, J. (2012). "Credit, housing collateral, and consumption: Evidence from Japan, the UK, and the US." *Review of Income and Wealth*, 58(3), 397–423.

Atkinson, A. (2019). "Rethinking credit as social provision." *Stanford Law Review*, 71(5), 1093–1162.

Avramenko, R. and Boyd, R. (2013). "Subprime virtues: The moral dimensions of American housing and mortgage policy." *Perspectives on Politics*, 11(1), 111–131.

Baccaro, L., Blyth, M. and Pontusson, J. (eds.). (2022). *Diminishing Returns: The New Politics of Growth and Stagnation*. New York: Oxford University Press.

Baccaro, L. and Hadziabdic, S. (2023). "Operationalizing growth models." *Quality & Quantity*, 58(2), 1325–1360.

Baccaro, L. and Höpner, M. (2022). "The political-economic foundations of export-led growth: An analysis of the German case," in Baccaro, L., Blyth, M. and Pontusson, J. (eds.). *Diminishing Returns: The New Politics of Growth and Stagnation*. New York: Oxford University Press, pp. 238–267.

Baccaro, L. and Pontusson, J. (2016). "Rethinking comparative political economy: The growth model perspective." *Politics & Society*, 44(2), 175–207.

Bacher, J. C. (1993). *Keeping to the Marketplace: The Evolution of Canadian Housing Policy*. Montreal: McGill-Queen's University Press.

Baker, D. (2012). *The Impact of the First-Time Homebuyer Tax Credit*. Center for Economic and Policy Research, Retrieved March 15, 2025, from https://cepr.net/documents/publications/housing-2012-04.pdf.

Baker, D. (2018). "The housing bubble and the Great Recession: Ten years later." *Center for Economic and Policy Research*. Retrieved May 16, 2024, from https://cepr.net/report/the-housing-bubble-and-the-great-recession-ten-years-later/.

Bakker, B. (1999). "Crisis and Recovery," in Watson, M., Bakker, B., Martijn, J. K., and Halikias, I. (eds.). *The Netherlands: Transforming a Market Economy*. Washington, DC: International Monetary Fund (IMF), pp. 4–15.

Baldenius, T., Kohl, S. and Schularick, M. (2020). "Die neue Wohnungsfrage: Gewinner und Verlierer des deutschen Immobilienbooms." *Leviathan*, 48(2), 195–236.

Bardhan, A. D. and Jaffee, D. M. (2007). "Global capital flows, foreign financing and US interest rates." *Fisher Center Working Papers*. Retrieved May 8, 2024, from https://escholarship.org/uc/item/9rd107b3.

Bayer, P., Ferreira, F., and Ross, S. L. (2016). "The vulnerability of minority homeowners in the housing boom and bust." *American Economic Journal: Economic Policy*, 8(1), 1–27.

Bayer, P., Ferreira, F. and Ross, S. L. (2018). "What drives racial and ethnic differences in high-cost mortgages? The role of high-risk lenders." *The Review of Financial Studies*, 31(1), 175–205.

Becker, U. (2005). "An example of competitive corporatism? The Dutch political economy 1983–2004 in critical examination." *Journal of European Public Policy*, 12(6), 1078–1102.

Béland, D. and Waddan, A. (2007). "Conservative ideas and social policy in the United States." *Social Policy and Administration*, 41(7), 768–786.

Béland, D., Campbell, A. L. and Weaver, R. K. (2022). *Policy Feedback: How Policies Shape Politics*. Cambridge: Cambridge University Press.

Bengtsson, B., Ruonavaara, H. and Sørvoll, J. (2017). "Home ownership, housing policy and path dependence in Finland, Norway and Sweden," in Dewilde, C. and Ronald, R. (eds.). *Housing Wealth and Welfare*. Cheltenham, UK: Edward Elgar Publishing, pp. 60–84.

Benson, C. and Tomkin, R. (2010). "A Housebound Economy." *Congressional Quarterly Weekly*, March 8, 2010, pp. 544–52.

Beramendi, P., Häusermann, S., Kitschelt, H. and Kriesi, H. (eds.). (2015). *The Politics of Advanced Capitalism*. New York: Cambridge University Press.

Berrill, P., Wilson, E. J. H., Reyna, J. L., Fontanini, A. D. and Hertwich, E. G. (2022). "Decarbonization pathways for the residential sector in the United States." *Nature Climate Change*, 12(8), 712–718.

Biedenkopf, K. and Miegel, M. (1978). *Wohnungsbau am Wendepunkt: Wohnungspolitik in der sozialen Marktwirtschaft*. Stuttgart: Bonn Aktuell.

Binder, S. and Spindel, M. (2017). *The Myth of Independence: How Congress Governs the Federal Reserve*. Princeton, NJ: Princeton University Press.

Birnbaum, J. and Murray, A. (1988). *Showdown at Gucci Gulch: Lawmakers, Lobbyists, and the Unlikely Triumph of Tax Reform*. New York: Vintage.

Bittle, J. (2023). *The Great Displacement: Climate Change and the Next American Migration*. New York: Simon & Schuster.

Blackwell, T. (2021). "Power, production and disorder: The decline of Sweden's housing industrial complex and the origins of the present housing discontents." *European Urban and Regional Studies*, 28(4), 338–352.

Blackwell, T. and Bengtsson, B. (2023). "The resilience of social rental housing in the United Kingdom, Sweden and Denmark. How institutions matter." *Housing Studies*, 38(2), 269–289.

Blau, E. (1999). *The Architecture of Red Vienna, 1919–1934*. Cambridge, MA: MIT Press.

Blyth, M. (2002). *Great Transformations: Economic Ideas and Institutional Change in the Twentieth Century*. New York, NY: Cambridge University Press.

Blyth, M. and Matthijs, M. (2017). "Black swans, lame ducks, and the mystery of IPE's missing macroeconomy." *Review of International Political Economy*, 24(2), 203–231.

Boelhouwer, P. (2002). "Trends in Dutch housing policy and the shifting position of the social rented sector." *Urban Studies*, 39(2), 219–235.

Böick, M. (2018). *Die Treuhand: Idee-Praxis-Erfahrung 1990–1994*. Göttingen: Wallstein Verlag.

Bohle, D. and Regan, A. (2021). "The comparative political economy of growth models: Explaining the continuity of FDI-led growth in Ireland and Hungary." *Politics & Society*, 49(1), 75–106.

Bökenkamp, G. (2010). *Das Ende des Wirtschaftswunders: Geschichte der Sozial-, Wirtschafts- und Finanzpolitik in der Bundesrepublik 1969–1998*. Stuttgart: Lucius & Lucius.

Bokhorst, D. J. (2019). *Governing imbalances in the economic and monetary union: A political economy analysis of the macroeconomic imbalance procedure*. PhD thesis, University of Amsterdam, Amsterdam.

Boleat, M. (1984). *National Housing Finance Systems: A Comparative Study*. London: Croom Helm.

Bordo, M. (2017). "The Operation and Demise of the Bretton Woods System; 1958 to 1971." *National Bureau of Economic Research Working Paper Series*. Retrieved May 8, 2024, from http://nber.org/papers/w23189.

Borgaes, H.-U. and Koopmann, W. (1978). "Die neue Sonderabschreibung für Wohngebäude." *Kritische Justiz*, 11(4), 389–403.

Börsch-Supan, A. (1994). "Housing market regulations and housing market performance in the United States, Germany, and Japan." in Blank, R. (ed.). *Social Protection versus Economic Flexibility: Is There a Trade-Off?* Chicago: University of Chicago Press, pp. 119–156.

Börsch-Supan, A. and Stahl, K. (1991). "Do savings programs dedicated to home-ownership increase personal savings? An analysis of the West German Bausparkassen system." *Journal of Public Economics*, 44(3), 265–297.

Braun, B. (2020). "Central banking and the infrastructural power of finance: The case of ECB support for repo and securitization markets." *Socio-Economic Review*, 18(2), 395–418.

Braun, R. (2020). "Bedeutung des Wohneigentums für die Altersvorsorge," in Depenheuer, O., Hertzsch, E. and Voigtländer, M. (eds.). *Wohneigentum für breite Schichten der Bevölkerung*. Berlin: Springer, pp. 213–232.

Brocker, M. and Hanes, C. (2014). "The 1920s American real estate boom and the downturn of the Great Depression: Evidence from city cross-sections," in White, E. N., Snowden, K. and Fishback, P. (eds.). *Housing and Mortgage Markets in Historical Perspective*. Chicago: University of Chicago Press, pp. 161–202.

Brounen, D. and Eichholtz, P. (2012). "House prices and market institutions: The Dutch experience," in Bardhan, A., Edelstein, R. H. and Kroll, C. A. (eds.). *Global Housing Markets: Crises, Policies, and Institutions*. Hoboken, NJ: John Wiley & Sons, pp. 135–155.

Brunnström, P., Håkansson, G. and Uppenberg, C. (2021). "Migration and housing regimes in Sweden 1739–1982." *Scandinavian Journal of History*, 46(3), 353–382.

Bunker, N. (2014). "A post-war history of U.S. economic growth: An examination of the contributions to growth of the components of gross domestic product." *Washington Center for Equitable Growth*. Retrieved May 16, 2024, from https://equitablegrowth.org/post-war-history-u-s-economic-growth/.

Busemeyer, M. R., Abrassart, A. and Nezi, R. (2021). "Beyond positive and negative: New perspectives on feedback effects in public opinion on the welfare state." *British Journal of Political Science*, 51(1), 137–162.

Calomiris, C. W., Longhofer, S. D. and Miles, W. (2013). "The housing wealth effect: The crucial roles of demographics, wealth distribution and wealth shares." *Critical Finance Review*, 2(1), 49–99.

Campbell, A. L. (2012). "Policy makes mass politics." *Annual Review of Political Science*, 15(1), 333–351.

Carlin, W. and Soskice, D. (2009). "German economic performance: Disentangling the role of supply-side reforms, macroeconomic policy and coordinated economy institutions." *Socio-Economic Review*, 7(1), 67–99.

Case, K. E., Quigley, J. M. and Shiller, R. J. (2013). "Wealth effects revisited 1975–2012." *Critical Finance Review*, 2(1), 101–128.

Chen, J. (2006). "Re-evaluating the association between housing wealth and aggregate consumption: New evidence from Sweden." *Journal of Housing Economics*, 15(4), 321–348.

Chisholm, S. and Hulchanski, D. (2019). "Canada's housing story," in Maclennan, D., Pawson, H., Gibb, K., Chisholm, S. and Hulchanski, D. (eds.). *Shaping Futures: Changing the Housing Story*. Glasgow: Policy Scotland, University of Glasgow.

Christophers, B. (2013). "A monstrous hybrid: The political economy of housing in early twenty-first century Sweden." *New Political Economy*, 18(6), 885–911.

Cloyne, J., Huber, K., Ilzetzki, E. and Kleven, H. (2019). "The effect of house prices on household borrowing: A new approach." *American Economic Review*, 109(6), 2104–2136.

Cohen, L. (2003). *A Consumer's Republic: The Politics of Mass Consumption in Postwar America*. New York: Vintage.

Cohen, L. (2004). "A consumers' republic: The politics of mass consumption in postwar America." *Journal of Consumer Research*, 31(1), 236–239.

Conradi, P., and Zöpel, C. (1994). *Wohnen in Deutschland: Not im Luxus*. Hamburg: Hoffmann und Campe.

Cooper, A. and Kurzer, P. (2023). "Similar origins–divergent paths: The politics of German and Dutch housing markets." *German Politics*, 32(2), 341–360.

Crouch, C. (2009). "Privatised Keynesianism: An unacknowledged policy regime." *The British Journal of Politics and International Relations*, 11(3), 382–399.

Davies, J. (1958). *Real Estate in American History*. Washington, DC: Public Affairs Press.

Desmond, M. (2016). *Evicted: Poverty and Profit in the American City*. New York: Crown.

Deutsch, E. and Tomann, H. (1995). "Home ownership finance in Austria and Germany." *Real Estate Economics*, 23(4), 441–474.

Dewilde, C. and Flynn, L. B. (2021). "Post-crisis developments in young adults' housing wealth." *Journal of European Social Policy*, 31(5), 580–596.

Di Carlo, D. and Höpner, M. (2022). "Germany is likely to shift toward wage restraint as inflation concerns mount." *LSE EUROPP Blog*, Retrieved January 20, 2025, from https://blogs.lse.ac.uk/europpblog/2022/07/25/germany-is-likely-to-shift-toward-wage-restraint-as-inflation-concerns-mount/.

Diefendorf, J. M. (1993). *In the Wake of War: The Reconstruction of German Cities after World War II*. New York: Oxford University Press.

Dougherty, C. (2020). *Golden Gates: Fighting for Housing in America*. New York: Penguin.

Dreier, P. (2000). "Labor's love lost? Rebuilding unions' involvement in federal housing policy." *Housing Policy Debate*, 11(2), 327–392.

Dreier, P. (2023). "Los Angeles' housing revolution." *Poverty & Race*, 32(1), 5–23.

Drukker, A. J., Gayer, T. and Rosen, H. S. (2021). "The mortgage interest deduction: Revenue and distributional effects." *Journal of Housing Research*, 30(1), 1–33.

Dustmann, C., Fitzenberger, B., Schönberg, U. and Spitz-Oener, A. (2014). "From sick man of Europe to economic superstar: Germany's resurgent economy." *Journal of Economic Perspectives*, 28(1), 167–188.

Eccles, M. S. *Beckoning Frontiers: Public and Personal Recollections*. New York: Alfred A. Knopf, 1951.

Ederer, S., Stockhammer, E. and Ćetković, P. (2015). "20 Jahre Österreich in der EU – Neoliberale Regulationsweise und exportgetriebenes Akkumulationsregime," in Beigewum (ed.). *Politische Ökonomie Österreichs: Kontinuitäten und Veränderungen seit dem EU-Beitritt*. Vienna: Mandelbaum Verlag, pp. 34–58.

Égert, B. and Kierzenkowski, R. (2014). "Exports and property prices in France: Are they connected?" *World Economy*, 37(3), 387–409.

Egner, B. (2014). "Wohnungspolitik seit 1945." *Aus Politik und Zeitgeschichte*, 64(20–21), 13–19.

Egner, B., Georgakis, N., Heinelt, H. and Bartholomäi, R. C. (2004). *Wohnungspolitik in Deutschland: Positionen. Akteure. Instrumente*. Darmstadt: Schader-Stiftung.

Eichengreen, B. (1994). *Reconstructing Europe's Trade and Payments: The European Payments Union*. Manchester: Manchester University Press.

Eichengreen, B. (2008). *The European Economy since 1945: Coordinated Capitalism and Beyond*. Princeton, NJ: Princeton University Press.

Eichengreen, B. (2011). *Exorbitant Privilege: The Rise and Fall of the Dollar and the Future of the International Monetary System*. Oxford: Oxford University Press.

Einstein, K. L., Glick, D. and Palmer, M. (2020). *Neighborhood Defenders: Participatory Politics and America's Housing Crisis*. New York: Cambridge University Press.

Elliott, R. (2021). *Underwater: Loss, Flood Insurance, and the Moral Economy of Climate Change in the United States*. New York: Columbia University Press.

Elsinga, M., Priemus, H. and Boelhouwer, P. (2016). "Milestones in housing finance in the Netherlands, 1988–2013," in Lunde, J. and Whitehead, C. (eds.). *Milestones in European Housing Finance*. West Sussex: John Wiley & Sons, pp. 255–272.

Engelen, E., Konings, M. and Fernandez, R. (2010). "Geographies of financialization in disarray: The Dutch case in comparative perspective." *Economic Geography*, 86(1), 53–73.

Erixon, L. and Pontusson, J. (2022). "Rebalancing balanced growth: The evolution of the Swedish growth model since the mid-1990s," in Baccaro, L., Blyth, M. and Pontusson, J. (eds.). *Diminishing Returns: The New Politics of Growth and Stagnation*. New York: Oxford University Press, pp. 268–292.

Esping-Andersen, G. (1978). "Social class, social democracy, and the state: Party policy and party decomposition in Denmark and Sweden." *Comparative Politics*, 11(1), 42–58.

Esping-Andersen, G. (1990). *Three Worlds of Welfare Capitalism*. Princeton, NJ: Princeton University Press.

Faber, J. W. (2013). "Racial dynamics of subprime mortgage lending at the peak." *Housing Policy Debate*, 23(2), 328–349.

Falck, O. and Wölfl, A. (2018). "Productivity weaknesses in the German service sector." *ifo Schnelldienst*, 71(1), 46–52.

Fecht, R. (1983). "Zur Einkommensbesteuerung der Selbstnutzung von Wohnungseigentum." *FinanzArchiv/Public Finance Analysis*, 41(3), 476–485.

Fergus, D. (2018). *Land of the Fee: Hidden Costs and the Decline of the American Middle Class*. New York: Oxford University Press.

Fetter, D. K. (2013). "How do mortgage subsidies affect home ownership? Evidence from the mid-century GI bills." *American Economic Journal: Economic Policy*, 5(2), 111–147.

Fetter, D. K. (2016). "The home front: Rent control and the rapid wartime increase in home ownership." *Journal of Economic History*, 76(4), 1001–1043.

Field, A. J. (2014). "The interwar housing cycle in the light of 2001–2012: A comparative historical perspective," in White, E. N., Snowden, K. and Fishback, P. (eds.). *Housing and Mortgage Markets in Historical Perspective*. Chicago: University of Chicago Press, pp. 39–80.

Financial Crisis Inquiry Commission. (2011). *The Financial Crisis Inquiry Report: Final Report of the National Commission on the Causes of the Financial and Economic Crisis in the United States*. Washington, DC: U.S. Government Printing Office.

Fischel, W. A. (2001). *The Homevoter Hypothesis: How Home Values Influence Local Government Taxation, School Finance, and Land-use Policies*. Cambridge, MA: Harvard University Press.

Fishback, P., Fleitas, S., Rose, J. and Snowden, K. (2020). "Collateral damage: The impact of foreclosures on new home mortgage lending in the 1930s." *Journal of Economic History*, 80(3), 853–885.

Fishback, P., Rose, J. and Snowden, K. (2013). *Well Worth Saving: How the New Deal Safeguarded Home Ownership*. Chicago: University of Chicago Press.

Fligstein, N. (2021). *The Banks Did It: An Anatomy of the Financial Crisis*. Cambridge, MA: Harvard University Press.

Fligstein, N. and Goldstein, A. (2012). "A long strange trip: The state and mortgage securitization, 1968–2010," in Knorr Cetina, K. and Preda, A. (eds.). *The Oxford Handbook of the Sociology of Finance*. Oxford: Oxford University Press, pp. 339–356.

Fligstein, N. and Goldstein, A. (2015). "The emergence of a finance culture in American households, 1989–2007." *Socio-Economic Review*, 13(3), 575–601.

Fogelson, R. M. (2013). *The Great Rent Wars: New York, 1917–1929*. New Haven: Yale University Press.

Förster, W. (1996). "Austria," in Balchin, P. (ed.). *Housing Policy in Europe*. London: Routledge, pp. 113–124.

Frame, W. S., Fuster, A., Tracy, J. and Vickery, J. (2015). "The rescue of Fannie Mae and Freddie Mac." *Journal of Economic Perspectives*, 29(2), 25–52.

Freund, D. M. (2007). *Colored Property: State Policy and White Racial Politics in Suburban America*. Chicago: University of Chicago Press.

Frieden, B. J. (1979). *The Environmental Protection Hustle*. Cambridge, MA: MIT Press.

Frydl, K. (2009). *The GI Bill*. New York: Cambridge University Press.

Führer, K. C. (1995). *Mieter, Hausbesitzer, Staat und Wohnungsmarkt: Wohnungsmangel und Wohnungszwangswirtschaft in Deutschland 1914–1969*. Stuttgart: F. Steiner.

Führer, K. C. (2015). *Die Stadt, das Geld und der Markt: Immobilienspekulation in der Bundesrepublik 1960–1985*. Berlin: De Gruyter Oldenbourg.

Fuller, G. (2015). "Who's borrowing? Credit encouragement vs. credit mitigation in national financial systems." *Politics & Society*, 43(2), 241–268.

Fuller, G. W. (2019). *The Political Economy of Housing Financialization*. Newcastle upon Tyne: Agenda Publishing.

Fuller, G. W., Johnston, A. and Regan, A. (2020). "Housing prices and wealth inequality in Western Europe." *West European Politics*, 43(2), 297–320.

Gabor, D. and Kohl, S. (2022). *My home is an asset class*. The Greens/EFA in the European Parliament. Retrieved March 15, 2025, from www.greens-efa.eu/en/article/document/my-home-is-an-asset-class.

Galbraith, J. K. (1979). *The Great Crash, 1929*. Boston: Houghton Mifflin.

Geiger, F., Muellbauer, J. and Rupprecht, M. (2016). "The housing market, household portfolios and the German consumer." *European Central Bank Working Paper Series*. Retrieved May 14, 2024, from www.ecb.europa.eu//pub/pdf/scpwps/ecbwp1904.en.pdf.

Germain, R. and Schwartz, H. M. (2017). "The political economy of currency internationalisation: The case of the RMB." *Review of International Studies*, 43(4), 765–787.

Germann, J. (2014). "German 'grand strategy' and the rise of neoliberalism." *International Studies Quarterly*, 58(4), 706–716.

Geselbracht, R. H. (ed.). (2019). *The Memoirs of Harry S. Truman: A Reader's Edition*. Columbia, MO: University of Missouri Press.

Gibb, K. (2019). "The UK housing story," in Maclennan, D., Pawson, H., Gibb, K., Chisholm, S. and Hulchanski, D. (eds.). *Shaping Futures: Changing the Housing Story*. Glasgow: Policy Scotland, University of Glasgow.

Giersch, H., Paqué, K.-H. and Schmieding, H. (1992). *The Fading Miracle: Four Decades of Market Economy in Germany*. New York: Cambridge University Press.

Gjerstad, S. and Smith, V. L. (2014). "Consumption and investment booms in the 1920s and their collapse in 1930," in White, E. N., Snowden, K. and Fishback, P. (eds.). *Housing and Mortgage Markets in Historical Perspective*. Chicago: University of Chicago Press, pp. 81–114.

Glaeser, E. L. (2011). "Rethinking the federal bias toward homeownership." *Cityscape: A Journal of Policy Development and Research*, 13(2), 5–37.

Glaeser, E. L. (2013). "A nation of gamblers: Real estate speculation and American history." *American Economic Review*, 103(3), 1–42.

Glaeser, E. L. and Gyourko, J. (2008). *Rethinking Federal Housing Policy: How to Make Housing Plentiful and Affordable*. Washington, DC: AEI Press.

Glaeser, E. L. and Gyourko, J. (2018). "The economic implications of housing supply." *Journal of Economic Perspectives*, 32(1), 3–30.

Glaeser, E. L. and Kahn, M. E. (2010). "The greenness of cities: Carbon dioxide emissions and urban development." *Journal of Urban Economics*, 67(3), 404–418.

Glaeser, E. L. and Shapiro, J. (2003). "The benefits of the home mortgage interest deduction." *Tax Policy and the Economy*, 17, 37–82.

Glock, J. (2021). *The Dead Pledge: The Origins of the Mortgage Market and Federal Bailouts, 1913–1939*. New York: Columbia University Press.

Goetz, E. G. (2013). *New Deal Ruins: Race, Economic Justice, and Public Housing Policy*. Ithaca, NY: Cornell University Press.

Goldstein, B., Gounaridis, D., & Newell, J. P. (2020). "The carbon footprint of household energy use in the United States." *Proceedings of the National Academy of Sciences*, 117(32), 19122–19130.

Goodman, L. S. and Mayer, C. (2018). "Homeownership and the American dream." *Journal of Economic Perspectives*, 32(1), 31–58.

Gotham, K. F. (2006). "The secondary circuit of capital reconsidered: Globalization and the U.S. real estate sector." *American Journal of Sociology*, 112(1), 231–275.

Gourevitch, P. A. (1986). *Politics in Hard Times: Comparative Responses to International Economic Crises*. Ithaca, NY: Cornell University Press.

Gourevitch, J. D., Kousky, C., Liao, Y., Nolte, C., Pollack, A. B., Porter, J. R. and Weill, J. A. (2023). "Unpriced climate risk and the potential consequences of overvaluation in US housing markets." *Nature Climate Change*, 13, 250–257.

Grebler, L. (1960). *Housing Issues in Economic Stabilization Policy*. New York: National Bureau of Economic Research.

Grebler, L., Blank, D. M. and Winnick, L. (1956). *Capital Formation in Residential Real Estate: Trends and Prospects*. Princeton, NJ: Princeton University Press.

Grebler, L. and Mittelbach, F. G. (1979). *The Inflation of House Prices, Its Extent, Causes, and Consequences*. Lexington, MA: Lexington Books.

Green, R. K. and Wachter, S. M. (2005). "The American mortgage in historical and international context." *Journal of Economic Perspectives*, 19(4), 93–114.

Green, R. K. and Wachter, S. M. (2010). "The housing finance revolution," in Smith, S. J. and Searle, B. A. (eds.). *The Blackwell Companion to the Economics of Housing: The Housing Wealth of Nations*. Oxford: Wiley-Blackwell, pp. 414–446.

Greenspan, A. and Kennedy, J. (2008). "Sources and uses of equity extracted from homes." *Oxford Review of Economic Policy*, 24(1), 120–144.

Gromis, A., Fellows, I., Hendrickson, J. R., Edmonds, L., Leung, L., Porton, A. and Desmond, M. (2022). "Estimating eviction prevalence across the United States." *PNAS*, 119(21), 1–8.

Haas, H. (2020). "Paradigmenwandel der Wohnungspolitik," in Depenheuer, O., Hertzsch, E. and Voigtländer, M. (eds.). *Wohneigentum für breite Schichten der Bevölkerung*. Berlin: Springer, pp. 35–50.

Hacker, J. S. (2002). *The Divided Welfare State: The Battle over Public and Private Social Benefits in the United States*. New York: Cambridge University Press.

Hacker, J., Hertel-Fernandez, A., Pierson, P., and Thelen, K. (eds.). (2021). *The American Political Economy: Politics, Markets, and Power*. New York: Cambridge University Press.

Hackley, H. H. (1973). *Lending Functions of the Federal Reserve Banks: A History*. Washington, DC: Board of Governors of the Federal Reserve System.

Haffert, L. and Mertens, D. (2021). "Between distribution and allocation: Growth models, sectoral coalitions and the politics of taxation revisited." *Socio-Economic Review*, 19(2), 487–510.

Hall, P. A. (1986). *Governing the Economy: The Politics of State Intervention in Britain and France*. New York: Oxford University Press.

Hall, P. A. (2020). "The electoral politics of growth regimes." *Perspectives on Politics*, 18(1), 185–199.

Hall, P. A. (2021). "How growth strategies evolve in the developed democracies," in Hassel, A. and Palier, B. (eds.). *Growth and Welfare in Advanced Capitalist Economies: How Have Growth Regimes Evolved?* Oxford: Oxford University Press, pp. 57–97.

Hall, P. A. (2024). "Growth Regimes." *Business History Review*, 98(1), 259–283.

Hall, P. A. and Franzese, R. J. (1998). "Mixed signals: Central bank independence, coordinated wage bargaining, and European monetary union." *International Organization*, 52(3), 505–535.

Hall, P. A. and Soskice, D. (eds.). (2001). *Varieties of Capitalism: The Institutional Foundations of Comparative Advantage*. Oxford: Oxford University Press.

Hall, T. and Vidén, S. (2005). "The Million Homes Programme: A review of the great Swedish planning project." *Planning Perspectives*, 20(3), 301–328.

Haltom, R. C. and Sharp, R. (2014). "The first time the Fed bought GSE debt." *Richmond Fed Economic Brief*, 14(4), 1–7.

Hanchett, T. W. (1996). "U.S. tax policy and the shopping-center boom of the 1950s and 1960s." *American Historical Review*, 101(4), 1082–1110.

Hancock, D. and Passmore, W. (2015). "How does the Federal Reserve's large-scale asset purchases (LSAPs) influence mortgage-backed securities (MBS) yields and U.S. mortgage rates?" *Real Estate Economics*, 43(4), 855–890.

Hankinson, M. (2018). "When do renters behave like homeowners? High rent, price anxiety, and NIMBYism." *American Political Science Review*, 112(3), 473–493.

Hansen, R. (2009). *Fire and Fury: The Allied Bombing of Germany, 1942–1945*. Toronto: Anchor Canada.

Hansen, R. (2023). *War, Work, and Want: How the OPEC Oil Crisis Caused Mass Migration and Revolution*. New York: Oxford University Press.

Harlander, T. (1995). *Zwischen Heimstätte und Wohnmaschine: Wohnungsbau und Wohnungspolitik in der Zeit des Nationalsozialismus*. Basel: Birkhäuser.

Harloe, M. (1995). *The People's Home? Social Rented Housing in Europe and America*. Oxford: Blackwell.

Harris, R. (2024). "Completing the picture of the Depression housing crisis." *Enterprise & Society*, 25(3), 789–812.

Hassel, A. and Palier, B. (eds.). (2021). *Growth and Welfare Reforms in Advanced Capitalist Economies: How Have Growth Regimes Evolved?* Oxford: Oxford University Press.

Hassel, A. and Schiller, C. (2010). *Der Fall Hartz IV: Wie es zur Agenda 2010 kam und wie es weitergeht*. Frankfurt: Campus Verlag.

Häußermann, H. and Siebel, W. (1996). *Soziologie des Wohnens: Eine Einführung in Wandel und Ausdifferenzierung des Wohnens*. Weinheim: Juventa.

Hawley, E. W. (1995). *The New Deal and the Problem of Monopoly: A Study in Economic Ambivalence*. New York: Fordham University Press.

Hay, C. (2013). *The Failure of Anglo-liberal Capitalism*. London: Palgrave Macmillan.

Heinelt, H. and Egner, B. (2006). "Wohnungspolitik – von der Wohnraumzwangsbewirtschaftung zur Wohnungsmarktpolitik," in Schmidt, M. and Zohlnhöfer, R. (eds.). *Regieren in der Bundesrepublik Deutschland: Innen- und Außenpolitik seit 1949*. Wiesbaden: VS Verlag für Sozialwissenschaften, pp. 203–220.

Herrigel, G. (1996). *Industrial Constructions: The Sources of German Industrial Power*. New York: Cambridge University Press.

Higgs, R. (1999). "From central planning to the market: The American transition, 1945–1947." *Journal of Economic History*, 59(3), 600–623.

Hilber, C. A. L. (2023). "How can we make homes more affordable?" *London School of Economics British Politics & Policy Blog*, retrieved March 15, 2025, from https://blogs.lse.ac.uk/politicsandpolicy/how-can-we-make-homes-more-affordable/.

Hilber, C. A. L. and Schöni, O. (2016). "Housing policies in the United Kingdom, Switzerland, and the United States: Lessons learned." *Cityscape*, 18(3), 291–332.

Hilber, C. A. L. and Turner, T. M. (2014). "The mortgage interest deduction and its impact on homeownership decisions." *Review of Economics and Statistics*, 96(4), 618–637.

Hoeller, P., Ziemann, V., Cournède, B. and Bétin, M. (2023). "Home, green home: Policies to decarbonise housing." *OECD Economics Department Working Papers No. 1751*. Retrieved May 16, 2024, from https://dx.doi.org/10.1787/cbda8bad-en.

Hoffmann, S. M. and Cassell, M. K. (2010). *Mission Expansion in the Federal Home Loan Bank System*. Albany: State University of New York Press.

Honhart, M. (1990). "Company housing as urban planning in Germany, 1870–1940." *Central European History*, 23(1), 3–21.
Hopkin, J. and Alexander Shaw, K. (2016). "Organized combat or structural advantage? The politics of inequality and the winner-take-all economy in the United Kingdom." *Politics & Society*, 44(3), 345–371.
Höpner, M. (2019). "The German undervaluation regime under Bretton Woods: How Germany became the nightmare of the world economy." *MPIfG Discussion Paper*, 19(1). Max Planck Institute for the Study of Societies. Retrieved December 6, 2024, from www.econstor.eu/handle/10419/192948.
Hornstein, J. M. (2005). *A Nation of Realtors: A Cultural History of the Twentieth-Century American Middle Class*. Durham, NC: Duke University Press.
Howard, C. (1997). *The Hidden Welfare State: Tax Expenditures and Social Policy in the United States*. Princeton, NJ: Princeton University Press.
Hsieh, C.-T. and Moretti, E. (2019). "Housing constraints and spatial misallocation." *American Economic Journal: Macroeconomics*, 11(2), 1–39.
Hyman, L. (2011). *Debtor Nation: The History of America in Red Ink*. Princeton, NJ: Princeton University Press.
Immergluck, D. (2009). *Foreclosed: High-Risk Lending, Deregulation, and the Undermining of America's Mortgage Market*. Ithaca: Cornell University Press.
International Monetary Fund (2011). *Global Financial Stability Report: Grappling with Crisis Legacies*. Washington, DC: IMF.
Iversen, T. and Soskice, D. (2012). "Modern capitalism and the advanced nation state: Understanding the causes of the crisis," in Bermeo, N. and Pontusson, J. (eds.). *Coping with Crisis: Government Reactions to the Great Recession*. New York: Russell Sage Foundation, 35–64.
Iversen, T. and Soskice, D. (2019). *Democracy and Prosperity: Reinventing Capitalism through a Turbulent Century*. Princeton: Princeton University Press.
Jackson, K. T. (1985). *Crabgrass Frontier: The Suburbanization of the United States*. New York: Oxford University Press.
Jacobides, M. G. (2002). "Mortgage banking unbundling: Structure, automation and profit." *Housing Finance International*, 16(4), 3–13.
Jacobs, A. M. and Weaver, R. K. (2015). "When policies undo themselves: Self-undermining feedback as a source of policy change." *Governance*, 28(4), 441–457.
Jacobs, L. R. and King, D. (2021). *Fed Power: How Finance Wins* (2nd ed.). New York: Oxford University Press.
Jacobs, M. (2007). *Pocketbook Politics: Economic Citizenship in Twentieth-century America*. Princeton: Princeton University Press.
Jaedicke, W. and Wollmann, H. (1990). "Wohnungspolitik zwischen Staatsintervention und Markt," in von Beyme, K. and Schmidt, M (eds.). *Politik in der Bundesrepublik Deutschland*. Berlin: Springer, pp. 203–226.
Jaedicke, W. and Wollmann, H. (1991). "Wohnungspolitik und Regierungswechsel," in Blanke, B. and Wollmann, H. (eds.). *Die alte Bundesrepublik: Kontinuität und Wandel*. Opladen: Westdeutscher Verlag, pp. 420–436.
Johnston, A. and Kurzer, P. (eds.). (2021). *Bricks in the Wall: The Politics of Housing in Europe*. Abingdon: Routledge.
Johnston, A. and Regan, A. (2017). "Global finance, labor politics, and the political economy of housing prices." *Politics & Society*, 45(3), 327–358.

Johnston, A., Fuller, G. W. and Regan, A. (2021). "It takes two to tango: Mortgage markets, labor markets and rising household debt in Europe." *Review of International Political Economy*, 28(4), 843–873.

Jones, O. and Grebler, L. (1961). *The Secondary Mortgage Market: Its Purpose, Performance, and Potential.* Los Angeles, CA: University of California Press.

Jordà, Ò., Schularick, M. and Taylor, A. M. (2016a). "Macrofinancial history and the new business cycle facts." *NBER Macroeconomics Annual*, 31, 213–263.

Jordà, Ò., Schularick, M. and Taylor, A. M. (2016b). "The great mortgaging: Housing finance, crises and business cycles." *Economic Policy*, 31(85), 107–152.

Kahn, C. H. (1960). *Personal Deductions in the Federal Income Tax.* Princeton, NJ: Princeton University Press.

Katzenstein, J. (1985). *Small States in World Markets: Industrial Policy in Europe.* Ithaca, NY: Cornell University Press.

Katznelson, I. (2005). *When Affirmative Action Was White: An Untold History of Racial Inequality in Twentieth-Century America.* New York: W. W. Norton & Company.

Katznelson, I. (2013). *Fear Itself: The New Deal and the Origins of Our Time.* New York: W. W. Norton & Company.

Kemeny, J. (1981). *The Myth of Home-Ownership: Private versus Public Choices in Housing Tenure.* London: Routledge & Kegan Paul.

Kemeny, J. (1995). *From Public Housing to the Social Market.* London: Routledge.

King, D. and Lieberman, R. C. (2009). "Ironies of state building: A comparative perspective on the American state." *World Politics*, 61(3), 547–588.

King, D. S. and Smith, R. M. (2011). *Still a House Divided: Race and Politics in Obama's America.* Princeton, NJ: Princeton University Press.

Kirkegaard, J. F. (2014). "Making labor market reforms work for everyone: Lessons from Germany." *Peterson Institute for International Economics Policy Briefs*, (14)1. Retrieved May 18, 2024, from www.piie.com/publications/policy-briefs/making-labor-market-reforms-work-everyone-lessons-germany.

Knoll, K., Schularick, M. and Steger, T. (2017). "No price like home: Global house prices, 1870–2012." *The American Economic Review*, 107(2), 331–353.

Kofner, S. (2004). *Wohnungsmarkt und Wohnungswirtschaft.* Munich: R. Oldenbourg Verlag

Kofner, S. (2014). "The German housing system: Fundamentally resilient?" *Journal of Housing and the Built Environment*, 29(2), 255–275.

Kohl, S. (2017). *Homeownership, Renting and Society: Historical and Comparative Perspectives.* Abingdon: Routledge.

Kohl, S. (2020). "The political economy of homeownership: A comparative analysis of homeownership ideology through party manifestos." *Socio-Economic Review*, 18(4), 913–940.

Kohl, S. (2021). "Too much mortgage debt? The effect of housing financialization on housing supply and residential capital formation." *Socio-Economic Review*, 19(2), 413–440.

Kohl, S. and Sørvoll, J. (2021). "Varieties of social democracy and cooperativism: Explaining the historical divergence between housing regimes in Nordic and German-speaking countries." *Social Science History*, 45(3), 561–587.

Kohl, S. and Spielau, A. (2022). "Centring construction in the political economy of housing: variegated growth regimes after the Keynesian construction state." *Cambridge Journal of Economics*, 46(3), 465–490.

Kohler, K. and Stockhammer, E. (2020). "Growth models in advanced countries before and after the 2008 crisis: Competitiveness, financial cycles and austerity." Working Paper 2008, *Post-Keynesian Economics Society*. Retrieved May 18, 2024, from www.postkeynesian.net/downloads/working-papers/Kohler_Stockhammer_2020_PKES-WP_-_Growth_models_after_2008_qNpvogn.pdf.

Köpfler, T. (1996). "Die Wohnungsbaufinanzierung," in Jenkis, H. W. (ed.). *Kompendium der Wohnungswirtschaft* (3rd ed.). Munich: Oldenbourg, pp. 627–647.

Koppell, J. G. S. (2003). *The Politics of Quasi-Government: Hybrid Organizations and the Dynamics of Bureaucratic Control*. New York, NY: Cambridge University Press.

Kramper, P. (2008). *Neue Heimat: Unternehmenspolitik und Unternehmensentwicklung im gewerkschaftlichen Wohnungs- und Städtebau 1950–1982*. Stuttgart: Franz Steiner Verlag.

Krampf, A. (2019). "Monetary power reconsidered: The struggle between the Bundesbank and the Fed over monetary leadership." *International Studies Quarterly*, 63(4), 938–951.

Kreile, M. (1977). "West Germany: The dynamics of expansion." *International Organization*, 31(4), 775–808.

Krippner, G. R. (2011). *Capitalizing on Crisis: The Political Origins of the Rise of Finance*. Cambridge, MA: Harvard University Press.

Krippner, G. R. (2017). "Democracy of credit: Ownership and the politics of credit access in late twentieth-century America." *American Journal of Sociology*, 123(1), 1–47.

Krishnamurthy, A. and Vissing-Jorgensen, A. (2011). "The Effects of Quantitative Easing on Interest Rates: Channels and Implications for Policy." NBER Working Paper Series, no. 17555, *National Bureau of Economic Research*. Retrieved May 19, 2024, from www.nber.org/papers/w17555.

Krummacher, M. (1981). "Wohnungspolitik in der BRD-Leitlinien und Entwicklungsphasen." *PROKLA. Zeitschrift für kritische Sozialwissenschaft*, 11(45), 75–111.

Krummacher, M. (1988). "Sozialer Wohnungsbau in der Bundesrepublik in den fünfziger und sechziger Jahren," in Schildt, A. and Sywottek, A. (eds.). *Massenwohnung und Eigenheim: Wohnungsbau und Wohnen in der Großstadt seit dem Ersten Weltkrieg*. Frankfurt: Campus, pp. 440–460.

Leamer, E. E. (2015). "Housing really is the business cycle: What survives the lessons of 2008–09?" *Journal of Money, Credit and Banking*, 47(S1), 43–50.

Lebowitz, N. H. (1981). "'Above party, class, or creed': Rent control in the United States, 1940–1947." *Journal of Urban History*, 7(4), 439–470.

Leutner, B. (ed.). (1990). *Wohnungspolitik nach dem 2.* Weltkrieg. Bonn: Bundesminister für Raumordnung, Bauwesen und Städtebau.

Levy, J. (2020). *Ages of American Capitalism: A History of the United States*. New York: Random House.

Light, M. A. (1999). "Different ideas of the city: Origins of metropolitan land-use regimes in the United States, Germany, and Switzerland." *Yale Journal of International Law*, 24, 577–611.

Lindenthal, T. and Eichholtz, P. (2012). "Prolonged crisis: Housing in Germany and Berlin," in Bardhan, A., Edelstein, R. H. and Kroll, C. A. (eds.). *Global Housing Markets: Crises, Policies, and Institutions*. Hoboken, NJ: John Wiley & Sons, pp. 69–99.

Lindlar, L. and Holtfrerich, C.-L. (1997). "Geography, exchange rates and trade structures: Germany's export performance since the 1950s." *European Review of Economic History*, 1(2), 217–246.

Lindvall, J. (2006). "The politics of purpose: Swedish economic policy after the golden age." *Comparative Politics*, 38(3), 253–272.

Link, S. J. (2020). *Forging Global Fordism: Nazi Germany, Soviet Russia, and the Contest over the Industrial Order*. Princeton, NJ: Princeton University Press.

Listerborn, C. (2023). "The new housing precariat: Experiences of precarious housing in Malmö, Sweden." *Housing Studies*, 38(7), 1304–1322.

Logemann, J. L. (2012). *Trams or Tailfins? Public and Private Prosperity in Postwar West Germany and the United States*. Chicago: University of Chicago Press.

Lüning, H. (2005). *Das Eigenheim-Land: Der öffentlich geförderte Soziale Wohnungsbau in Niedersachsen während der 1950er Jahre*. Hannover: Hahnsche Buchhandlung.

Maier, C. S. (1977). "The politics of productivity: Foundations of American international economic policy after World War II." *International Organization*, 31(4), 607–633.

Maki, D. M. (2001). "Household debt and the Tax Reform Act of 1986." *American Economic Review*, 91(1), 305–319.

Malpass, P. and Rowlands, R. (eds.). (2010). *Housing, Markets and Policy*. Abingdon: Routledge.

Manger, M. S. and Sattler, T. (2020). "The origins of persistent current account imbalances in the post-Bretton Woods era." *Comparative Political Studies*, 53(3–4), 631–664.

Mann, M. (1984). "The autonomous power of the state: Its origins, mechanisms and results." *European Journal of Sociology/Archives européennes de sociologie*, 25(2), 185–213.

Manow, P. (2020). *Social Protection, Capitalist Production: The Bismarckian Welfare State in the German Political Economy, 1880–2015*. New York: Oxford University Press.

Manow, P. and Seils, E. (2000). "Adjusting badly: The German welfare state, structural change, and the open economy," in Scharpf, F. W. and Schmidt, V. A. (eds.). *Diverse Responses to Common Challenges in Twelve Countries*. Vol. II of Welfare and Work in the Open Economy. Oxford: Oxford University Press, pp. 264–307.

Marble, W. and Nall, C. (2021). "Where self-interest trumps ideology: Liberal homeowners and local opposition to housing development." *Journal of Politics*, 83(4), 1747–1763.

Martin, C. J. (1991). *Shifting the burden: The Struggle over Growth and Corporate Taxation*. University of Chicago Press.

Martin, I. W. (2008). *The Permanent Tax Revolt: How the Property Tax Transformed American Politics*. Stanford, CA: Stanford University Press.

Mason, D. L. (2004). *From Buildings and Loans to Bail-Outs: A History of the American Savings and Loan Industry, 1831–1995*. New York: Cambridge University Press.

Matthijs, M. and Blyth, M. (eds.) (2015). *The Future of the Euro*. New York: Oxford University Press.

Mazzucato, M. (2015). *The Entrepreneurial State: Debunking Public vs. Private Sector Myths*. New York: PublicAffairs.

McCabe, B. J. (2016). *No Place Like Home: Wealth, Community and the Politics of Homeownership*. New York: Oxford University Press.
McCarty, N., Poole, K. T. and Rosenthal, H. (2013). *Political Bubbles: Financial Crises and the Failure of American Democracy*. Princeton, NJ: Princeton University Press.
McDonald, O. (2012). *Fannie Mae and Freddie Mac: Turning the American Dream into a Nightmare*. London: Bloomsbury Academic.
McDonnell, T. L. (1957). *The Wagner Housing Act: A Case Study of the Legislative Process*. Chicago: Loyola University Press.
McKenzie, E. (1994). *Privatopia: Homeowner Associations and the Rise of Residential Private Government*. New Haven, CT: Yale University Press.
McKernan, S.-M., Ratcliffe, C., Steuerle, E. and Zhang, S. (2014). "Disparities in wealth accumulation and loss from the Great Recession and beyond." *American Economic Review*, 104(5), 240–244.
McLean, B. (2015). *Shaky Ground: The Strange Saga of the U. S. Mortgage Giants*. New York: Columbia Global Reports.
McLure, C. E., Jr. (1986). "The tax treatment of owner-occupied housing: The Achillies' heel of tax reform," in Follain, J. R. (ed.). *Tax Reform and Real Estate*. Washington, DC: Urban Institute Press, pp. 219–232.
McLure, C. E., Jr., and Zodrow, G. R. (1987). "Treasury I and the Tax Reform Act of 1986: The economics and politics of tax reform." *Journal of Economic Perspectives*, 1(1), 37–58.
Mertens, D. (2015). *Erst sparen, dann kaufen? Privatverschuldung in Deutschland*. Frankfurt: Campus.
Mertens, D. (2017). "Borrowing for social security? Credit, asset-based welfare and the decline of the German savings regime." *Journal of European Social Policy*, 27(5), 474–490.
Mettler, S. (2005). *Soldiers to Citizens: The G.I. Bill and the Making of the Greatest Generation*. New York: Oxford University Press.
Mettler, S. (2010). "Reconstituting the submerged state: The challenges of social policy reform in the Obama era." *Perspectives on Politics* 8(3), 803–824.
Mettler, S. and SoRelle, M. (2018). "Policy feedback," in Sabatier, A. and Weible, C. M. (eds.). *Theories of the Policy Process* (4th ed.). New York: Routledge, pp. 103–134.
Mian, A. and Sufi, A. (2011). "House prices, home equity–based borrowing, and the US household leverage crisis." *American Economic Review*, 101(5), 2132–2156.
Mian, A. and Sufi, A. (2014). *House of Debt: How They (and You) Caused the Great Recession, and How We Can Prevent It from Happening Again*. Chicago: University of Chicago Press.
Mian, A., Rao, K. and Sufi, A. (2013). "Household balance sheets, consumption, and the economic slump." *Quarterly Journal of Economics*, 128(4), 1687–1726.
Michelsen, C. and Weiß, D. (2010). "What happened to the East German housing market? A historical perspective on the role of public funding." *Post-Communist Economies*, 22(3), 387–409.
Mierzejewski, A. C. (2004). *Ludwig Erhard: A Biography*. Chapel Hill, NC: University of North Carolina Press.
Mishkin, F. (2007). "Housing and the Monetary Transmission Mechanism." NBER Working Paper Series, no. 13518, *National Bureau of Economic Research*. Retrieved May 19, 2024, from www.nber.org/papers/w13518.

Morgan, K. J. and Orloff, A. S. (eds.) (2017). *The Many Hands of the State: Theorizing Political Authority and Social Control*. New York: Cambridge University Press.

Morgan, K. J. and Prasad, M. (2009). "The origins of tax systems: A French-American comparison." *American Journal of Sociology*, 114(5), 1350–1394.

Morgan, K. J. and Reisenbichler, A. (2022). "Riding the tiger: Managing risk in U.S. housing finance and health insurance welfare markets." *Socio-Economic Review*, 20(3), 1315–1338.

Muellbauer, J. (1992). "Anglo-German differences in housing market dynamics: The role of institutions and macro economic policy." *European Economic Review*, 36(2–3), 539–548.

Muellbauer, J. (2018). "Housing, debt and the economy: A tale of two countries." *National Institute Economic Review*, 245, R20–R33.

Nahm, J. (2021). *Collaborative Advantage: Forging Green Industries in the New Global Economy*. New York: Oxford University Press.

Nelson, S. and Katzenstein, P. J. (2014). "Uncertainty, risk, and the financial crisis of 2008." *International Organization*, 68(2), 361–392.

Nicolaides, B. and Wiese, A. (2017). "Suburbanization in the United States after 1945". In Butler, J. (ed.). *Oxford Research Encyclopedia of American History*. Oxford University Press.

Nölke, A. (2021). *Exportismus: Die deutsche Droge*. Frankfurt: Westend Verlag.

Opie, R. G. (1960). "Competition and growth – The lesson of West Germany: Comment." *American Economic Review*, 50(5), 1022–1025.

Oren, T. and Blyth, M. (2019). "From big bang to big crash: The early origins of the UK's finance-led growth model and the persistence of bad policy ideas." *New Political Economy*, 24(5), 605–622.

Ornston, D. (2016). *Good Governance Gone Bad: How Nordic Adaptability Leads to Excess*. Ithaca: Cornell University Press.

Ornston, D. and Vail, M. I. (2016). "The developmental state in developed societies: Power, partnership, and divergent patterns of intervention in France and Finland." *Comparative Politics*, 49(1), 1–21.

Öst, C.E. and Johansson, P. (2023). "The consequences of the Swedish rent control system on labor income: Evidence from a randomized apartment lottery." *Journal of Public Economics*, 221(article 104864), 1–12.

Palier, B. and Thelen, K. (2010). "Institutionalizing dualism: Complementarities and change in France and Germany." *Politics & Society*, 38(1), 119–148.

Parrott, J. and Zandi, M. (2015). "Privatizing Fannie and Freddie: Be careful what you ask for." *Moody's Analytics & Urban Institute*. Retrieved May 19, 2024, from www.urban.org/sites/default/files/publication/52861/2000229-Privatizing-Fannie-and-Freddie.pdf.

Persons, C. E. (1930). "Credit expansion, 1920 to 1929, and its lessons." *Quarterly Journal of Economics*, 45(1), 94–130.

Pfeiffer, U. and Ammann, M. (1994). *Wohnungspolitik in Ostdeutschland*. Bonn: Friedrich-Ebert-Stiftung.

Pierson, P. (1993). "When effect becomes cause: Policy feedback and political change." *World Politics*, 45(4), 595–628.

Pierson, P. (1994). *Dismantling the Welfare State? Reagan, Thatcher and the Politics of Retrenchment*. New York, NY: Cambridge University Press.

Piketty, T. (2014). *Capital in the Twenty-First Century*. Cambridge, MA: Belknap Press of Harvard University Press.

Pizzo, S. Fricker, M. and Muolo, P. (1989). *Inside Job: The Looting of America's Savings and Loans*. New York: McGraw-Hill.
Poterba, J. M. and Sinai, T. (2011). "Revenue costs and incentive effects of the mortgage interest deduction for owner-occupied housing." *National Tax Journal*, 64(2), 531–564.
Poterba, J. M., Weil, D. N. and Shiller, R. (1991). "House price dynamics: The role of tax policy and demography." *Brookings Papers on Economic Activity*, 1991(2), 143–203.
Prasad, M. (2012). *The Land of Too Much: American Abundance and the Paradox of Poverty*. Cambridge, MA: Harvard University Press.
Quinn, S. L. (2019). *American Bonds: How Credit Markets Shaped a Nation*. Princeton, NJ: Princeton University Press.
Radford, G. (1996). *Modern Housing for America: Policy Struggles in the New Deal Era*. Chicago, IL: University of Chicago Press.
Radford, G. (2013). *The Rise of the Public Authority: Statebuilding and Economic Development in Twentieth-Century America*. Chicago, IL: University of Chicago Press.
Rajan, R. (2010). *Fault Lines: How Hidden Fractures Still Threaten the World Economy*. Princeton, NJ: Princeton University Press.
Raymond, E., Kyungsoon, W. and Immergluck. D. (2016). "Race and uneven recovery: Neighborhood home value trajectories in Atlanta before and after the housing crisis." *Housing Studies*, 31(1), 324–339.
Reid, C. K., Bocian, D., Li, W. and Quercia, R. G. (2017). "Revisiting the subprime crisis: The dual mortgage market and mortgage defaults by race and ethnicity." *Journal of Urban Affairs*, 39(4), 469–487.
Reisenbichler, A. (2020a). "Housing finance markets between social welfare and growth strategies," in Hassel, A. and Palier, B. (eds.). *Growth and Welfare in Advanced Capitalist Economies: How Have Growth Regimes Evolved?* Oxford: Oxford University Press, pp. 320–347.
Reisenbichler, A. (2020b). "The politics of quantitative easing and housing stimulus by the Federal Reserve and European Central Bank, 2008–2018." *West European Politics*, 43(23), 464–484.
Reisenbichler, A. (2022). "Entrenchment or retrenchment: The political economy of mortgage debt subsidies in the United States and Germany." *Comparative Politics*, 54(4), 717–740.
Reisenbichler, A. and König, P. (2024). "Cause for celebration or concern? Voter reactions to rising house prices." *Comparative Political Studies* (online first).
Reisenbichler, A. and Morgan, K. J. (2012). "From 'sick man' to 'miracle' Explaining the robustness of the German labor market during and after the financial crisis 2008–09." *Politics & Society*, 40(4), 549–579.
Reisenbichler, A. and Wiedemann, A. (2022). "Credit-driven and consumption-led growth models in the United States and United Kingdom," in Baccaro, L., Blyth, M. and Pontusson, J. (eds.). *Diminishing Returns: The New Politics of Growth and Stagnation*. Oxford: Oxford University Press, pp. 213–237.
Rognlie, M. (2015). "Deciphering the fall and rise in the net capital share: Accumulation or scarcity?". *Brookings Papers on Economic Activity, Spring 2015*.
Ronald, R. (2008). *The Ideology of Home Ownership: Homeowner Societies and the Role of Housing*. Basingstoke: Palgrave Macmillan.

Rothstein, R. (2017). *The Color of Law: A Forgotten History of How Our Government Segregated America*. New York: Liveright Publishing.
Ryan, A., Trumbull, G. and Tufano, P. (2011). "A brief postwar history of U.S. consumer finance." *Business History Review*, 85(3), 461–498.
Salet, W. G. M. (1999). "Regime shifts in Dutch housing policy." *Housing Studies*, 14(4), 547–557.
Sattler, F. (2019). *Der Pfandbrief 1769–2019: Von der Preußischen Finanzinnovation zur Covered Bond Benchmark*. Stuttgart: Steiner.
Scharpf, F. W. (1991). *Crisis and Choice in European Social Democracy*. Ithaca, NY: Cornell University Press.
Scharpf, F. W. (2008). "Community, diversity and autonomy: The challenges of reforming German federalism." *German Politics*, 17(4), 509–521.
Scharpf, F. W., Reissert, B. and Schnabel, F. (1976). *Politikverflechtung: Theorie und Empirie des kooperativen Föderalismus in der Bundesrepublik*. Kronberg: Scriptor Verlag.
Schelkle, W. (2012). "A crisis of what? Mortgage credit markets and the social policy of promoting homeownership in the United States and in Europe." *Politics & Society*, 40(1), 59–80.
Schmidt-Hoepke, A. (1962). "Der Lücke-Plan hat sich bewährt." *Arbeit und Sozialpolitik*, 16(10), 294–297.
Schulz, G. (1994). *Wiederaufbau in Deutschland: Die Wohnungsbaupolitik in den Westzonen und der Bundesrepublik von 1945 bis 1957*. Düsseldorf: Droste.
Schwartz, A. F. (2010). *Housing Policy in the United States* (2nd ed.). New York, NY: Routledge.
Schwartz, H. M. (2009). *Subprime Nation: American Power, Global Capital, and the Housing Bubble*. Ithaca, NY: Cornell University Press.
Schwartz, H. (2012). "Housing, the welfare state, and the global financial crisis: What is the connection?" *Politics & Society*, 40(1), 35–58.
Schwartz, H. M. (2020). "Covering the private parts: The (re-)nationalisation of housing finance." *West European Politics*, 43(2), 485–508.
Schwartz, H. M. and Blyth, M. (2022). "Four Galtons and a Minksy: Growth models from an IPE perspective," in Baccaro, L., Blyth, M. and Pontusson, J. (eds.). *Diminishing Returns: The New Politics of Growth and Stagnation*. New York, NY: Oxford University Press, pp. 98–114.
Schwartz, H. M. and Seabrooke, L. (2009). *The Politics of Housing Booms and Busts*. Basingstoke: Palgrave Macmillan.
Shaw, C. W. (2019). *Money, Power, and the People: The American Struggle to Make Banking Democratic*. Chicago, IL: University of Chicago Press.
Shonfield, A. (1965). *Modern Capitalism: The Changing Balance of Public and Private Power*. London: Oxford University Press.
Silverman, D. (1970). "A pledge unredeemed: The housing crisis in Weimar Germany." *Central European History*, 3(1–2), 112–139.
Simon, H. (1964). "Eigentumsförderung durch den Wohnungsbau – Aufgaben einer Dachorganisation der Heimstättenbewegung," in Schneider, H. K. (ed.). *Verbände der Wohnungswirtschaft: Der Einfluss organisierter Interessen auf die Wohnungspolitik*. Köln-Braunseld: Verlagsgesellschaft Rudolf Müller, pp. 41–54.
Slater, G. (2021). *Freedom to Discriminate: How Realtors Conspired to Segregate Housing and Divide America*. Berkeley, CA: Heyday.

Slemrod, J. (2018). "Is this tax reform, or just confusion?" *Journal of Economic Perspectives*, 32(4), 73–96.

Snowden, K. (2013). "Mortgage banking in the United States, 1870–1940." *Research Institute for Housing America Research Paper*, 13(02). Retrieved May 23, 2024, from https://papers.ssrn.com/sol3/papers.cfm?abstract_id=2349189.

Sommer, K. and Sullivan, P. (2018). "Implications of US tax policy for house prices, rents, and homeownership." *American Economic Review*, 108(2), 241–274.

SoRelle, M. E. (2020). *Democracy Declined: The Failed Politics of Consumer Financial Protection*. Chicago, IL: University of Chicago Press.

Soskice, D. (2022). "Rethinking varieties of capitalism and growth theory in the ICT era." *Review of Keynesian Economics*, 10(2), 222–241.

Spielberger, L. and Voss, D. (2024). "Financial adjustment as a driver of growth model change: A balance-sheet approach to comparative political economy." *Comparative European Politics*, 22(1), 5–30.

Stimpel, R. (1990). *Der verbaute Markt: Villenglück und Wohnungsnot*. Frankfurt: Fischer Taschenbuch Verlag.

Stockhammer, E. (2015). "Rising inequality as a cause of the present crisis." *Cambridge Journal of Economics*, 39(3), 935–958.

Stockhammer, E., Rabinovich, J. and Reddy, N. (2021). "Distribution, wealth and demand regimes in historical perspective: The USA, the UK, France and Germany, 1855–2010." *Review of Keynesian Economics*, 9(3), 337–367.

Streeck, W. (1997). "German capitalism: Does it exist? Can it survive?" *New Political Economy*, 2(2), 237–256.

Streeck, W. (2009). *Re-forming Capitalism: Institutional Change in the German Political Economy*. Oxford: Oxford University Press.

Streeck, W. and Trampusch, C. (2005). "Economic reform and the political economy of the German welfare state." *German Politics*, 14(2), 174–195.

Streeck, W. and Yamamura, K. (eds.). (2001). *The Origins of Nonliberal Capitalism: Germany and Japan in Comparison*. Ithaca, NY: Cornell University Press.

Strumpel, B. (1975). "Saving behavior in western Germany and the United States." *American Economic Review*, 65(2), 210–216.

Sugrue, T. J. (1996). *The Origins of the Urban Crisis: Race and Inequality in Postwar Detroit*. Princeton, NJ: Princeton University Press.

Surrey, S. S. (1973). *Pathways to Tax Reform: The Concept of Tax Expenditures*. Cambridge, MA: Harvard University Press.

Suttor, G. (2016). *Still Renovating: A History of Canadian Social Housing Policy*. Montreal: McGill-Queen's University Press.

Sveriges Riksbank. (2014). *From A to Z: The Swedish Mortgage Market and Its Role in the Financial System*. Stockholm: Sveriges Riksbank.

Taylor, K.-Y. (2019). *Race for Profit: How Banks and the Real Estate Industry Undermined Black Homeownership*. Chapel Hill, NC: University of North Carolina Press.

Temin, P. (1995). "The 'Koreaboom' in West Germany: Fact or fiction?" *Economic History Review*, 48(4), 737–753.

Tett, G. (2019). "Faith-based finance: How Wall Street became a cult of risk." *Foreign Affairs*, 98(4), 34–41.

Thelen, K. (2014). *Varieties of Liberalization and the New Politics of Social Solidarity*. New York, NY: Cambridge University Press.

Thelen, K. (2019). "Transitions to the knowledge economy in Germany, Sweden, and the Netherlands." *Comparative Politics*, 51(2), 295–315.

Thomas, T., Koch, P. and Schwarzbauer, W. (2020). "Mieterparadies Österreich? Mythos und Realität." *List Forum für Wirtschafts-und Finanzpolitik*, 45(3), 319–346.

Thompson, H. (2009). "The political origins of the financial crisis: The domestic and international politics of Fannie Mae and Freddie Mac." *Political Quarterly*, 80(1), 17–24.

Thompson, H. (2010). *China and the Mortgaging of America: Economic Interdependence and Domestic Politics*. London: Palgrave Macmillan.

Thompson, H. (2012). "The limits of blaming neo-liberalism: Fannie Mae and Freddie Mac, the American state and the financial crisis." *New Political Economy*, 17(4), 399–419.

Thurston, C. N. (2015). "Policy feedback in the public–private welfare state: Advocacy groups and access to government homeownership programs, 1934–1954." *Studies in American Political Development*, 29(2), 250–267.

Thurston, C. N. (2018). *At the Boundaries of Homeownership: Credit, Discrimination, and the American State*. New York, NY: Cambridge University Press.

Tooze, A. (2018). *Crashed: How a Decade of Financial Crises Changed the World*. New York, NY: Viking.

Torgersen, U. (1987). "Housing: The wobbly pillar under the welfare state." *Scandinavian Housing and Planning Research*, 4(sup1), 116–126.

Trounstine, J. (2018). *Segregation by Design: Local Politics and Inequality in American Cities*. New York, NY: Cambridge University Press.

Trumbull, G. (2014). *Consumer Lending in France and America: Credit and Welfare*. New York, NY: Cambridge University Press.

Vail, M. I. (2010). *Recasting Welfare Capitalism: Economic Adjustment in Contemporary France and Germany*. Philadelphia, PA: Temple University Press.

van Gent, W. (2010). "Housing policy as a lever for change? The politics of welfare, assets and tenure." *Housing Studies*, 25(5), 735–753.

van Gent, W. and Hochstenbach, C. (2020). "The neo-liberal politics and socio-spatial implications of Dutch post-crisis social housing policies." *International Journal of Housing Policy*, 20(1), 156–172.

van Gunten, T. and Navot, E. (2018). "Varieties of indebtedness: Financialization and mortgage market institutions in Europe." *Social Science Research*, 70, 90–106.

van Kersbergen, Kees. (1995). *Social Capitalism: A Study of Christian Democracy and the Welfare State*. London: Routledge.

Ventry, D. J. (2010). "The accidental deduction: A history and critique of the tax subsidy for mortgage interest." *Law & Contemporary Problems*, 73(1), 233–284.

Vestman, R., Bojeryd, J., Tyrefors, B. and Kessel, D. (2023). "The housing wealth effect: Quasi-experimental evidence." *Centre for Economic Policy Research*, DP18034. Retrieved May 23, 2024, from https://cepr.org/publications/dp18034.

Visser, J. and Hemerijck, A. (1997). *A Dutch Miracle: Job Growth, Welfare Reform and Corporatism in the Netherlands*. Amsterdam: Amsterdam University Press.

Vogel, S. K. (2018). *Marketcraft: How Governments Make Markets Work*. Oxford: Oxford University Press.

Voigtländer, M. (2009). "Why is the German homeownership rate so low?" *Housing Studies*, 24(3), 355–372.

Voigtländer, M. (2014). "The stability of the German housing market." *Journal of Housing and the Built Environment*, 29(4), 583–594.

Voigtländer, M. (2019). *Luxusgut Wohnen: Warum unsere Städte immer teurer werden und was jetzt zu tun ist* (2nd ed.). Wiesbaden: Springer.

von Beyme, K. (1987). *Der Wiederaufbau: Architektur und Städtebaupolitik in beiden deutschen Staaten*. Munich: Piper.

von Beyme, K. (1999). "Wohnen und Politik," in Flagge, I. (ed.). *Geschichte des Wohnens: Von 1945 bis heute*. Ludwigsburg: Wüstenrot Stiftung, pp. 81–152.

von Einem, E. (1982). "National urban policy – The case of West Germany." *Journal of the American Planning Association*, 48(1), 9–23.

Vonyó, T. (2018). *The Economic Consequences of the War: West Germany's Growth Miracle After 1945*. Cambridge: Cambridge University Press.

Walks, A. (2014). "Canada's housing bubble story: Mortgage securitization, the state, and the global financial crisis." *International Journal of Urban and Regional Research*, 38(1), 256–284.

Walks, A. (2016). "Homeownership, asset-based welfare and the neighbourhood segregation of wealth." *Housing Studies*, 31(7), 755–784.

Wallich, H. C. (1955). *Mainsprings of the German Revival*. New Haven, CT: Yale University Press.

Wallison, J. (2016). *Hidden in Plain Sight: What Really Caused the World's Worst Financial Crisis and Why It Could Happen Again*. New York, NY: Encounter Books.

Wandschneider, K. (2014). "Lending to lemons: Landschaft credit in eighteenth-century Prussia," in White, E. N., Snowden, K. and Fishback, P. (eds.). *Housing and Mortgage Markets in Historical Perspective*. Chicago, IL: University of Chicago Press, pp. 305–326.

Wandschneider, K. (2015). "Landschaften as credit purveyors: The example of East Prussia." *Journal of Economic History*, 75(3), 791–818.

Wansleben, L. (2022). *The Rise of Central Banks: State Power in Financial Capitalism*. Cambridge, MA: Harvard University Press.

Warnock, F. E. and Warnock, V. C. (2009). "International capital flows and U.S. interest rates." *Journal of International Money and Finance*, 28(6), 903–919.

Watson, M. (2010). "House price Keynesianism and the contradictions of the modern investor subject." *Housing Studies*, 25(3), 413–426.

Weir, M. (2005). "States, race, and the decline of New Deal liberalism." *Studies in American Political Development*, 19(2), 157–172.

Weiss, M. A. (1987). *The Rise of the Community Builders: The American Real Estate Industry and Urban Land Planning*. New York, NY: Columbia University Press.

Wertheimer, R. G. (1958). "The miracle of German housing in the postwar period." *Land Economics*, 34(4), 338–345.

Wessel, D. (2009). *In Fed We Trust: Ben Bernanke's War on the Great Panic*. New York, NY: Currency.

White, E. N. (2014). "Lessons from the great American real estate boom and bust of the 1920s," in White, E. N., Snowden, K. and Fishback, P. (eds.). *Housing and Mortgage Markets in Historical Perspective*. Chicago, IL: University of Chicago Press, pp. 115–158.

Wickens, D. L. (1941). *Residential Real Estate, Its Economic Position as Shown by Values, Rents, Family Incomes, Financing, and Construction, Together with Estimates for All Real Estate*. New York, NY: National Bureau of Economic Research.

Wiedemann, A. (2021). *Indebted Societies: Credit and Welfare in Rich Democracies*. New York, NY: Cambridge University Press.

Wierts, P., Van Kerkhoff, H. and De Haan, J. (2014). "Composition of exports and export performance of Eurozone countries." *JCMS: Journal of Common Market Studies* 52(4), 928–941.

Wiese, A. (2004). *Places of Their Own: African American Suburbanization in the Twentieth Century*. Chicago, IL: University of Chicago Press.

Wijburg, G. and Aalbers, M. B. (2017). "The alternative financialization of the German housing market." *Housing Studies*, 32(7), 968–989.

Willis, J. W. (1950). "A Short history of rent control laws." *Cornell Law Quarterly*, 36(1), 54–92.

Wollmann, H. (1985). "Housing policy in West Germany – between state intervention and market," in von Beyme, K. and Schmidt, M. (eds.). *Policy and Politics in the Federal Republic of Germany*. Aldershot: Gower Publishing, pp. 132–155.

Wood, J. D. G. (2018). "The integrating role of private homeownership and mortgage credit in British neoliberalism." *Housing Studies*, 33(7), 993–1013.

Wood, J. D. G. (2019). "Mortgage credit: Denmark's financial capacity building regime." *New Political Economy*, 24(6), 833–850.

Wullkopf, U. (1982). "Wohnungsbau und Wohnungsbaupolitik in der Bundesrepublik Deutschland." *Aus Politik und Zeitgeschichte*, 10(82).

Zhang, L. (2019). "Do house prices matter for household consumption?" CPB Discussion Paper No. 396, *CPB Netherlands Bureau for Economic Policy Analysis*. Retrieved May 23, 2024, from https://ideas.repec.org/p/cpb/discus/396.html.

Zimmermann, C. (1991). *Von der Wohnungsfrage zur Wohnungspolitik: Die Reformbewegung in Deutschland 1845–1914*. Göttingen: Vandenhoeck & Ruprecht.

Zohlnhöfer, R. (2001). *Die Wirtschaftspolitik der Ära Kohl: Eine Analyse der Schlüsselentscheidungen in den Politikfeldern Finanzen, Arbeit und Entstaatlichung, 1982–1998*. Berlin: Springer.

Zündorf, I. (2006). *Der Preis der Marktwirtschaft: Staatliche Preispolitik und Lebensstandard in Westdeutschland 1948 bis 1963*. Stuttgart: Steiner.

Index

Cambridge Studies in Comparative Politics

OTHER BOOKS IN THE SERIES (*continued from page ii*)

Catherine Boone, *Inequality and Political Cleavage in Africa: Regionalism by Design*
Soledad Artiz Prillaman, *The Patriarchal Political Order: The Making and Unraveling of the Gendered Participation Gap in India*
Charlotte Cavaillé, *Fair Enough?: Support for Redistribution in the Age of Inequality*
Noah L. Nathan, *The Scarce State: Inequality and Political Power in the Hinterland*
Scott de Marchi and Michael Laver, *The Governance Cycle in Parliamentary Democracies: A Computational Social Science Approach*
Egor Lazarev, *State-Building as Lawfare: Custom, Sharia, and State Law in Postwar Chechnya*
Lorenza B. Fontana, *Recognition Politics: Indigenous Rights and Ethnic Conflict in the Andes*
Martha Wilfahrt, *Precolonial Legacies in Postcolonial Politics: Representation and Redistribution in Decentralized West Africa*
Sidney Tarrow, *Power in Movement: Social Movements and Contentious Politics*
Victor C. Shih, *Coalitions of the Weak: Elite Politics in China from Mao's Stratagem to the Rise of Xi*
Torben Iversen and Philipp Rehm, *Big Data and the Welfare State: How the Information Revolution Threatens Social Solidarity*
Eduardo Moncada, *Resisting Extortion: Victims, Criminals and States in Latin America*
Jacob S. Hacker, Alexander Hertel-Fernandez, Paul Pierson, and Kathleen Thelen, *The American Political Economy: Politics, Markets, and Power*
Lily Tsai, *When People want Punishment: Retributive Justice and the Puzzle of Authoritarian Popularity*
Kevin Mazur, *Revolution in Syria: Identity, Networks, and Repression*
Andreas Wiedemann, *Indebted Societies: Credit and Welfare in Rich Democracies*
Antje Ellerman, *The Comparative Politics of Immigration: Policy Choices in Germany, Canada, Switzerland, and the United States*
Michael Albertus, *Property without Rights: Origins and Consequences of the Property Rights Gap*
Ben W. Ansell and Johannes Lindvall, *Inward Conquest: The Political Origins of Modern Public Services*
Yanilda María González, *Authoritarian Police in Democracy: Contested Security in Latin America*
Robert H. Bates, *The Political Economy of Development: A Game Theoretic Approach*
Guillermo Trejo and Sandra Ley, *Votes, Drugs, and Violence: The Political Logic of Criminal Wars in Mexico*
Janet I. Lewis, *How Insurgency Begins: Rebel Group Formation in Uganda and Beyond*
David Szakonyi *Politics for Profit: Business, Elections, and Policymaking in Russia*
Mai Hassan, *Regime Threats and State Solutions: Bureaucratic Loyalty and Embeddedness in Kenya*
Daniel C. Mattingly, *The Art of Political Control in China*
Adam Michael Auerbach, *Demanding Development: The Politics of Public Goods Provision in India's Urban Slums*
Gwyneth H. McClendon and Rachel Beatty Riedl, *From Pews to Politics in Africa: Religious Sermons and Political Behavior*
David Rueda and Daniel Stegmueller, *Who Wants What? Redistribution Preferences in Comparative Perspective*

Yue Hou, *The Private Sector in Public Office: Selective Property Rights in China*
Thad Dunning et al., *Information, Accountability, and Cumulative Learning: Lessons from Metaketa I*
Ignacio Sánchez-Cuenca, *The Historical Roots of Political Violence: Revolutionary Terrorism in Affluent Countries*
G. Bingham Powell Jr., *Ideological Representation Achieved and Astray: Elections, Institutions, and the Breakdown of Ideological Congruence in Parliamentary Democracies*
Noah L. Nathan, *Electoral Politics and Africa's Urban Transition: Class and Ethnicity in Ghana*
S. Erdem Aytaç and Susan C. Stokes, *Why Bother? Rethinking Participation in Elections and Protests*
Deborah J. Yashar, *Homicidal Ecologies: Illicit Economies and Complicit States in Latin America*
Simeon Nichter, *Votes for Survival: Relational Clientelism in Latin America*
Santiago Anria, *When Movements Become Parties: The Bolivian MAS in Comparative Perspective*
Benjamin Lessing, *Making Peace in Drug Wars: Crackdowns and Cartels in Latin America*
Richard A. Nielsen, *Deadly Clerics: Blocked Ambition and the Paths to Jihad*
Kanchan Chandra, *Why Ethnic Parties Succeed: Patronage and Ethnic Head Counts in India*
Mary E. Gallagher, *Authoritarian Legality in China: Law, Workers, and the State*
Karen Jusko, *Who Speaks for the Poor? Electoral Geography, Party Entry, and Representation*
Alisha C. Holland, *Forbearance as Redistribution: The Politics of Informal Welfare in Latin America*
John D. Huber, *Exclusion by Elections: Inequality, Ethnic Identity, and Democracy*
Laia Balcells, *Rivalry and Revenge: The Politics of Violence during Civil War*
Daniel Ziblatt, *Conservative Parties and the Birth of Democracy*
Gretchen Helmke, *Institutions on the Edge: The Origins and Consequences of Inter-Branch Crises in Latin America*
Ana Arjona, *Rebelocracy: Social Order in the Colombian Civil War*
Rory Truex, *Making Autocracy Work: Representation and Responsiveness in Modern China*
Daniel Corstange, *The Price of a Vote in the Middle East: Clientelism and Communal Politics in Lebanon and Yemen*
Philipp Rehm, *Risk Inequality and Welfare States: Social Policy Preferences, Development, and Dynamics*
Prerna Singh, *How Solidarity Works for Welfare: Subnationalism and Social Development in India*
Alberto Diaz-Cayeros, Federico Estévez, and Beatriz Magaloni, *The Political Logic of Poverty Relief: Electoral Strategies and Social Policy in Mexico*
Sarah Zukerman Daly, *Organized Violence after Civil War: The Geography of Recruitment in Latin America*
Melanie Manion, *Information for Autocrats: Representation in Chinese Local Congresses*
Kate Baldwin, *The Paradox of Traditional Chiefs in Democratic Africa*
Michael Albertus, *Autocracy and Redistribution: The Politics of Land Reform*
Jesse Driscoll, *Warlords and Coalition Politics in Post-Soviet States*
Isabela Mares, *From Open Secrets to Secret Voting: Democratic Electoral Reforms and Voter Autonomy*
Carles Boix, *Political Order and Inequality: Their Foundations and their Consequences for Human Welfare*

Kenneth M. Roberts, *Changing Course in Latin America: Party Systems in the Neoliberal Era*
Yuhua Wang, *Tying the Autocrat's Hand: The Rise of the Rule of Law in China*
Ben W. Ansell and David J. Samuels, *Inequality and Democratization: An Elite-Competition Approach*
Kevin M. Morrison, *Nontaxation and Representation: The Fiscal Foundations of Political Stability*
Tariq Thachil, *Elite Parties, Poor Voters: How Social Services Win Votes in India*
Timothy Hellwig, *Globalization and Mass Politics: Retaining the Room to Maneuver*
Roger Schoenman, *Networks and Institutions in Europe's Emerging Markets*
Kathleen Thelen, *Varieties of Liberalization and the New Politics of Social Solidarity*
Catherine Boone, *Property and Political Order in Africa: Land Rights and the Structure of Politics*
Ken Kollman, *Perils of Centralization: Lessons from Church, State, and Corporation*
Michael Hechter, *Alien Rule*
Susan C. Stokes, Thad Dunning, Marcelo Nazareno, and Valeria Brusco, *Brokers, Voters, and Clientelism: The Puzzle of Distributive Politics*
Ben Ross Schneider, *Hierarchical Capitalism in Latin America: Business, Labor, and the Challenges of Equitable Development*
Richard M. Locke, *The Promise and Limits of Private Power: Promoting Labor Standards in a Global Economy*
Christopher Adolph, *Bankers, Bureaucrats, and Central Bank Politics: The Myth of Neutrality*
Stephen B. Kaplan, *Globalization and Austerity Politics in Latin America*
Edward L. Gibson, *Boundary Control: Subnational Authoritarianism in Federal Democracies*
Andreas Wimmer, *Waves of War: Nationalism, State Formation, and Ethnic Exclusion in the Modern World*
Leonardo R. Arriola, *Multi-Ethnic Coalitions in Africa: Business Financing of Opposition Election Campaigns*
Milan W. Svolik, *The Politics of Authoritarian Rule*
Guillermo Trejo, *Popular Movements in Autocracies: Religion, Repression, and Indigenous Collective Action in Mexico*
Cathie Jo Martin and Duane Swank, *The Political Construction of Business Interests: Coordination, Growth, and Equality*
Pablo Beramendi, *The Political Geography of Inequality: Regions and Redistribution*
Roger D. Petersen, *Western Intervention in the Balkans: The Strategic Use of Emotion in Conflict*
Jane R. Gingrich, *Making Markets in the Welfare State: The Politics of Varying Market Reforms*
Sidney Tarrow, *Power in Movement: Social Movements and Contentious Politics, Revised and Updated Third Edition*
Pepper D. Culpepper, *Quiet Politics and Business Power: Corporate Control in Europe and Japan*
Eric C. C. Chang, Mark Andreas Kayser, Drew A. Linzer, and Ronald Rogowski, *Electoral Systems and the Balance of Consumer-Producer Power*
Karen E. Ferree, *Framing the Race in South Africa: The Political Origins of Racial Census Elections*
Layna Mosley, *Labor Rights and Multinational Production*
Pauline Jones Luong and Erika Weinthal, *Oil is Not a Curse: Ownership Structure and Institutions in Soviet Successor States*

Dan Slater, *Ordering Power: Contentious Politics and Authoritarian Leviathans in Southeast Asia*
Sven Steinmo, *The Evolution of Modern States: Sweden, Japan, and the United States*
Stephen E. Hanson, *Post-Imperial Democracies: Ideology and Party Formation in Third Republic France, Weimar Germany, and Post-Soviet Russia*
Timothy Frye, *Building States and Markets After Communism: The Perils of Polarized Democracy*
Lauren M. MacLean, *Informal Institutions and Citizenship in Rural Africa: Risk and Reciprocity in Ghana and Côte d'Ivoire*
Ben W. Ansell, *From the Ballot to the Blackboard: The Redistributive Political Economy of Education*
Herbert Kitschelt, Kirk A. Hawkins, Juan Pablo Luna, Guillermo Rosas, and Elizabeth J. Zechmeister, *Latin American Party Systems*
James Mahoney, *Colonialism and Postcolonial Development: Spanish America in Comparative Perspective*
Monika Nalepa, *Skeletons in the Closet: Transitional Justice in Post-Communist Europe*
Orit Kedar, *Voting for Policy, Not Parties: How Voters Compensate for Power Sharing*
Maria Victoria Murillo, *Political Competition, Partisanship, and Policy Making in Latin American Public Utilities*
Henry Farrell, *The Political Economy of Trust: Institutions, Interests, and Inter-Firm Cooperation in Italy and Germany*
Andy Baker, *The Market and the Masses in Latin America: Policy Reform and Consumption in Liberalizing Economies*
Mark Hallerberg, Rolf Ranier Strauch, and Jürgen von Hagen, *Fiscal Governance in Europe*
Mark Irving Lichbach and Alan S. Zuckerman, eds., *Comparative Politics: Rationality, Culture, and Structure, 2nd edition*
John M. Carey, *Legislative Voting and Accountability*
Thad Dunning, *Crude Democracy: Natural Resource Wealth and Political Regimes*
Scott Gehlbach, *Representation through Taxation: Revenue, Politics, and Development in Postcommunist States*
Margarita Estevez-Abe, *Welfare and Capitalism in Postwar Japan: Party, Bureaucracy, and Business*
Henry E. Hale, *The Foundations of Ethnic Politics: Separatism of States and Nations in Eurasia and the World*
Bonnie M. Meguid, *Party Competition between Unequals: Strategies and Electoral Fortunes in Western Europe*
Austin Smith et al, *Selected Works of Michael Wallerstein*
Robert H. Bates, *When Things Fell Apart: State Failure in Late-Century Africa*
Lily L. Tsai, *Accountability without Democracy: How Solidary Groups Provide Public Goods in Rural China*
Aníbal Pérez-Liñán, *Presidential Impeachment and the New Political Instability in Latin America*
Daniel Treisman, *The Architecture of Government: Rethinking Political Decentralization*
Christian Davenport, *State Repression and the Domestic Democratic Peace*
Marc Howard Ross, *Cultural Contestation in Ethnic Conflict*
Anna Grzymala-Busse, *Rebuilding Leviathan: Party Competition and State Exploitation in Post-Communist Democracies*
José Antonio Cheibub, *Presidentialism, Parliamentarism, and Democracy*
Jeremy M. Weinstein, *Inside Rebellion: The Politics of Insurgent Violence*

Beatriz Magaloni, *Voting for Autocracy: Hegemonic Party Survival and its Demise in Mexico*
Alberto Diaz-Cayeros, *Federalism, Fiscal Authority, and Centralization in Latin America*
Julia Lynch, *Age in the Welfare State: The Origins of Social Spending on Pensioners, Workers, and Children*
Stathis Kalyvas, *The Logic of Violence in Civil War*
Regina Smyth, *Candidate Strategies and Electoral Competition in the Russian Federation: Democracy without Foundation*
Jason Wittenberg, *Crucibles of Political Loyalty: Church Institutions and Electoral Continuity in Hungary*
Isabela Mares, *Taxation, Wage Bargaining, and Unemployment*
Joshua Tucker, *Regional Economic Voting: Russia, Poland, Hungary, Slovakia and the Czech Republic, 1990–1999*
M. Steven Fish, *Democracy Derailed in Russia: The Failure of Open Politics*
Charles Tilly, *Trust and Rule*
Torben Iversen, *Capitalism, Democracy, and Welfare*
Gretchen Helmke, *Courts Under Constraints: Judges, Generals, and Presidents in Argentina*
Yoshiko Herrera, *Imagined Economies: The Sources of Russian Regionalism*
Michael Bratton, Robert Mattes, and E. Gyimah-Boadi, *Public Opinion, Democracy, and Market Reform in Africa*
Kathleen Thelen, *How Institutions Evolve: The Political Economy of Skills in Germany, Britain, the United States, and Japan*
Joseph Jupille, *Procedural Politics: Issues, Influence, and Institutional Choice in the European Union*
Stephen I. Wilkinson, *Votes and Violence: Electoral Competition and Ethnic Riots in India*
Daniele Caramani, *The Nationalization of Politics: The Formation of National Electorates and Party Systems in Europe*
Kanchan Chandra, *Why Ethnic Parties Succeed: Patronage and Ethnic Headcounts in India*
Catherine Boone, *Political Topographies of the African State: Territorial Authority and Institutional Change*
Junko Kato, *Regressive Taxation and the Welfare State*
Evan Lieberman, *Race and Regionalism in the Politics of Taxation in Brazil and South Africa*
Elisabeth J. Wood, *Insurgent Collective Action and Civil War in El Salvador*
Carles Boix, *Democracy and Redistribution*
Beverly Silver, *Forces of Labor: Workers' Movements and Globalization since 1870*
Lyle Scruggs, *Sustaining Abundance: Environmental Performance in Industrial Democracies*
Layna Mosley, *Global Capital and National Governments*
James Mahoney and Dietrich Rueschemeyer, eds., *Historical Analysis and the Social Sciences*
John D. Huber and Charles R. Shipan, *Deliberate Discretion? The Institutional Foundations of Bureaucratic Autonomy*
Roger D. Petersen, *Understanding Ethnic Violence: Fear, Hatred, and Resentment in Twentieth-Century Eastern Europe*
Lisa Baldez, *Why Women Protest? Women's Movements in Chile*
Fabrice E. Lehoucq and Ivan Molina, *Stuffing the Ballot Box: Fraud, Electoral Reform, and Democratization in Costa Rica*
Pauline Jones Luong, *Institutional Change and Political Continuity in Post-Soviet Central Asia*
Scott Morgenstern and Benito Nacif, eds., *Legislative Politics in Latin America*
Jefferey M. Sellers, *Governing from Below: Urban Regions and the Global Economy*

Anna Grzymala-Busse, *Redeeming the Communist Past: The Regeneration of Communist Parties in East Central Europe*
Robert F. Franzese, *Macroeconomic Policies of Developed Democracies*
Duane Swank, *Global Capital, Political Institutions, and Policy Change in Developed Welfare States*
Mark Beissinger, *Nationalist Mobilization and the Collapse of the Soviet State*
David C. Kang, *Crony Capitalism: Corruption and Capitalism in South Korea and the Philippines*
Amie Kreppel, *The European Parliament and the Supranational Party System*
Simona Piattoni, ed., *Clientelism, Interests, and Democratic Representation*
Joel S. Migdal, *State in Society: Studying How States and Societies Constitute One Another*
Nancy Bermeo, ed., *Unemployment in the New Europe*
Susan C. Stokes, *Mandates and Democracy: Neoliberalism by Surprise in Latin America*
Susan C. Stokes, ed., *Public Support for Market Reforms in New Democracies*
Richard Snyder, *Politics after Neoliberalism: Reregulation in Mexico*
Jeff Goodwin, *No Other Way Out: States and Revolutionary Movements*
Maria Victoria Murillo, *Labor Unions, Partisan Coalitions, and Market Reforms in Latin America*
Stefano Bartolini, *The Political Mobilization of the European Left, 1860–1980: The Class Cleavage*
Ton Notermans, *Money, Markets, and the State: Social Democratic Economic Policies since 1918*
Gerald Easter, *Reconstructing the State: Personal Networks and Elite Identity*
Ruth Berins Collier, *Paths toward Democracy: The Working Class and Elites in Western Europe and South America*
Wolfgang C. Müller and Kaare Strøm, *Policy, Office, or Votes?*
Herbert Kitschelt, Zdenka Mansfeldova, Radek Markowski, and Gabor Toka, *Post-Communist Party Systems*
Herbert Kitschelt, Peter Lange, Gary Marks, and John D. Stephens, eds., *Continuity and Change in Contemporary Capitalism*
Carles Boix, *Political Parties, Growth, and Equality: Conservative and Social Democratic Economic Strategies in the World Economy*
Sidney Tarrow, *Power in Movement: Social Movements and Contentious Politics, Revised and Updated Fourth Edition*
Geoffrey Garrett, *Partisan Politics in the Global Economy*
Anthony W. Marx, *Making Race, Making Nations: A Comparison of South Africa, the United States, and Brazil*
Michael Bratton and Nicolas van de Walle, *Democratic Experiments in Africa: Regime Transitions in Comparative Perspective*
J. Rogers Hollingsworth and Robert Boyer, eds., *Contemporary Capitalism: The Embeddedness of Institutions*
Miriam Golden, *Heroic Defeats: The Politics of Job Loss*
Robert O. Keohane and Helen B. Milner, eds., *Internationalization and Domestic Politics*
Frances Hagopian, *Traditional Politics and Regime Change in Brazil*
David Knoke, Franz Urban Pappi, Jeffrey Broadbent, and Yutaka Tsujinaka, eds., *Comparing Policy Networks*
Doug McAdam, John McCarthy, and Mayer Zald, eds., *Comparative Perspectives on Social Movements*
Donatella della Porta, *Social Movements, Political Violence, and the State*
Roberto Franzosi, *The Puzzle of Strikes: Class and State Strategies in Postwar Italy*

Ashutosh Varshney, *Democracy, Development, and the Countryside*
Marino Regini, *Uncertain Boundaries: The Social and Political Construction of European Economies*
Paul Pierson, *Dismantling the Welfare State? Reagan, Thatcher, and the Politics of Retrenchment*
Theda Skocpol, *Social Revolutions in the Modern World*
Joel S. Migdal, Atul Kohli, and Vivienne Shue, eds., *State Power and Social Forces: Domination and Transformation in the Third World*
Herbert Kitschelt, *The Transformation of European Social Democracy*
Thomas Janoski and Alexander M. Hicks, eds., *The Comparative Political Economy of the Welfare State*
Catherine Boone, *Merchant Capital and the Roots of State Power in Senegal, 1930–1985*
Sven Steinmo, Kathleen Thelen, and Frank Longstreth, eds., *Structuring Politics: Historical Institutionalism in Comparative Analysis*
David D. Laitin, *Language Repertoires and State Construction in Africa*

www.ingramcontent.com/pod-product-compliance
Lightning Source LLC
LaVergne TN
LVHW011806200926
848484LV00005B/1085